Words to
Make My
Dream Children
Live

By the same author

Crossing the Danger Water:
Three Hundred Years of African-American Writing

Words to Make My Dream Children Live

A Book of
African American Quotations

EDITED BY DEIRDRE MULLANE

ANCHOR BOOKS
DOUBLEDAY
NEW YORK LONDON TORONTO SYDNEY AUCKLAND

An Anchor Book
PUBLISHED BY DOUBLEDAY
a division of Bantam Doubleday Dell Publishing Group, Inc.
1540 Broadway, New York, New York 10036

Anchor Books, Doubleday, and the portrayal of an anchor
are trademarks of Doubleday, a division of Bantam Doubleday
Dell Publishing Group, Inc.

ISBN 0-385-42244-X

For Glen,

who was never at a loss for words

O God, give me words to make my dream-children live.

—JOSEPH COTTER, "A PRAYER"

Words are your business, boy. Not just the Word. *Words are everything. The key to the Rock, the answer to the Question.*

—RALPH ELLISON, "AND HICKMAN ARRIVES"

Contents

Introduction

This volume began to take shape some years ago after I had seen Henry Hampton's extraordinary documentary television series "Eyes on the Prize," and read the interviews on which the series was based, published in Hampton's volume *Voices of Freedom*. In the pages of this moving oral history were the accounts of such significant figures as Andrew Young, James Lewis, Joseph Lowery, James Farmer, Eldridge Cleaver, Ralph Abernathy, Betty Shabazz, and many other remarkable individuals who had played an active role in the events of the civil rights era. The clarity and force of this chorus of voices led me to seek out a collection of quotations by African American men and women, but I could find none.

I then discovered that, in other general books of quotations, African American speakers were markedly underrepresented. While *Bartlett's Quotations,* for example, included the sentiments of sometimes dubious cultural figures, it recorded no words by the great jurist Thurgood Marshall, the Nobel Prize–winner Ralph Bunche, or the controversial Congressman Adam Clayton Powell; significant gaps existed in this reference standard. I began to collect quotations for this volume, a process that continued while I compiled an anthology of African American writings, subsequently published.

The more than three thousand quotations culled from this process are the result of a great deal of selection and compromise. I wanted to include, of course, well-known figures like Frederick Douglass, W. E. B. Du Bois, Langston Hughes, and Alice Walker, while finding room for those whose significance has been sometimes overlooked. I also wanted to represent a broad spectrum of professions, from sports to politics, religion to the arts. The selection of quotations for some speakers was the result of a deliberate search through their major works, while those of others—such as the blues musician Junior Parker or the baseball player Chester Brown—were found during the course of research and were simply too good to be omitted.

For each speaker here I have tried to include both well-known quotations, frequently cited, as well as unexpected sentiments that express a telling aspect of personality. For professional writers, most material is taken from novels, nonfiction, and autobiography, representing their most polished and considered work. For individuals known best in other contexts—sports, politics, or music—there is a greater reliance on speeches and interviews. Some quotes will be chiefly of historical interest, such as Dred Scott's petition or Denmark Vesey's statement to the court, while others are marked by their power, lyricism, and timeliness.

I have also tried to compile a balanced collection, including both public statements and personal reflections, capturing moments of struggle and celebrations of triumph. While certain themes emerge— the importance of history and heritage, the joys of love and friendship, the bonds of family, the pervasiveness of racism and hopes for the future—so do the concerns and characteristics unique to each author.

For writers, students, public speakers, and other readers searching for an apt quotation on a particular topic, an index of subjects is provided, as is a brief index of famous quotations that readers may recognize but can't identify. The original source of each quotation has been given as specifically as possible, but as quotations have been passed down from writer to writer and referenced in secondary works, their exact origins have sometimes become clouded.

Of course the final collection can represent only a small portion of the work of many of the individuals included here, not to mention others finally omitted entirely. The work of prolific writers like James Baldwin and Toni Morrison can really only be touched upon; entire volumes have been devoted to the speeches and writings of Malcolm X and Martin Luther King, Jr. The challenge was to represent as many significant speakers as possible within a small amount of space. Readers are referred to the Bibliography for sources of additional information.

Finally, for support in the preparation of this volume, I would like to thank my publisher, Anchor Books, who displayed such enthusiasm when I first proposed the book, and especially my editor, Charles Flowers, who diligently shaped the manuscript to achieve the right balance. I would also like to thank those speakers whose powerful words live on in these pages.

Quotations
A–Z

Hank Aaron

(1 9 3 4 –   )

With his 715th home run, on April 8, 1974, Henry Louis Aaron surpassed Babe Ruth's long-standing record. One observer noted, "Trying to sneak a pitch past Hank Aaron is like trying to sneak the sunrise past a rooster." Born in Mobile, Alabama, Aaron played for the Negro League briefly before joining the Milwaukee Braves organization in 1952. He had a career total of 755 home runs and was elected to the Baseball Hall of Fame in 1982.

I had to break that record. I had to do it for Jackie and my people and myself and for everybody who ever called me nigger.
—IN COLUMBUS SALLEY, THE BLACK 100 *(1993)*

I've tried a lot of things in the off season, but the only thing I know is baseball.
—THE MILWAUKEE JOURNAL, *JULY 31, 1956*

The pitcher has got only a ball. I've got a bat. So the percentage in weapons is in my favor and I let the fellow with the ball do the fretting.
—*IBID.*

On the field, blacks have been able to be super giants. But once our playing days are over, this is the end of it and we go back to the back of the bus again.
—HAMMERIN' HANK *(1974)*

You can only milk a cow so long, and then you're left holding the pail.
—ON HIS RETIREMENT IN *1976*, WIDELY ATTRIBUTED

I never doubted my ability, but when you hear all your life you're inferior, it makes you wonder if the other guys have something you've never seen before. If they do, I'm still looking for it.

—I Had a Hammer *(1992)*

I never want them to forget Babe Ruth. I just want them to remember Aaron.

—*on being inducted into the Hall of Fame, 1982*

I'm hoping someday that some kid, black or white, will hit more home runs than myself. Whoever it is, I'd be pulling for him.

—*c. 1974. (No one ever has.)*

In 2007 Barry Bonds hit 756

Kareem Abdul-Jabbar

(1947 –)

Born Ferdinand Lewis Alcindor, Jr., in New York, Abdul-Jabbar had reached over seven feet in height while still in high school. He led his UCLA team to three NCAA championships and was twice selected college player of the year. In 1960 he joined the Milwaukee Bucks and was chosen Rookie of the Year. After moving to Los Angeles in 1975, he led the L.A. Lakers to five NBA championships. Influenced by Malcolm X, he converted to Islam in the 1960s, and in 1989 retired from professional basketball, at the age of forty-two, after a record-breaking twenty-year career.

You can't win unless you learn how to lose.

—Kareem *(1990)*

You go all the way back to the great black kings of Africa. Esteem came from presence. That's in me.

Ibid.

I learned early on that there's a place inside oneself that no one else can violate, that no one else can enter, and that we have a right to protect that place.

IBID.

When you're trying to horn in on the American pie, people just don't want to give up their share easily.

IBID.

Malcolm was talking about real people doing real things, black pride, and Islam. I just grabbed on to it. And I have never looked back.

IBID.

I'm not comfortable being preachy, but more people have to start spending as much time in the library as they do on the basketball court. If they took the idea that they could escape poverty through education, I think it would make a more basic and long-lasting change in the way things happen . . . What we need are positive, realistic goals and the willingness to work. Hard work and practical goals.

IBID.

All the courage and competitiveness of Jackie Robinson affects me to this day. If I patterned my life after anyone, it was him, not because he was the first black baseball player in the majors but because he was a hero.

IBID.

The sport goes on. People will find new heroes. And I'm flattered they'll be compared with me.

—*ON HIS RETIREMENT, IBID.*

ℛeverend ℛalph ᴀbernathy

(1926 – 1991)

The grandson of slaves, Ralph David Abernathy was born in Alabama and served in World War II. Ordained a Baptist minister at twenty-two, he received an M.A. in sociology from Atlanta University and became pastor of the First Baptist Church in Montgomery, where he first met Dr. Martin Luther King, Jr., during the bus boycott in 1955. He was one of the founders of the Southern Christian Leadership Conference and after King's death in 1968 led the SCLC until 1976.

You may be assured that we won't ever let your words die. Like the words of our Master, Jesus Christ, they will live in our minds and our hearts and in the souls of black men and white men, brown men and yellow men as long as time shall last.

— "MY LAST LETTER TO MARTIN"

There has been a crucifixion in our nation, but here in this spring season as we see the blossoms and smell the fresh air we know that the Resurrection will shortly appear.

—IBID.

Malcolm may not have believed what we believe and he may not have preached, but he was a child of God and he was concerned about the welfare of his people.

—AND THE WALLS CAME TUMBLING DOWN (1989)

Bring on your tear gas, bring on your grenades, your new supplies of Mace, your state troopers and even your national guards. But let the record show we ain't going to be turned around.

—IBID.

I don't know what the future may hold, but I know who holds the future.

—IN ANDREW YOUNG, A WAY OUT OF NO WAY (1994)

Clifford L. Alexander

(1 9 3 3 –)

*B*orn *in New York, Alexander attended Harvard University and Yale Law School and was named chairman of the Equal Employment Opportunity Commission by President Johnson. He was Secretary of the Army under President Carter, and he now practices law in Washington.*

This is the most prestigious segregated body in America . . . You see us as less than you are. You think that we are not as smart, not as energetic, not as well suited to supervise you as you are to supervise us. And yes, if you see a black man, you think that you had better cross the street before something bad happens to you.

—TESTIMONY TO THE SENATE BANKING, HOUSING, AND URBAN AFFAIRS COMMITTEE FOR THE 21ST-CENTURY COMMISSION ON AFRICAN AMERICAN MALES, MAY 21, 1991

Muhammad Ali

(1 9 4 2 –)

*C*assius *Marcellus Clay won his first title at fourteen and captured the Olympic Gold Medal in 1960. In 1964, he won the heavyweight title from Sonny Liston. When he became a member of the Nation of Islam, he changed his name, and in 1966 he was convicted of draft evasion for his conscientious objection to the Vietnam War. He was given a five-year jail term and stripped of his title, but on June 28, 1970, the Supreme Court threw out the conviction. He regained the title in 1978 and retired from boxing in 1981, but continued to be an outspoken critic of social injustice.*

I'm the greatest.

—HIS SLOGAN, INSPIRED BY THE BOXER GEORGEOUS GEORGE WAGNER

Float like a butterfly, sting like a bee.

—ANOTHER MOTTO

I'm so fast I can turn out the light and be in bed before it gets dark.

• • •

It's hard to be humble when you're as great as I am.

—SIGNATURE BOASTS

I started boxing because I thought this was the fastest way for a black person to make it in this country.

—IN JOSÉ TORRES, STING LIKE A BEE (1971)

I'm going to put him flat on his back,
so that he'll start acting Black

—ON HIS BOUT WITH FORMER HEAVYWEIGHT CHAMPION FLOYD PATTERSON, NOVEMBER 22, 1965.
(ALI WON.)

I am an astronaut of boxing. Joe Louis and Dempsey were just jet pilots. I'm in a world of my own.

—AFTER HIS DEFEAT OF ERNIE TERRELL, FEBRUARY 6, 1967, IN JOHN COTTRELL, MAN OF DESTINY:
THE STORY OF MUHAMMAD ALI (1967)

Maybe this will shock and amaze ya, but I'm gonna retire that Joe Frazier.

—BEFORE THE ALI–FRAZIER FIGHT ON MARCH 8, 1971. (THOUGH FRAZIER WON IN FIFTEEN ROUNDS,
BOTH MEN ENDED UP IN THE HOSPITAL, AND FRAZIER DIDN'T FIGHT FOR ANOTHER TEN MONTHS.)

I never thought of losing, but now that it's happened, the only thing is to do it right. That's my obligation to all the people who believe in me. We all have to take defeats in life.

—AFTER LOSING HIS FIRST FIGHT TO KEN NORTON, MARCH 31, 1973

It was like death. The closest thing to dyin' that I know of.

—AFTER DEFEATING FRAZIER IN THE THRILLA IN MANILA, SEPTEMBER 30, 1975, THOUGHT BY SOME
TO BE THE GREATEST FIGHT IN HISTORY

I believe in the religion of Islam. I believe in Allah and peace.
—*ANNOUNCING HIS CONVERSION, FEBRUARY 26, 1964*

Cassius Clay is a slave name. I didn't choose it and I don't want it. I am Muhammad Ali, a free man—it means "Beloved of God"—and I insist that people use it in speaking of and to me.
—*c. 1966*

Keep asking me no matter how long—
On the war in Vietnam I sing this song—
I ain't got no quarrel with the Viet Cong.
—*PRESS CONFERENCE IN MIAMI, FEBRUARY 1966*

I am not going ten thousand miles from here to help murder and kill and burn another poor people simply to help continue the domination of white slave masters over the darker people . . . I strongly object to the fact that so many newspapers have given the American public and the world the impression that I have only two alternatives in taking this stand—either I go to jail or go into the Army. There is another alternative, and that is justice.
—*AFTER REFUSING INDUCTION, APRIL 28, 1967*

Who is this descendant of the slave masters to order a descendant of slaves to fight other people in their own country?
—*THE GREATEST (1975)*

When my title was taken away, boxing died.
—*BBC INTERVIEW, 1971*

Life is a gamble. You can get hurt, but people die in plane crashes, lose their arms and legs in car accidents; people die every day. Same with fighters: some die, some get hurt, some go on. You just don't let yourself believe it will happen to you.
—*I AM KING (1975)*

The man who views the world at fifty the same as he did at twenty has wasted thirty years of his life.
—*PLAYBOY, NOVEMBER 1975*

I shall return.

—AFTER LOSING THE HEAVYWEIGHT TITLE TO LEON SPINKS, FEBRUARY 15, 1978. HE REGAINED THE TITLE FROM SPINKS SEVEN MONTHS LATER.

I am America. I am the part you won't recognize. But get used to me. Black confident, cocky; my name, not yours; my religion, not yours; my goals, my own; get used to me.

—THE GREATEST

Richard Allen

(1 7 6 0 – 1 8 3 1)

One of the most significant leaders of the post-revolutionary period, Allen was born a slave in Philadelphia and purchased his own freedom at the age of twenty. A founder of the Free African Society (1787), in 1794 he established the Mother Bethel Church and in 1816 the African Methodist Episcopal Church. In later life, he was an advocate of colonization to Canada and a leader in the convention movement.

The Lord was pleased to strengthen us, and remove all fear from us, and disposed our hearts to be as useful as possible.

—RECOUNTING AN EPIDEMIC THAT STRUCK PHILADELPHIA, DURING WHICH AFRICAN AMERICANS NURSED MUCH OF THE POPULATION; IN A NARRATIVE OF THE PROCEEDINGS OF THE BLACK PEOPLE, DURING THE LATE AWFUL CALAMITY IN PHILADELPHIA, IN THE YEAR 1793, WITH ABSALOM JONES

If you love your children, if you love your country, if you love the God of love, clear your hands from slaves, burden not your children or country with them.

—IBID.

We were *stolen* from our mother country, and brought *here*. We have *tilled* the ground and made fortunes for thousands, and still they are not weary of our services. *But they who stay to till the ground must be slaves.* Is there not land enough in America or "corn enough in Egypt"? . . . This land, which we have watered with our *tears* and *our blood,* is now our *mother country,* and we are well satisfied to stay where wisdom abounds and the gospel is free.

—FREEDOM'S JOURNAL, *NOVEMBER 2, 1827*

However great the debt which these United States may owe to injured Africa, and however unjustly her sons have been made to bleed, and her daughters to drink of the cup of affliction, still we who have been born and nurtured on this soil, we, whose habits, manners, and customs are the same in common with other Americans, can never consent to take our lives in our hands, and be the bearers of the redress offered by that Society to that much afflicted country.

—*OPPOSING THE AMERICAN COLONIZATION SOCIETY, CONVENTION OF COLOURED CITIZENS OF PHILADELPHIA, SEPTEMBER 20–24, 1830*

We will never separate ourselves voluntarily from the slave population in this country; they are our brethren by the trees of consanguinity, of suffering, and of wrong; and we feel there is more virtue in suffering privations with them than fancied advantage for a season.

—THE LIFE EXPERIENCE AND GOSPEL LABORS OF RICHARD ALLEN *(1887)*

Marian Anderson

(1 9 0 2 – 1 9 9 3)

Born in Philadelphia, Anderson performed with the New York Philharmonic and toured in Europe before she was barred from performing at Constitution Hall in Washington, D.C., in 1939. First Lady Eleanor Roosevelt resigned from the DAR in protest and staged a concert with Anderson on April 9 at the Lincoln Memorial in front of 75,000 people. In 1955, "the Philadelphia Lady" made her debut with the Metropolitan Opera. She was awarded the Presidential Medal of Freedom in 1963 and a Congressional Gold Medal in 1978.

It is easy to look back self-indulgently, feeling pleasantly sorry for oneself and saying I didn't have this and I didn't have that. But it is only the grown woman regretting the hardships of a little girl who never thought they were hardships at all . . . She had the things that really mattered.

—My Lord, What a Morning *(1956)*

A singer starts by having his instrument as a gift from God . . . When you have been given something in a moment of grace, it is sacrilegious to be greedy.

—*Ibid.*

I had gone to Europe . . . to reach for a place as a serious artist, but I never doubted that I must return. I was—and am—an American.

—Famous American Women *(1970)*

I just can't talk. I can't tell you what you have done for me today. I thank you from the bottom of my heart again and again.

—*statement after her concert on the Mall, April 9, 1939*

I could see that my significance as an individual was small in this affair. I had become, whether I liked it or not, a symbol representing my people.

—*Ibid.*

Fear is a disease that eats away at logic and makes man inhuman.

—My Lord, What a Morning

I suppose I might insist on making issues of things. But that is not my nature, and I always bear in mind that my mission is to leave behind me the kind of impression that will make it easier for those who follow.

—*Ibid.*

I have great belief in the future of my people and my country.

—*c. 1960*

Maya Angelou

(1 9 2 8 –)

Writer, poet, dancer, and actress, Marguerite Johnson was born in Saint Louis and grew up in Arkansas and California. Her best-selling autobiography, I Know Why the Caged Bird Sings, *was the first of more than ten books of poetry and prose. In 1993, she delivered the inaugural poem for President Bill Clinton.*

I write because I am a Black woman, listening attentively to her talking people.

—*"Shades and Slashes of Light," in Mari Evans,* Black Women Writers *(1984)*

My grandmother, who was one of the greatest human beings I've ever known, used to say, "I am a child of God and I'm nobody's creature." That to me defined the Black woman through the centuries.

—*interview,* Essence, *December 1992*

Of all the needs (there are none imaginary) a lonely child has, the one that must be satisfied, if there is going to be hope and a hope of wholeness, is the unshaken need for an unshakable God.

—I Know Why the Caged Bird Sings *(1970)*

> Because of Your mercy,
> Falling down on me like rain,
> Because of Your mercy,
> When I die I'll live again
> —*"Thank You, Lord"*

By no amount of agile exercising of a wistful imagination could my mother have been called lenient. Generous she was; indulgent, never. Kind, yes; permissive, never. In her world, people she accepted paddled their own canoes, pulled their own weight, put their own shoulders to their own plows and pushed like hell.

—Gather Together in My Name *(1974)*

Every person I knew had a hellish horror of being "called out of his name."

—I Know Why the Caged Bird Sings

The Black woman in the South who raises sons, grandsons, and nephews had her heartstrings tied to a hanging noose.

—*Ibid.*

I find it interesting that the meanest life, the poorest existence, is attributed to God's will, but as human beings become more affluent, as their living standard and style begin to ascend the material scale, God descends the scale of responsiblity at a commensurate speed.

—*Ibid.*

Nobody, but nobody
Can make it out here alone.

—*"Alone"*

The needs of society determine its ethics, and in the Black American ghettos the hero is that man who is offered only the crumbs from his country's table but by ingenuity and courage is able to take for himself a Lucullan feast.

—I Know Why the Caged Bird Sings

Bringing the gifts that my ancestors gave,
I am the dream and the hope of the slave.
I rise
I rise
I rise.

—*"Still I Rise"*

A slough of young cats riding that
cold, white horse,
a grey old monkey on their back, of course

—*"Letter to an Aspiring Junkie"*

The Black female is assaulted in her tender years by all those common forces of nature at the same time that she is caught in the tripartite crossfire of masculine prejudice, white illogical hate, and Black lack of power. The fact that the adult American Negro female emerges a formidable character is often met with amazement, distaste, and even belligerence. It is seldom accepted as an inevitable outcome of the struggle won by survivors and deserves respect.

—I Know Why the Caged Bird Sings

I lay down in my grave
and watch my children
grow proud blooms
above the weeds of death.

—"Elegy"

Everybody, his brother, and his dog thinks he can walk a road in a colored woman's behind. But you remember this, now. Your mother raised you. You're full grown. Let them catch it like they find it. If you haven't been trained at home to their liking, tell them to get stepping.

—Gather Together in My Name

If you're for the right thing, then you do it without thinking.

—I Know Why the Caged Bird Sings

I could moan some salty songs. I had been living with empty arms and rocks in my bed.

—The Heart of a Woman *(1981)*

I made the decision to quit show business. Give up the skintight dresses and manicured smiles. The false concern over sentimental lyrics. I would never again work to make people smile inanely and would take on the responsibility of making them think.

—*Ibid.*

If we lose [our] love and self-respect and respect for each other, this is how we will finally die.

—Essence, *December 1992*

You're Africa to me
At brightest dawn

—"To a Husband"

I am overwhelmed by the grace and persistence of my people.

—Essence, *December 1992*

When you see me walking, stumbling,
Don't study and get it wrong.
'Cause tired don't mean lazy
And every goodbye ain't gone.
— *"On Aging"*

Chant for us a new song. A song
Of Southern peace.
— *"A Georgia Song"*

If they want to learn how to live life right,
they ought to study me on Saturday night.
— *"Weekend Glory"*

You, the Ashanti, the Yoruba, the Kru, bought,
Sold, stolen, arriving on the nightmare
Praying for a dream.
Here, root yourselves beside me . . .
History, despite its wrenching pain,
Cannot be unlived, but if faced
With courage, need not be lived again.
— *"On the Pulse of Morning," delivered at the inauguration of Bill Clinton,
January 21, 1993*

I alone am responsible to God for my spirit. Not you, unless I give it
to you. And I would be a fool.
—Essence, *December 1992*

I had no idea what I was going to make of my life, but I had given a
promise and found my innocence. I swore I'd never lose it again.
—Gather Together in My Name

Lil Hardin Armstrong

(1 8 9 8 – 1 9 7 1)

Born in Memphis, the jazz pianist Lil Hardin studied classical music at Fisk University and was playing in prominent jazz bands in Chicago when she met Louis Armstrong, to whom she was married from 1924 to 1938. In the 1930s she formed an "all-girl" band, and died onstage in 1971, playing a tribute to her late former husband.

I encouraged him to develop himself, which was all he needed. He's a fellow who didn't have much confidence in himself to begin with. He didn't believe in himself. So I was sort of standing at the bottom of the ladder holding it, and watching him climb.
—IN BILL CROW, JAZZ ANECDOTES *(1990)*

If you want to hear Louis play, just hear him play when he's *angry*.
—IBID.

I beat out a background rhythm that put the Bechuana tribes of Africa to shame.
—IN NAT SHAPIRO AND NAT HENTOFF, HEAR ME TALKIN' TO YA *(1955)*

Louis Armstrong

(1 9 0 1 – 1 9 7 1)

Daniel Louis (Pops) Armstrong largely raised himself in the red-light district of Storyville in New Orleans and began playing cornet in clubs when he was thirteen. In the early 1920s he joined King Oliver in Chicago and Fletcher Henderson in New York. Among his

four wives was the accomplished pianist Lil Hardin, and he collaborated frequently with pianist Earl Hines. Through his recordings, European tours, and film appearances, Satchmo achieved worldwide popularity.

The memory of things gone is important to a jazz musician. Things like old folks singing in the moonlight in the back yard on a hot night or something said long ago.
—The New Yorker, *July 8, 1944*

After Storyville closed down, the people of that section spread out all over the city . . . So we turned out nice and reformed.
—*in Nat Shapiro and Nat Hentoff,* Hear Me Talkin' to Ya

There are some people that if they don't know, you can't tell 'em.
—*c. 1956*

We all do "do, re, mi," but you have got to find the other notes yourself.
—*on jazz, c. 1956*

They know I'm there in the cause of happiness.
—*quoted in Albert Murray's* Good Morning Blues *(1985)*

Red beans and ricely yours . . .
—*his signature closing*

Molefi Kete Asante

(1 9 4 2 –   )

Born Arthur Lee Smith, Asante is a leading proponent of the doctrine of Afrocentricity. He received his Ph.D. from UCLA and assumed his new name in 1968. He has taught at Purdue, UCLA, Howard, and other institutions, and is now the chairman of the

Department of African American Studies at Temple University, in Philadelphia. He has written more than twenty volumes and is the founding editor of The Journal of Black Studies.

We have a formidable history, replete with the voice of God, the ancestors, and the prophets.

—*"THE ESSENTIAL GROUNDS," AFROCENTRICITY, REVISED EDITION (1988)*

As a people, our most cherished and valuable achievements are the achievements of spirit. With an Afrocentric spirit, all things can be made to happen; it is the source of genuine revolutionary commitment.

—*"THE CONSTITUENTS OF POWER," IBID.*

A wise person speaks carefully and with truth, for every word that passes between one's teeth is meant for something.

—*"NIJA: THE WAY," IBID.*

The person who strays away from the source is unrooted and is like dust blown about by the wind.

—*IBID.*

Your power is in your faith. Keep it and pass it on to other bloods.

—*IBID.*

Arthur Ashe

(1 9 4 3 – 1 9 9 3)

The first African American to be named to the United States Davis Cup Team, Ashe was the only black tennis player to win the singles title at the U.S. Open (twice), the Australian Open, and Wimbledon. He was an outspoken critic of rights abuses in the United States and South Africa and was the author of a three-volume history of African

American athletes, A Hard Road to Glory. *In April 1992, Ashe revealed that he had contracted the AIDS virus during coronary bypass surgery, and the public education work he embarked upon before his death in February 1993 is continued by the Arthur Ashe AIDS Foundation.*

It's an abnormal world I live in. It's like I'm floating down the middle. I'm never quite sure where I am.

—*ON BEING THE ONLY PROMINENT BLACK TENNIS PLAYER,* SPORTS ILLUSTRATED, *1966*

Being black is the greatest burden I've had to bear.

—NEW YORK TIMES

If contemporary black athletes' exploits are more well known, few fully appreciate their true Hard Road to Glory. Discrimination, vilification, incarceration, dissipation, ruination, and ultimate despair have dogged the steps of the mightiest of these heroes.

—A HARD ROAD TO GLORY *(1988)*

We were once a people of dignity and morality; we wanted the world to be fair to us, and we tried, on the whole, to be fair to the world. Now I was looking at the new order, which is based squarely on revenge, not justice, with morality discarded. Instead of settling on what is right, or just, or moral, the idea is to get even.

—*ON THE RIOTS IN LOS ANGELES IN 1991,* DAYS OF GRACE *(1993)*

Racism is not an excuse to not do the best you can.

—SPORTS ILLUSTRATED, *JULY 1991*

Our national destiny, which at times seems as bright as in the past, sometimes also appears tragically foreshortened, even doomed, as the fabric of our society is threatened by endless waves of crime, by the weakening of our family structures, by the deterioration of our schools, and by the decline of religion and spiritual values. AIDS then takes on a specifically ominous cast, as if in its savagery and mystery it mirrors our fate.

—DAYS OF GRACE

Pearl Bailey

(1 9 1 8 – 1 9 9 0)

Born in Newport News, Virginia, Bailey sang with the Count Basie Orchestra and toured with the USO during World War II. She starred on Broadway in Saint Louis Woman *in 1946, as well as in the films* Carmen Jones, Porgy and Bess, *and others. In 1967 she received a Tony award for the title role in* Hello, Dolly *and in 1975 was appointed special adviser to the U.S. Mission to the United Nations.*

There is a way to look at the past. Don't hide from it. It will not catch you if you don't repeat it.

—*IN ERIC V. COPAGE*, BLACK PEARLS *(1993)*

People see God every day; they just don't recognize Him.

—*IBID.*

I see their souls, and I hold them in my hands, and because I love them they weigh nothing.

—*ON HER AUDIENCES*, THE RAW PEARL *(1968)*

Josephine Baker

(1 9 0 6 – 1 9 7 5)

Baker began performing professionally at the age of thirteen and became an international star after her extraordinary reception in Paris in the 1920s, in the Revue Nègre and at the Folies Bergère. Having witnessed violent riots in Saint Louis in her youth, she

worked for the French Resistance and was outspoken about civil rights as she gathered around herself a large, multiracial family.

Driven by dark forces I didn't recognize, I improvised, crazed by the music, the overheated theater filled to the bursting point, the scorching eye of the spotlights. Even my teeth and eyes burned with fever. Each time I leaped I seemed to touch the sky and when I regained earth it seemed to be mine alone.

—ON HER PERFORMANCE WITH THE *REVUE NÈGRE*, C. *1925*, JOSEPHINE *(1977)*

J'ai deux amours;
Mon pays et Paris

—BAKER'S THEME SONG, WRITTEN BY VINCENT SCOTTO *(1930)*

The rear end exists. I see no reason to be ashamed of it. It's true there are rear ends so stupid, so pretentious, so insignificant that they're good only for sitting on.

—LES MÉMOIRES DE JOSEPHINE BAKER

I believe in prayer. It's the best way we have to draw strength from heaven.

—JOSEPHINE

I was learning the importance of names—having them, making them—but at the same time I sensed the dangers. Recognition was followed by oblivion, a yawning maw whose victims disappeared without a trace.

—JOSEPHINE

France made me what I am. I will be grateful forever. The people of Paris have given me everything. They have given me their hearts, and I have given them mine.

—ON JOINING THE FRENCH RESISTANCE, LA GUERRE SECRÈTE DE JOSEPHINE BAKER *(1948)*

My ideal is so simple, yet so many people view it as a crazy dream. Surely the day will come when color means nothing more than skin tone; when religion is seen uniquely as a way to speak one's soul; when birth places have the weight of the dice and all men are born free; when understanding breeds loves and brotherhood.

—STATEMENT IN *1969* ON LOSING HER BELOVED CHÂTEAU, LES MILANDES, WHERE HER MIXED FAMILY

SOUGHT TO LIVE AS AN EXAMPLE OF RACIAL UNITY

A violinist had his violin, a painter his palette. All I had was myself. *I was the instrument that I must care for.*

—JOSEPHINE

Not bad for sixty-eight, eh?

—<small>AT HER STUNNING APPEARANCE IN</small> JOSEPHINE, *PARIS, 1975*

I am moral; They said I was the reverse.

—THE DEFENDER, *OCTOBER 10, 1931*

We can dance it a thousand times, only to find during the thousand and first that we can no longer limit ourselves to dancing. The music has swept us away, two souls who can rejoin their bodies only by fleeing together and making love.

—<small>ON THE TANGO WITH HER FIRST FUTURE MANAGER,</small> *PEPITO*

The things we truly love stay with us always, locked in our hearts as long as life remains.

—*c. 1940*

Beautiful? It's all a question of luck. I was born with good legs. As for the rest . . . beautiful, no. Amusing, yes.

—*c. 1969*

James Baldwin

(1 9 2 4 – 1 9 8 7)

Born in Harlem, Baldwin was a preacher for a short time during his teens. In 1948, after his early reviews and essays were published in The Nation *and* The New Leader, *he moved to Paris, where his first novel,* Go Tell It on the Mountain, *was written, followed by his career-making works,* Notes of a Native Son *and* The Fire Next Time. *A prolific author, he left an important legacy of plays, novels, and essays.*

I would have to appropriate these white centuries, I would have to make them mine . . .

—Notes of a Native Son *(1955)*

The black man has functioned in the white man's world as a fixed star, as an immovable pillar: and as he moves out of his place, heaven and earth are shaken to their foundations.

—*"Down at the Cross,"* The Fire Next Time *(1962)*

All over Harlem, Negro boys and girls are growing into stunted maturity, trying desperately to find a place to stand; and the wonder is not that so many are ruined but that so many survive.

—*"The Harlem Ghetto"*

Which of us has overcome his past?

—*"Alas, Poor Richard" (1961)*

Our crown has been bought and paid for; all we have to do is wear it.

—*c. 1961*

There is never time in the future in which we will work out our salvation. The challenge is in the moment; the time is always now.

—Nobody Knows My Name *(1961)*

People pay for what they do, and still more for what they have allowed themselves to become. And they pay for it very simply; by the lives they lead.

—*Ibid.*

The world is before you and you need not take it or leave it as it was when you came in.

—*Ibid.*

Where there is no vision, the people perish.

—*Ibid.*

I imagine that one of the reasons people cling to their hates so stubbornly is because they sense, once hate is gone, that they will be forced to deal with pain.

—Notes of a Native Son

No people come into possession of a culture without having paid a heavy price for it.

—*"Equal in Paris"*

The rage of the disesteemed is personally fruitless, but it is also absolutely inevitable.

—*"Stranger in the Village"*

This world is white no longer, and it will never be white again.

—*Ibid.*

I am what time, circumstance, history, have made of me, certainly, but I am also, much more than that. So are we all.

—*c. 1984*

A devotion to humanity . . . is too easily equated with a devotion to a Cause; and Causes . . . are notoriously bloodthirsty.

—Notes of a Native Son

I want to be an honest man and a good writer.

—*Ibid.*

To be sensual, I think, is to respect and rejoice in the force of life, of life itself, and to be *present* in all that one does, from the effort of loving to the breaking of bread.

—The Fire Next Time

When a white man faces a black man, especially if the black man is helpless, terrible things are revealed.

—*Ibid.*

For the horrors of the American Negro's life there has been almost no language.

—*Ibid.*

The power of the white world is threatened whenever a black man refuses to accept the white world's definitions.

—*Ibid.*

The most dangerous creation of any society is that man who has nothing to lose.

—*Ibid.*

The glorification of one race and the consequent debasement of another—or others—always has been and always will be recipe for murder.

—*Ibid.*

Life is tragic simply because the earth turns and the sun inexorably rises and sets, and one day, for each of us, the sun will go down for the last, last time.

—*Ibid.*

One is responsible to life: It is the small beacon in that terrifying darkness from which we come and to which we shall return.

—*Ibid.*

The only thing white people have that black people need, or should want, is power—and no one holds power forever.

—*Ibid.*

If one is continually surviving the worst that life can bring, one eventually ceases to be controlled by a fear of what life can bring; whatever it brings must be borne.

—*Ibid.*

A bill is coming in that I fear America is not prepared to pay.

—*Ibid.*

Color is not a human or a personal reality; it is a political reality.

—*Ibid.*

If we had not loved each other none of us would have survived.

—*"Down at the Cross,"* The Fire Next Time

To have been where we were, to have paid the price we have paid, to have survived, and to have shaken up the world the way we have is a rare journey.

—*"Why I Left America,"* Essence, *October 1970*

Not only was I not born to be a slave; I was not born to hope to become the equal of the slave master.

—THE PRICE OF THE TICKET *(1985)*

It is a terrible, an inexorable law that one cannot deny the humanity of another without diminishing one's own. In the face of one's victim one sees oneself.

—*IBID.*

Know whence you came. If you know whence you came, there is really no limit to where you can go.

—THE FIRE NEXT TIME *(1962)*

Toni Cade Bambara

(1 9 3 9 –)

Best known for her acclaimed short stories of the urban black experience, collected in Gorilla My Love *(1972) and* The Sea Birds Are Still Alive *(1977), Bambara is also the author of* The Salt Eaters, *a novel that received the American Book Award in 1980. Born in New York City, she is the editor of two anthologies of black literature and has taught at Rutgers, City College, and elsewhere.*

Immunity to the serpent's sting can be found in our tradition of struggle and our faculty for synthesis. The issue is salvation. I work to produce stories that save our lives . . . Writing is a legitimate way, an important way, to participate in the empowerment of the community that names me.

—*"SALVATION IS THE ISSUE," IN MARI EVANS,* BLACK WOMEN WRITERS *(1984)*

The responsibility of an artist representing an oppressed people is to make revolution irresistible.

—*CONFERENCE AT HOWARD UNIVERSITY, 1974*

The really hurtful thing about the complex of -isms that characterize America, its satellites, and captive territories—racism, narcissism, opportunism, speciism, materialism, sexism—is that they disfigure the spirit and cripple the capacity to grow, to imagine, to act.

—*"BEAUTY IS JUST CARE—LIKE UGLY IS CARELESSNESS,"* ESSENCE, *JANUARY 1978*

Are you, sure, sweetheart, that you want to be well?

—THE SALT EATERS *(1980)*

There are times, of course, in between intensely sociable periods and hospitable fits and collaborative work, when any visitor—in person, by mail—is an intruder, a burglar, a space hogger, an oxygen taker, a chaos maker, a conflict inducer, a mood chaser, and a total drag.

—*"SALVATION IS THE ISSUE"*

You know as well as I, Old Wife, that we have not been scuffling in this waste-howling wilderness for the right to be stupid.

—THE SALT EATERS

It's not the water in front that pulls the river. It's the rear guard that is the driving force.

—*"THE SEA BIRDS ARE STILL ALIVE"*

The dream is real, my friends. The failure to make it work is the unreality.

—THE SALT EATERS

Benjamin Banneker

(1 7 3 1 – 1 8 0 6)

Born free on the Eastern Shore of Maryland, Banneker was a naturalist, astronomer, inventor, poet, and early American scientific and mathematical genius. He helped design the city plan of Washington, D.C., and, starting in 1792, published an annual almanac.

I am of the African race, and in the colour which is natural to them of the deepest dye; and it is under a sense of the most profound gratitude to the Supreme Ruler of the Universe.

—LETTER TO THOMAS JEFFERSON, SECRETARY OF STATE, AUGUST 19, 1791

Sir, how pitiable it is to reflect, that although you were so fully convinced of the benevolence of the Father of Mankind, and of his equal and impartial distribution of these rights and privileges, which he hath conferred upon them, that you should at the same time counteract his mercies, in detaining by fraud and violence so numerous a part of my brethren, under groaning captivity, and cruel oppression, that you should at the same time be found guilty of that most criminal act, which you professedly detested in others, with respect to yourselves.

—COMPARING PRINCIPLES OF THE AMERICAN REVOLUTION TO THE PRACTICE OF SLAVERY, IBID.

The colour of the skin is in no way connected with strength of the mind or intellectual powers.

—BANNEKER'S ALMANAC, 1796

Presumption should never make us neglect that which appears easy to us, nor despair make us lose courage at the sight of difficulties.

—C. 1794

Among the many defects which have been pointed out in the federal constitution, it is much to be lamented that no person has taken notice of its total silence upon the subject of an office of the utmost important to the welfare of the United States, that is, an office for promoting and preserving perpetual peace in our country . . . PEACE ON EARTH—GOOD WILL TO MAN. AH! WHY WILL MEN FORGET THAT THEY ARE BRETHREN?

—"A PLAN OF PEACE OFFICE FOR THE UNITED STATES"

*A*miri *B*araka

(1 9 3 4 –   )

A protean talent—the author of more than twenty volumes of poetry, fiction, drama, autobiography, and criticism—Baraka, born LeRoi Jones in Newark, emerged during the 1960s as a poet of enormous power, taking the name Imamu (spiritual leader) Amiri (blessed one) Baraka (prince). With Larry Neal and Don Lee, he was a leader of the Black Arts Movement, and his work has continued to evolve, and remain heavily engaged, over time.

> African blues
> does not know me. . . .
> You are
> as any other sad man here
> american.
> —*"Notes for a Speech"*

> Lately, I've become accustomed to the way
> The ground opens up and envelops me
> Each time I go out to walk the dog.
> —*"Preface to a Twenty-Volume Suicide Note"*

May the people accept you as the ghost of the future. And love you, that you might not kill them when you can.
—*Lula*, Dutchman *(1964)*

You don't know anything except what's there for you to see. An act. Lies. Device. Not the pure heart, the pumping black heart.
—*Clay, Ibid.*

If Bessie Smith had killed some white people she wouldn't have needed that music . . . Crazy niggers turning their backs on sanity.

When all it needs is that simple act. Murder. Just murder! Would make us all sane.

—CLAY, IBID.

I am fully conscious all the time that I am an American Negro because it's part of my life. But I know also that if I want to say, "I see a bus full of people," I don't have to say, "I am a Negro seeing a bus full of people."

—THE SULLEN ART: INTERVIEW WITH MODERN AMERICAN POETS *(1963)*

We do not want a Nation, we are a Nation . . . We are a people. We are unconscious captives unless we realize this.

—"THE LEGACY OF MALCOLM X, AND THE COMING OF THE BLACK NATION" *(1965)*

These have been our White Ages, and all learning has suffered . . . What the Black Man must do now is look down at the ground upon which he stands, and claim it as his own.

—IBID.

As I stared at the books, I suddenly understood that I didn't know a hell of a lot about anything. What it was that seemed to move me then was that learning was *important* . . . I vowed, right then, to learn something new every day. It was a deep revelation, something I felt throughout my whole self.

—THE AUTOBIOGRAPHY OF LEROI JONES / AMIRI BARAKA *(1984)*

Despair sits on this country in most places like a charm, but there is a special gray death that loiters in the streets.

—COLD HURT AND SORROW *(1966)*

> The fair are
> fair, and death
> ly white.
>
> The day will not save them
> and we own
> the night.
>
> —"STATE / MEANT"

We want "poems that kill."

—"BLACK ART"

It is a narrow nationalism that says the white man is the enemy . . . Nationalism, so called, when it says "all non-blacks are our enemies," is sickness or criminality, in fact, a form of fascism.

—*INTERVIEW,* New York Times *(1974)*

Even if I wasn't strong enough to *act,* I would become strong enough to SPEAK what had to be said, for all of us, for Black people, yes, particularly for Black people, because they were the root and origin of my conviction, but for anyone anywhere who wanted justice!

—THE AUTOBIOGRAPHY OF LEROI JONES / AMIRI BARAKA *(1984)*

The Black Artist's role in America is to aid in the destruction of America as he knows it.

—*"STATE / MEANT"*

Charles Barkley

(C . 1 9 7 2 –)

One of the most talented, and controversial, players in the NBA, the somewhat outrageous Barkley has made it a point that his public role extends to playing basketball, period.

If I weren't earning more than $3 million a year to dunk a basketball, most people on the street would run in the other direction if they saw me coming.

—*IN KEVIN NELSON,* TALKIN' TRASH *(1993)*

I don't care what people think. People are stupid.

—*ON CHANGING HIS TEAM UNIFORM NUMBER TO HONOR MAGIC JOHNSON*

Do I want to stay in a 100 degree room with three or four room-mates? Of course I don't. I think that's a stupid question.

—*RESPONSE TO A REPORTER'S QUESTION ON WHETHER THE DREAM TEAM SHOULDN'T STAY WITH THE OTHER ATHLETES*

It's a ghetto thing. He hit me. I hit him. Something you guys don't understand.

—*RESPONSE TO A REPORTER ON HIS WIDELY CRITICIZED ELBOWING OF AN ANGOLAN PLAYER DURING THE 1992 OLYMPICS*

Kids are great. That's one of the best things about our business, all the kids you get to meet. It's a shame they have to grow up to be regular people and come to the games and call you names.

—*TALKIN' TRASH*

I am not a role model.

—*OFTEN STATED*

Count Basie

(1 9 0 4 – 1 9 8 4)

Born in Red Bank, New Jersey, the pianist and band leader Basie spent his early career in Kansas City. His lush swing orchestra emerged in the 1930s and was home to such musicians as Lester Young, Walter Page, Buck Clayton, and the singers Billie Holiday and Sarah Vaughan. The supremely polished Basie performed actively until his death.

I knew about King Oliver, and I also knew that Paul Whiteman was called the King of Jazz. Duke Ellington was also getting to be one of the biggest new names in Harlem and also on records and on the radio, and Earl Hines and Baron Lee were also important names. So I decided that I would be one of the biggest new names; and I actually had some little fancy business cards printed up to announce it, COUNT BASIE. Beware the Count Is Here.

—GOOD MORNING BLUES *(1985)*

Of course, there are a lot of ways you can treat the blues, but it will still be the blues.

—*IBID.*

Duke's whole thing was always so *beautiful.* It's so melodic and it took in everything—prettiness, swing—everything. It was just so wonderful . . . If he wanted something to swing, it was going to *swing,* and he was going to swing your behind right on *out* of there.

—*ON DUKE ELLINGTON, IBID.*

Old Pops. He was *everybody's* main man. One of a kind.

—*ON LOUIS ARMSTRONG, IBID.*

It's the way you play that makes it . . . Play like you play. Play like you *think,* and then you got it, if you're going to get it. And whatever you get, that's you, so that's your story.

—*IBID.*

If I haven't spent a lot of time complaining about all of these things, it's not because I want anybody to get the impression that all of that was not also a part of it. It was. So what? Life is a bitch, and if it's not one damn thing, it's going to be something else . . . I'll just say that I didn't intend to let anything stop me if I could help it, and that should tell you something.

—*ON THE DAYS OF JIM CROW, IBID.*

I was always willing to say, "Let's see what happens," when something came up that looked like it might help me get a little closer to where I wanted to be, and since that's the way I still am, that really is old Count Basie right on up to date . . . I'm saying: *to be continued, until we meet again.* Meanwhile, keep on listening and tapping your feet.

—*IBID.*

Daisy Bates

(1 9 2 0 –)

Civil rights activist and president of the Arkansas NAACP, Bates accompanied the nine children who desegregated Central High School in Little Rock, Arkansas, in the fall of 1957. She continued to be politically active, and in 1985 her newspaper, the Arkansas State Press, *which she had founded in the 1940s, was revived.*

The crowd moved in closer and then began to follow me, calling me names. I still wasn't afraid. Just a little bit nervous, whether I could make it to the center entrance a block away. It was the longest block I ever walked in my whole life.

   —THE LONG SHADOW OF LITTLE ROCK *(1962)*

We've got to decide if it's going to be this generation or never.

   —c. 1975

Kathleen Battle

(1 9 4 8 –)

Born in Portsmouth, Ohio, Battle sang in a gospel choir as she grew up and received her master's degree from the University of Cincinnati's College Conservatory. She made her debut at the Metropolitan Opera in 1977 in Tannhäuser *and has since sung with major companies and in music festivals around the world. She is also an immensely popular recording artist.*

The culture I come from is just as rich as any Western European culture. Therefore, I believe what I'm bringing to it only enriches opera. Many times I am asked, "How can you be from a small town in the Midwest and sing Mozart?" Mozart was a human being with emotions and a sense of humor . . . We all share these qualities as human beings.

—*1987 TELEVISION INTERVIEW*

Melba Pattillo Beals

(c .   1 9 4 3 –   )

Beals was one of the nine children who desegregated Central High School in Little Rock, Arkansas, in the fall of 1957. She went on to earn a graduate degree from the Columbia University School of Journalism and become a reporter for NBC. She is now a communications consultant and author.

You just realize that survival is day to day and you start to grasp your own spirit, you start to grasp the depth of the human spirit, and you start to understand your own ability to cope no matter what.

—*IN HENRY HAMPTON,* VOICES OF FREEDOM *(1990)*

If my Central High School experience taught me one lesson, it is that we are not separate. The effort to separate ourselves whether by race, creed, color, religion, or status is as costly to the separator as to those who would be separated . . . The task that remains is to cope with our interdependence—to see ourselves reflected in every other human being and to respect and honor our differences.

—WARRIORS DON'T CRY *(1994)*

Romare Bearden

(1914 – 1988)

Born in Charlotte, North Carolina, Bearden moved to New York to study art at the height of the Harlem Renaissance, and later attended the Sorbonne in Paris. Known particularly for his collages, Bearden captured the changing currents of twentieth-century black life in his work, which was celebrated by a one-man show at the Museum of Modern Art in New York in 1970.

Modern art has borrowed heavily from Negro sculpture . . . the fine surface qualities of the sculpture, the vitality of the work, and the unsurpassed ability of the artist to create such significant forms. Of great importance has been the fact that the African would distort his figure, if by so doing he could achieve a more expression form. This is one of the cardinal principles of the modern artist.

—*"The Negro Artist and Modern Art,"* Opportunity, *December 1934*

Practically all the great artists have accepted the influence of others. But the difference lies in the fact that the artist with vision sees his material, chooses, changes, and by integrating what he has learned with his own experiences, finally molds something distinctly personal.

—*Ibid.*

I am a man concerned with truth, not flattery, who shares a dual culture that is unwilling to deny the Harlem where I grew up or the Haarlem of the Dutch masters that contributed its element to my understanding of art.

—Art News, *October 1964*

There are roads out of the secret place within us which we must all move as we go to touch others.

—*c. 1975*

You see, this is also not just about painting: it was a history of something that is gone, and people should know about it.

—*ON HIS DEPICTION OF RURAL BLACK LIFE, IN* ROMARE BEARDEN *(1993)*

Well, it's like jazz; you *do* this and then you improvise.

—*ON HIS ARTISTIC METHOD, IBID.*

I create social indentities so far as the subjects are Negro, but I have not created protest images, because the world within the collage, if it is authentic, retains the right to speak for itself.

—ART NEWS, *OCTOBER 1964*

The artist must be the medium through which humanity expresses itself. In this sense the greatest artists have faced the realities of life, and have been profoundly social . . . If it is the race question, the social struggle, or whatever else that needs expression, it is to that the artist must surrender himself.

—*"THE NEGRO ARTS AND MODERN ART"*

I want to see how life can triumph.

—*IN ERIC V. COPAGE,* BLACK PEARLS *(1993)*

$\mathcal{D}$errick $\mathcal{B}$ell

(1 9 3 0 –)

A leading legal scholar, Bell was a tenured professor at Harvard University Law School until he was dismissed for refusing to end a leave of absence until a minority woman was appointed to the faculty. He is now a visiting professor at New York University Law School.

It appears that my worst fears have been realized: we have made progress in everything yet nothing has changed.

—AND WE ARE NOT SAVED *(1987)*

Black people are the magical faces at the bottom of society's well. Even the poorest whites, those who must live their lives only a few levels above, gain their self-esteem by gazing down on us. Surely, they must know that their deliverance depends on letting down their ropes.

—FACES AT THE BOTTOM OF THE WELL *(1992)*

We yearn that our civil rights work will be crowned with success, but what we really want—want even more than success—is meaning . . . This engagement and commitment is what black people have had to do since slavery: making something out of nothing. Carving out a humanity for oneself with absolutely nothing to help—save imagination, will, and unbelievable strength and courage . . . It is a story less of success than survival through an unremitting struggle that leaves no room for giving up. We are all part of that history, and it is still unfolding.

—*IBID.*

Philip A. Bell

(1 8 0 9 – 1 8 8 9)

A prominent activist all his life, Bell was a delegate to the important black political conventions of the mid-1800s, contributed to the black press, founded The Weekly Advocate *in 1837, and served as a U.S. Commissioner of Civil Rights.*

The time must come when the Declaration of Independence will be felt in the heart, as well as uttered from the mouth, and when the rights of all shall be properly acknowledged and appreciated. God hasten that time. This is our home, and this is our country. Beneath its sod lie the bones of our fathers; for it, some of them fought, bled, and died. Here we were born, and here we will die.

—*ADDRESS PROTESTING THE AMERICAN COLONIZATION SOCIETY, NEW YORK, JANUARY 24, 1831*

Be righteous, be honest, be just, be economical, be prudent, offend not the laws of your country—in a word, live in . . . the constant pursuit of that moral and intellectual strength, which will invigorate your understandings, and render you illustrious in the eyes of the civilized nations, when they will assert, that all that illustrious worth, which was once possessed by the Egyptians, and slept for ages, has now arisen in their descendants, the inhabitants of the new world.

—ADDRESS TO THE FREE COLORED INHABITANTS OF THESE UNITED STATES, SECOND ANNUAL
NATIONAL NEGRO CONVENTION, PHILADELPHIA, JUNE 4–13, 1832

This is *Our* own,
Our native land.
—*IBID.*

Gwendolyn Bennett

(1 9 0 2 – 1 9 8 1)

Born in Giddings, Texas, Bennett studied at Teachers College at Columbia University and was graduated from the Pratt Institute in Brooklyn in 1924. She taught in the Fine Arts Department at Howard University, studied art for a year in France, and edited "The Ebony Flute," a column of "literary chit-cat and artistic what-not," for Opportunity, *before returning to Howard University in 1926.*

Brushes and paints are all I have
To speak the music in my soul . . .
—*"QUATRAINS"*

I shall sing a lullaby
To the song I have made
Of your hair and eyes . . .
And you will never know
That deep in my heart

I shelter a song of you
Secretly . . .
—*"Secret"*

Something of old forgotten queens
Lurks in the lithe abandon of your walk . . .
—*"To a Dark Girl"*

Silence is a sounding thing
To one who listens hungrily.
—*"Your Songs"*

I sailed in my dreams to the Land of the Night
Where you were the dusk-eyed queen
—*"Fantasy"*

I shall hate you
Like a dart of singing steel
Shot through still air
At even-tide.
—*"Hatred"*

Chuck Berry

(1 9 2 6 –)

Charles Edward Anderson Berry was born in San Jose, California, and grew up in Saint Louis. Raised in the gospel tradition, he was drawn to the blues and especially the work of Muddy Waters. Waters introduced him to the Chess record label, which released his rock-and-roll classics "Maybelline," "Roll Over Beethoven," "Johnny B. Goode," and others.

Roll over Beethoven
And tell Tchaikovsky the news.
—*"ROLL OVER BEETHOVEN," 1956*

He never learned to read or write so well
But he could play a guitar just like ringing a bell.
—*"JOHNNY B. GOODE," 1958*

Mary McLeod Bethune

(1875–1955)

The educator and reformer Bethune founded Bethune-Cookman College, which she headed from 1904 to 1942, and helped organize the National Association of Colored Women's Clubs. She was an adviser to Presidents Roosevelt and Truman, served as a consultant to the conference to draft the UN Charter, and was awarded the Spingarn Medal of the NAACP.

The true worth of a race must be measured by the character of its womanhood.
—*"A CENTURY OF PROGRESS OF NEGRO WOMEN" CHICAGO WOMEN'S FEDERATION, JUNE 30, 1935*

Whatever the achievements of the Negro man in letters, business, art, pulpit, civic progress, and moral reform, he cannot but share them with his sister of darker hue. Whatever glory belongs to the race for a development unprecedented in history for the given length of time, a full share belongs to the womanhood of the race.
—*IBID.*

There is a place in God's sun for the youth "farthest down" who has the vision, the determination, and the courage to reach it.
—*c. 1935*

If our people are to fight their way out of bondage we must arm them with the sword and the shield and the buckler of pride—belief in themselves and their possibilities based upon a sure knowledge of the past. That knowledge and pride we must give them—if it breaks every back in the kingdom.

—*"Clarifying Our Vision with the Facts,"* The Journal of Negro History, *January 1938*

When they learn the fairy tales of mythical kings and queens, we must let them hear of the pharaohs and African kings and the brilliant pageantry of the Valley of the Nile; when they learn of Caesar and his legions, we must teach them of Hannibal and his Africans, when they learn of Shakespeare and Goethe, we must teach them of Pushkin and Dumas . . . Whatever the white man has done, we have done, and often better.

—*Ibid.*

We are not blind to what is happening. We are not humiliated. We are incensed.

—*speech to the National Council of Negro Women, November 26, 1938*

It was almost impossible for a Negro child, especially in the South, to get education . . . Mr. Lincoln had told our race we were free, but mentally we were still enslaved.

—*"Faith That Moved a Dump Heap,"* Who, the Magazine about People, *June 1941*

"For God so loved the world that He gave His only begotten Son, that whosoever believeth in Him should not perish, but have everlasting life" . . . These words stored up a battery of faith and confidence and determination in my heart which has not failed me to this day.

—*Ibid.*

I plunged into the job of creating something from nothing . . . Though I hadn't a penny left, I considered cash money as the smallest part of my resources. I had faith in a living God, faith in myself, and a desire to serve.

—*Ibid.*

I am my mother's daughter and the drums of Africa still beat in my heart. They will not let me rest while there is a single Negro boy or girl without a chance to prove his worth.

—*Ibid.*

What does the Negro want? His answer is very simple. He wants only what all other Americans want. He wants opportunity to make real what the Declaration of Independence and the Constitution and the Bill of Rights say, what the Four Freedoms establish. While he knows these ideals are open to no man completely, he wants only his equal chance to obtain them.

—*"Certain Inalienable Rights,"* What the Negro Wants *(1944)*

I am Mary McLeod Bethune, I am black, I am a Negro, and I am going somewhere.

—*her common salutation, in Bouthane,* Negro Orators and Their Orations *(1968)*

Knowledge is the prime need of the hour.

—*"My Last Will and Testament,"* Ebony, *August 1955*

ℬlack 𝒫anther 𝒫arty

Rising out of the dissolution of the civil rights movement and the rage engendered by the deaths of Martin Luther King, Jr., and Malcolm X, the BPP was organized in 1968 in Oakland, California, and spread to other parts of the nation. Among its leaders were Huey P. Newton, Bobby Seale, Eldridge Cleaver, and Fred Hampton.

We believe that black people will not be free until we are able to determine our destiny. . . . We believe in an education system that will give to our people a knowledge of self. If a man does not have a knowledge of himself and his position in society and the world, then he has little chance to relate to anything else.

—*Black Panther Ten-Point Party Platform, October 1966*

We want land, bread, housing, education, clothing, justice, and peace.

—*Ibid.*

Unita Blackwell

(c. 1940–)

At the forefront of the civil rights struggle, Blackwell was mayor of Mayersville, Mississippi. Like Fannie Lou Hamer, she was a member of the Mississippi Freedom Democratic Party, which was denied seating at the Democratic National Convention in 1964, but Blackwell spoke before the convention in 1984.

I can remember a woman told me one time . . . "Well, the reason I won't vote for you is because they going to kill you." The whites had told her that they were going to kill me and she thought she was saving my life. And when I stood on that podium twenty years later, that I was still living, that feeling that I was standing there for this woman, to understand that she had a right to register to vote for whomever she wanted to, and that we as a people were going to live.

—*IN CLAYBORNE CARSON, ET AL.,* THE EYES ON THE PRIZE CIVIL RIGHTS READER *(1991)*

We wanted something for ourselves and for our children, so we took a chance with our lives.

—*IN JANET CHEATHAM BELL,* FAMOUS BLACK QUOTATIONS *(1991)*

Eubie Blake

(1883–1983)

Born in Baltimore, J. Hubert Blake was the tenth child of former slaves and the only one to survive infancy. He began studying the piano at six and was playing in clubs by the age of seventeen. Begin-

ning with Shuffle Along *in 1921, he wrote a series of Broadway hits that also included* Chocolate Dandies *and* Blackbirds. *He retired in 1946 to enter college, and his life was the subject of the 1978 Broadway musical* Eubie!

Don't love nobody, it ain't worthwhile
All alone runnin' wild.
—*"Runnin' Wild," from* Shuffle Along *(1921)*

I don't have any bad habits. They might be bad habits for other people, but they're all right for me.
—Eubie *(1979)*

If I'd known I was going to live this long, I'd have taken better care of myself.
—*WIDELY ATTRIBUTED*

Vida Blue

(1 9 4 9 –)

Born in Mansfield, Louisiana, Vida Rochelle Blue was a star high school athlete and was recruited for the minors in 1967. He pitched a no-hitter in his rookie season with the Oakland A's in 1970, and the following year threw eight shut-outs and became the first black Cy Young Award winner in the American League. He later played for San Francisco and Kansas City and rebounded from a cocaine possession conviction in 1983 to be restored briefly in the majors.

I keep telling myself, don't get cocky. Give your services to the press and the media, be nice to the kids, throw a baseball into the stands once in a while.
—*IN Richard Deming,* Vida *(1972)*

I think I have already signed some scrap of paper for every man, woman, and child in the United States. What do they do with all those scraps of paper with my signature on it?

—*FROM* VIDA: HIS OWN STORY *(1972)*

It's easy, man. I just take the ball and throw. Hard! It's a God-given talent! No one can teach it to you. They either hit it or they don't.

—*IBID.*

It's a weird scene. You win a few baseball games and all of a sudden you're surrounded by reporters and TV men with cameras asking you about Vietnam and race relations.

—LOS ANGELES TIMES, *APRIL 14, 1982*

When I'm throwing good, I don't think there's a man in the world who can hit me.

—*WIDELY ATTRIBUTED*

Sometimes in this game it's as good to be lucky as it is to be good.

—VIDA: HIS OWN STORY

The Blues

Originating after the Civil War, and expanding in the 1890s in Texas and the Mississippi Delta, the blues grew out of work songs, love songs, and stomps to express the worldly lament of a people newly free. The familiar three-cornered lyrics came to have a major impact not only on black music and culture but on the work of such writers as Langston Hughes, Sterling Brown, Amiri Baraka, August Wilson, and others.

Now when a woman gets the blues,
Lord, she hangs her head and cries.
But when a man gets the blues,
Lord, he grabs a train and rides

. . . .

When you see me comin', h'ist yo' window high,
When you see me comin', h'ist yo' window high,
You know damn well I ain't gonna pass you by.

When you see me goin', hang yo' head an' cry,
When you see me goin', hang yo' head an' cry.
Gonna love you til the day I die.
                    —*"Easy Rider Blues"*

Dey tell me Joe Turner's come an' gone—
Tell me Joe Turner's come an' gone—
Got my man—an'—gone.
Come wid his fo'ty links of chain—
Come wid his fo'ty links of chain—
Got my man an' gone.
                    —*"Joe Turner Blues"*

Wake up this mawnin',
Blues all round my bed.
Went to eat breakfuss,
Blues all in my bread.
           —*"The Blues Come from Texas"*

I've had a man for fifteen years,
Give him his room and board;
Once he was like a Cadillac,
Now he's like an old worn-out Ford.
      —*"Put It Right Here or Keep It Out There"*

Ah, you hear me talking to you
I don't bite my tongue
You wants to be my man
You got fetch it with you when you come.
           —*"Hear Me Talkin' to You"*

Got de blues, but am too damn mean to cry.

The man I'll marry ain't born yet—an' his mammy's dead.

Been down so long, down don't worry me.

> I've got a belly full o' whiskey an' a head full o' gin
> The doctors say it'll kill me, but they don't say when.

Blues ain't nothing' but a po' man's heart disease.

Did you ever wake up in de mo'nin', yo' mind rollin' two different ways
One mind to leave your baby, and one mind to stay?

See also W. C. Handy; Skip James; Blind Lemon Jefferson; Robert Johnson; John Lee Hooker; Son House; Memphis Minnie; Ma Rainey; Bessie Smith

Bobby Bonilla

(1 9 6 4 –)

Born in New York City, Bonilla played for several years in the late 1980s for the Pittsburgh Pirates, where he was elected to the all-star team for three consecutive years. In 1991, he left the Pirates to join his hometown Mets for a then-record $29 million five-year contract.

Kids today are looking for idols, but sometimes they look too far . . . They don't have to look any farther than their home because those are the people that love you. They are the real heroes.
—USA Today, *March 30, 1989*

Marita Bonner

(1 8 9 9 – 1 9 7 1)

A graduate of Radcliffe College, Bonner won the 1925 essay prize in The Crisis *with the memorable "On Being Young—a Woman—and Colored" and contributed stories to* The Crisis *and* Opportunity. *She taught in Washington, D.C., and her collected works were published as* Frye Street and Environs.

If you have never lived among your own, you feel prodigal. Some warm untouched current flows through them—through you—and drags you out into the deep waters of a new sea of human foibles and mannerisms; of a peculiar psychology and prejudices. And one day you find yourself entangled—enmeshed—pinioned in the seaweed of a Black Ghetto.

—*"ON BEING YOUNG—A WOMAN—AND COLORED,"* THE CRISIS, *December 1925*

You wonder and you wonder until you wander out into Infinity, where—if it is to be found anywhere—Truth really exists.

—*IBID.*

You can, when Time is ripe, swoop to your feet—at your full height—at a single gesture. Ready to go where? Why . . . Wherever God motions.

—*IBID.*

Arna Bontemps

(1 9 0 2 – 1 9 7 3)

Born in Louisiana, Bontemps attended college in California and taught at the Harlem Academy in New York. His poems were published in Opportunity, The Crisis, *and other magazines, and he is the author of the novels* God Sends Sunday *and* Black Thunder.

I have sown beside all waters in my day.
I planted deep, within my heart the fear
That wind or fowl would take the grain away.
I planted safe against this stark, lean year.
   —"A Black Man Talks of Reaping"

Let us kept the dance of rain our fathers kept
And tread our dreams beneath the jungle sky.
   —"The Return"

Is there something we have forgotten? some precious thing
We have lost, wandering in strange lands?
   —"Nocturne at Bethesda"

Yet I hope, still I long to live.
And if there can be returning after death
I shall come back. But it will not be here;
If you want me you must search for me
Beneath the palms of Africa.
   —Ibid.

Dust shall yet devour the stones
But we shall be here when they are gone.
   —"Golgotha Is a Mountain"

Yet would we die as some have done,
Beating a way for the rising sun.
—*"THE DAY-BREAKERS"*

How dare anyone, parent, schoolteacher, or merely literary critic, tell me not to act *colored?*
—*QUOTED IN* HENRY LOUIS GATES, JR., COLORED PEOPLE *(1994)*

William Stanley Braithwaite

(1 8 7 8 – 1 9 6 2)

Born in Boston of West Indian parents, Braithwaite was a distinguished poet and critic and taught for more than two decades at Atlanta University. The author of three volumes of poetry and two novels, Braithwaite was one of the first to articulate, in his celebrated anthologies and critical studies, the canonical works of black letters.

Art alone has kept her covenant with democracy.
—THE CRISIS, *1915*

There was something in me grieves—
That was never born, and died.
—*"TURN ME TO MY YELLOW LEAVES"*

I am glad daylong for the gift of song,
For time and change and sorrow;
For the sunset wings and the world-end things
Which hang on the edge of tomorrow.
—*"RHAPSODY"*

Heart free, hand free,
Blue above, brown under,

All the world to me
Is a place of wonder.
—*"Sic Vita"*

North or south is there never a sign?
—*"The Watchers"*

Negro poetic expression hovers for the moment, pardonably perhaps, over the race problem, but its highest allegiance is to Poetry—it must soar.
—*"The Negro in American Literature,"* The Crisis, *1924*

The Souls of Black Folk [by Langston Hughes] was the book of an era; it was a painful book, a book of tortured dreams woven into the fabric of the sociologist's document. This book has more profoundly influenced the spiritual temper of the race than any other written in its generation.
—*Ibid.*

Cane is a book of gold and bronze, of dusk and flame, of ecstasy and pain, and Jean Toomer is a bright morning star of a new day of the race of literature.
—*Ibid.*

Chester Brewer, Jr.

(Negro League player— dates unknown)

For much of its early history, the sport of baseball remained strictly segregated and the feats of its black stars went unrecorded. In the 1920s, the first organized Negro National League was formed, but it disbanded in 1931 with the Great Depression. Throughout the 1930s, new Negro League teams sprang up, the playing ground of folk heroes like Satchel Paige, Josh Gibson, and James Thomas "Cool Papa"

Bell. While baseball would not become fully integrated until Jackie Robinson was signed to the majors in 1947, the Negro Leagues did provide what Bell called "a brotherhood of friendship which will last forever."

Drugs take you further than you want to go,
Keep you there longer than you want to stay,
And cost you more than you can ever pay.

ℒou ℬrock

(1 9 3 9 –)

Born in El Dorado, Arkansas, the left-hander Louis Clark Brock quickly established his reputation in the late 1960s as an aggressive player, first for the Chicago Cubs and later for the Saint Louis Cardinals. In 1974, he stole a record 118 bases, and he held the all-time stolen-base record of 938 until 1991. He played in three World Series for the Cardinals, where he tied the record for stolen bases, and in 1985 was elected to the Baseball Hall of Fame.

Jim Crow was king . . . and I heard a game in which Jackie Robinson was playing, and I felt pride in being alive. The baseball field was my fantasy of what life offered.
—INTERNATIONAL HERALD TRIBUNE, *JANUARY 30, 1985*

Competition is what keeps me playing—the psychological warfare of matching skill against skill and wit against wit. If you're successful in what you do over a period of time, you'll start approaching records, but that's not what you're playing for. You're playing to challenge and be challenged.
—CHRISTIAN SCIENCE MONITOR, *JANUARY 20, 1975*

You can't be afraid to make errors! You can't be afraid to be naked before the crowd, because no one can ever master the game of baseball, or conquer it. You can only challenge it.

—IN ROGER ANGELL, LATE INNINGS *(1977)*

Gwendolyn Brooks

(1 9 1 7 –)

The author of more than fifteen volumes of poetry, Brooks won early acclaim with her volumes A Street in Bronzeville *(1945) and* Annie Allen *(1949), which received the Pulitzer Prize. The author of the novel* Maud Martha *and several volumes of autobiography, she has taught at Columbia, City College, Northeastern, and elsewhere, and has served as a mentor to many younger poets.*

I want to write poems that will be non-compromising.

—c. 1969

Abortions will not let you forget.

—"THE MOTHER"

What shall I give my children? who are poor,
Who are adjudged the leastwise of the land

—"WHAT SHALL I GIVE MY CHILDREN?"

Art hurts. Art urges voyages—and it is easier to stay at home.

—"THE CHICAGO PICASSO"

This is the urgency: Live!
and have your blooming in the noise of the whirlwind.

—"THE SECOND SERMON ON THE WARPLAND"

Blackness
is a going to essences and to unifyings.
—*"Young Heroes: Keorapetse Kgositsile (Willie)"*

Your voice is the listened-for music.
—*"Young Heroes: To Don at Salaam"*

Fire.
That is their way of lighting candles in the darkness.
—*"Riot: The Third Sermon on the Warpland"*

Lies are told and legends made.
Phoenix rises unafraid.
—*Ibid.*

You are direct and self-accepting as a lion
in African velvet.
—*"Riot: An Aspect of Love, Alive in the Ice and Fire"*

To be in love
Is to touch things with a lighter hand.
—*"To Be in Love"*

Beware
the easy griefs
—*"Boys Black"*

Make of my Faith an engine
Make of my Faith
a Black Star. I am Beckoning.
—*Ibid.*

I—who have "gone the gamut" from an almost angry rejection of my dark skin by some of my brainwashed brothers and sisters to a surprised queenhood in the new Black sun—am qualified to enter at least the kindergarten of new consciousness now. New consciousness and trudge-toward-progress. I have hopes for myself.
—Report from Part One: An Autobiography *(1972)*

To die is to stop. Somebody else goes on or begins. The big, the middle, the little jobs are through. One may or may not have worked the puzzle, seen the comet, minimized, mastered, established, or tamed. One may or may not have managed the Miracle. What was to be done to be done to be done is done or not done.

—*tribute to Mayor Harold Washington, Chicago, February 1988*

What else is there to say but everything?

—*"In the Mecca"*

Claude Brown

(1 9 3 7 –   )

Brown, born in Harlem, spent his youth in the world of crime, gang wars, drugs, and reform schools he describes in his classic autobiography, Manchild in the Promised Land. *He attended Howard University and became a lawyer and is also a playwright and the author of* The Children of Ham *(1976).*

For where does one run to when he's already in the promised land?

—Manchild in the Promised Land *(1965)*

Man, you not givin' us another chance. You givin' us the same chance we had before.

—*Ibid.*

You don't mess with a man's money; you don't mess with a man's woman; you don't mess with a man's family or his manhood—these were a man's principles . . .

—*Ibid.*

Despite everything that Harlem did to our generation, I think it gave something to a few. It gave them a strength that couldn't be obtained anywhere else.

—*Ibid.*

H. Rap Brown

(1 9 4 3 –)

A prominent activist during the 1960s, in 1967 Brown became head of the Student Non-Violent Coordinating Committee. The following year he was convicted on a gun-possession charge and in 1972 he was shot and arrested for armed robbery. While in prison he converted to the Islamic faith and took the name Jamil Abdullah Al-Amin. He now leads a community mosque in Atlanta.

Violence is as American as cherry pie.
> —STATEMENT AT A PRESS CONFERENCE, JULY 27, 1967

Being a man is the continuing battle for one's life. One loses a bit of manhood with every stale compromise to the authority of any power in which one does not believe.
> —DIE NIGGER DIE *(1969)*

James Brown

(1 9 3 3 –)

Born in rural South Carolina and raised in Georgia, "the Godfather of Soul" left school at fifteen to begin his professional career, singing gospel and rhythm and blues with the Flames. He made his first recording in 1956, and over the years "the Hardest Working Man in Show Business" has had a string of hits that include "Out of Sight," "Papa's Got a Brand New Bag," "Living in America," and others.

"Say It Loud: I'm Black and I'm Proud."
—SONG TITLE, 1979

Sometimes you struggle so hard to feed your family one way, you forget to feed them the other way, with spiritual nourishment. Everybody needs that.
—JAMES BROWN: THE GODFATHER OF SOUL *(1986)*

Hair is the first thing. And teeth the second. Hair and teeth. A man got those two things he's got it all.
—*IBID.*

It doesn't matter how you travel it, it's the same road. It doesn't get any easier when you get bigger, it gets harder. And it will kill you if you let it.
—*IBID.*

You can't accomplish anything by blowing up, burning up, stealing, and looting. Don't terrorize. Organize. Don't burn. Give kids a chance to learn . . . The real answer to race problems in this country is education. Not burning and killing. Be ready. Be qualified. Own something. Be somebody. That's Black Power.
—*STATEMENT ON NATIONAL TELEVISION DURING THE RIOTS IN WASHINGTON, D.C., 1968*
(AFTER MARTIN LUTHER KING'S DEATH)

When I'm on stage, I'm trying to do one thing: bring people joy. Just like church does. People don't go to church to find trouble, they go there to lose it.
—JAMES BROWN: THE GODFATHER OF SOUL

Honors and gold records and all that aren't what I'm proudest of. I'm proudest of what I have become, as opposed to what I *could* have become, and I'd like to be remembered as someone who brought people together.
—*IBID.*

There's something wrong with the system. It's designed for you not to make it. And if you make it, it's designed for you not to keep it.
—DETROIT FREE PRESS, *FEBRUARY 12, 1989*

I've been in slavery all my life. Ain't nothing changed for me but the address.

—DETROIT FREE PRESS, *MARCH 12, 1989*

$\mathcal{S}$terling $\mathcal{B}$rown

(1 9 0 1 – 1 9 8 9)

*E*ducated at Williams and Harvard, Sterling Brown tapped a rich poetic source in the folk songs and blues of his people and began his long career as a poet with the publication of Southern Road *in 1932. A critic and teacher, he also co-edited the important anthologies* The Book of American Negro Poetry *(with James Weldon Johnson, revised in 1931), and* The Negro Caravan *(with Arthur Davis and Ulysses Lee).*

Dialect or the speech of the people is capable of expressing whatever the people are.

—THE NEGRO CARAVAN *(1941)*

I have . . . a deep concern with the development of a literature worthy of our past, and of our destiny; without which literature certainly, we can never come to much. I have a deep concern with the development of an audience worthy of such a literature.

—*"OUR LITERARY AUDIENCE,"* OPPORTUNITY, *FEBRUARY 1930*

Propaganda, however legitimate, can speak no louder than the truth.

—*IBID.*

One manifest truth . . . is this: the sincere, sensitive artist, willing to go beneath the clichés of popular belief to get at an underlying reality, will be wary of confining a race's entire characters to a half-dozen narrow grooves. He will hardly have the temerity to say that his necessarily limited observation of a few Negroes in a restricted envi-

ronment can be taken as the last word about some mythical *the* Ne-
gro.
—*"Negro Character as Seen by White Authors,"* The Journal of Negro Education,
April 1933

> The place was Dixie
> That I took for hell.
> —*"Slim in Hell"*

> They got the shotguns
> They got the rope
> We git the justice
> In the end
> —*"Old Lem"*

> Chain gang nevah—hunh—Let me go;
> Chain gang nevah—hunh—Let me go.
> —*"Southern Road"*

> Ain't no call at all, sweet woman,
> Fo' to carry on—
> Jes' my name and jes' my habit
> To be long Gone . . .
> —*"Long Gone"*

An embattled people used literature as a weapon.
—*"A Century of Negro Portraiture in American Literature"*—The Massachusetts Review,
Winter 1966

> *One thing they cannot prohibit—*
> The strong men . . . coming on
> The strong men gittin' stronger.
> Strong men. . . .
> Stronger. . . .
> —*"Strong Men"*

Cracker, your breed ain't exegetical.
—*response to Robert Penn Warren ("Nigger, your breed ain't metaphysical" in "Pondy
Woods") interview, 1973*

I wanted to understand my people. I wanted to understand what it meant to be a Negro, what the qualities of life were. With their imgination, they combine two great loves: the love of words and the love of life. Poetry results.

—New York Times Book Review, *January 11, 1981*

William Wells Brown

(1 8 1 5 – 1 8 8 4)

Antislavery lecturer and author of more than sixteen volumes, William Wells Brown was among the most prominent African Americans of his day. In addition to his several works on early black American history, he wrote Narrative, *the story of his escape from slavery; it is a classic work in this genre. He was the first black author to write a novel (*Clotel*) and play (*The Escape*).*

When I alone thought myself lost my dungeon shook, my chains fell off.

—Narrative *(1847)*

We may search history in vain to find a people who have sunk themselves as low, and made themselves appear as infamous by their treatment of their fellow men, as have the people of the United States . . . This is emphatically an age of discoveries; but I will venture the assertion, that none but an American slaveholder could have discovered that a man born in a country was not a citizen of it.

—*letter from England to Wendell Phillips,* The Liberator, *November 22, 1849*

The duty I owe to the slave, to truth, and to God, demands that I should use my pen and tongue so long as life and health are vouchsafed to me to employ them, or until the last chain shall fall from the limbs of the last slave in America and the world.

—LETTER TO HIS FORMER MASTER, ENOCH PRICE, THE LIBERATOR, DECEMBER 14, 1849

I will not yield to you in affection for America, but I hate her institution of slavery. I love her, because I am identified with her enslaved millions by every tie that should bind man to his fellow-man.

—IBID.

Society does not frown upon the man who sits with his mulatto child upon his knee, whilst its mother stands a slave behind his chair.

—CLOTEL (1853)

Oh, how the moonlight oppressed him with its friendly sadness! It was like the plaintive eye of his forsaken one, like the music of sorrow echoed from an unseen world.

—IBID.

You may place the slave where you please; you may dry up to your utmost the fountains of his feelings, the springs of his thought; you may yoke him to your labour, as an ox which liveth only to work, and workest only to live; you may put him under any process which, without destroying his value as a slave, will debase and crush him as a rational being; you may do this, and *the idea that he was born to be free will survive it all*. It is allied to his hope of immortality; it is the ethereal part of his nature, which oppression cannot reach; it is a torch lit up in his soul by the hand of Deity, and never meant to be extinguished by the hand of man.

—IBID.

Sad to say, Jefferson is not the only American statesman who has spoken high-sounding words in favour of freedom, and then left his own children to die slaves.

—IBID.

No country has produced so much heroism in so short a time, connected with escapes from peril and oppression, as has occurred in the United States among fugitive slaves.

—IBID.

The prejudice that exists in the Free States against coloured persons, on account of their colour, is attributable solely to the influence of slavery, and is but another form of slavery itself.

—*IBID.*

Despotism increases in severity with the number of despots; the responsibility is more divided, and the claims more numerous.

—*IBID.*

We, as individuals, are fast losing our reputation for honest dealing. Our nation is losing its character. The loss of a firm national character, or the degradation of a nation's honour, is the inevitable prelude to her destruction.

—*IBID.*

Behold the Mayflower anchored at Plymouth Rock, the slave-ship in James River. Each a parent, one of the prosperous, labour-honouring, law-sustaining institutions of the North; the other the mother of slavery, idleness, lynching, ignorance, upaid labour, poverty, and duelling, despotism, the ceaseless swing of the whip; and the peculiar institutions of the South. These ships are the representation of good and evil in the New World, even to our day. When shall one of these parallel lines come to an end?

—*IBID.*

I would have the Constitution torn in shreds and scattered to the four winds of heaven. Let us destroy the Constitution and build on its ruins the temple of liberty.

—THE LIBERATOR, *MAY 18, 1855*

All I demand for the black man is, that the white people shall take their heels off his neck, and let him have a chance to rise by his own efforts.

—SPEECH TO THE AMERICAN ANTI-SLAVERY SOCIETY, NEW YORK, *MAY 6, 1862*

The last struggle for our rights, the battle for our civilization is entirely with ourselves.

—CIRCA *1881*

I was not only hunting for my liberty, but also hunting for my name.

—IN HENRY LOUIS GATES, JR., FIGURES IN BLACK *(1987)*

Blanche K. Bruce

(1 8 4 1 – 1 8 9 8)

Born into slavery in Virginia, Bruce remained a fugitive throughout the Civil War. He later traveled to Mississippi and, after holding a series of political offices, was elected to the United States Senate in 1875. Though Southern politicians spurned him, Bruce served until 1881.

The only distinctions upon which parties can be safely organized and in harmony with our institutions are differences of opinion relative to principles and policies of government, and that differences of religion, nationality, or race can neither with safety nor propriety be permitted for a moment to enter into the party contests of the day . . .

—SPEECH TO THE SENATE MARCH 31, 1876, AFTER FRAUDULENT ELECTIONS IN MISSISSIPPI

I have confidence, not only in my country and her institutions, but in the endurance, capacity, and destiny of my people . . . Whatever our ultimate position in the composite civilization of the Republic and whatever varying fortunes attend our career, we will not forget our instincts for freedom nor our love for country.

—IBID.

Ralph J. Bunche

(1 9 0 4 – 1 9 7 1)

A Phi Beta Kappa graduate of the University of California, Bunche received his Ph.D. from Harvard and taught briefly at Howard University. After serving in the military in World War II, he joined the State Department and participated in the planning conferences for

the formation of the UN, where he worked until his resignation in 1971. He was instrumental in the resolution of the postwar conflict in the Middle East and in 1950 was awarded the Nobel Peace Prize.

The Constitution of the United States is a very flexible instrument and it cannot be anything more than the controlling elements that the American society wish it to be . . . We must adhere staunchly to the basic principle that anything less than full equality is not enough. If we compromise on that principle, our soul is dead.

— *"Critical Analysis of the Tactics and Programs of Minority Groups,"* The Journal of Negro Education, *July 1935*

We must fight as a race for everything that makes for a better country and a better world. We are dreaming idiots and trusting fools to do anything less.

— *c. 1944*

There is no doubt that overwhelmingly the sympathy of the members of the UN, from all sections of the world and people of all colors, is for the American Negro in his heroic struggle for justice. The eyes of the world are focused on this problem, on what happens in the United States. This has a tremendous effect on the United States' image abroad. I have always been confident that the Negro will win this struggle, but it is not the Negro, really, but the nation that must win it.

— *Ibid.*

The impatience of the Negro about the lack of *decisive* and *immediate* progress—and that is the *only* kind of progress that can now have meaning in the removal of racial shackles—is increasing and will continue to increase until all of the racial shackles are removed.

— *Ibid.*

Nuclear weapons, the death and destruction of war, are color-blind, and in that context, there is complete equality among the races. The entire world will be living on borrowed time until peace is finally made secure . . .

— *in* Columbus Salley, The Black 100 *(1993)*

ℳannie ℬurroughs

(1 8 8 3 – 1 9 6 1)

Born in Washington, D.C., Nannie Helen Burroughs trained as a teacher and was active in the Women's Auxiliary of the National Colored Baptist Convention. She founded the National Training School for Girls, was a member of the National Association of Colored Women's Clubs and the NAACP, and was a frequent contributor to the press.

We specialize in the wholly impossible.

—*MOTTO OF THE NATIONAL TRAINING SCHOOL FOR GIRLS, WASHINGTON, D.C.*

The Negro woman carries the moral destiny of two races in her hand. Had she not been the woman of unusual moral stamina that she is, the black race would have been made a great deal whiter, and the white race a great deal blacker, during the past fifty years.

—THE CRISIS, *AUGUST 1915*

This nation openly endorses, tolerates, and legalizes the very abuses against which she originally waged a bloody revolution . . . Day after day, year after year, decade after decade, black people have been robbed of their inalienable rights. They have been goaded, hounded, driven around, herded, held down, kicked around, and roasted alive, by America's homemade Reds. In Harlem the cornered rats fought back.

—*"DECLARATION OF 1776 IS CAUSE OF HARLEM RIOT,"* THE AFRO-AMERICAN, *APRIL 13, 1935*

It will profit the Negro nothing to enter into ungodly competition for material possessions when he has gifts of greater value. The most valuable contribution which he can make to American civilization must be made out of his spiritual endowment.

—*"WITH ALL THEY GETTING,"* THE SOUTHERN WORKMAN, *JULY 1927*

When the Negro learns what manner of man he is spiritually, he will wake up all over. He will stop playing white even on the stage. He will rise up in the majesty of his own soul. He will glorify the beauty of his own brown skin . . . No race is richer in soul quality and color than the Negro. Someday he will realize and glorify them; he will popularize black.

—*IBID.*

Anything that is as old as racism is in the blood line of the nation. It's not any superficial thing—that attitude is in the blood and we have to educate it out.

—*"UNLOAD YOUR UNCLE TOMS,"* THE LOUISIANA WEEKLY, *DECEMBER 23, 1933*

Human beings are equipped with divinely planted yearnings and longings. That's what the Constitution meant by "certain unalienable rights"! There must be no substitute for them in the form of charity, philanthropy, or any man-made institution. There must be no compromise.

—*IBID.*

What we need are mental and spiritual giants who are aflame with a purpose . . . We're a race ready for crusade, for we've recognized that we're a race on this continent that can work out its own salvation.

—*IBID.*

Get used to being colored. Have faith in yourselves and in your race. Negroes who buy Cadillacs to bolster their ego are whistling in the dark. They are confused and don't want to be left out of things. The Negro must stop apologizing for not being white. He must qualify for the position that he wants . . . Aspire to be, and all that we are not, God will give us credit for trying.

—OPPORTUNITY, *MAY 1924*

"Moses, my servant is dead. Therefore arise and go over Jordan." There are no deliverers. They're all dead. We must arise and go over Jordan. We can take the promised land.

—*"UNLOAD YOUR UNCLE TOMS"*

Cab Calloway

(1 9 0 7 – 1 9 9 4)

*K*nown as much for his style as for his skills as a musician, Calloway
and his big band reigned after Ellington at the Cotton Club during
the 1930s. He featured such soloists as Dizzie Gillespie, and appeared
in numerous films, including Stormy Weather.

Hi-De-Hi-De-Hi-De-Ho.
> —*HIS TRADEMARK*

My audience was my life. What I did and how I did it, was all for my
audience.
> —*c. 1988*

Roy Campanella

(1 9 2 1 – 1 9 9 3)

*C*ampanella began playing professionally at sixteen and won four
National League pennants with the Brooklyn Dodgers in the 1950s.
His career was cut short when he was paralyzed in a car accident in
1958. In 1969, he became the second black player inducted into the
Baseball of Fame.

You didn't get hurt when you played in the Negro leagues. You played
no matter what happened to you because if you didn't play, you didn't
get paid.
> —*QUOTED ON HIS DEATH*, NEW YORK TIMES, *JUNE 28, 1993*

I never want to quit playing ball. They'll have to cut this uniform off me to get me out of it.

—IN MEL ALLEN, IT TAKES HEART (1959)

This completes my baseball career. All my disappointments are behind me. There is nothing more I could ask for in baseball.

—ON BEING INDUCTED INTO THE HALL OF FAME, 1969

Stokely Carmichael

(1 9 4 1 –)

At a demonstration in Jackson, Mississippi, in May 1966, Stokely Carmichael, the head of the Student Nonviolent Coordinating Committee (SNCC), first used the Black Power slogan. Meant to describe grass-roots efforts at political and economic self-empowerment, the slogan was much misunderstood as a declaration of militancy. Carmichael is now known as Kwame Ture.

Our grandfathers had to run, run, run. My generation's out of breath. We ain't running no more.

—c. 1963

Politically, black power means what it has always meant . . . the coming-together of black people to elect representatives and to force those representatives to speak to their needs. It does not mean merely putting black faces into office.

—"WHAT WE WANT," THE NEW YORK REVIEW OF BOOKS, SEPTEMBER 22, 1966

[T]he economic foundations of this country must be shaken if black people are to control their lives. The colonies of the United States— and this includes the black ghettoes within its borders, north and south—must be liberated. . . . The society we seek to build among black people, then, is not a capitalist one. It is a society in which the spirit of community and humanistic love prevail.

—*Ibid.*

To most whites, black power seems to mean that the Mau Mau are coming to the suburbs at night . . . Black people do not want to "take over" this country. They don't want to "get whitey"; they just want to get him off their backs . . . The white man is irrelevant to blacks, except as an oppressive force.

—*Ibid.*

For decades, black people had been taught to believe that voting, politics, is "white folks' business." And the white folks had indeed monopolized that business, by methods which ran the gamut from economic intimidation to murder.

—Black Power: The Politics of Liberation in America *(1967)*

The *act* of registering to vote . . . marks the beginning of political modernization by broadening the base of participation. It also does something the existentialists talk about: it gives one a sense of being. The black man who goes to register is saying to the white man, "No."

—*Ibid.*

We had no more courage than Harriet Tubman or Marcus Garvey had in their times. We just had a more vulnerable enemy.

—*"What Became of the Prophets of Rage,"* Life, Spring *1988*

For racism to die, a totally different America must be born.

—*"What We Want"*

Betty Carter

(1 9 3 0 –   )

Born in Flint, Michigan, Carter began her career as a be-bop singer after she won amateur night at the Apollo. A preeminent scat singer, she has worked with Dizzy Gillespie, Ray Charles, Charlie Parker, and Lionel Hampton, among others.

If you wanted to get into jazz, you had to go downtown where the pimps, prostitutes, hustlers, gangsters, and gamblers supported the music. If it wasn't for them there wouldn't be no jazz! They supported the club owners who bought the music. It wasn't the middle-class people who said "Let's go hear Charlie Parker tonight."

—Jazz Forum, *January 1979*

This is our culture, and I don't care who the musician is, if he avoids black people, then he is scared of something. He doesn't have confidence in himself or else he doesn't believe in what he's doing.

—*1972 interview in Arthur Taylor,* Notes and Tones *(1977)*

Billie Holiday was a stylist with a particular and unique sound of her own. She was untrained, unabashed, and uninhibited.

—*Ibid.*

If you're sitting in that audience ready to fight me from the very beginning, I'm going to have a hard time getting to you. But if you've got a heart at all, I'm going to get it.

—*in Nat Hentoff,* Books and Art, *September 14, 1979*

After me there are no more jazz singers . . . It's a crime that no little singer is back there sockin' it to me in my field. To keep it going, to keep it alive, because I'm not going to live forever. I'm going to die eventually, and I don't want it to die with me; I want it to keep on.

—Notes and Tones

Stephen L. Carter

(1 9 5 4 –)

Stephen L. Carter is William Nelson Cromwell Professor of Law at Yale University. Once a clerk to former Supreme Court Justice Thurgood Marshall, today he is one of the nation's leading experts on constitutional law. Carter is the author of Reflections of an Affirmative Action Baby: The Culture of Disbelief *and* The Confirmation Mess: Cleaning Up the Federal Appointments Process.

One sees a trend in our political and legal cultures toward treating religious beliefs as arbitrary and unimportant, a trend supported by a rhetoric that implies that there is something wrong with religious devotion.

—The Culture of Disbelief, *1993*

A religion is, at its heart, a way of denying the authority of the rest of the world. It is a way of saying to fellow human beings and to the state those fellow humans have erected, "No, I will *not* accede to your will." This is a radically destabilizing proposition.

—*Ibid.*

George Washington Carver

(1 8 6 4 ? – 1 9 4 3)

Born to slave parents in Missouri during the Civil War, Carver received a master's degree in science in 1896 from Iowa State College, where he taught briefly before Booker T. Washington brought him, later that year, to Tuskegee, where he remained for the rest of his life. A deeply religious man, "The Wizard of Tuskegee" is best known for his work in developing products from the peanut plant.

No individual has any right to come into the world and go out of it without leaving behind him distinct and legitimate reasons for having passed through it.

—CORRESPONDENCE, MAY 25, 1915

I wanted to know the name of every stone and flower and insect and bird and beast. I wanted to know where it got its color, where it got its life—but there was no one to tell me.

—AMERICAN LIFE, *November 1923*

Our Creator is the same and never changes despite the names given Him by people here and in all parts of the world. Even if we gave Him no name at all, He would still be there, within us, waiting to give us good on this earth.

—GEORGE WASHINGTON CARVER: MAN OF GOD *(1954)*

Fear of something is at the root of hate for others and hate within will eventually destroy the hater.

—*IBID.*

He who puts . . . a product upon the market as it demands, controls that market, regardless of color. It is simply a survival of the fittest.

—*"THE NEGRO AS FARMER," IN* TWENTIETH-CENTURY NEGRO LITERATURE *(1905?)*

We have become ninety-nine percent money mad. The method of living at home modestly and within our income, laying a little by systematically for the proverbial rainy day which is due to come, can almost be listed among the lost arts.

—*"Are We Starving in the Midst of Plenty?," December 1931*

More and more as we come closer and closer in touch with nature and its teachings are we able to see the Divine and are therefore fitted to interpret correctly the various languages spoken by all forms of nature about us . . . the little windows through which God permits me to commune with Him, and to see much of His glory, majesty, and power by simply lifting the curtain and looking in.

—*"How to Search for Truth," February 1930*

My work is that of keeping every operation down so that the farmer and the man fartherest down can get hold of it.

—*correspondence, March 29, 1940*

The beating on the tail of the snake may stop his progress a little, but the more vital parts must be struck before his poisonous death-dealing venom will be wiped out. Just so with the poisonous venom of prejudice and race hatred.

—*correspondence, April 2, 1929*

My people must get credit.

—*correspondence, July 1, 1929*

Ray Charles

(1 9 3 0 –)

Born in Albany, Georgia, Ray Charles Robinson suffered total loss of his eyesight by the age of seven. On the death of his mother, when he was fifteen, he left school to begin performing, and in the fifty years since he has enjoyed enormous popularity as a pianist and vocalist in

*a career that has arced from blues and jazz to soul, country, and pop.
He was one of the original inductees in the Rock and Roll Hall of
Fame in 1986, and received a Kennedy Center honor in 1986 and the
Grammy Lifetime Achievement Award in 1988.*

I was born with music inside me . . . Music was one of my parts.
Like my ribs, my liver, my kidneys, my heart. Like my blood. It was a
force already within me when I arrived on the scene. It was a necessity
for me—like food or water.

—BROTHER RAY *(1978)*

Going blind. Sounds like a fate worse than death, doesn't it? Seems
like something which would get a little kid down, make him afraid,
and leave him half-crazy and sad. Well, I'm here to tell you that it
didn't happen that way—at least not with me.

—*IBID.*

Those tunes got dark all over again—in a hurry—when I got my
hands on them. I reclaimed them and brought 'em back to where they
started out.

—*ON RE-RECORDING SONGS COMPOSED BY BLACK ARTISTS THAT HAD LATER BEEN RECORDED
BY WHITE PERFORMERS; IBID.*

I couldn't see the people looking back at me. So I just tried to please
myself. I figured if I could please Ray, that was good enough.

—*IBID.*

Affluence separates people. Poverty knits 'em together. You got some
sugar and I don't; I borrow some of yours. Next month you might not
have any flour; well, I'll give you some of mine.

—*IBID.*

I never learned to stop at the skin. If I looked at a man or woman, I
wanted to see inside. Being distracted by shading or coloring is stupid. It gets in the way. It's something I just can't see.

—*IBID.*

My music had roots which I'd dug up from my own childhood, musical roots buried in the darkest soil.

—*IBID.*

Charles W. Chesnutt

(1858 – 1932)

A major figure in nineteenth-century letters, Chesnutt was born in Cleveland, studied classics and modern literature, and became a teacher and court stenographer before his first stories, written in dialect, which he later abandoned, appeared in The Atlantic Monthly. *Two collections of stories were followed by three novels, numerous speeches, essays, and reviews.*

I think I must write a book. It has been my cherished dream and I feel an influence that I cannot resist calling me to the task . . . The object of my writings would be not so much the elevation of the colored people as the elevation of the whites—for I consider the unjust spirit of caste which is so insidious as to pervade a whole nation, and so powerful as to subject a whole race and all connected with it to scorn and social ostracism—I consider this a barrier to the moral progress of the American people; and I would be one of the first to head a determined, organized crusade against it.

—JOURNAL, MAY 29, 1880

En ha' ter be a monst'us cloudy night when a dollar get by him in de dakhness.

—ON HIS MASTER, UNCLE JULIUS MCADOO, "THE GOOPHERED GRAPEVINE" (1887)

Impossibilities are merely things of which we have not learned, or which we do not wish to happen.

—THE MARROW OF TRADITION (1901)

The race which at last will inherit the earth—the residuary legatee of civilization—will be the race which remains longest upon it. The Negro was here before the Anglo-Saxon was evolved, and his thick lips and heavy lidded eyes looked out from the inscrutable face of the Sphinx across the sands of Egypt while yet the ancestors of those who now oppress him were living in caves, practicing human sacrifices, and painting themselves with woad—and the Negro is here yet.

—*IBID.*

The workings of the human heart are the profoundest mystery of the universe. One moment they make us despair of our kind, and the next we see in them the reflection of the divine image.

—*IBID.*

Selfishness is the most constant of human motives. Patriotism, humanity, or the love of God may lead to sporadic outbursts which sweep away the heaped-up wrongs of centuries; but they languish at times, while the love of self works on ceaselessly, unwearyingly, burrowing always at the very roots of life, and heaping up fresh wrongs for other centuries to sweep away.

—*IBID.*

Sins, like chickens, come home to roost.

—*IBID.*

Surely, God had put his curse not alone upon the slave, but upon the stealer of men! . . . The weed had been cut down, but its root remained, deeply imbedded in the soil, to spring up and trouble a new generation.

—*IBID.*

The Negro who died for the common rights of humanity might look for no need of admiration or glory . . . they would applaud his courage while they stretched his neck, or carried off the fragments of his mangled body as souvenirs, in much the same way that savages preserve the scalps or eat the hearts of their enemies.

—*IBID.*

Race prejudice is the devil unchained.

—*IBID.*

As a man sows, so shall he reap. In works of fiction, such men are sometimes converted. More often, in real life, they do not change their natures until they are converted into dust.

—*IBID.*

Our boasted civilization is but a veneer which cracks and scrubs off at the first impact of primal passions.

—*IBID.*

When the pride of intellect and caste is broken; when we grovel in the dust of humiliation; when sickness and sorrow come, and the shadow of death falls upon us, and there is no hope elsewhere—we turn to God, who sometimes swallows the insult, and answers the appeal.

—*IBID.*

There's time enough, but none to spare.

—*IBID.*

It never occurred to me to claim any merit because of it, and I have always resented the denial of anything because of it.

—ON RACE, *"POST-BELLUM—PRE-HARLEM," 1931*

Alice Childress

(1 9 2 0 – 1 9 9 4)

Born in South Carolina and raised in Harlem, Childress had a successful career as an actress and director before turning her hand to playwrighting. Her plays include Florence *(1950) and* Trouble in Mind *(1955), which won an Obie Award, and she is the author of* A Hero Ain't Nothin' but a Sandwich *and other novels.*

The Black writer explains pain to those who inflict it.

—*"A CANDLE IN A GALE WIND," IN MARI EVANS,* BLACK WOMEN WRITERS *(1984)*

Writers are encouraged to "keep 'em laughing" and complain "with good humor" in order to "win" allies. The joke is always on ourselves.

—*IBID.*

Like snowflakes, the human pattern is never cast twice. We are uncommonly and marvelously intricate in thought and action, our problems are most complex and, too often, silently borne.

—*Ibid.*

I continue to create because writing is a labor of love and also an act of defiance, a way to light a candle in a gale wind: "In the beginning was the Word, and the Word was God, and the Word was God."

—*Ibid.*

Life is just a short walk from the cradle to the grave—and it sure behooves us to be kind to one another along the way.

—A SHORT WALK *(1979)*

*S*hirley *C*hisholm

(1 9 2 4 –)

Born in Brooklyn and educated at Columbia University, Chisholm taught and held local office before becoming the first black woman elected to Congress, in 1969. Though she was unsuccessful in her attempt to gain the Democratic nomination for president in 1972, she remained in Congress until 1982, continuing to fight for programs to benefit women and the underprivileged.

Our children, our jobless men, our deprived, rejected, and starving fellow citizens must come first. For this reason, I intend to vote *No* on every money bill that comes to the floor of this House that provides any funds for the Department of Defense.

—*HER FIRST SPEECH TO CONGRESS, MARCH 26, 1969*

I am, as is obvious, both black and a woman. And that is a good vantage point from which to view at least two elements of what is becoming a social revolution: the American black revolution and the women's liberation movement. But it is also a horrible disadvantage.

It is a disadvantage because America as a nation is both racist and antifeminist.

—ADDRESS TO THE CONFERENCE ON WOMEN'S EMPLOYMENT, U.S. HOUSE OF REPRESENTATIVES, 91ST CONGRESS, 1970

The law cannot do it for us. *We must do it for ourselves.* Women in this country must become revolutionaries.

—IBID.

I believe that women have a special contribution to make to help bring order out of chaos in our nation because they have special qualities of leadership which are greatly needed today. And these qualities are the patience, tolerance, and perseverance which have developed in many women because of suppression. And if we can add to these qualities a reservoir of information about the techniques of community action, we can indeed become effective harbingers for change.

—IBID.

When I decided to run for Congress, I knew I would encounter both antiblack and antifeminist sentiments. What surprised me was the much greater virulence of the sex discrimination . . . I was constantly bombarded by both men and women exclaiming that I should return to teaching, a woman's vocation, and leave politics to the men.

—IN COLUMBUS SALLEY, THE BLACK 100 (1993)

Kenneth B. Clark

(1 9 1 4 –)

Kenneth Bancroft Clark moved to Harlem in 1918, at the dawn of the Harlem Renaissance, attended Howard University, and received his Ph.D. from Columbia in 1940. The studies conducted by Dr. Clark on the psychological effect of institutional racism on black children profoundly affected the outcome of the landmark Brown v. Board of

Education *ruling on school segregation, and he is the author of a number of important studies on race.*

Are children born with racial feelings? Or do they have to learn, first, what color they are and, second, what color is "best"? . . . Learning about races and racial differences, learning one's own racial identity, learning which race is to be preferred and which rejected—all these are assimilated by the child as part of the total pattern of ideas he acquires about himself and the society in which he lives.
—*"How Children Learn About Race,"* Prejudice and Your Child *(1955)*

The dark ghettos are social, political, educational, and—above all—economic colonies. Their inhabitants are subject peoples, victims of the greed, cruelty, insensitivity, guilt, and fear of their masters.
—Dark Ghetto *(1965)*

I read that report . . . of the 1919 riot in Chicago, and it is as if I were reading the report of the investigating committee on the Harlem riot of '35, the report of investigating committee on the Harlem riot of '43, the report of the McCone Commission on the Watts riot. I must again in candor say to you members of this commission—it is a kind of Alice in Wonderland—with the same moving picture re-shown over and over again, the same analysis, the same recommendations, and the same inaction.
—*testimony to the Kerner Commission, 1968*

Pride, like humility, is destroyed by one's insistence that he possess it.
—The Pathos of Power *(1974)*

It is questionable whether the *masses* of an oppressed group can in fact "love" their oppressor. The natural reactions to injustice, oppression, and humiliation are bitterness and resentment.
—*in* Columbus Salley, The Black 100 *(1993)*

The Negro remains the constant, and at times irritating reality that is America. He remains the essential psychological reality with which America must continuously seek to come to terms—and in so doing is formed by.
—*Ibid.*

Eldridge Cleaver

(1 9 3 5 –)

Born in Little Rock, Arkansas, Cleaver spent much of his youth in trouble and was eventually interned in Soledad Prison, where he read voraciously and began writing; in 1968, his collection of essays, Soul on Ice, *was published. After he was paroled in 1966, he became Minister of Information for the Black Panthers, but fled the country after a clash between the Panthers and the police.*

You're either part of the solution or part of the problem.
—SPEECH, SAN FRANCISCO, *1968*

History could pass for a scarlet text, its jot and tittle graven red in human blood.
—SOUL ON ICE *(1968)*

From my prison cell, I have watched America slowly come awake.
—*"ON BECOMING," IBID.*

White blood is the coin of freedom in a land where for four hundred years black blood has been shed unremarked and with impunity. America has never truly been outraged by the murder of a black man, woman, or child.
—*"THE WHITE RACE AND ITS HEROES," IBID.*

What America demands in her black champions is a brilliant, powerful body and a dull, bestial mind.
—*"LAZARUS COMES FORTH," IBID.*

Respect commands itself and it can neither be given nor withheld when it is due.
—*"THE WHITE RACE AND ITS HEROES," IBID.*

And we had thought that our hard climb out of that cruel valley led to some cool, green, and peaceful, sunlit place—but it's all jungle here, a wild and savage wilderness that's overrun with ruins.

> —"TO ALL BLACK WOMEN, FROM ALL BLACK MEN," *IBID.*

The white heroes, their hands dripping with blood, are dead.

> —"THE WHITE RACE AND ITS HEROES," *IBID.*

The question of the Negro's place in America, which for a long time could actually be kicked around as a serious question, has been decisively resolved: he is here to stay.

> —"RALLYING ROUND THE FLAG," *IBID.*

The enemies of Black people have learned something from history and they're discovering new ways to divide us faster than we are discovering new ways to unite.

> —OPEN LETTER TO STOKELY CARMICHAEL, *1969*

You don't have to teach people to be human. You have to teach them how to stop being inhuman.

> —CONVERSATIONS WITH ELDRIDGE CLEAVER *(1970)*

The price of hating other human beings is loving oneself less.

> —"ON BECOMING," SOUL ON ICE

Lucille Clifton

(1 9 3 6 –)

Born in New York, Lucille Clifton attended Howard University before publishing her first book of poetry in 1969. Since then she has written more than twenty books for children and adults (several of them featuring the young Everett Anderson), one of which was nominated for a Pulitzer Prize. She received a fellowship from the National Endowment for the Arts and has taught at various colleges.

we have always loved each other
children all ways
pass it on.
—*"LISTEN CHILDREN,"* GOOD NEWS ABOUT THE EARTH

I have always known that being very poor, which we were, had nothing to do with lovingness or familyness or character or any of that . . . We were quite clear that what we had didn't have anything to do with what we were.
—*"A SIMPLE LANGUAGE," IN MARI EVANS,* BLACK WOMEN WRITERS *(1984)*

. . . i got a long memory
and i come from a line
of black and going on women
—*"FOR DE LAWD,"* GOOD TIMES

Things hold. Lines connect in ways that last and last and lives become generations made out of pictures and words just kept.
—*"GENERATIONS," IBID.*

mine already is
an afrikan name
—*"LIGHT," IBID.*

children
when they ask you
why your mama so funny
say
she is a poet
she don't have no sense.
—*"ADMONITIONS," IBID.*

Sometimes I think that the most anger comes from ones who were late in discovering that when the world said nigger it meant them too.
—*"A SIMPLE LANGUAGE"*

We have a generation enslaving itself to drugs, young men and women doing to our race what slavery couldn't.
—*"LETTER TO FRED,"* ESSENCE, *NOVEMBER 1989*

when a man
walk manly
he don't stumble
even in the lion's den.
—*"DANIEL,"* GOOD NEWS ABOUT THE EARTH

me and you be sisters.
we be the same.
me and you
coming from the same place.
—*"SISTERS,"* AN ORDINARY WOMAN

other people think they know
how long life is.
how strong life is.
we know.
—*"NEW BONES,"* IBID.

men will be gods
if they want it.
—*"GOOD FRIDAY,"* IBID.

Daniel Coker

(f l .   1 8 0 0 s)

A minister of the African Methodist Episcopal Church in Baltimore, the Reverend Coker was elected the first bishop of the newly independent A.M.E. Church in 1816, but soon ceded the position to Richard Allen and went to serve as a missionary in Africa.

While you have prayed that Ethiopia might stretch out her hands unto God, now when God seems to be answering your prayers, and opening the door for you to enjoy all that you could wish, many of you rise up and say, the time is not yet come; and it is thought by some a mark of arrogance and ostentation, in us who are embracing the opportunity that is now offered to us of being free. May the time speedily come, when we shall see our brethren come flocking to us like doves to their windows. And we as a band of brethren, shall sit down under our own vine to worship, and none to make us afraid.

—ON THE ROLE OF THE NEW *A.M.E. CHURCH; SERMON DELIVERED AT THE AFRICAN BETHEL CHURCH IN BALTIMORE, JANUARY 21, 1816*

Johnetta B. Cole

(1 9 3 6 –)

Born into a prominent family in Jacksonville, Florida, Cole attended Fisk and Oberlin universities and received her M.A. and Ph.D. in anthropology from Northwestern University. The recipient of numerous honorary doctorates and other awards, she taught at Washington State University, the University of Massachusetts, and Hunter College before being named the first female president of Spelman College in 1987.

Here we stand on the edge of the twenty-first century and still we are not free.

—*"BEING BLACK IN AMERICA," CONVERSATIONS (1993)*

While it is true that without a vision the people perish, it is doubly true that without action the people and their vision perish as well.

—*IBID.*

The victory is not in asking to be treated equally, but in being treated equally.

—*"BETWEEN A ROCK AND A HARD PLACE," IBID.*

In the long run . . . the real horror of oppression is that it can rob people of their will to try, and make them take themselves out of the running of life.

—*"LET'S DO WINDOWS ON THE WORLD," IBID.*

Making do when DON'T prevails is, quite simply, a kind of genius.

—*"STURDY BLACK BRIDGES," IBID.*

The histories of the poor and the powerless are as important as those of their conquerors, their colonizers, their kings and queens.

—*"SHE WHO LEARNS MUST TEACH," IBID.*

In an atmosphere relatively free of racism and sexism, where teachers care and expect the very best, parents and kinfolks are involved, and the curriculum and those around the students reflect in positive ways who the students are—there are no limits to what individuals can learn and what they can become.

—*IBID.*

When you educate a man you educate an individual, but when you educate a woman, you educate a nation.

—*IBID.*

Like many, I found the best therapy in the world is work. Lots of it!

—*"WILL THE CIRCLE BE UNBROKEN?," IBID.*

Spelman, as an institution and environment that promotes equality, justice, and human decency, has given me an opportunity to see and experience a touch of the ideal society for which I have struggled most of my life.

—*IBID.*

Nat (King) Cole

(1919–1965)

*B*orn *Nathaniel Adams Coles in Montgomery, Alabama, Cole moved with his family to Chicago when he was a boy and began playing piano in the church where his father was a minister. In 1936 he joined a touring company of* Shuffle Along, *and he followed his first record, "Straighten Up and Fly Right," in 1943 with a string of popular hits like "Mona Lisa," "Too Young," "The Christmas Song." He acted in several films and briefly hosted a network television show in 1957 before his death from cancer at the age of forty-five.*

I am an American citizen, and I feel that I am entitled to the same rights as any other citizen . . . we intend to stay there the same as any other American citizen would.

> —DURING PROTESTS AGAINST HIS FAMILY'S MOVE TO BEVERLY HILLS, SUMMER *1948*

I felt something impossible for me to explain in words. Then when they took her away, it hit me. I got scared all over again and began to feel giddy. Then it came to me—I was a father.

> —ON THE BIRTH OF HIS FIRST CHILD, NATALIE COLE, EBONY, MARCH *1950*

I got the message. All of us get the message, sooner or later. If you get it before it's too late or before you're too old, you'll pull through all right.

> —ON HIS TROUBLES WITH THE IRS IN *1949,* EBONY INTERVIEW

I just came here to entertain you. That was what I thought you wanted. I was born here.

> —ON BEING ATTACKED ONSTAGE IN BIRMINGHAM, ALABAMA, APRIL *10, 1956*

I can't come in on a one-night stand and overpower the law. The whites come to applaud a Negro performer like the colored do. When you've got the respect of white and colored, you can erase a lot of things . . . I can help ease the tension by gaining the respect of both races all over the country.

—ON PLAYING SEGREGATED VENUES IN THE SOUTH, c. 1956

Sponsors don't have guts. Madison Avenue is afraid of the dark.

—ON THE CANCELATION OF THE "NAT KING COLE SHOW" FOR LACK OF ADVERTISERS, DECEMBER 1957

I'm a businessman. I work for business people. The kind of thing they say is: Now we've sold a lot of records, let's sell some more.

—BRITISH INTERVIEW, 1963

Critics don't buy records. They get 'em free.

—ON CRITICISM THAT HE WAS BECOMING TOO "COMMERCIAL," IN JAMES HASKINGS, NAT KING COLE (1990)

Ornette Coleman

(1 9 3 0 -)

Born in Fort Worth, Texas, the alto sax player and master improvisor sought in the late 1950s to infuse jazz with new life in such albums as The Shape of Jazz to Come *and* Tomorrow Is the Question. *He is also a composer; his 1972 symphony* Skies of America *displays his notion of "harmelody," in which harmony, melody, and rhythm share equal emphasis.*

I only knew blues in B-flat. I was a B-flat man.

—INTERVIEW, PARIS, OCTOBER 1969, IN ARTHUR TAYLOR, NOTES AND TONES (1977)

I'm interested in music, not in my image. If someone plays something fantastic, that I could never have thought of, it makes me happy to know it exists. Only America makes you feel that everybody wants to be like you. That's what success is: Everybody wants to be like you.

—IBID.

We live in a world where someone can ask who the richest man in the world is and be given a name. But you can't name the poorest man in the world. They come in the millions.

—*IBID.*

Harmelody allows everybody to be an individual who does not have to imitate anybody else.

—*c. 1972*

I decided, if I'm going to be poor and black and all, the least thing I'm going to do is to try and find out who I am. I created everything about me.

—NEW YORK TIMES, *JUNE 23, 1991*

John Coltrane

(1 9 2 6 – 1 9 6 7)

Raised in Philadelphia, Coltrane played briefly with Dizzy Gillespie before working with Monk, Miles Davis, and later his own quartet. In such albums as Giant Steps, My Favorite Things, Love Supreme, *and* Ascension, *Trane incorporated Eastern and African influences while his deepening spirituality freed him from addiction to alcohol and drugs and allowed him "a glimpse into the unfathomed abyss of what has not yet become."*

I think I was first awakened to musical exploration by Dizzy Gillespie and Bird. It was through their work that I began to learn about musical structures and the more theoretical aspects of music.

—*"COLTRANE ON COLTRANE,"* DOWN BEAT, *SEPTEMBER 29, 1960*

Working with Monk brought me close to a musical architect of the highest order.

—*IBID.*

It took me that long to get it all in.

—*ON HIS INFAMOUS SOLOS,* COLTRANE'S SOUND *(1960)*

Usually, I like to get familiar with a new piece before I record it, but you never have to *worry about the blues.*

—COLTRANE "LIVE" AT THE VILLAGE VANGUARD *(1961)*

During the year 1957, I experienced by the grace of God a spiritual awakening which was to lead me to a richer, fuller, more productive life. At that time, in gratitude, I humbly asked to be given the means and privilege to make others happy through music.

—A LOVE SUPREME *(1964)*

No matter what . . . it is with God, He is gracious and merciful. His way is through love in which we all are. It is truly—a Love SUPREME.

—*IBID.*

There are so many things to be considered in making music. The whole question of life itself . . . I know that I want to produce beautiful music, music that does things to people that they need.

—*INTERVIEW, 1962*

All a musician can do is to get closer to the sources of nature, and so feel that he is in communion with the natural laws.

—*IBID.*

I never even thought about whether or not they understand what I'm doing . . . the emotional reaction is all that matters—as long as there's some feeling of communication, it isn't necessary that it be understood.

—*"FOR COLTRANE THE TIME IS NOW,"* MELODY MAKER, *DECEMBER 19, 1964*

There is never any end . . . There are always new sounds to imagine; new feelings to get at. And always, there is the need to keep purifying these feelings and sounds so that we can really see what we've discovered in its pure state. So that we can see more clearly where we are. In that way we can give to those who listen the essence, the best of what we are. But to do that at each stage, we have to keep on cleaning the mirror.

—MEDITATIONS *(1975)*

I want to be a force for real good. In other words, I know that there are bad forces put here that bring suffering to others and misery to the world, but I want to be the force which is truly for good.

—BLACK NATIONALISM AND THE REVOLUTION IN MUSIC *(1970)*

By this point I don't know what else can be said in words about what I'm doing. Let the music speak for itself.

—EXPRESSION, *1967*

James Cone

(1 9 3 8 –)

A leading black theologian, Cone was born in Arkansas and received his M.A. and Ph.D. from Northwestern University. Based at Union Theological Seminary in New York since 1969, he is the author of several important works on liberation theology, including Black Theology and Black Power *(1969).*

Anger and humor are like the left and right arm. They complement each other. Anger empowers the poor to declare their uncompromising opposition to oppression, and humor prevents them from being consumed by their fury.

—MARTIN AND MALCOLM AND AMERICA *(1991)*

Testimony is an integral part of the Black religious tradition. It is the occasion where the believer stands before the community of faith in order to give account of the hope that is in him or her.

—MY SOUL LOOKS BACK *(1993)*

To sing about freedom and to pray for its coming is not enough. Freedom must be actualized in history by oppressed peoples who accept the intellectual challenge to analyze the world for the purpose of changing it.

—SPEAKING THE TRUTH *(1986)*

Truth knows no color; it appeals to intelligence.

—*IBID.*

Anna Julia Cooper

(1 8 5 8 – 1 9 6 4)

Born to a slave mother in Raleigh, North Carolina, Cooper was well educated as a child. After she was widowed, at the age of twenty-one, she attended Oberlin College, from which she received her B.A. and M.A. She later studied at Columbia and the Sorbonne, was active in the women's and Pan-African movements, and was also a teacher.

Only the BLACK WOMAN can say "when and where I enter, in the quiet, undisputed dignity of my womanhood, without violence and without suing or special patronage, then and there the whole *Negro race enters with me.*"

—A VOICE IN THE SOUTH *(1892)*

One needs occasionally to stand aside from the hum and rush of human interests and passions to hear the voices of God.

—*IBID.*

Woman, Mother—your responsibility is one that might make angels tremble and fear to take hold!

—*IBID.*

The cause of freedom is not the cause of a race or a sect, a party or a class—it is the cause of human kind, the very birthright of humanity.

—*IBID.*

A nation or an individual may be at peace because all opponents have been killed or crushed; or, nation as well as individual may have found the secret of true harmony in the determination to live and let live.

—*IBID.*

Bullies are always cowards at heart and may be credited with a pretty safe instinct in scenting their prey.

—*IBID.*

It is not the intelligent woman vs. the ignorant woman; nor the white woman vs. the black, the brown, and the red—it is not even the cause of woman vs. man. Nay, 'tis woman's strongest vindication for speaking that *the world needs to hear her voice.*

—IBID.

To be a woman of the Negro race in America, and to be able to grasp the deep significance of the possibilities of the crisis, is to have a heritage, it seems to me, unique in the ages.

—IBID.

$\mathcal{S}$amuel $\mathcal{E}$. $\mathcal{C}$ornish

(1 7 9 5 – 1 8 5 8)

Together with John B. Russwurm, the Reverend Cornish was a founding editor of the African-American press, establishing the first black paper, Freedom's Journal, *on March 16, 1827. After a split with Russwurm, Cornish continued the paper briefly as* The Rights of All *and was editor of the* Colored American. *A Presbyterian minister, he was also active in the black political convention movement of the mid-1800s.*

We wish to plead our own cause. Too long have others spoken for us. Too long has the publick [sic] been deceived by misrepresentations in things which concern us dearly, though in the estimation of some mere trifles.

—FREEDOM'S JOURNAL, *MARCH 30, 1827*

From the press and the pulpit we have suffered much by being incorrectly represented. Men whom we equally love and admire have not hesitated to represent us disadvantageously, without becoming personally acquainted with the true state of things, nor discerning between virtue and vice among us.

—*IBID.*

Bill Cosby

(1 9 3 7 -)

Born in Philadelphia, William Henry Cosby served in the navy and then attended Temple University on an athletic scholarship. While still in school he began performing and in the mid-1960s starred in the television series "I Spy," for which he received three Emmy Awards. His later series, "The Bill Cosby Show" and "The Cosby Show," and his autobiographical books extol the joys of marriage and family life, and he has shared his success with generous philanthropic gifts to numerous black colleges and charities.

There is hope for the future because God has a sense of humor and we are funny to God.

—*c. 1978*

Poets have said the reason to have children is to give yourself immortality . . . Immortality? Now that I have had five children, my only hope is that they are all out of the house before I die.

—FATHERHOOD *(1986)*

Always end the name of your child with a vowel, so that when you yell, the name will carry.

—*IBID.*

The truth is that parents are not really interested in justice. They just want quiet.

—ON METING OUT DISCIPLINE, *IBID.*

When my oldest one went [to college], the bill for her first year had already reached thirteen thousand dollars. I looked hard at this bill and then said to her, "Thirteen thousand dollars. Will you be the only student?"

—*Ibid.*

Human beings are the only creatures on earth that allow their children to come back home.

—*Ibid.*

I recently turned fifty, which is young for a tree, midlife for an elephant, and ancient for a quarter-miler, whose son now says, "Dad, I just can't run the quarter with you anymore unless I bring something to read."

—Time Flies *(1987)*

Like everyone else who makes the mistake of getting older, I begin each day with coffee and obituaries.

—*Ibid.*

The past is a ghost, the future a dream, and all we ever *have* is now.

—*Ibid.*

Let us now set forth one of the fundamental truths about marriage: the wife is in charge.

—Love and Marriage *(1989)*

Men and women belong to different species, and communication between them is a science still in its infancy.

—*Ibid.*

The heart of marriage is memories; and if the two of you happen to have the same ones and can savor your reruns, then your marriage is a gift from the gods.

—*Ibid.*

I am certainly not an authority on love because there are no authorities on love, just those who've had luck with it and those who haven't.

—*Ibid.*

My childhood should have taught me lessons for my own fatherhood, but it didn't because parenting can be learned only by people who have no children.
—CHILDHOOD *(1991)*

Civilization had too many rules for me, so I did my best to rewrite them.
—*IBID.*

The essence of childhood, of course, is play, which my friends and I did endlessly on streets that we reluctantly shared with traffic.
—*IBID.*

Children today know more about sex than I *or* my father did.
—*IBID.*

Racism has always been alive, well, and living in America. But the real issue has always been: How are you going to let it or not let it affect you? I chose not to let it get to me by learning to do business.
—*c. 1986*

Joseph Seamon Cotter, Jr.

(1 8 9 5 – 1 9 1 9)

Born in Louisville, Kentucky, Cotter attended Fisk University and demonstrated enormous promise as a young poet before his death, from tuberculosis, at the age of twenty-four. His volume The Band of Gideon *was published in 1918.*

O God, give me words to make my dream-children live.
—*"A PRAYER"*

I am so tired and weary,
So tired of endless fight,
So weary of waiting the dawn
And finding endless night.
— *"SUPPLICATION"*

Train your head and hands to do, your head and heart to dare.
—LINKS OF FRIENDSHIP *(1898)*

Let lessons of stern yesterdays . . . be your food, your drink, your rest.
—NEGRO TALES *(1912)*

Alexander Crummell

(1819–1898)

Born free in New York, Crummell was educated at the New York African Free School, Oneida Institute, and Cambridge University and became an ordained Episcopal minister. He spent twenty years in Liberia before returning to the United States in 1873 and was an early advocate of colonization. An outspoken critic of the limited educational opportunities available to African Americans, in 1897 he founded the American Negro Academy to recognize and promote scholarship.

We are Americans. We were born in no foreign clime. Here, where we behold the noble rivers and the rich fields, and the healthful skies, that may be called America; here, amid the institutions that now surround us, we first beheld the light of the impartial sun.
—*ADDRESS TO NEW YORK CONVENTION OF BLACK MEN, ALBANY, AUGUST 18–20, 1840*

[Our] blood is mingled with the soil of every battle field, made glorious by revolutionary reminiscence; and [our] bones have enriched the most productive lands of the country . . . For no vested rights, for no peculiar privileges, for no extra-ordinary prerogatives, do we ask. We merely put forth our appeal for a republican birthright.

IBID.

Color is nothing, anywhere. Civilized *condition* differences men, all over the globe.

—THE RELATIONS AND DUTIES OF FREE COLORED MEN IN AMERICA TO AFRICA *(1861)*

[We] are becoming awake to the conviction that, *as a race,* we have a great work to do. The zeal of England and of America, for Africa, is opening our eyes. Our own thoughtful men begin to feel the binding tie which joins them in every interest and feeling, with the negro race, all over the globe . . . You should claim with regard to this continent that "THIS IS OUR AFRICA," in all her gifts, and in her budding grace and glory.

—*IBID.*

Let our posterity know that we their ancestors, uncultured and un-learned, amid all trials and temptations, were men of integrity; recognized with gratefulness their truest friends, dishonoured and in peril; were enabled to resist the seductions of ease and the intimidations of power; were true to themselves, the age in which they lived, their object race, and the cause of man; shrunk not from trial, nor from sufferings—but conscious of Responsibility and impelled by Duty, gave themselves up to the vindication of the high hope, and the lofty aims of true Humanity!

—*"THE DIGNITY OF LABOR, ITS VALUE TO A NEW PEOPLE," WORKING MEN'S CLUB, PHILADELPHIA, 1881*

I do not stand here to-day to plead for the black *man.* He is a man; and if he is weak he must go the wall. He is a man; he must fight his own way, and if he is strong in mind and body, he can take care of himself. But for the mothers, sisters, and daughters of my race I have a right to speak. And when I think of their sad condition down South . . . [A] true civilization can only then be attained when the life of woman is reached, her whole being permeated by noble ideas, her fine taste enriched by culture, her tendencies to the beautiful gratified and developed, her singular and delicate nature lifted up to its full capacity.

—*"THE BLACK WOMAN OF THE SOUTH," ADDRESS TO THE FREEDMAN'S AID SOCIETY, OCEAN GROVE, NEW JERSEY, AUGUST 15, 1883*

Blind men! For they fail to see that neither property, nor money, nor station, nor office, nor lineage, are fixed factors, in so large a thing as the destiny of man; that they are not vitalizing qualities of humanity. The greatness of peoples springs from their ability to grasp the grand conceptions of being. It is the absorption of a people, of a nation, of a race, in large majestic and abiding things which lifts them up to the skies.

—ON THE FOUNDING OF THE NEGRO ACADEMY, MARCH 1897

Whatever rivalries and dissensions may divide man in the social or political world, let generosity govern *us*. Let us emulate one another in the prompt recognition of rare genius, or uncommon talent. Let there be no tardy acknowledgment of worth in *our* world of intellect.

—IBID.

Cheapness characterizes almost all the donations of the American people to the Negro . . . cheap wages and cheap food, cheap and rotten huts; cheap and dilapidated schools; cheap and stinted weeks of schooling; cheap meeting houses for worship; cheap and ignorant ministers; cheap theological training; and now, cheap learning, culture and civilization!

—"THE ATTITUDE OF THE AMERICAN MIND TOWARD THE NEGRO INTELLECT," 1898

There is no repugnance to the Negro buffoon, and the Negro scullion; but so soon as the Negro stands forth as an intellectual being, this toad of American prejudice, as at the touch of Ithuriel's spear, starts up a devil! . . . The Negro mind, imprisoned for nigh three hundred years, needs breadth and freedom, largeness, altitude, and elasticity . . .

—IBID.

The Almighty does not preserve, rescue, and build up a lowly people merely for ignoble ends.

—IN ANNA JULIA COOPER, VOICE FROM THE SOUTH (1892)

It is a sad reflection . . . that a sense of responsibility which comes with power is the rarest of things.

—c. 1894

Countee Cullen

(1903 – 1946)

One of the first writers to signal the Harlem Renaissance, Cullen published important poems while still in college. His volumes Color *and* Copper Sun *remain his best known works, though he also published fiction, drama, and books for children. For a brief time, at the height of the Renaissance, he was married to the daughter of W. E. B. Du Bois.*

If I am going to be a poet at all, I am going to be POET and not NEGRO POET.

—BROOKLYN DAILY NEWS, *FEBRUARY 10, 1924*

Yet do I marvel at this curious thing:
To make a poet black, and bid him sing!
—*"YET DO I MARVEL"*

No less, once in a land of scarlet suns
And brooding winds, before the hurricane
Bore down upon us, long before this pain,
We found a place where quiet water runs . . .
—*"BROWN BOY TO BROWN GIRL"*

What if his glance is bold and free,
His mouth the lash of whips?
So should the eyes of lovers be,
And so a lover's lips.
—*"TO A BROWN GIRL"*

Virtue still is stooping down
To cast the first hard stone.
—*"BLACK MAGDALENS"*

What is Africa to me:
Copper sun or scarlet sea,

Jungle star or jungle track,
Strong bronzed men, or regal black
Women from whose loins I sprang
When the birds of Eden sang?
One three centuries removed
From the scenes his fathers loved,
Spicy grove, cinnamon tree,
What is Africa to me?
—"HERITAGE"

This lovely flower fell to seed;
Work gently, sun and rain;
She held it as her dying creed
That she would grow again.
—"FOR MY GRANDMOTHER"

God and the devil still are wrangling
Which should have her, which repel;
God wants no discord in his heaven;
Satan has enough in hell.
—"FOR A MOUTHY WOMAN"

The key to all strange things is in thy heart. . . .
My spirit has come home, that sailed the doubtful seas.
—"THE SHROUD OF COLOR"

The play is done, the crowds depart; and see
That twisted tortured thing hung from a tree,
Swart victim of a newer Calvary.
—"COLORS"

The loss of love is a terrible thing;
They lie who say that death is worse.
—"VARIATIONS ON A THEME (THE LOSS OF LOVE)"

For we must be one thing or the other, an asset or a liability, the
sinew in your wing to help you soar, or the chain to bind you to earth.
—LEAGUE OF YOUTH ADDRESS, THE CRISIS, AUGUST 1923

My poetry, I should think, has become the way of my giving out what music is within me.

—CHRISTIAN SCIENCE MONITOR, *OCTOBER 23, 1925*

Without in the least depreciating the beauty of Negro spirituals or the undeniable fact that Negro singers do them, as it were, to the manner born, we have always resented the natural inclination of most white people to demand spirituals the moment it is known that a Negro is about to sing. So often the request has seemed to savor of the feeling that we could do this and this alone.

—*"THE DARK TOWER" COLUMN,* OPPORTUNITY, *JUNE 1927*

As our train whirled deeper and deeper into what we could not help considering the fastnesses of a benighted country, we felt that the hand of the rioter had dug its nails deep into the soil of this land, leaving it red and raw with the welt of oppression.

—*ON TRAVELING IN THE SOUTH, "THE DARK TOWER,"* OPPORTUNITY *APRIL 1928*

There is no secret to success except hard work and getting something indefinable which we call the "breaks." In order for a writer to succeed, I suggest three things—read and write—and wait.

—*INTERVIEW BY JAMES BALDWIN, DE WITT CLINTON HIGH SCHOOL* MAGPIE, *WINTER 1942*

Waring Cuney

(1 9 0 6 –)

Born in Washington, D.C., Cuney attended Howard and Lincoln universities before studying at the New England Conservatory of Music in Boston. His first published poem, "No Images," won the first-place Opportunity *prize in 1926, and his work appeared in numerous magazines and William Stanley Braithwaite's anthologies.*

She thinks her brown body
Has no glory.

If she could dance
Naked,
Under palm trees,
And see her image in the river
She would know.
      —*"No Images"*

O Death,
Did you ever
Fall on your knees
In tears an' cry?
      —*"Wake Cry"*

Angela Davis

(1944 –   )

Raised in a Birmingham neighborhood so torn with integration strife that it was called Dynamite Hill, Davis, a Phi Beta Kappa graduate of Brandeis, studied philosophy in Europe before teaching at UCLA, where her job was threatened by her membership in the Communist Party. She was a proponent of mass organization rather than violence, but when a shoot-out erupted during the controversy surrounding the Soledad Brothers, she was suspected of being an accomplice. Acquitted of murder in 1972, she continues to teach and to remain politically engaged.

Thousands of my ancestors had waited, as I had done, for nightfall to cover their steps, had leaned on one true friend to help them, had felt, as I did, the very teeth of the dogs at the heels. It was simple. I had to be worthy of them.

      —*ON BECOMING A FUGITIVE*, Angela Davis *(1974)*

Jails and prisons are designed to break human beings, to convert the population into specimens in a zoo—obedient to our keepers, but dangerous to each other. In response, imprisoned men and women will invent and continually invoke various and sundry defenses . . . In an elemental way, this culture is one of resistance, but a resistance of desperation.

—*Ibid.*

Liberation is a dialectical movement—the Black man cannot free himself as a Black man unless the Black woman can liberate herself . . . Women's liberation in the revolution is inseparable from the liberation of the male.

—*Ibid.*

When white people are indiscriminantly viewed as the enemy, it is virtually impossible to develop a political solution.

—*Ibid.*

"Justifiable Homicide"—these innocuously official words conjured up the untold numbers of unavenged murders of my people.

—*Ibid.*

Work. Struggle. Confrontation lay before us like a rock-strewn road. We would walk it . . . If we saw this moment of triumph as a conclusion and not as a point of departure, we would be ignoring all the others who remained draped in chains.

—*Ibid.*

Revolution is a serious thing, the most serious thing about a revolutionary's life. When one commits oneself to the struggle, it must be for a lifetime.

—*Ibid.*

Same struggle. Same enemies.

—*Ibid.*

Nothing in the world made me angrier than inaction, than silence. I never felt I had the right to look upon myself as being any different from my sisters and brothers who did *all* the suffering, for *all* of us.

—*Ibid.*

Miles Davis

A jazz innovator for more than four decades, while still a teenager Davis played with Charlie Parker and Dizzy Gillespie. In 1945 he studied briefly at Juilliard before playing professionally with the musicians on 52nd Street. In 1955 he formed a quartet with John Coltrane which led to the innovative albums "Miles Ahead" and "Kind of Blue." Known for his cool stage presence, he has played over the years with Herbie Hancock, Chick Corea, Keith Jarrett, and other musicians.

Trane would sit there and say nothing but play his ass off. He never did say much. He was just like Bird when it came to talking about music. They both just played with talked with their horns.

—MILES *(1989)*

That was my gift . . . having the ability to put certain guys together that would create a chemistry and then letting them go; letting them play what they knew, and above it.

—*IBID.*

As a musician and an artist, I have always wanted to reach as many people as I could through my music. And I have never been ashamed of that. Because I never thought that the music called "jazz" was ever meant to reach just a small group of people, or become a museum thing locked under glass like all other dead things that were once considered artistic.

—*IBID.*

Bebop was about change, about evolution. It wasn't about standing still and becoming safe. If anybody wants to keep creating they have to be about change.

—*IBID.*

For me, music and life are all about style.

—*IBID.*

When kids don't learn about their own heritage in school, they just don't care about school . . . But you won't see it in the history books unless we get the power to write our own history and tell our story ourselves. Nobody else is going to do it for us and do it like it is supposed to be done.

—*IBID.*

It's always been a gift with me hearing music the way I do. I don't know where it comes from, it's just there and I don't question it.

—*IBID.*

When you work with great musicians, they are always a part of you . . . their spirits are walking around in me, so they're still here and passing it on to others.

—*IBID.*

Nothing is out of the question the way I think and live my life. I'm always thinking about creating. My future starts when I wake up every morning . . . Every day I find something creative to do with my life. Music is a blessing and a curse. But I love it and wouldn't have it no other way.

—*IBID.*

Ossie Davis

(1 9 1 7 –)

Born in Waycross, Georgia, Davis attended Howard University, where Alain Locke urged him to pursue a career in theater. While performing in his first role in 1946 he met the actress Ruby Dee, whom he married two years later. During the 1950s and 1960s, he performed in numerous film and stage roles, including the play Purlie Victorious, *which he had written. He has also directed such films as* Cotton Comes to Harlem *(1970), been involved with educational television, and more recently appeared in the films of Spike Lee.*

I find, in being black, a thing of beauty: a joy; a strength; a secret cup of gladness.

—Purlie Victorious *(1961)*

Any form of art is a form of power; it has impact, it can affect change —it can not only move us, it makes us move.

—*in Jeanne Noble,* Beautiful, Also, Are the Souls of My Black Sisters *(1978)*

Material deprivation is horrible, but it does not compare to spiritual deprivation.

—City Arts Quarterly, *Spring 1988*

If you knew him you would know why we must honor him: Malcolm was our manhood, our living black manhood! This was his meaning to his people. And, in honoring him, we honor the best in ourselves . . . And we will know him then for what he was and is—a Prince—our own black shining Prince!—who didn't hesitate to die, because he loved us so.

—*eulogy for Malcolm X, February 1965*

$\mathcal{R}$uby $\mathcal{D}$ee

(1 9 2 3 –)

*B*orn in Cleveland, Dee grew up in Harlem and attended Hunter College before beginning her acting career. She married the actor Ossie Davis in 1947 and she has often worked with her husband on the stage (Raisin in the Sun, Purlie Victorious) and screen, including most recently the films of Spike Lee. Together, she and Davis have recorded albums for children and have established several foundations to encourage the careers of young people in the arts.

Among whom the gods bless, high on the list are the music people, who tune into celestial vibe-brations and give mortals a taste of immortal sensations. Paradise is to be the ultimate instrument, fulfilling God's desperate intent that we love each other. The music people . . . they give thanks for the gift and reflect the love.

—*TRIBUTE TO LIONEL HAMPTON, MARCH 1978*

Martin Delany

(1 8 1 2 – 1 8 8 5)

The grandson of an African chieftain, "the father of black nationalism" was born free in Virginia and attended the African Free School in New York and Harvard Medical School. A cofounder of Douglass's North Star, *he served in the Union Army during the Civil War and was active in Southern politics during Reconstruction. His ideas on the benefits of emigration are outlined in his seminal work,* The Condition, Elevation, and Destiny of the Colored People of the United States, *and he was also the author of one of the first African American novels,* Blake, or the Huts of Africa *(1859).*

Every people should be the originators of their own destiny, the projectors of their own schemes, and creators of the events that lead to their destiny—the consummation of their own desires.

—THE CONDITION, ELEVATION, EMIGRATION, AND DESTINY OF THE COLORED PEOPLE OF THE UNITED STATES, POLITICALLY CONSIDERED *(1852)*

A serpent is a serpent, and none the less a viper, because nestled in the bosom of an honest hearted man.

—*ON THE AMERICAN COLONIZATION SOCIETY, IBID.*

The argument that man must pray for what he receives, is a mistake, and one that is doing the colored people, especially, incalculable injury . . . There are no people more religious in this Country, than the colored people, and none so poor and miserable as they.

—*Ibid.*

Let us have an education, that shall practically develop our thinking faculties and manhood; and then, and only then, shall we be able to vie with our oppressors, go where we may . . . We desire accomplishments, but they must be *useful.*

—*Ibid.*

The claims of no people, according to established policy and usage, are respected by any nation, until they are presented in a national capacity.

—*Ibid.*

We must MAKE AN ISSUE, CREATE an EVENT, and ESTABLISH A NATIONAL POSITION for OURSELVES: and never may expect to be respected as men and women, until we have undertaken some fearless, bold, and adventurous deeds of daring—contending against every odds—regardless of every consequence.

—*Ibid.*

Go—or stay—of course each is free to do as he pleases—one thing is certain; our Elevation is the work of our own hands.

—*Ibid.*

The Delany Sisters

Sarah Louise (Sadie, 1889) and Annie Elizabeth (Bessie, 1891) Delany were born into a family that had risen from slavery to prominence within decades. Their father was elected the country's first black Episcopal bishop in 1918, and in 1920 Sadie earned a master's degree in education from Columbia University, while Bessie became a doctor of dental surgery. They knew many prominent figures during the Harlem Renaissance and after, and their autobiography, Having Our Say, *became a national best seller.*

Sometimes, when I realize I am 101 years old, it hits me right between the eyes. I say, "Oh Lord, how did this happen?" Turning one hundred was the worst birthday of my life. I wouldn't wish it on my worst enemy. Turning 101 was not so bad. Once you're past that century mark, it's just not as shocking.

—BESSIE, HAVING OUR SAY: THE DELANY SISTERS' FIRST 100 YEARS *(1993)*

Oh, Mama was a smart woman. It takes a smart woman to fall in love with a good man.

—SADIE AND BESSIE

Once in a while, God sends a good white person my way, even to this day. I think it's God's way of keeping me from becoming too mean. And when he sends a nice one to me, then I have to eat crow. And honey, crow is a tough old bird to eat, let me tell you.

—BESSIE

I thought I could change the world. It took me a hundred years to figure out I *can't* change the world. I can only change Bessie. And, honey, that ain't easy, either.

—BESSIE

Life is short, and it's up to you to make it sweet.

—*Sadie*

Funny thing is, some days I feel like a young girl and other days I'm feeling the grave, just a-feeling the grave.

—*Bessie*

I can't imagine having so little faith in the Lord, and so much faith in money, that you would end your life over a little thing like losing your fortune.

—*Bessie*

When you get real old, honey, you realize there are certain things that just don't matter anymore. You lay it all on the table. There's a saying: Only little children and old folks tell the truth.

—*Bessie*

Ain't nobody going to censor *me,* no, sir! I'm a hundred and one years old, and at my age, honey, I can say what I want!

—*Bessie*

In our dreams, we are always young.

—*Sadie*

David Dinkins

(1 9 2 7 –)

Born in New Jersey, Dinkins attended Howard Law School, and after holding several political offices, including Manhattan borough president, in 1989 he was elected the first black mayor of New York, a post he held from 1990 to 1994.

I stand before you today as the elected leader of the greatest city of a great nation, to which my ancestors were brought, chained and whipped in the hold of a slave ship. We have not finished the journey toward liberty and justice, but surely we have come a long way.

—ON TAKING THE OATH OF OFFICE, JANUARY 1, 1990

There are a lot of folks who don't want me to be right, no how, under any circumstances.

—WLIB INTERVIEW, 1991

It is so unfair to these young people for somebody to suggest to them that the solutions to the problem include violence and unlawful behavior . . . We're not being fair to them if we permit them to believe this is the way to get it done.

—ON THE RIOTS IN CROWN HEIGHTS, AUGUST 23, 1991

People need to respect each other's concerns and differences. And frankly, there's far more in common than divides us.

—ON THE RELATIONSHIP BETWEEN AFRICAN-AMERICANS AND JEWS, IBID.

I suppose some folks are so used to seeing us in dungarees and overalls—you know, out on the plantation or something.

—DEFENDING HIS SARTORIAL ELEGANCE, NEW YORK TIMES, SEPTEMBER 12, 1993

Those who bemoan the death of the old neighborhood . . . reject the economics of upward mobility for all New Yorkers. They fail to understand, or refuse to understand, that the old neighborhood is alive and well in our city, that little has changed in our New York neighborhoods except the faces, the names, and the languages spoken. The same decent values of hard work and accomplishment and service to city and nation still exist.

—POLICY SPEECH, SEPTEMBER 13, 1993

Whether we like it or not, race is the silent visitor . . . Race relations can be an appropriate issue . . . but only if you want to craft solutions, and not catalogue complaints. If we use the issue appropriately, we can transform it from the cancer of our society into the cure.

—SPEECH, OCTOBER 14, 1993

You can be anything you want to be. You can be a street sweeper, if you want. Just be the best blasted street sweeper you can be . . . And, you *know* you can be mayor.

—*OFTEN REPEATED CHALLENGE*

If I were to look back on my tenure as mayor . . . great pride must be taken in our efforts to strengthen our neighborhoods and to help lift all our people up . . . I'm proud of what I've done in New York City. We've proved that even in tough times you can make a difference, through compassion and innovation.

—*AFTER HIS ELECTORAL DEFEAT, NEW HAVEN, NOVEMBER 17, 1993*

Father Divine

(1 8 7 7 – 1 9 6 5)

The charismatic preacher is thought to have been born George Baker in rural Georgia. In 1919 he moved to New York, where some of his followers believed him to be God incarnate. His Peace Mission flourished during the 1930s and 1940s and provided much needed food and shelter during the Depression.

I am *joy, peace, life,* and *love* and everything else that is good.

—*IN MARCUS HANNA BOULWARE, ED., THE ORATORY OF NEGRO LEADERS: 1900–1968 (1969)*

Peace brother—it is wonderful.

—*HIS SLOGAN*

Frederick Douglass

Born Frederick August Washington Bailey on the Eastern Shore of Maryland, Douglass escaped from slavery in 1838. He was soon recognized in the North as a speaker of unusual power, and his famous Narrative was published in 1845. As the editor of numerous journals, he was among the first to urge free blacks to take up the Union cause. After the war he was a strong advocate for the Fifteenth Amendment and women's rights, and served as minister to Haiti from 1889 to 1891.

The songs of the slaves represent the sorrows of his heart; and he is relieved by them, only as an aching heart is relieved by its tears.

— *FROM* NARRATIVE OF THE LIFE OF FREDERICK DOUGLASS *(1845)*

From my earliest recollection, I date the entertainment of a deep conviction that slavery would not always be able to hold me within its foul embrace . . .

— *IBID.*

You have seen how a man was made a slave; you shall see how a slave was made a man.

— *IBID.*

I now resolved that, however long I might remain a slave in form, the day had passed forever when I could be a slave in fact. I did not hesitate to let it be known of me, that the white man who expected to succeed in whipping, must also succeed in killing me.

— *ON "THE TURNING-POINT" OF HIS LIFE, IBID.*

In coming to a fixed determination to run away, we did more than Patrick Henry when he resolved upon liberty or death. With us it was a doubtful liberty at most, and almost certain death if we failed. For my part, I should prefer death to hopeless bondage.

—*IBID.*

We had talked long enough; we were now ready to move; if not now, we never should be; and if we did not intend to move now, we had as well fold our arms, sit down, and acknowledge ourselves fit only to be slaves.

—*IBID.*

I have observed this in my experience of slavery—that whenever my condition was improved, instead of its increasing my contentment, it only increased my desire to be free, and set me to thinking of plans to gain my freedom. I have found that, to make a contented slave, it is necessary to make a thoughtless one. It is necessary to darken his moral and mental vision, and, as far as possible, to annihilate the power of reason. He must be able to detect no inconsistencies in slavery; he must be made to feel that slavery is right; and he can be brought to that only when he ceases to be a man.

—*IBID.*

I love the pure, peaceable, and impartial Christianity of Christ: I therefore hate the corrupt, slaveholding, women-whipping, cradle-plundering, partial, and hypocritical Christianity of this land.

—*IBID.*

What to the American slave is your Fourth of July? I answer, a day that reveals to him more than all other days of the year, the gross injustice and cruelty to which he is the constant victim. To him your celebration is a sham; your boasted liberty an unholy license; your national greatness, swelling vanity; your sounds of rejoicing are empty and heartless; your denunciation of tyrants, brass-fronted impudence; your shouts of liberty and equality, hollow mockery; your prayers and hymns, your sermons and thanksgivings, deception, impiety, and hypocrisy—a thin veil to cover up crimes which would disgrace a nation of savages. There is not a nation of the earth guilty of practices more shocking and bloody than are the people of these United States at this very hour . . . This Fourth of July is *yours,* not *mine.*

—*INDEPENDENCE DAY ORATION, ROCHESTER, NEW YORK, JULY 1852*

There is not a man beneath the canopy of heaven who does not know that slavery is wrong *for him.*

—*Ibid.*

That which is inhuman can not be divine.

—*Ibid.*

It is not light that is needed, but fire; it is not the gentle shower, but thunder. We need the storm, the whirlwind, and the earthquake. The feeling in the nation must be quickened, the conscience of the nation must be roused, the propriety of the nation must be startled, the hypocrisy of the nation must be exposed: and its crimes against God and man must be denounced.

—*Ibid.*

In leaving you, I took nothing but what belonged to me, and in no way lessened your means for obtaining an *honest* living.

—*LETTER TO FORMER MASTER, THOMAS AULD, SEPTEMBER 22, 1848*

We want to live in the land of our birth, and to lay our bones by the side of our fathers'; and nothing short of an intense love of personal freedom keeps us from the South. For the sake of this, most of us would live on a crust of bread and a cup of cold water.

—*Ibid.*

There is no roof under which you would be more safe than mine, and there is nothing in my house which you might need for your comfort, which I would not readily grant. Indeed, I should esteem it a privilege, to set you an example as to how mankind ought to treat each other. I am your fellow man, but not your slave.

—*Ibid.*

The ground which a colored man occupies in this country is, every inch of it, sternly disputed.

—*SPEECH AT AMERICAN FOREIGN ANTI-SLAVERY SOCIETY, NEW YORK CITY, MAY 1853*

If there is no struggle, there is no progress. Those who profess to favor freedom and yet deprecate agitation, are men who want crops without plowing up the ground, they want rain without thunder and lightning. They want the ocean without the awful roar of its many waters. This struggle may be a moral one, or it may be a physical one, and it may be both moral and physical, but it must be a struggle. Power concedes nothing without a demand. It never did and it never will. Find out just what any people will quietly submit to and you have found out the exact measure of injustice and wrong that will continue till they are resisted with either words of blows or with both. The limits of tyrants are prescribed by the endurance of those whom they oppress . . . Men may not get all they pay for in this world, but they must certainly pay for all they get.

—CONFERENCE IN CANADAIGUA, NEW YORK, 1857

The destiny of the colored American . . . is the destiny of America.

—SPEECH TO THE EUROPEAN LEAGUE, BOSTON, FEBRUARY 12, 1962

When men sow the wind it is rational to expect that they will reap the whirlwind. It is evident to my mind that the Negro will not alway rest a passive subject to the violence and bloodshed by which he is now pursued. If neither the law nor public sentiment shall come to his relief, he will devise methods of his own.

—THE NORTH AMERICAN REVIEW, JULY 1892

The Negro was not a coward at Bunker Hill; he was not a coward in Haiti; he was not a coward in the late war for the Union; he was not a coward at Harpers Ferry, with John Brown; and care should be taken against goading him to acts of desperation by continuing to punish him for heinous crimes of which he is not legally convicted.

—IBID.

Let the press and the pulpit of the South unite their power against the cruelty, disgrace, and shame that is settling like a mantle of fire upon these lynch-law states, and lynch law itself will soon cease to exist.

—IBID.

The sin against the Negro is both sectional and national, and until the voice of the North shall be heard in emphatic condemnation and withering reproach against these continued ruthless mob-law murders, it will remain equally involved with the South in this common crime.

—IBID.

A little learning, indeed, may be a dangerous thing, but the want of learning is a calamity to any people.

—COMMENCEMENT ADDRESS, THE COLORED HIGH SCHOOL, BALTIMORE, MARYLAND, JUNE 22, 1894

No man can put a chain about the ankle of his fellow man, without at least finding the other end of it about his own neck.

—LIFE AND TIMES OF FREDERICK DOUGLASS (1895)

> I am the Smoke King
> I am black
> I am darkening with song
> I am hearkening with wrong
> I will be black as blackness can
> the blacker the mantle the mightier the man.
>
> —"THE SONG OF THE SMOKE," 1899

Rita Dove

(1 9 5 2 –)

Dove is the author of a novel, a collection of short stories, and four volumes of poetry, including Thomas and Beulah, *which was awarded the Pulitzer Prize in 1987. A professor of English at the University of Virginia, Dove was chosen poet laureate at the Library of Congress in 1993.*

> Sometimes
> a word is found so right it trembles
> at the slightest explanation.
>
> —"O," THE YELLOW HOUSE ON THE CORNER

Under adversity, under oppression, the words begin to fail, the easy words begin to fail. In order to convey things accurately, the human being is almost forced to find the most precise words possible, which is a precondition for literature.

—*INTERVIEW ON HER BEING NAMED POET LAUREATE*, NEW YORK TIMES, *JUNE 20, 1993*

It's a crazy feeling that carries through the night; as if the sky were an omen we could not understand, the book that, if we could read, would change our lives.

—*"KENTUCKY, 1833,"* THE YELLOW HOUSE ON THE CORNER

What's invisible
sings, and we bear witness.

—*"THE HILL HAS SOMETHING TO SAY,"* MUSEUM

The terror of waking is a trust
drawn out unbearably
until nothing, not even love,
makes it easier, and yet
I love this life.

—*"THREE DAYS OF FOREST, A RIVER, FREE,"* IBID.

There are ways
to make of the moment

a topiary
so the pleasure's in

walking through.

—*"FLIRTATION,"* IBID.

Who discovered usefulness?
Who forgot how to sing, simply?

—*"EXEUNT THE VIOLS,"* IBID.

Any fear, any

memory will do: and if you've
got a heart at all, someday
it will kill you.

—*"PRIMER FOR THE NUCLEAR AGE,"* IBID.

W. E. B. Du Bois

(1 8 6 8 – 1 9 6 3)

The dominant African American intellectual of his time, William Edward Burghardt Du Bois was born in Great Barrington, Massachusetts, and studied at Harvard and in Europe. While continuing his work as an academic, journalist, and author, he helped organize the Niagara Movement and the NAACP, and served as editor of its journal, The Crisis. *In later life he was active in pacifist and African independence movements and became a citizen of Ghana, where he lived until his death.*

The problem of the Twentieth Century is the problem of the color line.

— *"To the Nations of the World," Pan-African Congress, London, 1900*

The Negro is a sort of seventh son, born with a veil, and gifted with second-sight in this American world—a world which yields him no true self-consciousness, but only lets him see himself through the revelation of the other world. It is a peculiar sensation, this double-consciousness, this sense of always looking at one's self through the tape of a world that looks on in amused contempt and pity. One ever feels his twoness—an American, a Negro; two souls, two thoughts, two unreconciled strivings; two warring ideals in one dark body, whose dogged strength alone keeps it from being torn asunder.

—The Souls of Black Folk *(1903)*

Merely a concrete test of the underlying principles of the great republic is the Negro Problem, and the spiritual striving of the freedmen's sons is the travail of souls whose burden in almost beyond the measure of their strength, but who bear it in the name of an historic race, in the name of this land of their fathers' fathers, and in the name of human opportunity.

—*Ibid.*

The South believed an educated Negro to be a dangerous Negro. And the South was not wholly wrong; for education among all kinds of men always has had, and always will have, an element of danger and revolution, of dissatisfaction and discontent.

—*IBID.*

There was scarcely a white man in the South who did not honestly regard Emancipation as a crime, and its practical nullification as a duty.

—*IBID.*

The Negro folk song—the rhythmic cry of the slave—stands to-day not simply as the sole American music, but as the most beautiful expression of human experience born this side the seas. It has been neglected, it has been, and is, half despised, and above all it has been persistently mistaken and misunderstood; but notwithstanding, it still remains as the singular spiritual heritage of the nation and the greatest gift of the Negro people.

—*IBID.*

If somewhere in this whirl and chaos of things there dwells Eternal God, pitiful yet masterful, then anon in His good time America shall rend the Veil and the prisoned shall go free.

—*IBID.*

Bewildered we are, and passion-tost, mad with the madness of a mobbed and mocked and murdered people straining at the armposts of Thy Throne, we raise our shackled hands and charge Thee, God, by the bones of our stolen fathers, by the tears of our dead mothers, by the very blood of Thy crucified Christ: *What meaneth this?* Tell us the Plan; give us the Sign! *Keep not Thou silence, O God!*

—A LITANY OF ATLANTA *(1906)*

Sit no longer blind, Lord God, deaf to our prayer and dumb to our dumb suffering. Surely Thou too are not white, O Lord, a pale, bloodless, heartless thing?

—*IBID.*

The cost of liberty is less than the price of repression.

—*"THE LEGACY OF JOHN BROWN," JOHN BROWN (1909)*

If we expect to gain our rights by nerveless acquiescence in wrong, then we expect to do what no other nation ever did. What must we do then? We must complain. Yes, plain, blunt, complain, ceaseless agitation, unfailing exposure of dishonesty and wrong—this is the ancient, unerring way to liberty, and we must follow it.

—*c. 1910*

The dark world is going to submit to its present treatment just as long as it must and not one moment longer.

—*"The Souls of White Folk,"* Darkwater *(1920)*

Negro art is today plowing a difficult row. We want everything that is said about us to tell of the best and highest and noblest in us. We insist that our Art and Propaganda be one. We fear that evil in us will be called racial, while in others it is viewed as individual. We fear that our shortcomings are not merely human.

—*"Negro Art,"* The Crisis, *June 1921*

Where in heaven's name do we Negroes stand? If we organize separately for anything—"Jim Crow!" scream all the Disconsolate; if we organize with white people—"Traitors! Pressure! They're betraying us!" yell all the Suspicious. If, unable to get the whole loaf, we seize half to ward off starvation—"Compromise!" yell all the Scared. If we let the half loaf go and starve—"Why don't you *do* something?" yell those same critics, dancing about on their toes.

—The Crisis, *April 1933*

This the American Black man knows: his fight is a fight to the finish. Either he dies or he wins. He will enter modern civilization in America as a Black man on terms of perfect and unlimited equality with any white man, or he will enter not at all. Either extermination root and branch, or absolute equality. There can be no compromise.

—Black Reconstruction *(1935)*

Believe in life! Always human beings will live and progress to greater, broader, and fuller life.

—*"Last Message to the World,"* 1957, *read at his funeral in 1963*

Paul Laurence Dunbar

(1 8 7 2 – 1 9 0 6)

*B*orn in Dayton, Ohio, the son of former slaves, Dunbar became the first African American poet to gain a national audience. *Writing in both dialect and the standard English he preferred but found no audience for, he was the author of four volumes of poetry, including* Oak and Ivy *and* Lyrics of Lowly Life, *four novels, including* The Sport of the Gods, *and several volumes of short stories.*

*P*eople are taking it for granted that [the Negro] ought not to work with his head. And it is so easy for these people among whom we are living to believe this; it flatters and satisfies their self-complacency.

—*c. August 1898*

> We wear the mask that grins and lies,
> It hides our cheeks and shades our eyes,
> This debt we pay to human guile . . .
> But let the world dream otherwise,
> We wear the mask!
>
> —*"We Wear the Mask"*

> If my tongue were trained to measures,
> I would sing a stirring song.
>
> —*"The Colored Soldiers"*

> I know why the caged bird sings, ah me,
> When his wing is bruised and his bosom sore,
> When he beats his bars and he would be free;
> It is not a carol of joy or glee,
> But a prayer that he sends from his heart's deep core.
>
> —*"Sympathy"*

It's easy 'nough to titter w'en de/stew is smokin' hot,
But it's mighty ha'd to giggle we'n/dey's nuffin' in de pot.
—*"PHILOSOPHY"*

A crust of bread and a corner to sleep in,
A minute to smile and an hour to weep in,
A pint of joy to a peck of troubles
And never a laugh but the moans come double;
And that is life.
—*"LIFE"*

Wisht you could allus know ease an' cleah skies;
Wisht you could stay jes' a chile on my breas'—
Little brown baby wif spa'klin' eyes!
—*"LITTLE BROWN BABY"*

Jump back, honey, jump back.
—*"A NEGRO LOVE SONG"*

He kept his counsel as he kept his path;
'Twas for his race, not for himself he spoke.
—*"FREDERICK DOUGLASS"*

. . . dem wu'ds so sweetly murmured
Seem to tech de softes' spot,
When my manny says de blessin',
An' de co'n pone's hot.
—*"WHEN DE CO'N PONE'S HOT"*

Because I had loved so deeply,
Because I had loved so long,
God in His great compassion
Gave me the gift of song.

Because I had loved so vainly,
And sung with such faltering breath,
The Master in infinite Mercy
Gave me the boon of Death.
—*"COMPENSATION"*

Oh, how with more than dreams the soul is torn,
Ere sleep comes down to soothe the weary eyes.

—*"Ere Sleep Comes Down to Soothe the Weary Eyes"*

This is the debt I pay
Just for one riotous day,
Years of regret and grief,
Sorrow without relief.

—*"The Debt"*

He sang of love when earth was young,
And Love, itself, was in his lays.
But ah, the world, it turned to praise
A jingle in a broken tongue.

—*"The Poet"*

With our short sight we affect to take a comprehensive view of eternity. Our horizon is the universe.

—The Uncalled *(1908)*

With it all, I cannot help being overwhelmed by self-doubts. I hope there is something worthy in my writings and not merely the novelty of a black face associated with the power to rhyme that has attracted attention.

—*in* Valerie Smith, *et al.,* African-American Writers *(1991)*

Alice Dunbar-Nelson

(1 8 7 5 – 1 9 3 5)

*Alice Ruth Moore published her first book—*Violets and Other Tales, *a collection of poems, essays, and stories—when she was twenty, followed by* The Goodness of Saint Roque and Other Stories. *She remains best known, however, for her poetry. From 1898 to his death in 1906 she was married to the poet Paul Laurence Dunbar. In later life, she was active in politics and the women's club movement.*

I sit and sew—a useless task it seems,
My hands grown tired, my head weighed down with dreams . . .
—*"I Sit and Sew"*

Winter had stretched
Long chill fingers into the brown, streaming hair
Of fleeing October.
—*"Snow in October"*

It's punishment to be compelled to do what one doesn't wish.
—Give Us Each Day *(1984)*

In every race, in every nation, and in every clime in every period of
history there is always an eager-eyed group of youthful patriots who
seriously set themselves to right the wrongs done to their race or
nation or sect or sometimes to art or self-expression. No race or
nation can advance without them.
—The Messenger, *March 1927*

*K*atherine *D*unham

(1 9 1 0 –)

*The pioneering choreographer was born in Joliet, Illinois, and at-
tended the University of Chicago, where she majored in anthropology.
She pursued her studies in the Caribbean and Brazil and drew on
native rhythms and rituals in many of her dances, which include Le
Jazz Hot (1938), Plantation Dances (1940), and Afrique du North
(1953), among others. She also appeared in the 1940 film* Cabin in
the Sky, *which she choreographed with George Balanchine.*

This night she felt stirred by the multiple raw potentialities; and the music that drifted out from every doorway . . . struck so far down into a substance that had never stirred or made itself known before that now, at this moment, began a possession by the blues, a total immersion in the baptismal font of Race . . . Single road to freedom.

—A Touch of Innocence *(1959)*

The choreography of her inner being stirred at this instant, Dionysus took possession of her, and she rose to her knees and looked full into the silver radiance. Breathlessly she poured into the night the prayer that was to be worded almost identically for the rest of her life . . . "Help me. Make me strong, give me courage, make me know the right thing to do."

—*Ibid.*

We weren't pushing Black is beautiful. We just showed it.

—American Visions, *February 1987*

Go within every day and find the inner strength so that the world will not blow your candle out.

—*Ibid.*

I used to want the words "She tried" on my tombstone. Now I want "She did it."

—*in Eric V. Copage,* Black Pearls *(1993)*

Marian Wright Edelman

(1 9 3 9 –)

A graduate of Yale Law School, Marian Wright Edelman was born in South Carolina and became active in the civil rights protests of the 1960s. She headed the NAACP Legal Defense and Educational Fund from 1964 to 1968 and in 1973 founded the Children's Defense Fund, which lobbies for social programs for children and families. She has also written several books on the subject.

Don't feel entitled to anything you don't sweat and struggle for.
— THE MEASURE OF OUR SUCCESS *(1992)*

If our children run into bad weather on the way, they will not have the protective clothing to withstand the wind and the rain, lightning and thunder that have characterized the Black sojourn in America.
— SPEECH TO THE CONGRESSIONAL BLACK CAUCUS, SEPTEMBER 26, 1987

People who don't vote have no line of credit with people who are elected and thus pose no threat to those who act against our interests.
— IBID.

Education is a precondition to survival in America today.
— c. 1988

Never work just for money or for power. They won't save your soul or help you sleep at night.
— THE MEASURE OF OUR SUCCESS

Service is the rent we pay for living. It is the very purpose of life and not something you do in your spare time.
— IBID.

No one, Eleanor Roosevelt said, can make you feel inferior without your consent. *Never* give it.

—*IBID.*

First World privilege and Third World deprivation and rage are struggling to coexist not only in our nation's capital but all over an America that has the capacity but not the moral commitment and political will to protect all its young . . . We need to stop punishing children because we don't like their parents.

—*IBID.*

What unites us is far greater than what divides us as families and friends and Americans and spiritual sojourners on this Earth.

—*IBID.*

The question is not whether we can afford to invest in every child; it is whether we can afford not to.

—*IBID.*

I am not fighting just for myself and my people in the South when I fight for freedom and equality. I realize now that I fight for the moral and political health of America as a whole and for her position in the world at large.

—*IN COLUMBUS SALLEY, THE BLACK 100 (1993)*

Speak truth to power.

—THE MEASURE OF OUR SUCCESS

Joycelyn Elders

(1 9 3 3 –)

The daughter of Arkansas sharecroppers, Elders received her medical training in pediatrics and became director of public health in Arkansas under Governor Bill Clinton. When Clinton was elected president, he nominated her to the position of surgeon general. Despite criticism of her support of sex education for young people, she won confirmation in September 1993.

Well, I'm not going to put them on their lunch trays, but yes.

— *RESPONSE AT A NEWS CONFERENCE THAT SHE SUPPORTED DISTRIBUTION OF CONDOMS IN SCHOOLS,*
AS DIRECTOR OF THE ARKANSAS HEALTH DEPARTMENT, 1987

We taught them what to do in the front seat of a car. Now it's time to teach them what to do in the back seat.

— *ON EDUCATING TEENAGERS ABOUT THE HEALTH RISK OF SEX, WIDELY QUOTED*

When you're dancing with a bear, you have to make sure you don't get tired and sit down. You've got to wait till the bear is tired before you get a rest.

— *ON THE PROBLEMS SHE FACES IN PUBLIC HEALTH,* NEW YORK TIMES, *SEPTEMBER 14, 1993*

I came to Washington as prime steak, and after being there a little while I feel like low-grade hamburger.

— *AFTER HER DIFFICULT SENATE CONFIRMATION HEARINGS, SEPTEMBER 1993*

Duke Ellington

(1 8 9 9 – 1 9 7 4)

*B*orn *in Washington, D.C., Edward Kennedy Ellington formed his first band soon after he left high school and moved to New York in 1923. From 1927 to 1932, he gained international fame as a composer and band leader based at the Cotton Club in Harlem. The author of such well-known pieces as "Mood Indigo," "Sophisticated Lady," "Solitude," and others, he wrote nearly a thousand compositions and was elected to the National Institute of Arts and Letters in 1970.*

"It Don't Mean a Thing If It Ain't Got That Swing."
—SONG TITLE, 1932

By and large, jazz has always been like the kind of man you wouldn't want your daughter to associate with.
—ON THE MORALITY OF JAZZ

Small's was the place to go, the one spot where everybody'd drop in . . . There was always plenty of whiskey around those places, and the music would jump and everything else besides.
—ON HARLEM IN THE EARLY 1920S

In our music we have been talking for a long time about what it is to be a Negro in our country. And we've never let ourselves be put into a position of being treated with disrespect. From 1934 to 1936 we went touring deep into the South, without the benefit of Federal judges, and we commanded respect.
—IN BILL CROW, JAZZ ANECDOTES (1990)

The common root, of course, comes out of Africa. That's the pulse. The African pulse. It's all the way back from what they first recognized as the old slave chants and up through the blues, the jazz, and up through the rock. And the avant-garde. And it's all got the African pulse.

—*Ibid.*

My mother told me I was blessed, and I have always taken her word for it. Being born of—or reincarnated from—royalty is nothing like being blessed. Royalty is inherited from another human being; blessedness comes from God.

—Music Is My Mistress *(1973)*

Critics have their purposes, and they're supposed to do what they do, but sometimes they get a little carried away with what they think someone should have done, rather than concerning themselves with what they did.

—*Ibid.*

$\mathcal{R}$alph $\mathcal{E}$llison

(1 9 1 4 – 1 9 9 4)

Born in Oklahoma City, Ralph Waldo Ellison studied music at Tuskegee but before graduating moved to New York, where he met Langston Hughes and Richard Wright in the 1930s. His highly acclaimed Invisible Man *remains one of the most significant novels of the postwar era, and he is also the author of two collections of essays,* Shadow and Act *and* Going to the Territory, *and numerous short stories. He was elected a member of the American Academy of Arts and Letters and was awarded the Medal of Freedom, the country's highest civilian honor.*

Harlem is a place where our folklore is preserved and transformed. It is the place where the body of our Negro myth and legend thrives. It is a place where our styles, musical styles, the many styles of Negro life, find continuity and metamorphosis.

—*"Harlem's America"*

Americans began to tell stories which emphasize the uncertain nature of existence in the new world, and as we did so, we allowed ourselves some relief from the pain of discovering that our bright hopes were going to be frustrated.

—IN VALERIE SMITH, ET AL., AFRICAN-AMERICAN WRITERS *(1991)*

I am not ashamed of my grandparents for having been slaves. I am only ashamed of myself for having at one time been ashamed.

—INVISIBLE MAN *(1952)*

I sings me some blues that might ain't never been sung before, and while I'm singin' them blues I makes up my mind that I ain't nobody but myself and ain't nothin' I can do but let whatever is gonna happen, happen. I made up my mind that I was goin' back home.

—*IBID.*

To Whom It May Concern: Keep This Nigger-Boy Running.

—*IBID.*

You have looked upon chaos and have not been destroyed.

—*IBID.*

The blues is an art of ambiguity, an assertion of the irrespressibly human over all circumstances whether created by others or by one's own human failing.

—*"REMEMBERING JIMMY," SHADOW AND ACT (1953)*

Please, a definition: A hibernation is a covert preparation for a more overt action.

—INVISIBLE MAN

This is just life; it's not to be cried over, just understood.

—*"AND HICKMAN ARRIVES" (1960)*

Words are your business, boy. Not just *the* Word. Words are everything. The key to the Rock, the answer to the Question.

—*IBID.*

When it comes to chillen, women just ain't gentlemen.

—*IBID.*

Ah, but though divided and scattered, ground down and battered into the earth like a spike being pounded by a ten-pound sledge, we were on the ground and in the earth and the earth was red and black like the earth of Africa. And as we moldered underground we were mixed with this land. We liked it. It fitted us fine. It was in us and we're in it. And then—praise God—deep in the ground, deep in the womb of this land, we began to stir!

—*"The Roof, the Steeple and the People" (1960)*

Don't come preaching me no sermon. Cause you know I can kick your butt.

—*Ibid.*

Space, time, and distance, like they say, I'm a yearning man who has to sit still . . . then I hear those train whistles talking to me, just to me, and in those times I know I have all in this world I'll ever need mama and papa and jellyroll.

—*"A Song of Innocence" (1970)*

I'm not a separatist. The imagination is integrative. That's how you make the new—by putting something else with what you've got. And I'm unashamedly an American integrationist.

—*c. 1960s*

All of us are part white, and all of y'all are part colored.

—*Harvard University, 1973*

When I discover who I am, I'll be free.

—*Invisible Man*

Eclecticism is the word. Like a jazz musician who creates his own style out of the styles around him, I play by ear.

—*"The Essential Ellison," interview with Ishmael Reed, Y'Bird (1978)*

Remember that the antidote to *hubris,* to overweening pride, is irony, that capacity to discover and systematize ideas. Or, as Emerson insisted, the development of consciousness, consciousness, *consciousness.* And with consciousness, a more refined conscientiousness and, most of all, that tolerance which takes the form of humor.

—*speech, 1974*

I am invisible, understand, simply because people refuse to see me.
—INVISIBLE MAN

The end is in the beginning and lies far ahead.
—*IBID.*

Mari Evans

Having come to prominence in the 1960s, Mari Evans has taught at Cornell, Purdue, Washington University, and elsewhere. She is the author of several volumes of poetry, and edited the critical anthology Black Women Writers: 1950–1980.

I
am a black woman
tall as a cypress . . .
Look
   on me and be
renewed.
—*"I AM A BLACK WOMAN"*

To identify the enemy is to free the mind.
—*"SPEAK TRUTH TO THE PEOPLE"*

Idiom is larger than geography; it is the hot breath of a people—singing, slashing, explorative. Imagery becomes the magic denominator, the language of a passage, saying the ancient unchanging particulars.
—*"MY FATHER'S PASSAGE," IN* BLACK WOMEN WRITERS

If we have the Word let us
   say it
If we have the Word let us
   be it
If we have the Word let us
   DO
     —"*NIGHTSTAR*"

   i'm
   gonna spread out
   over America
       intrude
   my proud blackness
   all
      over the place
    —"*VIVA NOIR*"

      I am a wisp of energy
flung from the core of the Universe
      housed
     in a temple
of flesh and bones and blood
     —"*CONCEPTUALITY*"

   who
   can be born
   black
   and not exult!
  —"*MY FATHER'S PASSAGE*"

As a Black writer embracing . . . responsibility, approaching my Black family/nation from within a commonality of experience, I try for a poetic language that says, "This is *who* we are, where we have been, *where* we are. This is where we must go. And *this* is what we must do."

    —"*MY FATHER'S PASSAGE*"

Medgar Evers

(1926 – 1963)

*B*orn in Mississippi, Evers served in World War II and on his return *became field secretary for the NAACP, leading fights against segregation at the University of Mississippi and public facilities in Jackson. He was assassinated in front of his home on June 12, 1963, and is buried in Arlington National Cemetery. In February 1994, the white supremacist Byron De La Beckwith was convicted of his murder, and his widow, Myrlie Evers, commented, "Perhaps Medgar did more in death than in life. But he lives on."*

Our only hope is to control the vote.

—*c. 1963*

The gifts of God . . . should be enjoyed by all citizens in Mississippi.

—IN COLUMBUS SALLEY, THE BLACK 100 *(1993)*

I'm looking to be shot any time I step out of my car . . . If I die, it will be in a good cause. I've been fighting for America just as much as the soldiers in Vietnam.

—IN LERONE BENNETT, JR., BEFORE THE MAYFLOWER *(1982)*

Louis Farrakhan

(1933 –)

*B*orn in Washington, D.C., Louis Eugene Walcott attended Winston-Salem Teachers' College and was a calypso singer before he converted to the Nation of Islam in the 1950s. He was an outspoken *opponent of Malcolm X after Malcolm split with Elijah Muhammad, and after Muhammad's death he formed his own branch of the Nation of Islam. Farrakhan gained national prominence during Jesse Jackson's 1984 presidential campaign and he continues to be a highly visible figure.*

Louis Farrakhan has become quite a controversial brother . . . Once you speak against the popular version of the truth, then you must be willing to pay the price for so doing.

—SPEECH AT THE KENNEDY CENTER, JULY 22, 1985

Islam has always been a force that dispels tyrants and tyranny, oppression and exploitation. Islam has always been a force that militates for justice.

—IBID.

Now we found out what the real deal is . . . ECONOMICS, ECONOMICS, ECONOMICS, ECONOMICS, ECONOMICS.

—IBID.

There is no need to cry, it's time. There is no need to weep, it is time. There is no need to lament, it is time. There is no need for despair, hopelessness, and bitterness. It is time.

—IBID.

History is our guide, and without a knowledge of history, we are lost!

—SPEECH AT PRINCETON UNIVERSITY, 1984

You are the ancient builders of civilization. Before there was civilization, you were there, and when civilization was built, your fathers built it.

—IBID.

God has ordained opposition. He never raises a prophet, or an apostle, or a teacher without opposition coming to that prophet, apostle, or that teacher. God ordains opposition so that he may prove to the opponents, who are many in number, to the few that God chooses to bless, that if God's hand is with that few, the many cannot oppose and be successful.

—SPEECH IN CHICAGO, APRIL 12, 1987

Never exalt people because they're in your family; never exalt people because they're your color; never exalt people because they're your kinfolk. Exalt them because they're worthy.

—*IBID.*

I am not a Prophet. I am not a Messenger. But I am a warner.

—SPEECH AT THE KENNEDY CENTER, JULY 22, 1985

Jessie Redmon Fauset

(1882–1961)

A significant figure of the Harlem Renaissance, Fauset was a Phi Beta Kappa graduate of Cornell University. She promoted the work of other writers as the literary editor of The Crisis *and was the author of four novels, most notably* There Is Confusion *and* Plum Bun, *as well as essays, poems, and short stories.*

The white world is feverishly anxious to know of our thoughts, our hopes, our dreams. Organization is our strongest weapon.

—"IMPRESSIONS OF THE SECOND PAN-AFRICAN CONGRESS," THE CRISIS, NOVEMBER–DECEMBER 1921

All the possibilities of all black men are needed to weld together the black men of the world against the day when black and white meet to do battle. God grant that when that day comes we shall be so powerful that the enemy will say, "But behold! these men are our brothers."

—*IBID.*

The remarkable thing about this gift of ours is that it has its rise, I am convinced, in the very woes which beset us . . . It is our emotional salvation.

—"THE GIFT OF LAUGHTER," THE NEW NEGRO, 1925

There is an unwritten law in America that though white may imitate black, black, even when superlatively capable, must never imitate white. In other words, grease-paint may be used to darken but never to lighten.

—*IBID.*

Like the French I am fond of dancing, and adore cards and the theatre probably because I am a minister's daughter.

—*IN COUNTEE CULLEN'S* CAROLING DUSK, *1927*

It was a curious business, this colour. It was the one god apparently to whom you could sacrifice everything.

—PLUM BUN *(1929)*

It's wrong for men to have both money and power; they're bound to make some woman suffer.

—*IBID.*

Men are always wanting women to give, but they don't want the women to want to give. They want to take—or at any rate to compel the taking . . . If we don't give enough we lose them. If we give too much we lose ourselves.

—*IBID.*

New York, it appeared, had two visages. It could offer an aspect radiant with promise or a countenance lowering and forbidding. With its flattering possibilities it could elevate to the seventh heaven, or lower to the depths of hell with its crushing negations. And loneliness! Loneliness such as that offered by the great, noisy city could never be imagined.

—*IBID.*

She thought then of black people, of the race of her parents and of all the odds against living which a cruel, relentless fate had called on them to endure. And she saw them as a people powerfully, almost overwhelmingly endowed with the essence of life. They had to persist, had to survive, because they did not know how to die.

—*IBID.*

142

Rudolph Fisher

(1 8 9 7 – 1 9 3 4)

Born in Washington, D.C., Fisher was educated at Brown, where he was elected to Phi Beta Kappa. He received a medical degree from Howard University in 1924 and during the Harlem Renaissance earned a reputation as an accomplished writer of short fiction.

In Harlem, black was white. You had rights that could not be denied you; you had privileges, protected by law. And you had money. Everybody in Harlem had money. It was a land of plenty.
—*"The City of Refuge," 1925*

He's from 'way down behind the sun an' ripe f' the pluckin'.
—*Ibid.*

Dickties is evil—don' never trust no dickty.
—Walls of Jericho *(1928)*

Maybe . . . she ain't so possible as she looks.
—*"Common Meter"*

The rhythm persisted, the unfaltering common meter of blues, but the blueness itself, the sorrow, the despair, began to give way to hope.
—*Ibid.*

Ella Fitzgerald

(1 9 1 7 –)

"The First Lady of Song" *was born in Newport News, Virginia, and as a child moved with her family to New York, where she sang in church choirs and enjoyed dancing in the clubs in Harlem. After her mother died, when Ella was sixteen, she was homeless and living in deprivation. In November 1934 she won an Apollo Amateur Night Contest and soon after joined the Chick Webb Orchestra. In 1938 the twenty-one-year-old singer had a number one hit with "A-Tisket, A-Tasket." For more than five decades she has been the pre-eminent interpreter of popular song; she was awarded eight Grammys, the Kennedy Center Honors, and the National Medal of Arts.*

The only thing better than singing is more singing.
—NEW YORK SUNDAY NEWS, *AUGUST 1, 1954*

I guess what everyone wants more than anything else is to be loved. And to know that you loved me for my singing is too much for me. Forgive me if I don't have all the words. Maybe I can sing it and you'll understand.
—*AT AN AWARDS CEREMONY CELEBRATING HER FIRST TWO DECADES IN SHOW BUSINESS,* NEWSWEEK, *JUNE 7, 1954*

Being on the road gets rough sometimes, but I'd sure miss singing to the people.
—NEW YORK SUNDAY NEWS, *SEPTEMBER 8, 1957*

Sometimes you can find you're way up on top and all by yourself. It can get pretty lonely up there, and you can miss all the kicks.
—NEW YORK POST, *OCTOBER 17, 1965*

I don't want to be considered, as the song goes, "as cold as yesterday's mashed potatoes." I want to stay with it.
—HOUSTON POST, *JANUARY 7, 1968*

I get a little tired sometimes, but whenever I get on stage and the public is there, I forget all the tiredness. Everything comes back and I feel good again.

—PHILADELPHIA INQUIRER, *JULY 4, 1971*

This is a wonderful evening for me, with all the greats. Best of all, I'm the only girl!

—*AT AN "ALL-STAR SWING FESTIVAL" AT NEW YORK'S PHILHARMONIC HALL, OCTOBER 23, 1972*

I always thank God. I'm here because this is what I love to do. When they say come and sing, that's the medicine.

—JET, *JUNE 27, 1988*

It isn't where you came from; it's where you're going that counts.

—*IN STUART NICHOLSON,* ELLA FITZGERALD *(1994)*

$\mathcal{F}$olk $\mathcal{P}$oetry

Gwineter mourn and never tire,
Mourn and never tire,
Mourn and never tire.
There's a great camp meeting in the Promised Land.

Oh, get you ready children,
Don't you get weary,
Get you ready children,
Don't you get weary.

—*"WALK TOGETHER CHILDREN"*

We raise de wheat,
Dey gib us de corn;
We bake de bread,
Dey gib us de crust;
We sif de meal,

Dey gib us de huss;
We peel de meat,
Dey gib us de skin;
And dat's de way
Dey take us in;
We skim de pot,
Dey gib us de liquor,
And say dat's good enough for nigger.
                    —*"We Raise de Wheat"*

The big bee flies high,
The little bee make the honey;
The black folks makes the cotton,
And the white folks gets the money.

My ole Mistiss promise me,
W'en she died, she'd set me free.
She lived so long dat 'er head got bal',
An' she give out'n de notion a dyin' at all.

Yes, my ole Mosser promise me;
But "his papers" didn't leave me free.
A dose of pizen he'ped 'im along.
May de Devil preach 'is funer'l song.
                    —*"Promises of Freedom"*

Dis sun are hot,
Dis hoe are heavy,
Dis grass grow furder dan I can reach;
An' as I looks
At dis cotton fiel',
I thinks I mus' 'a' been called to preach.
                    —*"This Sun Is Hot"*

Oh come 'long, chilluns, come 'long,
W'ile dat moon are shinin' bright.
Let's git on board, an' float down de river,
An' raise dat rucus to-night.
                    —*"Raise a 'Rucus' To-Night"*

John Henry said to his captain,
  "A man ain't nothin' but a man,
But before I'll let dat steam drill beat me down,
  I'll die wid my hammer in my hand,
    Die wid my hammer in my hand."

            . . .

When John Henry was laying there dying
  The people all by his side,
The very last words they heard him say,
  "Give me a cool drink of water 'fore I die,
    Cool drink of water 'fore I die."

            . . .

They took John Henry to the river,
  And buried him in the sand,
And every locomotive come a-roarin' by,
  Says "There lies a steel-drivin' man,
    Lawd, there lies a *steel*-drivin' man."
                —*"John Henry"*

Dark an' stormy may come de wedder;
I jines dis he-male an' dis she-male togedder.
Let none, but Him dat makes de thunder,
Put dis he-male an' dis she-male asunder.
I darfore 'nounce you bofe de same.
Be good, go 'long, an' keep up yo' name.
De broomstick's jumped, de worl's not wide.
She's now yo' own. Salute yo' bride!
            —*Slave Marriage Ceremony Supplement*

George Foreman

Born near Houston, Texas, Foreman was living a life of petty crime when he began boxing, but by 1968 he had won an Olympic Gold Medal. On January 22, 1973, he won the world heavyweight title from Joe Frazier, but lost it to Muhammad Ali in the Rumble in the Jungle in October 1974. He retired in 1977 to become a preacher, but returned to professional boxing in 1988.

I'm world heavyweight champion. I consider myself a citizen of the whole world.

—*AFTER WINNING THE TITLE IN 1973*

I don't even think about a retirement program because I'm working for the Lord, for the Almighty. And even though the Lord's pay isn't very high, his retirement program is, you might say, out of this world.

—*THE FORMER HEAVYWEIGHT CHAMP AND PREACHER*

I know how to make money. I went back and put on my boxing trunks.

—*ON HIS COMEBACK,* Sports Illustrated, *JULY 17, 1989*

Everybody wants to be somebody. The thing you have to do is give them confidence they can. You have to give a kid a dream.

—*ON COACHING YOUNG KIDS*

Leon Forrest

(1 9 3 7 –   )

*B*orn in Chicago, Forrest was educated at Roosevelt University and the University of Chicago. A former editor of the journal Muhammad Speaks, *he has taught at Yale, Rochester, Brown, and Northwestern, and his novels include* There Is a Tree More Ancient than Eden *and* Two Wings to Veil My Face.

How can a man live out the length of his fiery days without a vision-prize?

—*IN JANET CHEATHAM BELL,* FAMOUS BLACK QUOTATIONS *(1991)*

Why pose and posture a self that is other than you, when I know your true name?

—*IBID.*

James Forten

(1 7 6 6 – 1 8 4 2)

A prominent free black living in Philadelphia, Forten had fought in the Revolutionary War at the age of fifteen and was imprisoned in England for seven months. After his return, he became one of the most successful businessmen in the city. He was an early proponent of the political convention and abolition movements and, with Richard Allen, one of the founders of the Bethel African Methodist Episcopal Church.

Has the God who made the white man and the black left any record declaring us a different species? Are we not sustained by the same power, supported by the same food, hurt by the same wounds, wounded by the same wrongs, pleased with the same delights, and propagated by the same means? And should we not then enjoy the same liberty, and be protected by the same laws?

—PROTESTING PROPOSED LEGISLATION BASED ON RACE,
A SERIES OF LETTERS BY A MAN OF COLOR, *1813*

Many of our ancestors were brought here more than one hundred years ago; many of our fathers, many of ourselves, have fought and bled for the independence of our country. Do not then expose us to sale. Let not the spirit of the father behold the son robbed of that liberty which he died to establish, but let the motto of our legislature be: "The law knows no distinction."

—*IBID.*

We will never separate ourselves voluntarily from the slave population in this country; they are our brethren by the ties of consanguinity, of suffering, and of wrong; and we feel that there is more virtue in suffering privations with them, than fancied advantages for a season.

—FROM A RESOLUTION OPPOSING THE AMERICAN COLONIZATION SOCIETY, ADOPTED AT A MEETING
CHAIRED BY FORTEN, PHILADELPHIA, JANUARY *1817*

Whilst so much is being done in the world, to ameliorate the condition of mankind, and the spirit of Freedom is marching with rapid strides and causing tyrants to tremble, may America awake from the apathy in which she has long slumbered. She must, sooner or later, fall in with the irresistible current.

—LETTER TO WILLIAM LLOYD GARRISON, DECEMBER *31, 1830*

Our country asserts for itself the glory of being the freest upon the surface of the globe . . . She proclaimed freedom to all mankind— and offered her soil as a refuge to the enslaved of all nations. The brightness of her glory was radiant, but one dark spot still dimmed its lustre. Domestic slavery existed among a people who had themselves disdained to submit to a master.

—PETITION TO THE PENNSYLVANIA LEGISLATURE PROTESTING DISCRIMINATORY LEGISLATION,
JANUARY *1832*

T. Thomas Fortune

(1856 – 1928)

Timothy Thomas Fortune was born in Florida, where he saw, first-hand, violent raids by the Ku Klux Klan. He briefly attended Howard University before entering a career in journalism, and in 1879 he became editor of the New York Globe. *An ally of Booker T. Washington, he was a proponent of practical education, supported organized labor, and in the* Globe, *and later the* Freeman *and the* Age, *did not shrink from advocating meeting violence with violence.*

When the Negro who steals from society what society steals from him under the specious cover of invidious law is hung upon the nearest oak tree, and the white villain who shoots a Negro without provocation is not so much as arrested—when society tolerates such an abnormal state of things, what will the harvest be?

—GLOBE, *JANUARY 13, 1883*

Ours is supposed to be a government in which classes and distinctions melt into a harmonious whole. Until we reach this ideal of government, we will be a distracted, contentious people.

—GLOBE, *FEBRUARY 17, 1883*

Let the colored man stand his ground. There is far more honor in dying like a free man than living like a slave.

—GLOBE, *NOVEMBER 10, 1883*

Our history in this country dates from the moment that restless men among us became restless under oppression and rose against it . . . Agitation, contentions, ceaseless unrest, constant aspiring—a race so moved must prevail.

—GLOBE, *AUGUST 18, 1883*

Mental inertia is death.

—*IBID.*

We must learn to lean upon ourselves; we must learn to plan and execute business enterprises of our own; we must learn to venture our pennies if we would gain dollars.

—*Ibid.*

It is bad enough to be denied equal political rights, but to be murdered by mobs—denied the protection of life and limb and property—the thing is not to be endured without protest, and if violence must be met with violence, let it be met.

—Globe, *January 12, 1884*

The laboring men of the South, the North, and the West, have a common cause, and they will yet present a solid front to the masterful forces which press them down, will yet stand in solemn array against the men who revel in luxury while labor, the wealth creating power, shivers in the March winds and dies by the wayside.

—Globe, *April 5, 1884*

The great newspapers, which should plead the cause of the oppressed and the down-trodden, which should be the palladiums of the people's rights, are all on the side of the oppressor, or by silence preserve a dignified but ignominious neutrality. Day after day they weave a false picture of facts—facts which must measurably influence the future historian of the times in the composition of impartial history.

—Black and White: Land, Labor and Politics in the South *(1884)*

When a society fosters as much crime and destitution as ours, with ample resources to meet the actual necessities of every one, there must be something radically wrong, not in the society but in the foundation upon which society is reared.

—*Ibid.*

The colored man is in the South to stay there. He will not leave it voluntarily and he cannot be driven out. He had no voice in being carried into the South, but he will have a very loud voice in any attempt to put him out . . . the black man will remain in the South just as long as corn will tassel and cotton will bloom into whiteness.

—*Ibid.*

I have walked through the tenement wards of New York, and I have seen enough want and crime and blasted virtue to condemn the civilization which produced them and which fosters them in its bosom. I have looked upon the vast army of police which New York City maintains to protect life and so-called vested rights and I have concluded that there is something wrong in the social system which can only be kept intact by the expenditure of so much productive force, for this vast army.

—Ibid.

There can be no overproduction of anything as long as there are hungry mouths to be fed. It does not matter if the possessor of these hungry mouths are too poor to buy the bread; if they are hungry, there is no overproduction.

—Ibid.

I am an American citizen. I have a heritage in each and every provision incorporated in the Constitution of my country.

—Ibid.

Necessity knows no law and discrimination in favor of no man or race.

—Ibid.

The real problem is not the Negro but the Nation.

—Freeman, October 9, 1886

Was ever race more unjustly maligned than ours? Was ever race more shamelessly robbed than ours? Was ever race used to advance the political and pecuniary fortunes of others as ours? Was ever race so patient, so law abiding, so uncomplaining as ours? Ladies and gentlemen, it is time to call a halt. It is time to begin to fight fire with fire. It is time to stand shoulder to shoulder as men. It is time to rebuke the treachery of friends in the only way that treachery should be rebuked. It is time to face the enemy and fight him inch by inch for every right he denies us.

—address to the first convention of the National Afro-American League,
Chicago, January 1890

I am now and I have always been a race man and not a party man . . . We stand for the race, and not for this party or that party, and we should know a friend from a foe when we see him.

—Ibid.

As the agitation which culminated in the abolition of African slavery in this country covered a period of fifty years, so may we expect that before the rights conferred upon us by the war amendments are fully conceded, a full century will have passed away. We have undertaken no child's play. We have undertaken a serious work which will tax and exhaust the best intelligence and energy of the race for the next century.

—Ibid.

The sleepless agent of colonization . . . has penetrated the utmost bounds of the globe. It has wrenched from the weak their fertile valleys and luxuriant hillsides, and when they protested, when they resisted, it has enslaved them or cut their throats.

—"<small>The Nationalization of Africa," speech to the Africa and the Africans Congress,</small>
<small>Atlanta, December 12–13, 1896</small>

Aretha Franklin

(1942–)

"The Queen of Soul" was born in Memphis and raised in Detroit, the daughter of the well-known Reverend Charles L. Franklin. She left school at fourteen to begin singing gospel and at eighteen moved to New York to sing professionally. In a thirty-year career, she has earned fifteen Grammys, more than any other female artist, and in 1987 she was the first woman inducted into the Rock and Roll Hall of Fame.

R-E-S-P-E-C-T
Find out what it means to me.

—<small>her signature song, written by Otis Redding (1967)</small>

Trying to grow up is hurting, you know. You make mistakes. You try to learn from them, and when you don't, it hurts even more. And I've been hurt—hurt bad. I might be just twenty-six, but I'm an old woman in disguise—twenty-six goin' on sixty-five.

—TIME *INTERVIEW, JUNE 28, 1968*

I feel a real *kinship* with God, and that's what has helped me pull out of the problems I've faced. Anybody who has kept up with my career knows that I've had my share of problems and trouble, but look at me today . . . Through the years, no matter how much success I achieved, I never lost my faith in God.

—ESSENCE *INTERVIEW, 1971*

I believe that the black revolution certainly forced me and the majority of black people to begin taking a second look at ourselves. It wasn't that we were all that ashamed of ourselves, we merely started appreciating our *natural* selves . . . sort of, you know, falling in love with ourselves *just as we are.*

—*CIRCA 1972*

My heart is still there in gospel music. It never left . . . I'm gonna make a gospel record and tell Jesus I cannot bear these burdens alone.

—*IN MARK BEGO,* ARETHA FRANKLIN: THE QUEEN OF SOUL *(1989)*

Well, the doors are open, girls!

—*ON BEING INDUCTED INTO THE ROCK AND ROLL HALL OF FAME, JANUARY 1987*

Don't say Aretha is making a comeback, because I've never been away!

—*ON THE RELEASE OF HER GRAMMY-WINNING "WHO'S ZOOMIN' WHO?" (1985)*

John Hope Franklin

(1915 –)

Born in Oklahoma, Franklin attended Fisk University and received his M.A. and Ph.D. from Harvard. He is the author of numerous volumes of history, essay, and autobiography, including The Emancipation Proclamation *(1963) and* Reconstruction after the Civil War *(1961). He has taught at Fisk, Chicago, and Duke, and has served as president of several academic societies, including the American Historical Association and Phi Beta Kappa.*

If the house is to be set in order, one cannot begin with the present; he must begin with the past.

—*IN COLUMBUS SALLEY,* THE BLACK 100 *(1993)*

Racial segregation, discrimination, and degradation are no unanticipated accidents in this nation's history. They stem logically and directly from the legacy that the founding fathers bestowed upon contemporary America . . . [W]hen the colonists emerged victorious from their war with England, they had both their independence *and* their slaves.

—*"THE MORAL LEGACY OF THE FOUNDING FATHERS,"* UNIVERSITY OF CHICAGO MAGAZINE, *SPRING 1975*

The new Negro history, then, is the literary and intellectual movement that seeks to achieve the same justice in history that is sought in other spheres . . . and, in time, will provide *all America* with a lesson in the wastefulness, nay the wickedness of human exploitation and injustice that have characterized too much of this nation's past.

—*"THE NEW NEGRO HISTORY,"* THE CRISIS, *FEBRUARY 1957*

The South's historians served the cause of Southern nationalism with more lasting effect than did its armies . . . Southerners must win with the pen what they had failed to win with the sword.

—*"AS FOR OUR HISTORY,"* IN THE SOUTHERNER AS AMERICAN *(1960)*

When we also learn that this country and the Western world have no monopoly of goodness and truth or of skills and scholarship, we begin to appreciate the ingredients that are indispensable to making a better world. In a life of learning that is, perhaps, the greatest lesson of all.

—*"A LIFE OF LEARNING," DELIVERED BEFORE THE AMERICAN COUNCIL OF LEARNED SOCIETIES, NEW YORK, APRIL 14, 1988*

We must get beyond textbooks, go out into the bypaths and untrodden depths of the wilderness and travel and explore and tell the world the glories of our journey.

—*c. 1967*

It was necessary, as a black historian, to have a personal agenda.

—*"A LIFETIME OF LEARNING"*

Ɛ. ℐranklin ℐrazier

(1894 – 1962)

One of the most prominent sociologists of the twentieth century, Edward Franklin Frazier was born in Baltimore, attended Howard University, and received his Ph.D. from the University of Chicago in 1931. He was the author of the important works The Negro Family in the United States *(1939),* The Black Bourgeoisie *(1957), and* The Negro Church in America *(1962), among others. He also taught at Morehouse, Atlanta, and Fisk, and at Howard University from 1934 to 1959.*

America faces a new race that has awakened.

—*"NEW CURRENTS OF THOUGHT AMONG THE COLORED PEOPLE OF AMERICA," MASTER'S THESIS, CIRCA 1920*

The Negro does not want love. He wants justice . . . I believe it would be better for the Negro's soul to be seared with hate than dwarfed by self-abasement.

—"THE NEGRO AND NON-RESISTANCE" (1924)

The killing of a white man is always the signal for a kind of criminal justice resembling primitive tribal revenge.

—IBID.

Suppose there should arise a Gandhi to lead Negroes without hate in their hearts to stop tilling the fields of the South under the peonage system; to cease paying taxes to States that keep their children in ignorance; and to ignore the iniquitous disfranchisement and Jim-Crow laws. I fear we would witness an unprecedented massacre of defenseless black men and women in the name of Law and Order and there would scarcely be enough Christian sentiment in American to stay the flood of blood.

—ON NONRESISTANCE, THE CRISIS, JUNE 1924

The closer a Negro got to the ballot box, the more he looked like a rapist.

—ON EFFORTS TO KEEP BLACKS FROM VOTING, QUOTED BY STERLING BROWN, 1966

Joe Frazier

(1 9 4 4 –)

Smokin' Joe Frazier was born in Beaufort, South Carolina, and won an Olympic Gold Medal in 1964. He gained the world heavyweight title in 1968, but lost it to George Foreman in 1973, and his career included three epic bouts with Muhammad Ali. He was elected to the Boxing Hall of Fame in 1980 and retired in 1981.

I don't want to knock my opponents out, I want to hit him, step away, and watch him hurt. I want his heart.

—*IN HARRY MULLAN, THE BOOK OF BOXING QUOTATIONS (1988)*

This is just another man, another fight, another payday.

—*BEFORE HIS FIRST WITH ALI ON MARCH 8, 1971, IN WHICH HE RETAINED THE TITLE*

You one bad nigger. We both bad niggers. We don't do no crawlin'.

—*AFTER HIS LOSS TO ALI IN THE THRILLER IN MANILA, OCTOBER 1, 1975, IN HARRY CARPENTER,*
BOXING: AN ILLUSTRATED HISTORY

When I go out there, I have no pity on my brother. I'm out there to win.

—*MULLAN, THE BOOK OF BOXING QUOTATIONS*

Freedom Songs

Derived from the spirituals of the nineteenth century and the early protest songs of the 1930s and 1940s, the freedom song enjoyed wide popularity during the civil rights movement of the 1960s. As the lyrics were adapted to the present circumstances, they would be sung in sit-ins, bus trips, and jail cells.

Oh, deep in my heart,
I do believe, that
We shall overcome
Someday.

—*"WE SHALL OVERCOME"*

O Freedom!
O Freedom!
O Freedom over me!
And before I'd be a slave,
I'd be buried in my grave,
And go home to my Lord and be free!
—*"O Freedom"*

Free at last, free at last,
I thank God I'm free at last.
—*"Free at Last"*

If you miss me from the back of the bus,
And you can't find me nowhere,
Come on up to the front of the bus,
I'll be riding up there, I'll be riding up there.
—*"If You Miss Me from the Back of the Bus"*

The only thing that we did wrong
Stayed in the wilderness a day too long
Keep your Eyes on the Prize, Hold On

. . .

But the one thing we did right
Was the day we started to fight
Keep Your Eyes on the Prize, Hold On.
—*"Keep Your Eyes on the Prize"*

We're fighting for our freedom,
We shall not be moved.
—*"We Shall Not Be Moved"*

Ain't gonna let nobody turn me 'round,
I'm gonna keep on a-walkin', Lord,
Keep on a-talkin',
Marching up to freedom land.
—*"Ain't Gonna Let Nobody Turn Me 'Round"*

I'm gonna sit at the welcome table,
I'm gonna sit at the welcome table
one of these days, hallelujah.
—*"I'm Gonna Sit at the Welcome Table"*

Everybody sing freedom, freedom, freedom.

—*"Everybody Sing Freedom"*

See also **Spirituals**

Ernest J. Gaines

(1 9 3 3 –)

Gaines, the oldest of eleven children, was born in Louisiana and began working in the fields when he was nine. In 1948 his family moved to California, and, after serving in the army, he attended San Francisco State College and began writing award-winning stories and novels peopled with rural folk of enormous strength. His best-known works include The Autobiography of Miss Jane Pittman *and* A Gathering of Old Men.

I came from a place where people sat around and chewed sugarcane and roasted sweet potatoes and peanuts in the ashes and sat on ditch banks and told tales and sat on porches and went into the swamps and went into the fields—that's what I came from.

—*interview with Marcia Gaudet and Carol Wooton, in Valerie Smith, et al.*
African-American Writers *(1991)*

There will always be men struggling to change, and there will always be those who are controlled by the past.

—*interview with John O'Brien, in* African-American Writers

Question everything. Every stripe, every star, every word spoken. Everything.

—*"The Sky Is Gray"*

Words mean nothing. Action is the only thing. Doing. That's the only thing.

—*Ibid.*

I have learned as much about writing about my people by listening to blues and jazz and spirituals as I have by reading novels. The understatements in the tenor saxophone of Lester Young, the crying, haunting, forever searching sounds of John Coltrane, and the softness and violence of Count Basie's big band—all have fired my imagination as much as anything in literature.

—*in Smith, African-American Writers*

The mark of fear is not easily removed.

—*The Autobiography of Miss Jane Pittman (1971)*

I began with an idea, this point, this fact: some time in the past, we were brought from Africa in chains, put in Louisiana to work the rice, cane, and cotton fields. Some kind of way we survived.

—*"Miss Jane and I"*

We wait till now? Now, when we're old men, we get to be brave?

—*A Gathering of Old Men (1983)*

Sometimes you got to hurt something to help something. Sometimes you have to plow under one thing in order for something else to grow.

—*Ibid.*

Henry Highland Garnet

(1 8 1 5 – 1 8 8 2)

Born in Maryland, Garnet escaped from slavery with his parents and was educated and ordained a minister in New York. A prominent abolitionist, Garnet was an early proponent of armed revolt against slaveholders and was the first African American clergyman to deliver

a sermon in Congress. A supporter of colonization, in 1881 he was appointed ambassador to Liberia, where he died the following year.

Millions have come from eternity into time, and have returned again to the world of spirits, cursed and ruined by American slavery.

—An Address to the Slaves of the United States of America (Garnet's "Call to Rebellion") August 21, 1843

Slavery had stretched its dark wings of death over the land, the Church stood silently by—the priests prophesied falsely, and the people loved to have it so. Its throne is established, and now it reigns triumphant.

—Ibid.

Slavery! How much misery is comprehended in that single word.

—Ibid.

Neither God, nor angels, or just men, command you to suffer for a single moment. Therefore it is your solemn and imperative duty to use every means, both [sic] moral, intellectual, and physical, that promises success.

—Ibid.

The humblest peasant is as free in the sight of God as the proudest monarch that ever swayed a sceptre. Liberty is a spirit sent out from God and, like its great Author, is no respecter of persons.

—Ibid.

Think of the undying glory that hangs around the ancient name of Africa—and forget not that you are native-born American citizens, and as such, you are justly entitled to all the rights that are granted to the freest.

—Ibid.

However much you and all of us may desire it, there is not much hope of redemption without the shedding of blood. If you must bleed, let it all come at once—rather *die freemen, than live to be slaves.*

—Ibid.

Your dead fathers speak to you from their graves. Heaven, as with a voice of thunder, calls on you to arise from the dust. Let your motto be resistance! *resistance!* RESISTANCE!

—*Ibid.*

They endeavor to make you as much like brutes as possible. When they have blinded the eyes of your mind—when they have embittered the sweet waters of life—when they have shot out the light which shines from the word of God, then and not till then has American slavery done its perfect work.

—*from a Memorial Discourse Delivered in the Hall of the House of Representatives February 12, 1865*

The caged lion may cease to roar, and try no longer the strength of the bars of his prison, and lie with his head between his mighty paws and snuff the polluted air as though he heeded not. But is he contented? Does he not instinctively long for the freedom of the forest and the plain? Yes, he is a lion still.

—*Ibid.*

If such are the deeds of mercy wrought by angels, then tell me what works of iniquity there remain for devils to do?

—*Ibid.*

The destroying angel has gone forth throughout the land to execute the fearful penalties of God's broken law.

—*Ibid.*

The orators and statesmen of our own land, whether they belong to the past, or to the present age, will live and shine in the annals of history, in proportion as they have dedicated their genius and talents to the defence of Justice and man's God-given rights.

—*Ibid.*

If slavery has been destroyed merely from *necessity,* let every class be enfranchised at the dictation of *justice.*

—*Ibid.*

With the assurance of God's favor in all things done in obedience to his righteous will, and guided by day and by night by the pillars of cloud and fire, let us not pause until we have reached the other and safe side of the stormy and crimson sea. Let freemen and patriots mete out complete and equal justice to all men, and thus prove to mankind the superiority of our Democratic, Republican Government.

—Ibid.

$\mathcal{M}$arcus $\mathcal{G}$arvey

(1 8 8 7 – 1 9 4 0)

Born in Jamaica, Garvey traveled extensively in the Caribbean and went to London before founding the Universal Negro Improvement Association in 1914, editing its journal, Negro World, *and establishing the Black Star line for trade and emigration to Africa. Controversial among less activist black leaders, Garvey was convicted of defrauding his investors, and spent two years in prison before moving to London in 1935, where he attempted, largely unsuccessfully, to revive his movement.*

Up you mighty race,
you can accomplish
what you will.

. . .

One God! One Aim!
One Destiny!

. . .

Africa for the Africans.

—MOTTOES OF THE UNIVERSAL NEGRO IMPROVEMENT ASSOCIATION

I know no national boundary where the Negro is concerned. The whole world is my province until Africa is free.

—STATEMENT AT THE FIRST PAN-AFRICAN CONFERENCE, LONDON, 1900

As one who knows the people well, I make no apology for prophesying that there will soon be a turning point in the history of the West

Indies; and that the people who inhabit that portion of the Western Hemisphere will be the instruments of uniting a scattered race who, before the close of many centuries, will found an Empire on which the sun shall shine as ceaselessly as it shines on the Empire of the North today.

—The African Times and Orient Review, *October 1913*

I asked myself, Where is the black man's Government? Where is his President, his country, and his ambassador, his army, his navy, his men of big affairs? I could not find them, and then I declared, "I will help to make them."

—Philosophy and Opinions of Marcus Garvey *(1923)*

We must keep our business to ourselves. We must be as wise as the serpent and appear to be harmless as the dove. We must strike at the right moment.

—*Ibid.*

Lose not courage, lose not faith, go forward.

—*Ibid.*

This trial has been a conspiracy to ruin Marcus Garvey . . . I am satisfied to let the world judge me innocent or guilty. History will decide.

—*statement before his trial, 1923*

Now, understand me well, Marcus Garvey has entered the fight for the emancipation of race; Marcus Garvey has entered the fight for the redemption of a country. From the graves of millions of my forebears at this hour I heard the cry, and I am going to answer it even though hell is cut loose before Marcus Garvey. From the silent graves of millions who went down to make me what I am, I shall make for their memory, this fight that shall leave a glaring page in the history of man.

—*speech before entering the Tombs prison in Atlanta, June 17, 1923*

I did not bring myself here; they brought me from my silent repose in Africa three hundred years ago, and this is only the first Marcus Garvey. They have thought that they could for three hundred years brutalize a race. They have thought that they could for three hundred years steep the soul of a race in blood and darkness and let it go at that. They make a terrible mistake.

—Ibid.

We are no longer dogs; we are no longer peons; we are no longer serfs —we are men. Tell us about fear; we were not born with fear. Intimidation does not drive fear into the soul of Marcus Garvey. There is no fear but the fear of God. Man cannot drive fear into the heart of man, because man is but the equal of man.

—Ibid.

We must canonize our own saints, create our own martyrs, and elevate to positions of fame and honor black men and women who have made their distinct contributions to our racial history.

—"African Fundamentalism," UNIA pamphlet, 1925

If others laugh at you, return the laughter to them; if they mimic you, return the compliment with equal force . . . Honor them when they honor you, disrespect and disregard them when they vilely treat you. Their arrogance is but skin deep and an assumption that has no foundation in morals or in law.

—Ibid.

When we were embracing the arts and sciences on the banks of the Nile their ancestors were still drinking human blood and eating out of the skulls of their conquered dead; when our civilization had reached the noonday of progress they were still running naked and sleeping in holes and caves with rats, bats, and other insects and animals. After we had already fathomed the mystery of the stars and reduced the heavenly constellations to minute and regular calculus they were still backwoodsmen, living in ignorance and blatant darkness.

—Ibid.

Who can tell what tomorrow will bring forth? Did they not laugh at Moses, Christ, and Mohammed? Was there not a Carthage, Greece, and Rome? We see and have changes every day, so pray, work, be steadfast, and be not dismayed.

—Ibid.

God and Nature first made us what we are, and then out of our own created genius we make ourselves what we want to be. Follow always

167

that great law. Let the sky and God be our limit and Eternity our measurement.

—*IBID.*

When I am dead wrap the mantle of the Red, Black, and Green around me, for in the new life I shall rise with God's grace and blessing to lead the millions up the heights of triumph with the colors that you well know. Look for me in the whirlwind or the storm, look for me all around you, for, with God's grace, I shall come and bring with me countless millions of black slaves who have died in America and the East Indies and the millions in Africa to aid you in the fight for Liberty, Freedom and Life.

—*First Message to the Negroes of the World from Atlanta Prison, February 10, 1925*

I shall write the history that will inspire the millions that are coming and leave the posterity of our enemies to reckon with the hosts for the deeds of their fathers.

—*IBID.*

We are men; we have souls, we have passions, we have feelings, we have hopes, we have desires like any other race in the world. The cry is raised all over the world today of Canada for the Canadians, of America for the Americans, of England for the English, of France for the French, of Germany for the Germans. Do you think it unreasonable that we, the blacks of the world, should raise the cry of Africa for the Africans?

—*Speech at Royal Albert Hall, June 6, 1928*

You cannot scare the Negro anymore. The Negro is a man. We represent the new Negro. His back is not yet to the wall.

—*IBID.*

Liberate the minds of men and ultimately you will liberate the bodies of men.

—*IBID.*

You do not know Africa. Africa has been sleeping for centuries—not dead, only sleeping.

—*IBID.*

168

Henry Louis Gates, Jr.

(1 9 5 0 –)

*O*ne of the leading critics of African American letters, Gates was born in West Virginia and educated at Yale. A correspondent for Time before earning his Ph.D. at Cambridge University, he held teaching chairs at Cornell and Duke and is the author of several critical studies, including The Signifying Monkey, which won an American Book Award. A recipient of a MacArthur Foundation Award, he is chairman of Afro-American Studies at Harvard University. His memoir, Colored People, was published in 1994.

It has been the traditional role of the black poet . . . to be the consciousness, or superconsciousness, of his or her people. It is the black poet who bridges the gap in tradition, who modifies tradition when experience demands it, who translates experience into meaning and meaning into belief.

—*"Dis and Dat: Dialect and Descent," in Dexter Fisher and Robert B. Stepto, Afro-American Literature (1979)*

This is the challenge of the critic of Afro-American literature: not to shy away from literary theory, but rather to translate it into the black idiom, renaming principles of criticism where appropriate, but especially naming indigenous black principles of criticism and applying these to explicate our own texts.

—*Introduction, Figures in Black (1989)*

The creation of formal literature could be no mean matter in the life of the slave, since the sheer literacy of writing was the very commodity that separated animal from human being, slave from citizen, object from subject.

—*"Literary Theory and the Black Tradition," Ibid.*

We must begin to understand the nature of intertextuality . . . the manner by which texts—poems and novels—respond to other texts. After all, all cats may be black at night, but not to other cats.
—*IBID.*

Slavery's time was delineated by memory and memory alone. One's sense of one's existence, therefore, depended upon memory. It was memory, above all else, that gave a shape to being itself.
—*"FREDERICK DOUGLASS AND THE LANGUAGE OF THE SELF," THE YALE REVIEW, SUMMER 1981*

[Douglass] was Representative Man because he was Rhetorical Man, black master of the verbal arts. Douglass is our clearest example of the will to power as the will to write. The act of writing for the slave constituted the act of creating a public, historical self, not only the self of the individual author but also the self, as it were, of the race.
—*IBID.*

That the progenitor of the black literary tradition was a woman means, in the most strictly literal sense, that all subsequent black writers have evolved in a matrilinear line of descent, and that each, consciously or unconsciously, has extended and revised a canon whose foundation was the poetry of a black woman.
—*ON PHILLIS WHEATLEY, "IN HER OWN WRITE," FOREWORD TO THE SCHOMBURG LIBRARY OF NINETEENTH-CENTURY BLACK WOMEN WRITERS (1988)*

In literacy lay freedom for the black slave . . . No group of slaves anywhere, at any other period in history, has left such a large repository of testimony about the horror of becoming the legal property of another human being . . . This was no easy task. Nevertheless, the ex-slave met this challenge squarely, creating the largest body of literature ever created by ex-slaves and giving birth thereby to the Afro-American literary tradition.
—*INTRODUCTION, THE CLASSIC SLAVE NARRATIVES (1987)*

What hurt me most about the glorious black awakening of the late sixties and early seventies is that we lost our sense of humor. Many of us thought that enlightened politics excluded it.
—*COLORED PEOPLE (1994)*

Mama and I would go to a funeral and she'd stand up to read the dead person's eulogy. She made the ignorant and ugly sound like scholars and movie stars, turned the mean and evil into saints and angels. She knew what people had meant to be in their hearts, not what the world had forced them to become. She knew the ways in which working too hard for paltry wages could turn you mean and cold, could kill the thing that had made you laugh.

—*Ibid.*

We thought we had learned at last our unutterable, secret name, and that name was BLACK.

—*Ibid.*

Insofar as we, critics of the black tradition, master our craft, we serve both to preserve our own traditions and to shape their direction. All great writers demand great critics.

—*"Literary Theory and the Black Tradition"*

Marvin Gaye

(1939 – 1984)

Born the son of a strict Pentecostal minister, Marvin Pentz Gay sang with a number of groups in Washington and Chicago before moving to Detroit in 1960, where he signed with Motown and married the sister of its legendary founder, Barry Gordy. Both deeply religious and openly sensual, Gaye produced a string of classic soul hits. Long troubled by artistic frustrations, depression, and drug abuse, he was shot by his father in Los Angeles at the age of forty-four.

I hope to refine music, study it, try to find some area that I can unlock. I don't quite know how to explain it but it's there. These can't be the only notes in the world, there's got to be other notes some place, in some dimension, between the cracks on the piano keys.

—*Interview in* Crawdaddy, *c. 1971*

I think it was around 1968 and 1969 when I stopped thinking so much about my erotic fantasies and started to think about the war in Vietnam . . . It caused me to think hard about society, and something happened with me during that period, and I felt the strong urge to write music, and write lyrics that would touch the souls of men.

—ON HIS 1971 CONCEPT ALBUM WHAT'S GOING ON, IN SHARON DAVIS,
I HEARD IT THROUGH THE GRAPEVINE (1991)

Brother, brother, there are too many of us dying.

—WHAT'S GOING ON (1971)

Great artists suffer for the people.

—IN DAVID RITZ, DIVIDED SOUL (1985)

Maybe today is the result of yesterday spent in wooden churches, singing the praises of our Maker in joyous harmony and love. Part of it has to be the songs we sang, working under the blazing sun, to help pass the hard times. Yesterday was also Bessie Smith, New Orleans, and gospel choirs, folk songs, Bojangles. Yesterday was the birthplace of today . . . songs of protest and anger, songs of gentleness and songs of wounds left unattended for far too long, songs to march to, to fly to, to make love to. It's music pure and simple and soulful, and if you insist, full of promise and determination, unity and humanity; today is the birthplace of forever.

—AT THE CELEBRATION "MOTOWN 25: YESTERDAY, TODAY, FOREVER," MARCH 25, 1983

Music is one of the closest link-ups with God that we can probably experience. I think it's a common vibrating tone of the musical notes that holds all life together.

—IN DAVIS, I HEARD IT THROUGH THE GRAPEVINE (1991)

I would like to be remembered as one of the twelve music disciples, and as a man who was aware and conscious of his environment, and as a person who was full of sensuality, erotic, profound. A person who has depth, feeling, and concern for the needs of others. A man who tried to create music, a whole individual . . . I thank God for my wonderful life.

—HIS EPITAPH FOR HIMSELF, WRITTEN SHORTLY BEFORE HIS DEATH

Addison Gayle, Jr.

(1 9 3 2 –   )

Critic, academic, and author, Gayle has taught at City College in New York and has published numerous volumes, including The Way of the New World *and* Wayward Child, *and edited the important anthology* The Black Aesthetic.

Speaking honestly is a fundamental principle of today's black artist. He has given up the futile practice of speaking to whites, and has begun to speak to his brothers.
> —"CULTURAL STRANGULATON: BLACK LITERATURE AND THE WHITE AESTHETIC,"
> THE BLACK AESTHETIC *(1971)*

The extent of the cultural strangulation of Black literature by white critics has been the extent to which they have been allowed to define the terms in which the Black artist will deal with his own experience . . . the historic practice of bowing to other men's gods and definitions has produced a crisis of the highest magnitude, and brought us, culturally, to the limits of racial Armageddon.
> —*IBID.*

To evaluate the life and culture of black people, it is necessary that one live the black experience in a world where substance is more important than form, where the social takes precedence over the aesthetic, where each act, gesture, and movement is political, and where continual rebellion separates the insane from the sane, the robot from the revolutionary.
> —THE WAY OF THE NEW WORLD: THE BLACK WRITER IN AMERICA *(1975)*

To understand madness is to be a bit mad.
> —*IBID.*

Bob Gibson

(1 9 3 5 –)

Born in Omaha, Nebraska, Robert (Hoot) Gibson was unable to play on his high school's all-white baseball team but was a track and basketball star. After attending college, Gibson played briefly for the Harlem Globetrotters and spent several years in the minor leagues before joining the Saint Louis Cardinals in 1960. He pitched a record thirty-one strike-outs in the 1964 World Series, won the Cy Young Award in 1968 and 1970, and was inducted into the Baseball Hall of Fame in 1981.

A great catch is like watching girls go by—the last one you see is always the prettiest.

—SPORTS ILLUSTRATED, *JUNE 1, 1964*

It is not something I earned or acquired or bought. It is a gift. It is something that was given to me—just like the color of my skin.

—*ON HIS THROWING ABILITY,* FROM GHETTO TO GLORY: THE STORY OF BOB GIBSON *(1968)*

In a world filled with hate, prejudice, and protest, I find that I too am filled with hate, prejudice, and protest.

—*IBID.*

I guess I was never much in awe of anybody. I think you have to have that attitude if you're going to go far in this game.

—*IN ROGER ANGELL,* LATE INNINGS *(1982)*

When I was playing I never wished I was doing anything else. I think being a professional athlete is the finest thing a man can do.

—*IBID.*

Why do I have to be an example for your kid? *You* be an example for your own kid.

—*WIDELY ATTRIBUTED*

I always got by on my ability. I never learned the politics of the game. I found out that honesty just pisses people off.

—*INTERVIEW, MAY 1994*

$\mathcal{D}$izzy $\mathcal{G}$illespie

(1 9 1 7 – 1 9 9 3)

Master trumpeter John Birks Gillespie began his career in big bands and played with Charlie Parker in clubs on Fifty-second Street during the early 1940s. His 1948 concert in Paris did much to establish the popularity of jazz in Europe, and in the United States he helped introduce be-bop and Afro-Cuban jazz. With his upward-tilted instrument he liberated the trumpet solo, and he was also an accomplished scat singer. He will be remembered as well for his compositions, which include "Night in Tunisia" and "Anthropology." He was a devout member of the Baha'i faith.

Ideas, ideas, backward and forward. His influence is layers and layers of spirit.

—*ON CHARLIE PARKER, IN GÉRALD ARNAUD AND JACQUES CHESNEL, MASTERS OF JAZZ (1991)*

I don't care too much about music. What I like is sounds.

—*INTERVIEW IN STOCKHOLM, AUGUST 1970, IN ARTHUR TAYLOR, NOTES AND TONES (1977)*

I think the idea is now for blacks to write about the history of our music. It's time for that, because whites have been doing it all the time. It's time for us to do it ourselves and tell it like it is.

—*IBID.*

The one principle that holds true in the Baha'i faith is the Unity of Mankind. You must always keep that unity in mind . . . So that's what I'm about now.

—*IBID.*

What do you think we were doing up there, kidding?
—*c. 1980*

He was too fragile to last. It's terrible to be black in this society. If you let all these pressures reach you, they drag you down and they do you in.

—*on Charlie Parker, in Gérald Arnaud and Jacques Chesnel, Masters of Jazz (1991)*

cNikki Giovanni

(1 9 4 3 –)

Born in Lexington, Kentucky, Giovanni attended Fisk and the University of Pennsylvania. Coming to prominence first as a militant poet in the 1960s, she is the author of more than ten volumes of poetry and prose, including Sacred Cows and Other Edibles *and* Racism 101.

We ain't got to prove we can die
We got to prove we can kill.
—*"The True Impact of Present Dialogue: Black vs. Negro"*

perhaps these are not poetic
times
at all
—*"For Saundra"*

death is a slave's freedom.
—*"The Funeral of Martin Luther King, Jr."*

You, my children of battle, are your heroes
You must invent your own games and teach us old ones how to play
—*"Poem for Black Boys"*

we eat up artists like there's going to be a famine at the end.
—*"Poem for Aretha"*

I like to tell truth as I see it . . . That's why literature is so important. We cannot possibly leave it to history as a discipline nor to sociology nor science nor economics to tell the story of our people . . . It's not a ladder we're climbing, it's literature we're producing, and there will always be someone to read it.

—"An Answer to Some Questions on How I Write: In Three Parts," in Mari Evans,
Black Women Writers (1984)

I really don't think life is about the I-could-have-beens . . . Life is only about the I-tried-to-do. I don't mind the failure but I can't imagine that I'd forgive myself if I didn't try.

—Ibid.

We write because we believe that the human spirit cannot be tamed and should not be trained.

—Ibid.

if they kill me
it won't stop
the revolution
—"My Poem"

I only want to reclaim myself
—"The Dance Committee"

Dexter Gordon

(1 9 2 3 – 1 9 9 0)

*A master of the tenor saxophone and improvisation, Gordon worked with Lionel Hampton and Louis Armstrong, among others, and also acted in plays and film (*Round Midnight*).*

I'm looking forward to the day when I can have utter, complete chaos. Instead of semi. Instead of semi I want utter.

—interview in Paris, June 1967, in Arthur Taylor, Notes and Tones (1977)

Dick Gregory

(1 9 3 2 –)

*B*orn *in poverty in St. Louis, Gregory earned a track scholarship to Southern Illinois University and in 1953 was drafted into the army, where he began his career as a comedian. He opened his own club in the late 1950s and became active in the civil rights movement, participating in the marches in Selma, Birmingham, and Washington. He is the author of several volumes, including the autobiography,* Nigger, *and recently has become involved in issues of world health and hunger.*

We thought I was going to be a great athlete, and we were wrong, and I thought I was going to be a great entertainer, and that wasn't it, either. I'm going to be an American citizen. First class.

—Nigger *(1964)*

When you have a good mother and no father, God kind of sits in. It's not enough, but it helps.

—*Ibid.*

I never learned hate at home, or shame. I had to go to school for that.

—*Ibid.*

Freedom will run all over this town.

—*on the march on Selma, Ibid.*

This isn't a revolution of black against white, this is a revolution of right against wrong. And right has never lost . . . It started long before I came into it, and I may die before it's over, but we'll beat this thing and cut out this cancer. America will be as strong and beautiful as it should be, for black folks and white folks. We'll all be free then, free from a system that makes a man less than a man, that teaches hate and fear and ignorance.

—*Ibid.*

In America, with all of its evils and faults, you can still reach through the forest and see the sun. But we don't know yet whether that sun is rising or setting for our country.

—<small>IBID.</small>

I have to thank Martin Luther King for where I am now, Abernathy and that whole Movement, because in playing games with nonviolence, I had to either say that I was nonviolent or I wasn't.

—<small>IN HOWELL RAINES, MY SOUL IS RESTED</small> (1977)

Angelina Weld Grimke

(1 8 8 0 – 1 9 5 8)

Born and educated in Boston, Grimke taught at the prestigious Paul Laurence Dunbar High School in Washington, D.C. She was the author of the play Rachel, *poetry, and short stories.*

'Tis few, it is, that goes with the grey road
The straight road
All the way,
With the grey dust liftin' at ev'ry step.

—<small>"THE WAYS O' MEN"</small>

I should like to poise
On the very brink
Of the leaf-brown pools
That are your shadowed eyes . . .

—<small>"MONA LISA"</small>

If I might only grow small enough
To curl up into the hollow of your palm,
Your left palm,
Curl up, lie close and cling,

So that I might know myself always there
. . . Even if you forgot.
—*"Your Hands"*

Hushed by the hands of Sleep,
By the beautiful hands of Sleep.
—*"Hushed by the Hands of Sleep"*

Let us forget the past unrest—
We ask for peace.
—*"Surrender"*

I am not afraid to trust my sisters—not I.
—*in Eric V. Copage, Black Pearls (1993)*

Archibald H. Grimke

(active early twentieth century)

The president of the Washington NAACP branch, Grimke served as minister to Santo Domingo and president of the American Negro Academy and in 1919 was awarded the Spingarn Medal of the NAACP for public service.

We claim no more than what other American citizens claim and obtain, namely, access to your galleries and service in your restaurants—a privilege or a right which is denied to no class of citizens, to no race of men—not even to aliens or alien enemies . . . Has our country declared war against Germany merely to make the world safe for white people?
—*letter to the U.S. Senate, protesting segregation in the nation's capital, 1917*

Charlotte L. Forten Grimke

(1837–1914)

The granddaughter of early abolitionist James Forten and the niece of Robert B. Purvis, Charlotte Forten was born free in Philadelphia and was educated in Massachusetts. During the Civil War, she traveled to the Sea Islands in South Carolina, where she became the first black teacher to ex-slaves and began her "bequest to humanity," a detailed journal of the Civil War era (published in 1953). She eventually married Francis James Grimke, of the Southern abolitionist family.

Provoking, isn't it? that when one is most in need of sensible words, one finds them not.

—JOURNAL OF CHARLOTTE FORTEN *(1953)*

I wonder that every colored person is not a misanthrope. Surely we have everything to make us hate mankind.

—*IBID.*

Let me not forget again that I came not here for friendly sympathy or for anything else but to work, and to work hard. Let me do that faithfully and well.

—*IBID.*

What a victory the black troops had lately won on the Georgian coast, and what a great good they had done for their race in winning; they had proved to their enemies that the black man can and will fight for his freedom.

—ON THE BLACK *FIRST SOUTH CAROLINA VOLUNTEERS, IBID.*

Oh! it is hard to go through life meeting contempt with contempt, hatred with hatred, fearing, with too good reason, to love and trust hardly any one whose skin is white—however lovable, attractive, and congenial in seeming.

—*IBID.*

Ah, what a grand, glorious day this has been. The dawn of freedom which it heralds may not break upon us at once; but it will surely come, and sooner, I believe, than we have ever dared hope before . . . And to us all a year of such freedom as we have never yet known in this boasted but hitherto wicked land.

—*Emancipation Day, Thursday, New Year's Day, 1863, Ibid.*

Ah! this love. Tis a queer thing, but very amusing—to lookers-ons.

—*Ibid.*

It is all like a dream still, and will be for a long time, I suppose; a strange wild dream.

—*On Freedom, Ibid.*

On such a night as this, methought,
Angelic forms are near;
In beauty unrevealed to us
They hover in the air.

—*"The Angel's Visit"*

Francis J. Grimke

(1850–1937)

After his graduation from the Princeton Theological Seminary in 1878, Grimke became pastor of the Fifteenth Street Presbyterian Church in Washington, D.C. From the pulpit he was a frequent advocate of civil rights, particularly during the period of World War I. Four volumes of his writings were edited by Carter Woodson.

Race prejudice can't be talked down, it must be lived down.

—*c. 1914*

When the United States Government shows a proper appreciation of the services of the Negro who has never failed it in every crisis of its history to do his whole duty, to shed his blood freely in its behalf . . . then, and not till then, will I be heard.

—*ON WITHHOLDING PUBLIC SUPPORT FOR THE WAR EFFORT, JULY 1, 1917*

The white people in this country seem to be greatly concerned as to whether humanity or the savage is to rule in other lands but utterly indifferent as to which rules in this.

—*APRIL 16, 1918*

The Negro soldier might just as well lay down his life here in defense of the principles of democracy as to go abroad to do so . . . The greatest enemies to true democracy are not in Germany or Austria, but here in these United States of America.

—*AFTER AN ATTACK ON BLACK SOLDIERS IN CAMP MERRITT, NEW JERSEY, AUGUST 17, 1918*

Nothing so excites the ire of the white man in this country as an attempt on the part of a colored man to stand up for his rights as an American citizen and as a man . . . Liberty long since would have perished from the earth if her fate depended upon such defenders.

—*AFTER LYNCHINGS IN BROOKS AND LOWNDES COUNTIES, GEORGIA, MAY 1918*

You know now that the mean, contemptible spirit of race prejudice that curses this land is not the spirit of other lands: you know now what it is to be treated as a man.

—*ADDRESS TO BLACK SOLDIERS RETURNING FROM WORLD WAR I, APRIL 24, 1919*

The awful things that are going on in this nation—the wanton disregard of law, the exhibitions of brutality, of savagery—show, and show with a clearness which none can fail to see, that unless there comes to the Nation a greater emancipation than Lincoln's Proclamation effected, it is doomed, it is bound to go down.

—*AFTER THE CEREMONY DEDICATING THE LINCOLN MEMORIAL, DURING WHICH BLACK DIGNITARIES WERE SEGREGATED, MAY 1922*

It is only what is written upon the soul of man that will survive the wreck of time.

—*c. 1927*

Marvin Hagler

(1 9 5 4 –)

Born in Newark, New Jersey, Marvelous Marvin Hagler boxed for seven years before gaining the world middleweight title in his bout with Alan Minter in September 1980. He held the title until a split-decision fight with Sugar Ray Leonard in 1987.

When a man goes into the ring, he's going to war.
—IN HARRY MULLAN, THE BOOK OF BOXING QUOTATIONS *(1988)*

Nothing can intimidate me. I just go out and destruct and destroy.
—*IBID.*

Don't doubt me, because that's when I get stronger. I like to see the smiles on people's faces when I show them I can do the impossible.
—*c. 1985*

Clara McBride (Mother) Hale

(1 9 0 5 – 1 9 9 2)

Cited by Ronald Reagan in his 1985 State of the Union Address as an "American heroine," Hale was born in Philadelphia but spent most of her adult life in New York, where she cared for abandoned children, particularly those, in later years, with AIDS. Her work is continued at the nonprofit Hale House in Harlem.

I am not an American hero; I'm a person that loves children.

—c. 1986

If you can't hold them in your arms, please hold them in your heart.

—ON HER BABIES

Alex Haley

(1921–1992)

Haley was born in Ithaca, New York, and raised in Henning, Tennessee, the son of a college professor and grade-school teacher. After two years of college, he entered the coast guard and began writing. When he retired, twenty years later, he launched a career as a journalist and became a writer for Reader's Digest *and* Playboy, *where he initiated the Playboy Interviews.* The Autobiography of Malcolm X, *his 1965 collaboration with the civil rights leader, became a best seller, as did his 1976 novel,* Roots, *based on his twelve-year search to uncover his family's history. The book was made into a record-breaking miniseries in 1977 and was the source of additional books and television programs.*

I tried to be a dispassionate chronicler. But he was the most electric personality I have ever met, and I still can't quite conceive him dead. It still feels to me as if he has just gone into some next chapter, to be written by historians.

—IN THE AUTOBIOGRAPHY OF MALCOLM X *(1965)*

I acknowledge immense debt to the griots of Africa—where today it is rightly said that when a griot dies, it is as if a library has burned to the ground.

—ROOTS *(1976)*

He lifted up the infant and, as all watched, whispered three times into his son's ear the name he had chosen for him. It was the first time the name had ever been spoken as this child's name, for Omoro's people felt that each human being should be the first to know who he was.

—Ibid.

He walked to the edge of the village, lifted his baby up with his face to the heavens, and said softly, *"Fend kiling dorong leh warrata ka iteh tee."* (Behold—the only thing greater than yourself.)

—Ibid.

The more blackness a woman has, the more beautiful she is.

—Ibid.

Let me tell you something: I am a man.

—Ibid.

Prince Hall

(1735–1807)

An early advocate of abolition and colonization to Africa, Hall, according to some historians, may have fought in the Revolutionary War. In 1777 he petitioned the General Court of Massachusetts to end slavery and in 1787 sought educational opportunity for black children. In the same year, he founded the Masonic African Lodge in Boston, a fraternal self-help organization, and later chartered lodges in Philadephia and Providence.

We, or our ancestors, have been taken from all our dear connections, and brought from Africa and put into a state of slavery in this country . . . But we yet find ourselves, in many respects, in very disagreeable and disadvantageous circumstances; most of which must attend us, so long as we and our children live in America.

—PETITION TO THE GENERAL COURT, JANUARY 4, 1777

As we are willing to pay our equal part of these burdens, we are of the humble opinion that we have the right to enjoy the privileges of free men . . . We . . . fear for our rising offspring to see them in ignorance in a land of gospel light when there is provision made for them as well as others and yet can't enjoy them, and for no other reason can be given this they are black.

—PETITION TO THE MASSACHUSETTS LEGISLATURE, OCTOBER 1787

He that despises a black man for the sake of his colour, reproacheth his Maker.

—A CHARGE DELIVERED TO THE BRETHREN OF THE AFRICAN LODGE ON 25TH OF JUNE, 1792

Patience, I say, for were we not possess'd of a great measure of it, we could not bear up under the daily insults we meet with in the streets of Boston, much more on public days of recreation, how we are shamefully abus'd, and that at such a degree, that we may truly be said to carry our lives in our hands, and the arrows of death are flying about our heads.

—A CHARGE DELIVERED TO THE AFRICAN LODGE, JUNE 24, 1797

Fannie Lou Hamer

(1 9 1 7 – 1 9 7 7)

The youngest of twenty children in a family of sharecroppers in Ruleville, Missisipi, Fannie Lou Hamer began working at the age of six. Her decision to register to vote in 1962 left her unemployed, and she became a prominent organizer, leading the Mississippi Freedom Democratic Party (MFDP) in its unsuccessful attempt to be seated at the 1964 Democratic National Convention.

I'm sick and tired of being sick and tired.

—c. 1972, WIDELY ATTRIBUTED

We are here to work side by side with the black man in trying to bring liberation to all people.

—c. 1962, IN COLUMBUS SALLEY, THE BLACK 100 (1993)

We didn't come all the way up here for no two seats! When all of us is tired!

—ON THE "COMPROMISE" ALLOCATING SEATS TO TWO DELEGATES FROM THE MISSISSIPPI FREEDOM DEMOCRATIC PARTY AT THE 1964 DEMOCRATIC CONVENTION

What was the point of being scared? The only thing they could do to me was kill me and it seemed like they'd been trying to do that a little bit at a time ever since I could remember.

—TO PRAISE OUR BRIDGES (1967)

The question for black people is not when is the white man going to give us our rights, or when is he going to give us good education for our children, or when is he going to give us jobs. If the white man gives you anything—just remember when he gets ready he will take it right back. We have to take for ourselves.

—IBID.

Is this America?

—AT THE REFUSAL OF THE DEMOCRATIC NATIONAL CONVENTION TO SEAT DELEGATES OF MDFP, SUMMER 1964

White Americans today don't know what in the world to do because when they put us behind them, that's where they made their mistake. If they had put us in front, they wouldn't have let us look back. But they put us behind them, and we watched every move they made.

—IN JANET CHEATHAM BELL, FAMOUS BLACK QUOTATIONS (1991)

Black people know what white people mean when they say law and order.

—c. 1963

We have to build our own power. We have to win every single political office we can, where we have a majority of black people.
—To Praise Our Bridges

If this is a great society, I'd have to see a bad one.
—The Worker, *July 13, 1975*

When I liberate others, I liberate myself.
—*c. 1969*

William Hamilton

(fl. 1830s)

Abolitionist and prominent member of the convention movement, Hamilton delivered the address at the fourth annual convention, June 1834.

That society must be the most happy, where the good of one is the common good of the whole. Civilization is not perfect, nor has reason full sway, until the community shall see that a wrong done to one is a wrong done to the whole; that the interest of one is or ought to be the common interest of the whole. Surely that must be a happy state of society where the sympathies of all are to all alike.
—*Address to the Fourth National Negro Convention, New York, June 2–13, 1934*

They have put on the garb of angels of light. Fold back their covering, and you have in full array those of darkness.
—*On the American Colonization Society, Ibid.*

Jupiter Hammon

(c . 1 7 2 0 – c . 1 8 0 0)

Hammon's broadside "An Evening Thought" was the first poem published by an African American author. Hammon lived on Long Island, New York, and published many other works in his lifetime, most notably a tribute to Phillis Wheatley.

We cry as Sinners to the Lord,
Salvation to obtain;
It is firmly fixed, his holy Word,
Ye shall not cry in vain.
—*"An Evening Thought," 1761*

The humble soul shall fly to God,
And leave the things of time,
Start forth as 'twere at the first word,
To taste things more divine.
Behold! the soul shall waft away,
When'er we come to die,
And leave its cottage made of clay,
In twinkling of an eye.
—*"An Address to Miss Phillis Wheatly, Ethiopian Poetess"*

ℰred ℋampton

(1947-1969)

The son and grandson of ministers, charismatic and highly articulate, Hampton was one of the early leaders of the Black Panther Party outside California. He was killed while unarmed by police in a predawn attack in Chicago on December 4, 1969, and after years of litigation his heirs received a major settlement for wrongful death.

We understood that politics is nothing but war without bloodshed; and war is nothing but politics with bloodshed.
— *c. 1968*

The people have to have the power—it belongs to the people.
—FRED HAMPTON 20TH COMMEMORATION *(1989)*

We say that we need some guns. There's nothing wrong with the guns in our community; there's just been a misdirection of guns in our community. For some reason or another, the pigs have all the guns, so all we have to do is equally distribute them. So if you see one that has a gun and you don't have one, then when you leave you should have one.
— *IBID.*

You can jail a revolutionary, but you can't jail the revolution.
— *IBID.*

You have to understand that people have to pay the price for peace. You dare to struggle, you dare to win. If you dare not struggle, then goddammit you don't deserve to win. Let me say to you peace if you're willing to fight for it.
— *IBID.*

I believe I'm going to die doing the things I was born to do. I believe I'm going to die high off the people. I believe I'm going to die a revolutionary in the international revolutionary proletarian struggle.

—*Ibid.*

We some Marxist-Leninist cussin' niggers.

—*Ibid.*

$\mathcal{L}$ionel $\mathcal{H}$ampton

(1 9 0 8 –)

A widely popular entertainer, Hampton played with Benny Good-man's band in Chicago, in New York, and throughout Europe. He pioneered the jazz vibraharp (vibes) and led his own band for thirty-five years. A political conservative, he received the Kennedy Center Honors in 1992.

In those same towns where we couldn't get a hotel room or a meal in a decent restaurant—even if we could pay for it—the people treated us like kings once we got up on the stage.

—*on touring in the 1930s,* Hamp: An Autobiography *(1989)*

Every chance we got, we'd go over to Fifty-second Street—West Fifty-second Street, the street that never slept . . . We were all crazy, staying out late and drinking and doing all kinds of fool things . . . We didn't know when to go home.

—*Ibid.*

If you were a black entertainer of any kind—musician, singer, come-dian—being a headliner at the Apollo was your proudest achievement.

—*c. 1941*

I love music, perhaps as much as life itself, and it's given me a great deal of happiness as well as a comfortable living.

—New York Journal-American, *August 31, 1965, on thirty-five years of performing*

The young jazzmen who seem to resent having to perform, or to communicate with an audience, had better wrap up their horns and try another profession. All art is communication of the artists' ideas, sounds, thoughts; without that no one will support the artist.

—*Ibid.*

It went from the classics to ragtime to Dixieland to swing to bebop to cool jazz, and whatever you hear today, it's gone—and this is what you're going to hear tomorrow . . . But it's always jazz. You can put a new dress on her, a new hat on her, but no matter what kind of clothes you put on her, she's the same old broad.

—Hamp

The secret is keeping busy, and loving what you do.

—*on turning eighty, 1988*

Seemed to me that drumming was the best way to get close to God.

—Hamp

W. C. Handy

(1 8 7 3 – 1 9 5 8)

"The Father of the Blues," William Christopher Handy was born in Florence, Alabama, the son and grandson of Methodist ministers. Despite the disapproval of his strict father, he began to play trumpet and piano with a variety of quartets in Birmingham and Saint Louis. His first composition, "Mister Crump," was an immediate success, and with "Saint Louis Blues" he formed his own publishing company. In his music, Handy drew upon the work songs, love songs, and stomps of the Mississippi Delta to create a new American music, later

performed by Robert Johnson, Bessie Smith, Alberta Hunter,
Leadbelly, Ma Rainey, Jelly Roll Morton, Blind Lemon Jefferson, and
many others.

I said the Mississippi river's so deep and wide.
Man I love, he's on the other side.
—*"MEMPHIS BLUES" (1912)*

I hate to see de ev'nin' sun go down,
Hate to see de ev'nin' sun go down,
'Cause ma baby he done lef dis town.

Got de Saint Louis Blues jes as blue as ah can be,
Dat man got a heart lak a rock cast in the sea,
Or else he wouldn't have gone so far from me.
—*"SAINT LOUIS BLUES" (1914)*

Way down where the Southern cross' the Dog,
Money don't exactly grow on trees,
On cotton stalks it grows with ease.
—*"YELLOW DOG BLUES" (1914)*

Sometimes I feel like nothin,' somethin' throwed away,
Somethin' throwed away.
And then I get my guitar, play the blues all day.
—*"JOE TURNER BLUES" (1915)*

If Beale Street could talk, if Beale Street could talk,
Married men would have to take their beds and walk,
Except one or two, who never drink booze,
And the blind men on the corner who sings the Beale Street Blues.
—*"BEALE STREET BLUES" (1916)*

I got a man I keep right around my heels,
I got a man that want me like he want his meals,
Got one so slow he don't know how bad mistreatment feels.
—*"BLUE GUMMED BLUES" (1926)*

And in the wreckage of desire
We sigh for wings like Noah's dove,
Just to fly away from loveless love.

—"LOVELESS LOVE" (1921)

Conjuration in his socks and shoes,
Tomorrow he'll have those mean Sundown Blues.

—"SUNDOWN BLUES" (1923)

Hard times that's all we hear 'round this way.
Odd dimes they're growing thinner each day.
Good times, "Just 'round the corner," so they say.

—"WAY DOWN SOUTH WHERE THE BLUES BEGAN" (1932)

You can never tell what's in a woman's mind,
And if she's from Harlem, there's no use o' tryin'

—"HARLEM BLUES" (1922)

Lorraine Hansberry

(1930–1965)

*In her short life, Lorraine Hansberry made an indelible impression
on the American theater. When she was twenty-eight, her first play,* A
Raisin in the Sun, *was produced on Broadway and won the New York
Drama Critics Award. When she died of cancer at the age of thirty-
four, she left behind many essays, dramatic works, letters, and dia-
ries, published as* The Sign in Sidney Brustein's Window, To Be
Young, Gifted and Black, Les Blancs, *and other works.*

When you starts measuring somebody, measure him *right*, child,
measure him right. Make sure you done taken into account what hills
and valleys he come through before he got to wherever he is.

—*MAMA*, A RAISIN IN THE SUN *(1959)*

I come from five generations of people who were slaves and share-croppers—but ain't nobody in my family never let nobody pay 'em no money that was a way of telling us we wasn't fit to walk the earth. We ain't never been that poor.

MAMA, IBID.

The compelling obligation of the Negro writer, as writer and citizen of life, is participation in the intellectual affairs of all men, everywhere. The foremost enemy of the Negro intelligentsia of the past has been—and in a large sense remains—isolation.

—"THE NEGRO WRITER AND HIS ROOTS: TOWARD A NEW ROMANTICISM,"
SPEECH, MARCH 1, 1959

Despair? Did someone say "despair" was a question in the world? Well, then, listen to the sons of those who have known so little else if you wish to know the resiliency of this thing you would so quickly resign to mythhood, this thing called the human spirit!

—IBID.

As of today, if I am asked abroad if I am a free citizen in the United States of America, I must say only what is true: *No.*

—IBID.

I think that the human race does command its own destiny and that that destiny can eventually embrace the stars. If man is as small and ugly and grotesque as his most inhuman act, he is also as large as his most heroic gesture, and he is therefore a hero manyfold.

—IBID.

As we turn our full attention to the hearts and minds of men, we shall see that if man can fly—he can also be free.

—IBID.

The *why* of why we are here is an intrigue for adolescents; the *how* is what must command the living. Which is why I have lately become an insurgent again.

—THE SIGN IN SIDNEY BRUSTEIN'S WINDOW *(1972)*

One cannot live with sighted eyes and feeling heart and not know and read of the miseries which affect the world.

—IBID.

My people are poor. And they are tired. And they are determined to live.

—To Be Young, Gifted and Black *(1969)*

So many truths seem to be rushing at me as the result of things felt and seen and lived through. Oh what I think I must tell this world! Oh the time that I crave—and the peace—and the *power!*

—*Ibid.*

Will work or perish.

—*Ibid.*

No one, to my knowledge, has ever paid reparations to the descendants of black men; indeed, they have not yet *really* acknowledged the fact of the crime against humanity which was the conquest of Africa. But then—history has not been concluded either, has it?

—*Ibid.*

It is still yesterday in Africa. It will take millions of tomorrows to rectify what has been done here.

—Les Blancs *(1972)*

One does not glorify in romanticizing revolution. One cries.

—*Ibid.*

I wish to live because life has within it that which is good, that which is beautiful, and that which is love. Therefore, since I have known all of these things, I have found them to be reason enough and—I wish to live. Moreover, because this is so, I wish to live for generations and generations and generations and generations.

—"*The Negro Writer and His Roots*"

Though it be a thrilling marvelous thing to be merely young and gifted in such times, it is doubly so, doubly dynamic—to be young, gifted *and black*. Look at the work that awaits you!

—To Be Young, Gifted and Black

Frances Watkins Harper

(1825–1911)

Born free, Frances Ellen Watkins supported herself from the age of thirteen and became a prominent lecturer for the Anti-Slavery Society. A founding member of the National Association of Colored Women and a strong proponent of woman suffrage, during her long life Harper was the author of ten volumes of poetry; "The Two Offers," the first short story credited to a black author; and the classic novel Iola Leroy *(1892).*

Make me a grave where'er you will,
In a lowly plain, or a lofty hill;
Make it among earth's humblest graves,
But not in a land where men are slaves.
—"BURY ME IN A FREE LAND"

He is not hers, for cruel hands
May rudely tear apart
The only wreath of household love
That binds her breaking heart.
—"THE SLAVE MOTHER"

For she is a mother—her child is a slave—
And she'll give him his freedom, or find him a grave!
—"ELIZA HARRIS"

God wields national judgment on national sins.
—LETTER TO JOHN BROWN, NOVEMBER 25, 1859

The true aim of female education should be, not a development of one or two, but all the faculties of the human soul, because no perfect womanhood is developed by imperfect culture.
—"THE TWO OFFERS," 1859

198

The world was not so wealthy in love that it had no use for hers.
—*Ibid.*

The white race has yet work to do in making practical the political axiom of equal rights and the Christian idea of human brotherhood. The most important question before us colored people is not simply what the Democratic party may do against us or the Republican party do for us; but what are we going to do for ourselves?
—*Address on the Centennial Anniversary of the Pennsylvania Society for Promoting the Abolition of Slavery, 1875*

I find, by close observation, that the mothers are the levers which move in education. The men talk about it . . . but the women work most for it.
—*"The Coloured Women of America," 1878*

> Hope and joy, peace and blessing,
> Met me in my first-born child.
> —*"The Mother's Blessing"*

In dealing with the negro we wanted his labor; in dealing with the Indian we wanted his lands. For one we had weapons of war; for the other we had real and invisible chains, the coercion of force, and the terror of the unseen world.
—*Iola Leroy, or Shadows Uplifted (1892)*

Law is the pivot on which the whole universe turns; and obedience to law is the gauge by which a nation's strength or weakness is tried.
—*Ibid.*

They never burn a man in the South that they do not kindle a fire around my soul.
—*Ibid.*

Men who are deaf to the claims of mercy, and oblivious to the demands of justice, can feel when money is slipping from their pockets.
—*Ibid.*

Justice is always uncompromising in its claims and inexorable in its demands. The laws of the universe are never repealed to accommodate our follies.
—*Ibid.*

No man can feel the iron which enters another man's soul.

—*Ibid.*

There is material among us for the broadest comedies and the deepest tragedies, but, besides money and leisure, it needs patience, perseverance, courage, and the hand of an artist to weave it into the literature of the country.

—*Ibid.*

Old age turns to her for comfort, young girls for guidance, and mothers for counsel. Her life is full of blessedness.

—*Ibid.*

The shadows have been lifted from all their lives; and peace, like bright dew, has descended upon their paths. Blessed themselves, their lives are a blessing to others.

—*Ibid.*

What matters it if they do forget the singer, so they don't forget the song.

—*Ibid.*

Hubert H. Harrison

(1 8 8 3 – 1 9 2 7)

A black nationalist and Garveyite, Harrison was a frequent lecturer and orator during the Harlem Renaissance; he was best known for his collection of essays, When Africa Awakes *(1920).*

[The new Negro] is no longer begging or asking. He is demanding as a right that which he is in position to enforce . . . Any man today who aspires to lead the Negro race must set squarely before his face the idea of "Race First."

—"The New Politics for the New Negro," September 1917

The Negro will never be accepted by the white American democracy except in so far as he can by the use of force, financial, political, or other, win, seize, or maintain in the teeth of opposition that position which he finds necessary to is own security and salvation . . . We as Negroes are compelled to fight for what we want from the white world.

—"A Negro for President," June 1920

Robert Hayden

(1913–1980)

Born in Detroit, Hayden attended Detroit City College and joined the Federal Writers Project during the 1930s. He received his M.A. from the University of Michigan in 1944 and taught at Fisk University for twenty-two years. In 1975, he was elected to the American Academy of Poets and two years later became a poetry consultant to the Library of Congress.

> . . . voyage through death
> to life upon these shores.
>
> —"Middle Passage"

> And this was the way of it, brethren brethren,
> way we journeyed from Can't to Can.
>
> —"Runagate"

> She came out on the stage in ostrich feathers, beaded satin, and shone that smile on us and sang.
>
> —"Homage to the Empress of the Blues"

Oh who and oh who will sing Jesus down
to help with struggling and doing without and being colored
all through blue Monday?
Till way next Sunday?
—*"Mourning Poem for the Queen of Sunday"*

. . . your presence was shore where I rested
released from the hoodoo of that dance, where I spoke
with my true voice again.
—*"A Ballad of Remembrance"*

Mean mean mean to be free.
—*"Runagate"*

[My poetry is] a way of coming to grips with reality . . . a way of
discovery and definition. It is a way of solving for the unknowns.
—*Address at the Library of Congress, 1977*

We must not be frightened nor cajoled
into accepting evil as deliverance from evil.
We must go on struggling to be human,
though monsters of abstractions
police and threaten us.
—*"In the Mourning Time"*

Lemuel B. Haynes

(1 7 5 3 – 1 8 3 3)

*Haynes, born of a slave father and white mother, was abandoned as
a young child and raised by a white family in New York. He fought in
the Revolutionary War and was ordained a Congregational minister
in 1785. Though his sermons shed no light on the cause of abolition,
in his most famous oration he did have some instructive comments
about the devil.*

The serpent, before he set up preaching universal salvation, was a cunning, beautiful, and happy creature; but now his glory is departed.

—*"Universal Salvation—A Very Ancient Doctrine," 1805*

He is a very *laborious,* unwearied preacher. He has been in the ministry almost six thousand years, and yet his zeal is not in the least abated . . . He is a very *successful* preacher. He draws a great number after him. No preacher can command hearers like him . . . He mixes truth with error, in order to make it go well, or to carry his point.

—*on Satan, Ibid.*

He does not wish to have it known that he is a liar; therefore he conceals himself, that he can the better accomplish his design and save his own character.

—*Ibid.*

$\mathcal{D}$*orothy* $\mathcal{H}$*eight*

(1 9 1 2 –)

Born in Richmond, Height received her M.A. from New York University and has spent a lifetime of service with the YWCA and the Delta Sigma Theta Sorority. Since 1957, she has been president of the National Council of Negro Women. She served as a welfare adviser to the U.S. Department of Health and in 1986 helped develop Black Family Reunion Celebration programs.

When you're a black woman, you seldom get to do what you just want to do; you always do what you have to do.

—*in Columbus Salley,* The Black 100 *(1993)*

History reminds us that our life traditions were wholly emcompassed by our kinships and tribes. No children and mothers were ever unsheltered and unprotected.

—*c. 1982*

Jimi Hendrix

(1 9 4 2 – 1 9 7 0)

Johnny Allen Hendrix (renamed James Marshall Hendrix when he was four years old) experimented with science fiction and the visual arts as a child. He performed under the name Jimi James and later formed the Jimi Hendrix Experience, profoundly influencing the sound of the electric guitar before his death, thought to be due to a drug overdose, at the age of twenty-seven.

Purple haze was in my brain
Lately things don't seem the same,
Actin' funny, but I don't know why
'Scuse me while I kiss the sky.
—*"Purple Haze" (1967)*

Anita Hill

(1 9 5 6 –   )

*R*aised in rural Oklahoma, Hill received her law degree from Yale
and held several positions in law and government before she came to
national prominence during the Supreme Court confirmation hearings for Clarence Thomas, in October 1991. Then a professor of law
at the University of Oklahoma, she testified that she had been subjected to sexual harassment from Thomas when they both worked for
the Equal Employment Opportunity Commission during the early
1980s. For her reluctant testimony Hill was both vilified and praised
by the public and the press.

It would have been more comfortable to remain silent. I took no
initiative to inform anyone. But when I was asked by a representative
of this committee to report my experience, I felt that I had to tell the
truth. I could not keep silent.

—*STATEMENT TO THE SENATE JUDICIARY COMMITTEE ON THE NOMINATION OF CLARENCE THOMAS,*
OCTOBER 11, 1991

Chester Himes

(1 9 0 9 – 1 9 8 4)

*T*he author of more than a dozen novels and volumes of autobiography, Himes was born in Jefferson City, Missouri. He left Ohio State
University in his first year, and when he was in prison for armed
robbery, began writing for Esquire and other magazines. After his
release he went to California, the setting of his first novel, If He
Hollers Let Him Go (1945). After 1955, he spent much of the rest of

his life in Europe, where he first published the increasingly popular series of detective novels featuring Coffin Ed Smith and Gravedigger Jones.

There is an indomitable quality within the human spirit that cannot be destroyed; a face deep within the human personality that is impregnable to all assaults. They rest so deeply that prejudice, oppression, lynching riots, time, or weariness can never corrode or destroy them.

—BEYOND THE ANGRY BLACK *(1966)*

Man cannot live without some knowledge of the purpose of life. If he can find no purpose in life he creates one in the inevitability of death.

—*IBID.*

Martyrs are needed to create incidents. Incidents are needed to create revolutions. Revolutions are needed to create progress.

—THE CRISIS, *1943*

There can be only one (I repeat: *only one*) aim of revolution by Negro Americans. That is *the enforcement of the Constitution of the United States.* At this writing no one has yet devised a better way of existence than contained in the Constitution. *Therefore Negro Americans could not revolt for any other reason.* This is what a Negro American revolution will be: A revolution by a racial minority for the enforcement of the democratic laws already in existence.

—*IBID.*

When people become barbarians they can no longer govern themselves. They respect only might. The strongest, most deadly, most vicious, most cunning, most murderous, will become the ruler. He will rule as long as he is feared.

—*IBID.*

The first step backward is riots. *Riots are not revolutions* . . . No matter who passes the first blow or fires the first shot, riots between white and black occur for only one reason: *Negro Americans are firmly convinced that they have no access to any physical protection which they do not provide for themselves.*

—*IBID.*

America lives by violence, and violence achieves—regardless of what anyone says, regardless of the distaste of the white community—its own ends.

—IN RICHARD BARKSDALE AND KENETH KINNAMON, BLACK WRITERS OF AMERICA *(1972)*

Billie Holiday

(1 9 1 5 – 1 9 5 9)

Born to teenage parents in Baltimore, Eleonora Fagan endured an unhappy childhood amid prostitution and neglect and spent time in a home for "wayward girls" before she began her singing career in Harlem in 1931, fronting for Count Basie, Artie Shaw, and other prominent band leaders. Though Lady Day struggled with addiction to drugs and alcohol and was imprisoned for drug possession, her artistry has proven timeless.

Them that's got, shall get
Them that's not, shall lose
So the Bible says,
And it still is news
Mama may have
Papa may have
But God bless the child that's got his own
That's got his own.

—*"GOD BLESS THE CHILD"*

Southern trees bear strange fruit
Blood on the leaves and blood at the root
Black bodies swinging
In the southern breeze
Strange fruit hanging
From the poplar trees

—*"STRANGE FRUIT"*

Mom and Pop were just a couple of kids when they got married. He was eighteen, she was sixteen, and I was three.

—Lady Sings the Blues *(1956)*

Most of the . . . white people who came to Harlem those nights were looking for atmosphere. Damn few of them brought any along.

—*Ibid.*

You can be up to your boobies in white satin, with gardenias in your hair and no sugar cane for miles, but you can still be working on a plantation.

—*Ibid.*

You can't copy anybody and end with anything. If you copy, it means you're working without any real feeling. And without feeling, whatever you do amounts to nothing. No two people on earth are alike, and it's got to be that way in music or it isn't music.

—*Ibid.*

Some people is and some people ain't . . .

—*Ibid.*

Somebody once said we never know what is enough until we know what's more than enough.

—*Ibid.*

It's awful to be in trouble with someone who just doesn't have the heart for it.

—*Ibid.*

I've been told that nobody sings the word "hunger" like I do. Or the word "love." Maybe I remember what those words are all about . . . You've got to have something to eat and a little love in your life before you can hold still for any damn body's sermon on how to behave.

—*Ibid.*

All dope can do for you is kill you—and kill you the long slow hard way. And it can kill the people you love right along with you.

—*Ibid.*

God has blessed you when he lets you believe in somebody.

—*Ibid.*

Larry Holmes

(1 9 4 9 –)

Holmes won the WBC heavyweight title from Ken Norton in June 1978, and the IBF title from thirty-eight-year-old Muhammad Ali in 1980. He suffered defeats to Michael Spinks and Mike Tyson in the mid-1980s, but made a brief comeback in 1991 and holds one of the highest records for consecutive wins (48) for a career of 53 to 3.

It's hard being black. You ever been black? I was black once—when I was poor.

—IN JOYCE CAROL OATES, ON BOXING *(1987)*

It's going to be Everlast in his face all night long.

—BEFORE HIS FIGHT WITH GERRY COONEY, JUNE *1982*, IN WHICH HE RETAINED HIS TITLE

I don't want you guys to write, "Larry Holmes fought one too many."

—ON RETIREMENT, BEFORE HIS FIGHT WITH DAVID BEY, MARCH *1985*,

IN WHICH HE RETAINED HIS TITLE

There is no quit in me.

—BEFORE HIS DEFEAT TO MIKE TYSON, JANUARY *1988*

In the ring, I give it all I've got . . . I've paid my dues in this business.

—c. *1983*

John Lee Hooker

(1 9 2 0 –)

Born in Vance, Mississippi, the blues guitarist Hooker moved north to Detroit after the war. With more than five hundred tracks and a dozen albums, Hooker was especially popular during the 1960s blues revival and influenced many early rock musicians.

To you and all of my friends . . . especially my fellow mens . . . It's a big wide world . . . We come a long ways . . . We are here to pay our dues to the natural facts. You know . . . we have come a long ways . . . we all . . . we entertainers trying to reach you to bring you the message of the blues.

—AT THE NEWPORT JAZZ FESTIVAL, C. 1964 (ELLIPSIS IN ORIGINAL)

Everybody in the world has the blues . . .

—DETROIT FREE PRESS, SEPTEMBER 8, 1991

bell hooks

(1 9 6 1 –)

Born Gloria Watkins in rural Kentucky, but assuming her great-grandmother's name, hooks attended Stanford and taught at Yale before becoming professor of English and Women's Studies at Oberlin. She wrote her first book, Ain't I a Woman: Black Women and Feminism, *while still an undergraduate, and she is also the author of* Yearning: Race, Gender, and Cultural Politics, Sisters of the Yam, *and other volumes.*

Nineteenth-century black women were more aware of sexist oppression than any other female group in American society.

—Ain't I a Woman: Black Women and Feminism *(1981)*

She wants to express herself—to speak her mind. To them it is just talking back.

—Black Is a Woman's Color *(1989)*

It is poetry that changes everything.

—*Ibid.*

There is sorrow in every gesture, sorrow and pain. It is so thick she feels that she could gather it up in her hands. It is like dust collecting on everything.

—*Ibid.*

Secrets find a way out in sleep . . . It is the place where there is no pretense.

—*Ibid.*

It is crucial for the future of the Black liberation struggle that we remain ever mindful that ours is a shared struggle, that we are each other's fate.

—Breaking Bread *(1991)*

When we talk about that which will sustain and nurture our spiritual growth as a people, we must once again talk about the importance of community. For one of the most vital ways we sustain ourselves is by building communities of resistance, places where we know we are not alone.

—*Ibid.*

Benjamin L. Hooks

(1 9 2 5 –)

From Memphis, Hooks served in Italy during World War II and received his law degree from DePaul University in 1948. An ordained minister, he pursued a successful career in law and business before he was unanimously elected executive director of the NAACP in 1977, succeeding Roy Wilkins. Before his retirement in 1992, he led several successful legislative initiatives and was awarded the Spingarn Medal in 1986.

Once we thought there would come a time when our work would be finished. But racism still exists and inequality is still built into this society.

—The Crisis, *June 1986*

I don't think America was ready to end segregation. I don't think it has ever been ready to extend full equality. I can't think of anything we've gained as a black people that has not come without a struggle.

—*on civil contemporary civil rights legislation,* New York Times, *April 3, 1991*

We have moved from a president who said of civil rights, "We shall overcome," to president who vetoes civil rights bills and says, "You can't override."

—*on the nomination of Clarence Thomas, NAACP conference, Houston, July 7, 1991*

We've come a long way, but it's like nibbling at the edge of darkness.

—The Crisis, *March 1987*

John Hope

(1868 – 1936)

Born in Augusta, Georgia, and educated at Brown University, Hope was the first black president of Atlanta Baptist College (later Morehouse College). He was a proponent of liberal arts rather than industrial education, and served as president of the Association for the Study of Negro Life and History. The only Southern founding member of the Niagara Movement, he was also on the advisory board of the NAACP.

We have sat on the river bank and caught catfish with pin hooks. The time has come to harpoon a whale.

—*CIRCA 1900*

If we are not striving for equality, in heaven's name for what are we living? . . . If money, education, and honesty will not bring to me as much privilege, as much equality as they bring to any American citizen, then they are to me a curse, and not a blessing . . . Yes, my brothers, I want equality. Nothing less.

—The Story of John Hope *(1948)*

Rise, Brothers! Come let us possess this land. Never say: "Let well enough alone" . . . Be discontented. Be dissatisfied.

—*Ibid.*

Frank Horne

(1 8 9 9 – 1 9 7 4)

Horne was born in New York City and studied at City College. Though he was trained as an optometrist, he wrote that he "had a hankering to write as long as I can remember, but Charles Johnson, Editor of Opportunity, *and a certain Gwendolyn Bennett are responsible for my trying it openly." He is especially known for his long poem "Letters Found Near a Suicide."*

Here's to your heart
May it ever be full
of the love of loving . . .
Here's to your soul
as yet
unborn . . .
—*"Toast"*

Life—an infinite loving
Sweeping to the peak of anticipation
Trembling breathlessly at the brink
of realization . . .
—*"Immortality"*

Look you well,
You shall know this thing.
—*"On Seeing Two Brown Boys in a Catholic Church"*

For I have battered the stark stonewall
Before me . . .
I have kept faith with you
And now
I have called my signal,
Found my opening
And slipped through

Fighting and squirming
Over the line
To victory . . .

—"LETTERS FOUND NEAR A SUICIDE"

Lena Horne

(1917–)

Born into a prominent family in Brooklyn, New York, Horne began dancing at the Cotton Club when she was sixteen and toured as a singer and dancer with Noble Sissle, the creator of the popular review Shuffle Along. *In the 1940s she went to Hollywood, where she was the first black studio contract performer; she became a star after her roles in* Cabin in the Sky *and* Stormy Weather. *An outspoken social activitist, Horne continues her career to the present day and in 1981 received a special Tony citation for* Lena Horne: The Lady and Her Music.

When interested people began to try to give me different "images" of myself, I came to realize that nobody (and certainly not yet myself) had any sound image to give a woman who stood between the two conventional ideas of Negro womanhood: the "good" quiet, Negro woman who scrubbed and cooked and was a respectable servant—and the whore.

—LENA *(1965)*

I did not know whether to be proud of my color or ashamed of it . . . I was a changeling, presenting different faces to different people, and to this day, I am two or three people.

—*IBID.*

You have to be taught to be second class; you're not born that way.

—*IBID.*

It's an irony, but as true as anything in this world: when you're poor you need, in a deep, aching kind of way, luxuries. You need them, psychologically, as you never do when you're well off.

—*Ibid.*

As *Thousands Cheer* was the beginning of a long line of films where I was pasted to a pillar to sing my song.

—*Ibid.*

If patrons did not object to a Negro using the elevators or taking a shower or entertaining visitors in a suite, how could they object to her staying overnight? The contortions of logic which segregation forces on people would alone make it worthwhile to abandon.

—*ON THE CIRCUMSTANCES SURROUNDING HER PERFORMANCES, Ibid.*

Music was, and perhaps still is, the area of my life where the question of color comes second and the question of whether you play good or not is the one you have to answer as a test of admission into society.

—*Ibid.*

Up until Little Rock, when I suppose untold millions of small Negro children were confronted all at once with the word [nigger], on television, shouted by the charming fat white ladies in hair curlers as they tried to enter Central High School, it was the Negro parent's duty to face up all alone to the day when your baby wants to know what the word means and why it hurts so much.

—*Ibid.*

What an endless chain of unhappiness prejudice forges.

—*Ibid.*

Once I was talking to a very famous Negro athlete and he suddenly started a tirade about what the Negro men would do when they were free. He told me how they would take back their possessions and their women whom the white men have stolen and they would not let them go with white men again. I said to him: "What you mean is that even when black people are free, their women will still not be free."

—*Ibid.*

I don't think anyone is totally aware of it when her spirit starts to die.

—*Ibid.*

History has passed us by—the generation of celebrity symbols. We are free merely to be human, free to speak, frankly as individuals, not as examples, not as "credits" to our race. And so I do not have to measure myself against an impossible idea of Negro womanhood and feel shame over my failure to meet the standards. I can, at last, try to be myself.

—Ibid.

It's bad for a seventy-one-year-old broad to be singing about how bad she needs it.

—c. 1988

George Moses Horton

(c .   1 8 0 0 – c .   1 8 8 0)

The third published African American poet, Horton worked at the University of North Carolina, where he expressed his political sentiments in his works and sold love poems to students in an effort to buy his freedom, though he gained his liberty only with abolition. His volumes are Poems by a Slave *(1937),* Poetical Works *(1845), and* Naked Genius *(1865).*

> Oh! that my soul had winged its flight,
> When first I saw the morning light,
> To worlds of liberty!
> *—"Slavery"*

> My heart I shall ever twine about thee;
> Fare thee well—but think of me,
> Compell'd to live and die without thee
> *—"To Eliza"*

I leave my parents here behind
And all my friends to love resigned
'Tis grief to go, but death to stay
Farewell—I'm gone with love away.
—*"The Lover's Farewell"*

Must I dwell in Slavery's night,
And all pleasures take its flight,
Far beyond my feeble sight,
Forever?
—*The Slave's Complaint*

My genius from a boy
Has fluttered like a bird within my heart;
But could not thus confined her power employ,
Impatient to depart.
—*"Myself"*

Son House

(1 9 0 2 – 1 9 8 8)

A blues guitarist born in the Mississippi Delta, House remains best known for "Preachin' the Blues."

I says I got up this morning
with the jinx all 'round my bed
Know I thought about you and
it like to kill me dead
—*"The Jinx Blues"*

Oh, I have religion on this very day
But the women and whiskey, well they would not let me pray

. . .

Well I met the blues this morning
Walking just like a man
I said, Good morning blues
Now give me your right hand
                    —*"Preachin' the Blues"*

Charles Hamilton Houston

(1 8 9 5 – 1 9 5 0)

Dean of the law school at Howard University, Houston was head of the NAACP legal team that began the assault on the nation's system of segregated schools in the 1930s. Born in Washington, D.C., he was admitted to Amherst College at the age of fifteen. He served in World War I and in 1919 entered Harvard Law School, where he joined the Law Review. During World War II, he served on the President's Committee on Fair Employment Practices, but resigned that position in protest.

The individual college youth cannot wait forever until the problem of his education is decided.
                    —The Crisis, *January 1938*

A Negro has handicaps enough without having to pay taxes to support the education of white students to learn how to suppress him.
                    —*Ibid.*

Many white servicemen are talking about what they are going to do to put the Negro in his place as soon as they get back home. Many Negroes are getting to the point of disgust and desperation where they had just as soon die fighting one place as another.
    —*"Conference on America's Opportunity to Create and Maintain Lasting Peace," New York, October 7–8, 1944*

The American color bar unless speedily removed will be the rock on which our international Good Neighbor policy and our pious claims to moral leadership will founder. The moment the peoples of Asia, Africa, and India become convinced that our true war aims are to perpetuate the old colonial system with the white man's heel on the colored man's neck . . . that moment we might as well begin preparing for World War III.

—*Ibid.*

It is high time the country awakens to the fact that it is guaranteeing its own salvation by making a substantial down payment on the Four Freedoms at home.

—*Ibid.*

The failure of the government to enforce democratic practices and to protect minorities in its own capital makes its expressed concern for national minorities abroad somewhat specious, and the interference in the domestic affairs of other countries very premature.

—*letter of resignation from the FEPC, November 1945*

Whether elected or appointed, public officials serve those who put and keep them in office. We cannot depend upon them to fight our battles.

—*circa 1945*

Nathan Irvin Huggins

(1 9 2 7 –)

Born in Chicago and educated at the University of California at Berkeley, Huggins is now professor of history at Harvard University. His works include Black Odyssey *and the award-winning* Harlem Renaissance.

The vogue of the New Negro . . . had all of the character of a public relations promotion. The Negro had to be "sold" to the public in terms they could understand.

—HARLEM RENAISSANCE *(1977)*

How convenient! It was merely a taxi trip to the exotic for most white New Yorkers . . . Theirs had been thrill without danger.

—*IBID.*

The way that the Negro has been used by whites, and the way he has permitted himself to be used, exposes the deep moral tensions that have characterized American race relations.

—*IBID.*

Langston Hughes

(1 9 0 2 – 1 9 6 7)

Born in Joplin, Missouri, Hughes lived in various cities in the Midwest before he entered Columbia University in 1921. He left after a year and went to sea, where he continued writing for The Crisis, Opportunity, *and other journals. On his return he entered Lincoln University, and in 1926 his first volume of poems,* The Weary Blues, *was published. He lived for the rest of his life in Harlem, the backdrop for two volumes of autobiography,* The Big Sea *and* I Wonder as I Wander, *the stories in* The Ways of White Folks, *numerous volumes of poetry, the popular columns based on the character Jesse B. Semple, and other works.*

This is the mountain standing in the way of any true Negro art in America—this urge to whiteness, the desire to pour racial individuality into the mold of American standardization, and to be as little Negro and as much American as possible.

—"THE NEGRO ARTIST AND THE RACIAL MOUNTAIN," THE NATION, JUNE 23, 1926

Jazz to me is one of the inherent expressions of Negro life in America: the eternal tom-tom beating in the Negro soul—the tom-tom of revolt against weariness in a white world, a world of subway trains, and work, work, work; the tom-tom of joy and laughter, and pain swallowed in a smile.

—IBID.

An artist must be free to choose what he does, certainly, but he must also never be afraid to do what he might choose . . . We younger Negro artists who create now intend to express our individual dark-skinned selves without fear or shame. If white people are pleased we are glad. If they are not, it doesn't matter. We know we are beautiful. And ugly too.

—IBID.

I, too, sing America.

—"I, TOO"

I've known rivers;
I've known rivers ancient as the world and older than the flow of human blood in human veins.

—"THE NEGRO SPEAKS OF RIVERS"

I don't have to do nothing
but eat, drink, stay black, and die.

—"NECESSITY"

And farther down the coast it was more like the Africa I had dreamed about—wild and lovely, the people dark and beautiful, the palm trees tall, the sun bright, and the rivers deep. The great Africa of my dreams!

—THE BIG SEA (1940)

They seemed to me like the gayest and the bravest people possible—these Negroes from the Southern ghettos—facing tremendous odds, working and laughing and trying to get somewhere in the world.

—IBID.

. . . that fantastic period, when Harlem was in vogue.
—ON THE HARLEM RENAISSANCE, IBID.

For how long could a large and enthusiastic number of people be crazy about Negroes forever? But some Harlemites thought the millennium had come . . . I don't know what made any Negroes think that—except that they were mostly intellectuals doing the thinking. The ordinary Negroes hadn't heard of the Harlem Renaissance. And if they had, it hadn't raised their wages any.
—IBID.

We Negro writers, just by being black, have been on the blacklist all our lives . . . Censorship for us begins at the color line.
—NATIONAL ASSEMBLY OF AUTHORS AND DRAMATISTS SYMPOSIUM, MAY 7, 1957

What happens to a dream deferred?
—"HARLEM"

Alberta Hunter

(1895–1988)

Born in Memphis, Hunter left home at a very young age for Chicago, where she sang with artists like Eubie Blake, Fats Waller, and Louis Armstrong while still in her teens. In the early 1920s she moved to New York, where she starred on Broadway, and toured widely in Europe. In 1954, she withdrew abruptly from performing to become a nurse, but made a spectacular comeback in 1977.

Blues means what milk does to a baby. Blues is what the spirit is to the minister. We sing the blues because our hearts have been hurt, our souls have been disturbed.
—IN GILES OAKLEY, THE DEVIL'S MUSIC: A HISTORY OF THE BLUES (1977)

I've got the world in a jug
The stopper's in my hand.
— *"Down Hearted Blues" (1922)*

Now, children I'm goin' way down in the gutter and get those blues. Some people take a ballad and sing it real slow and say it's the blues. Don't believe 'em. I'm gonna sing some blues—so help me!
— *in performance, April 29, 1982*

[The musicians] that didn't know music could play the best blues. I know that I don't want no musicians who know all about music playin' for me.
— *in Nat Shapiro and Nat Hentoff, Hear Me Talkin' to Ya (1955)*

Can't a man alive mistreat me, 'cause I know who I am.
— *c. 1985*

Addie W. Hunton

(1 8 7 5 – 1 9 4 3)

Born in Norfolk, Virginia, Addie Hunton was one of the most active African American women of her day, participating in the YWCA, the women's club movement, the NAACP, and the Pan-African movement.

Resting upon the unified aim and spirit of 45,000 workers, quick to discern opportunities, what can the National Association of Colored Women not achieve?
— *The Crisis, May 1911*

Some will suffer in the evolution, but it is the only way to justice.
— *bulletin of the NAACP, April 1917*

Zora Neale Hurston

(1891 – 1960)

The author of four novels, two collections of black folklore, an auto-biography, and numerous stories and essays, Hurston was one of the most celebrated figures of the Harlem Renaissance. Born in Eaton-ville, Florida, she attended Howard University and studied anthropol-ogy at Barnard College with Franz Boas. She traveled to Florida, South Carolina, Jamaica, and Haiti to study black folklore and was awarded a Guggenheim Fellowship in 1936 to continue her research. Though Hurston died in obscurity, through the attention of Alice Walker she has found a new audience, and all of her work has been returned to print.

I am not tragically colored. There is no great sorrow dammed up in my soul, nor lurking behind my eyes. I do not mind at all. I do not belong to the sobbing school of Negrohood who hold that nature somehow has given them a lowdown dirty deal and whose feelings are all hurt about it. No, I do not weep at the world—I am too busy sharpening my oyster knife.

   —"COLORED ME," WORLD TOMORROW *(1928)*

When I pitched headforemost into the world I landed in the crib of negroism. From the earliest rocking of my cradle, I had known about the capers Brer Rabbit is apt to cut and what the Squinch Owl says from the house top. But it was fitting me like a tight chemise. I couldn't see it for wearing it. It was only when I was off in college, away from my surroundings, that I could see myself like somebody else and stand off and look at my garment. Then I had to have the spy-glass of Anthropology to look through at that.

   —MULES AND MEN *(1935)*

Nothing had been done in Negro folklore when the greatest cultural wealth of the continent was disappearing without the world ever real-izing it had ever been.

   —*IBID.*

225

The brother in black puts a laugh in every vacant place in his mind. His laugh has a hundred meanings.

—*Ibid.*

You come to de right place if lies is what you want. Ah'm gointer lie up a nation.

—*Ibid.*

Don't you know you can't git de best of no woman in de talkin' game? Her tongue is all de weapon a woman got.

—*Ibid.*

There's more work in de world than there is anything else. God made de world and de white folks made work.

—*Ibid.*

Some folks is born wid they feet on de sun and they kin seek out de inside meanin' of words.

—*Ibid.*

De wind is a woman, and de water is a woman too. They useter talk together a whole heap. Mrs. Wind useter go set down by de ocean and talk and patch and crochet. They was jus' like all lady people. They loved to talk about their chillun, and brag on 'em.

—*Ibid.*

> God Amighty, he took de bone out of his side
> So dat places de woman beside us.

—*Ibid.*

Belief in magic is older than writing.

—*Ibid.*

Three days my body must lie silent and fasting while my spirit went wherever spirits must go that seek answers never given to men as men.

—*on voodoo, Ibid.*

In order for you to reach the spirit somebody has got to suffer. I'll suffer for you because I'm strong.

—*Ibid.*

So de white man throw down de load and tell de nigger man tuh pick it up. He pick it up because he have to, but he don't tote it. He hand it to his womenfolks. De nigger woman is de mule uh de world so fur as Ah can see.
—Their Eyes Were Watching God *(1937)*

When you see uh woman doin' so much rakin' in her head, she's combin' at some man or 'nother.
—*Ibid.*

They seemed to be staring at the dark, but their eyes were watching God.
—*Ibid.*

No hour is ever eternity, but it has its right to weep.
—*Ibid.*

Two things everybody's got tuh do fuh theyselves. They got tuh go tuh God, and they got tuh find out 'bout livin' fuh theyselves.
—*Ibid.*

She pulled in her horizon like a great fish-net. Pulled it from around the waist of the world and draped it over her shoulder. So much of life in its meshes! She called in her soul to come and see.
—*Ibid.*

In the beginning there was neither nothing nor anything. Darkness hid in darkness—shrouded in nothingness.
—Moses, Man of the Mountain *(1939)*

Most things are born in the mothering darkness and most things die. Darkness is the womb of creation. But the sun with his seven horns of flame is the father of life.
—*Ibid.*

There is something about poverty that smells like death. Dead dreams dropping off the heart like leaves in a dry season and rotting around the feet; impulses smothered too long in the fetid air of underground caves. The soul lives in a sickly air. People can be slave-ships in shoes.
—Dust Tracks on the Road *(1942)*

The Master-Maker in His making had made Old Death. Made him with big, soft feet and square toes. Made him with a face that reflects the face of all things, but neither changes itself, nor is mirrored anywhere. Made the body of death out of infinite hunger. Made a weapon of his hand to satisfy his needs. This was the morning of the day of the beginning of things.

—*Ibid.*

It is one of the blessings of this world that few people see visions and dream dreams.

—*Ibid.*

Roll your eyes in ecstasy and ape his every move, but until we have placed something upon his street corner that is our own, we are right back where we were when they filed our iron collar off.

—*Ibid.*

I who are borne away to become an orphan, carry my parent with me.

—Jonah's Gourd Vine *(1934)*

Ice-T

(C . 1 9 6 2 –)

Born Tracy Marrow in Newark, New Jersey, but raised in South Central Los Angeles, Ice-T has often used controversial raps that place him squarely in the center of the debate over rap, violence, and freedom of speech.

I'm the rap trickster.

—*"I'm Your Pusher"*

I'm tryin' to walk the edge. I'm going to tell you what you need to hear, not what you want to hear.

—Los Angeles Weekly, *c. 1992*

I gave you a warning, that record was a warning . . . but now you've seen it's real.

—*about the record "Cop Killer," after the Los Angeles riots, 1993*

George Jackson

(1 9 4 1 – 1 9 7 1)

George Jackson had spent more than ten years in prison for a $70 robbery when his thoughtful, provocative letters were published in Soledad Brother in 1970. He was shot to death in San Quentin on August 21, 1971, while "trying to escape."

To determine how men will behave once they enter the prison it is of first importance to know that prison. Men are brutalized by their environment—not the reverse.

—Soledad Brother *(1970)*

We have been transformed into an implacable army of liberation . . . Believe me, my friend, with the time and incentive that these brothers have to read, study, and think, you will find no class or category more aware, more embittered, desperate, or dedicated to the ultimate remedy—revolution . . . Men who read Lenin, Fanon, and Che don't riot, "they mass," "they rage," they dig graves.

—*Ibid.*

Hurl me into the next existence; the descent into hell won't turn me . . . They won't defeat my revenge, never, never. I'm part of a righteous people who anger slowly but rage undamned. We'll gather at his door in such a number that the rumbling of our feet will make the earth tremble.

—*Ibid.*

Jesse Jackson

(1941–)

The great-grandson of slaves, Jesse Jackson was a college athlete before attending Chicago Theological Seminary. An associate of Martin Luther King, Jr., he founded Operation PUSH in Chicago in 1971 and was a keynote speaker at the National Black Political Convention in Gary, Indiana, in 1972. A presidential candidate in 1984 and 1988, he remains active in politics today.

We are not a perfect people. Yet, we are called to a perfect mission; our mission, to feed the hungry, to clothe the naked, to house the homeless, to teach the illiterate, to provide jobs for the jobless, and to choose the human race over the nuclear race.

—*ADDRESS TO THE DEMOCRATIC NATIONAL CONVENTION, JULY 17, 1984*

My constituency is the damned, disinherited, disrespected, and the despised.

—*Ibid.*

Only leadership—that intangible combination of gifts, discipline, information, circumstance, courage, timing, will, and divine inspiration —can lead us out of the crisis in which we find ourselves.

—*Ibid.*

This campaign has taught me much: that leaders must be tough enough to fight, tender enough to cry, human enough to make mistakes, humble enough to admit them, strong enough to absorb the pain, and resilient enough to bounce back and keep on moving.

—*Ibid.*

Our flag is red, white, and blue, but our nation is rainbow—red, yellow, brown, black, and white—we're all precious in God's sight. America is not like a blanket—one piece of unbroken cloth, the same color, the same texture, the same size. America is more like a quilt—many patches, many pieces, many colors, many sizes, all woven and held together by a common thread.

—*Ibid.*

My right and my privilege to stand here before you has been won—in my lifetime—by the blood and the sweat of the innocent.

—*Ibid.*

Many people, many cultures, many languages—with one thing in common, the yearning to breathe free. Common ground!

—*Ibid.*

The genius of America is that out of the many, we become one.

—*Address to the Democractic National Convention, July 20, 1988*

Reagan gave the rich and the powerful a multibillion-dollar party. Now, the party is over.

—*Ibid.*

I just want to take common sense to high places.

—*Ibid.*

If an issue is morally right, it will eventually be political. It may be political and never be right . . . If we're principled first, our politics will fall in place.

—*Ibid.*

War is irrational in this age and unwinnable.

—*Ibid.*

I was born in the slum, but the slum was not born in me. And it wasn't born in you, and you can make it. Wherever you are tonight, you can make it. Hold your head high, stick your chest out. You can make it. It gets dark sometimes, but the morning comes. Don't you surrender. Suffering breeds character. Character breeds faith. In the end faith will not disappoint.

—*IBID.*

The fact is, most of the American people have not been educated, therefore not inspired to awaken to the rightness of our quest for democracy. We know our case is morally right and legally sound and economically feasible . . . We know our arguments will prevail.

—*ON STATEHOOD FOR THE DISTRICT OF COLUMBIA, WASHINGTON POST, JULY 4, 1993*

We are far more threatened by the dope than the rope . . . We lose more lives annually to the crime of blacks killing blacks than the sum total of lynchings in the entire history of the country . . . What faces us today is preventable. It is within our power to change our behavior.

—*ADDRESS TO HIGH SCHOOL IN MANHATTAN, OCTOBER 18, 1993*

Keep hope alive. Keep hope alive. Keep hope alive.

—*IBID.*

Mahalia Jackson

(1 9 1 2 – 1 9 7 2)

Born in New Orleans, Jackson moved in her teens to Chicago, where she met the "Father of Gospel," Thomas A. Dorsey, who supported her early career. In 1947, her "Move on Up a Little Higher" became the first gospel record to sell a million copies, and "the queen of gospel" soon became an international figure. She sang in Montgomery during the bus boycott, at the March on Washington, and at the funeral of Dr. Martin Luther King, Jr. She also briefly had her own television show and appeared in several films.

No one can hurt the gospel because the gospel is strong, like a two-headed sword is strong.

—IN JULES SCHWERIN, GOTTA TELL IT *(1992)*

I'm goin' to drink from the crystal fountains . . .
And move on up a little higher!

—HER SIGNATURE SONG, *"MOVE ON UP A LITTLE HIGHER"*

How come, mister, you think you can tell me about that old song, when it was born in my mouth?

—ON PRODUCERS' ATTEMPTS TO *"POLISH"* HER RENDITIONS, IN GOTTA TELL IT

Time is important to me because I want to sing long enough to leave a message. I'm used to singing in churches where nobody would dare stop me until the Lord arrives!

—ON THE PRESSURES OF TELEVISION SCHEDULES, IBID.

How big does a person have to grow, down in this part of the country, before he's going to stand up and say—Let us stop treating other men and women and children with such cruelty just 'cause they're born colored!

—MOVIN' ON UP *(1966)*

I have nothing against intermarriage, except that it means a Negro man is leaving behind the Negro woman who has worked and suffered with him since slavery times.

—IBID.

As I sang the words, I heard a great murmur come rolling back to me from the multitude below, and I sensed I had reached out and touched a chord. I was moved to shout for joy, and I did!

—ON SINGING *"I BEEN 'BUKED AND I BEEN SCORNED"* AT THE MARCH ON WASHINGTON, AUGUST 28, 1963

Anybody that sings the blues is in a deep pit, yelling for help.

—IN MARK BEGO, ARETHA FRANKLIN *(1989)*

Sometimes you feel like you're so far from God, and *then* you know those deep songs have special meanings. They bring back the communication between yourself and God.

—<small>IN</small> G<small>OTTA</small> T<small>ELL</small> I<small>T</small>

It's easy to be independent when you've got money. But to be independent when you haven't got a thing—that's the Lord's test.

—M<small>OVIN'</small> O<small>N</small> U<small>P</small> *(1966)*

Maynard Jackson

(1 9 3 8 –)

Born in Dallas, Jackson moved to Atlanta with his family when he was seven. He entered law practice, but ran for a Senate seat in 1968, following the death of Martin Luther King, Jr. Though he was defeated, he was elected vice mayor the following year and held that position until, on October 18, 1973, he became the first black mayor of Atlanta. He initiated an aggressive affirmative action policy and was re-elected in 1977. Under his administration, the world's largest airport was opened in Atlanta in 1980.

It was hard-core segregation all the way, but we never bowed to it. It was against the family policy. We never walked in anybody's back door, ever.

—<small>ON GROWING UP IN</small> A<small>TLANTA, IN</small> H<small>ENRY</small> H<small>AMPTON,</small> V<small>OICES OF</small> F<small>REEDOM</small> *(1990)*

We must do more than *say* we are concerned and that we care. We must begin to translate that concern into action, because we know that injustice and inequality are not vague and shadowy concepts that have no tangible dimensions. Behind every unjust act and behind all unequal treatment there are conscious decisions made by conscious men and women who choose not to care.

—<small>INAUGURAL ADDRESS,</small> J<small>ANUARY</small> 7, *1974*

We must open our eyes if we are to begin to deal with the systematic eradication of poverty and the diminution of crime. We must render visible the invisible.

—Ibid.

This period of time is probably Atlanta's acid test. We're either going to live up to our advance billings, or we're going to flunk miserably. It all depends on whether black people and white people can get along with each other, and not become consumed in anxieties that are truly without basis in fact . . . So the issue is, can Atlanta succeed where America has failed?

—Interview after five hundred days in office, Atlanta magazine, June 1975

Being the first black mayor is what you would wish on your enemy, okay? . . . Every black mayor who's been the first black mayor, I'm sure, has felt the same thing. But it truly is part hell. All of a sudden I became the mayor not just of Atlanta, but of black people in Georgia and even some neighboring states. That was an extraordinary burden.

—Voices of Freedom

The reality is that we've got to prove ourselves more than others, not just to the white community but to the black community as well . . . I'm sorry, but black taxpayers want the same things as white taxpayers, and you better be able to deliver. You've got to be able to stand and deliver.

—Before his re-election in 1989.

Michael Jackson

(1 9 5 8 –)

One of nine children, Jackson was born in Gary, Indiana, and sang with four of his brothers as a member of the Jackson Five while he was growing up. The group signed with Motown in 1969 and produced a string of top ten hits while Michael also began performing as a solo artist in 1971. While filming The Wiz *in 1969, Jackson met*

Quincy Jones, who went on to produce Thriller, *the best-selling record of all time, and* Bad. *One of the world's most famous individuals, the "King of Pop" married Lisa Marie Presley in the summer of 1994.*

The stage was my home. Once I got off stage I was very sad . . . sad at having to face the popularity and all that . . . when I was little it was always work, work, work.

—*TELEVISED INTERVIEW WITH OPRAH WINFREY, FEBRUARY 1993*

I wake up from dreams and go "Wow, put this down on paper." The whole thing is strange. You hear the words, everything is right there in front of your face . . . That's why I hate to take credit for the songs I've written. I feel that somewhere, someplace, it's been done and I'm just a courier bringing it out into the world.

—*IN CATHERINE DINEEN, MICHAEL JACKSON (1993)*

Nothing can harm me when I'm on stage—nothing. That's really me. That's what I'm here to do. I'm totally at home on stage. That's where I live. That's where I was born. That's where I'm safe.

—*IBID.*

I hate it when I meet fans and they try and tear bits of my hair and clothing. It's like they're trying to tear your soul away.

—*IBID.*

The same music governs the rhythm of the seasons, the pulse of our heartbeats, the migration of the birds, the ebb and flow of ocean tides, the cycles of growth, evolution and dissolution. It's music, it's rhythm.

—*IBID.*

I want to live in a world with peace and without hunger. A world where mankind knows no suffering. I believe I can help achieve that goal if I stay healthy in mind and body. I believe that if I live correctly I can live to be 150.

—*IBID.*

I care about being paid fairly for what I do. When I approach a project, I put my whole heart and soul into it and expect to be paid. The guy who works should eat. It's that simple.

—*IBID.*

I happen to be color blind. I don't hire color. I hire competence.

—*IBID.*

For me, it's like the dawn of civilization. It's the first place where society existed . . . I guess there's that connection because it is the root of all rhythm. Everything. It's home.

—*ON HIS FIRST TRIP TO AFRICA*

There's so much garbage written about me. It's so untrue and they're complete lies . . . When people make up stories that I don't want to be who I am it hurts me.

—*INTERVIEW WITH OPRAH WINFREY, FEBRUARY 1993*

My goal in life is to give to the world what I was lucky to receive: the ecstasy of divine union through my music and dance.

—MICHAEL JACKSON

There are times when I wish I could be just like everybody else.

—*IBID.*

ℛeggie Jackson

(1 9 4 6 –   )

Reginald Martinez Jackson attended college on a football scholarship and began his professional baseball career with the Kansas City Athletics (later the Oakland A's) in 1966. He took the team to the World Series in 1973 and 1974, and moved to the Baltimore Orioles in 1976 and the New York Yankees in 1977. In the 1977 World Series, Mr. October hit three consecutive home runs and established or tied seven Series records. He joined the California Angels in 1982, retiring in 1987, and was inducted into the Hall of Fame in 1993.

Fans don't boo nobodies.
—AS OAKLAND A'S OUTFIELDER, 1974

I'll probably get a million more than I should, but I didn't make the rules. I'm just taking advantage of them.
—ON BECOMING A FREE AGENT, 1976

This team, it all flows from me. I've got to keep it going. I'm the straw that stirs the drink.
—NEW YORK YANKEES OUTFIELDER, 1977

He's so good, blind people come to the park just to hear him pitch.
—ON CINCINNATI REDS PITCHER TOM SEAVER, 1977

I don't want to be a hero; I don't want to be a star. It just works out that way.
—AS NEW YORK YANKEES OUTFIELDER, 1980

It boosted my ego, although mine probably doesn't need it.
—ON MATCHING LOU GEHRIG'S 493 HOME RUNS, 1984

Money lets you live better. It doesn't make you play better.
—AS AN ANNOUNCER, 1990

Love me or hate me, you can't ignore me.
—AS A NEW YORK YANKEES OUTFIELDER, 1977

Harriet Ann Jacobs

(1 8 1 3 – 1 8 9 7)

In 1861, Jacobs published the classic women's slave narrative Incidents in the Life of a Slave Woman *under the pseudonym Linda Brent. "I was twenty-one years in that cage of obscene birds," she wrote. "I can testify, from my own experience and observation, that slavery is a curse to the whites as well as to the blacks."*

We all know that the memory of a faithful slave does not avail much to save her children from the auction block.

        —Incidents in the Life of a Slave Woman

Alas, what mockery it is for a slave mother to try to pray back her dying child to life.

        —Ibid.

Slaveholders have been cunning enough to enact that "the child shall follow the condition of the *mother*," not of the *father*; thus taking care that licentiousness shall not interfere with avarice.

        —Ibid.

Slavery is terrible for men; but it is far more terrible for women. Superadded to the burden common to all, *they* have wrongs, and sufferings, and mortifications peculiarly their own . . . If God has bestowed beauty upon her, it will prove her greatest curse. That which commands admiration in the white woman only hastens the degradation of the female slave.

        —Ibid.

Why does a slave ever love?

        —Ibid.

Stand by your own children, and suffer with them till death.

        —Ibid.

My master had power and law on his side; I had a determined will. There is might in each.

—*IBID.*

There are no bonds so strong as those which are formed by suffering together.

—*IBID.*

Hot weather brings out snakes and slaveholders, and I like one class of the venomous creatures as little as I do the other.

—*IBID.*

It is a sad feeling to be afraid of one's native country.

—*IBID.*

There are wrongs which even the grave does not bury.

—*IBID.*

So I was *sold* at last! A human being *sold* in the free city of New York! The bill of sale is on record, and future generations will learn from it that women were articles of traffic in New York, late in the nineteenth century of the Christian religion.

—*IBID.*

Friend! It is a common word, often lightly used. Like other good and beautiful things, it may be tarnished by careless handling.

—*IBID.*

Skip James

(1902–1969)

Born Nehemiah James in the Mississippi Delta, the blues guitarist, noted for his falsetto voice and for playing in a minor key, recorded in the 1930s and enjoyed a resurgence in popularity during the 1960s blues revival.

When the sun gone down you know what you promised me
When the sun gone down you know what you promised me
And what's the matter baby, I can't see
—"Cypress Grove Blues"

The woman I love stoled her from my best friend
But he got lucky stoled her back again
—"Devil Got My Woman"

If I ever get off this killin' floor
I'll never get down this low no more
—"Hard Times Killin' Floor Blues"

After I got that much from those [other blues players], then I just used my own self: Skip. I don't pattern after anyone or either copycat.
—in Henry Louis Gates, Jr., Figures in Black *(1989)*

Roscoe Jameson

(1 8 8 8 – 1 9 1 8)

*B*orn in Winchester, Tennessee, the poet is best known for his work *"The Negro Soldiers."*

These truly are the Brave,
These men who cast aside
Old memories to walk the blood-stained pave
Of Sacrifice, joining the solemn tide
That moves away, to suffer and to die
For Freedom—when their own is yet denied!
—*"THE NEGRO SOLDIERS" (1917)*

Judith Jamison

(1 9 4 3 –)

*F*rom Philadelphia, Jamison began dancing at the age of six. She attended Fisk University and joined the Philadelphia Dance Company, where she was discovered by Agnes de Mille. In 1964 she began her famous collaboration with Alvin Ailey, of whom she wrote, "Alvin and I were like two limbs of a tree, growing and climbing together." With his troupe she toured Europe, Russia, Asia, and Africa before performing on Broadway in Sophisticated Ladies and forming her own dance group, the Jamison Project. In 1989 she returned to Ailey's company and assumed its directorship after his death in 1989.

Once you've danced, you always dance. You can't deny the gifts that God sends your way.

—Essence, *December 1988*

In each country I was drawn to the marketplaces, the landscape, the diversity of everyday life unfolding before me. I very much wanted to be identified as being from somewhere on the continent. I wanted to be identified with *somebody*, to see some something in that bone structure that said, "You're from here, your ancestors are from here."

—Dancing Spirit *(1993)*

I'm moved by contraries, by opposites, the strength that was my mother's eyes, the beauty of my father's hands.

—*Ibid.*

Our house was built with bricks, built with coal, and filled with love.

—*Ibid.*

A lot of young people I meet do not know what they want to do with the rest of their lives, while it's getting later and they're under pressure to make a decision. It's for them not to worry, but to be well prepared, open, and educated. Learn as much as you can about everything. It's hard to tell young people to be patient, but that's what they need to be.

—*Ibid.*

When I think of Alvin Ailey I think of rivers, the clarity and strength of water, carrying with it the memory of its source as it pushes forward. I think of winding rivers, water brimming with life . . . I am the catalyst, the conduit in this situation, and the one who is responsible for continuing that legacy. One + One + One.

—*Ibid.*

I felt the naïveté of a child in my dancing. I cherished that feeling. I had what I call a knowledgeable naïveté, and it worked for me.

—*Ibid.*

I remember always the need to know myself, because if I avoid knowing who I am deep inside, then I can't express what I have to say
through the talent that I have.

—IBID.

When I was a child I knew that I had whatever "spirit" there is in this
world. It's difficult to name because I believe His name has been
thrown all over kingdom come. I believe that this world was set about
for us to enjoy and to love and to experience and to have it all be, to a
certain extent, unpredictable. Ever since I was a child I have believed
that my life has been guided.

—IBID.

In places where people suffered, there's a residue of spirit you can
actually feel . . . You don't ever have to try to cry, because we've
been through it for such a long time, so that it's blood. You don't have
to make an effort to remember. It's in your genes.

—IBID.

Whenever someone leaves, there is always discovery.

—IBID.

So many people dwell on negativity and I've survived by ignoring it: it
dims your light and it's harder each time to turn the power up again.

—IBID.

Dance is about never-ending aspiration.

—IBID.

Blind Lemon Jefferson

(c. 1897 – 1930)

Blind from birth, "the King of The Country Blues" recorded during the 1920s. He died in Chicago, lost in the streets during a snowstorm.

Seem like you hungry, honey, come and lunch with me
I wanna stop these married-looking women from worrying me
—*"Rabbit Foot Blues"*

Back water rising, coming in my windows and doors
I leave with a prayer in my heart: back water won't rise no more
—*"Rising High Water Blues"*

My feets is so sore can't hardly wear my shoes
Out last night with wild women and it give me the big night blues
—*"Big Night Blues"*

I'm a stranger here just come in on the train
Won't some good man tell me some woman's name
—*"Stocking Feet Blues"*

Mmmmmmm mmmm black snake crawling in my room
And some pretty mama better come and get this black snake soon
—*"That Black Snake Moan"*

Woman rocks the cradle and I declare she rules her home
Many man rocks some other man's baby and the fool thinks he's rocking his own.
—*"That Crawling Baby Blues"*

Hey, mama, what have I said and done?
You treat me like my trouble has just begun
—*"Wartime Blues"*

Goodbye brown, what's the matter now
You trying your best to quit me, woman, and you don't know how
—*"Easy Rider Blues"*

Charles Johnson

(1 9 4 8 –)

Johnson received his M.A. in philosophy from Southern Illinois University and taught at the University of Washington in Seattle. An artist as well as a writer, he has published numerous short stories as well as the novels Faith and the Good Thing, Oxherding Tale, *and* Middle Passage, *which won a National Book Award in 1990.*

All art points to others with whom the writer argues about what is . . . He must have models with which to agree . . . or outright oppose . . . for Nature seems to remain silence.
—Being and Race *(1970)*

Our experience as Black men and women completely outstrips our perception—Black life is ambiguous, and a kaleidoscope of meanings, rich, multi-sided . . . we have frozen our vision in figures that caricature, at best, the complexity of our lives and leave the real artistic chore of interpretation unfinished.
— *"Philosophy and Black Fiction,"* Obsidian, *Spring-Summer 1980*

In a dangerous world, a realm of disasters, a place of grief and pain, a sensible man made *himself* dangerous, more frightening than all the social and political "accidents" that might befall him. He was, in a way, a specialist in survival.
—The Middle Passage *(1990)*

All bonds, landside or on ships, between masters and mates, women and men, it struck me, were a lie forged briefly in the name of convenience and just as quickly broken when they no longer served one's interest.

—<small>IBID.</small>

As long as each sees a situation differently there will be slaughter and slavery and the subordination of one to another 'cause two notions of things never exist side by side as equals.

—<small>IBID.</small>

No longer Africans, yet not Americans either. Then what? . . . The mills of the gods were still grinding, killing and remaking us all, and nothing I or anyone else did might stop the terrible forces and transformations our voyage had set free.

—<small>IBID.</small>

Wealth isn't what a man has, but what he is.

—<small>IBID.</small>

It came to me as I lay here, a nightmare, that this was the last hour of history.

—<small>IBID.</small>

We, forgetful of ourselves, gently crossed the Flood, and countless seas of suffering.

—<small>IBID.</small>

Writing is my refuge. It's where I go. It's where I find that integrity I have.

—<small>THE WORLD AND</small> I *(1990)*

I found my way to make my peace with the recent past by turning it into <small>WORD</small>.

—<small>MIDDLE PASSAGE</small>

Charles S. Johnson

(1 8 9 3 – 1 9 5 6)

Born in Virginia, Johnson received his Ph.D. from the University of Chicago and was a member of the committee that investigated the Chicago riot of 1919. He was director of research with the National Urban League and founded its journal, Opportunity. *In 1946, he became the first black president of Fisk University.*

White and black these cities lured, but the blacks they lured with a demoniac appeal.

—ON THE GREAT MIGRATION, "THE NEW FRONTAGE ON AMERICAN LIFE," IN THE NEW NEGRO
(1925)

There comes the testing of long-cherished desires, the thirst for forbidden fruit—and disillusionment, partial or complete, almost as inevitably.

—IBID.

Earvin (Magic) Johnson

(1 9 6 0 –   )

One of the best basketball players ever, Johnson was an all-American at Michigan State University and played for the Los Angeles Lakers from 1979 to 1992. The team took five NBA titles, and Johnson was a three-time MVP. He now heads the Magic Johnson Foundation, dedicated to AIDS research.

I was born to play this game.

—MY LIFE *(1992)*

You only thought it could happen to other people. It *has* happened. But I'm going to deal with it. Life is going to go on for me, and I'm going to be a happy man.

—HIS ANNOUNCEMENT TO THE PRESS ABOUT HIS *HIV* STATUS, NOVEMBER 7, 1991

You don't have to feel sorry for me. Because if I die tomorrow, I've had the greatest life that anybody can want.

—THE NEXT NIGHT, ON *"THE ARSENIO HALL SHOW"*

With the love and support of my family and friends, I'm going to fight this illness as best I can. And pass on to you the lessons I have learned the hard way.

—WHAT YOU CAN DO TO AVOID AIDS *(1992)*

After the announcement, I started working for God's agenda. I believe He's got a mission for me—to help make society more aware, and to get people to care.

—MY LIFE *(1992)*

Standing on that platform, I said a silent prayer. I thanked God for giving me the strength and the opportunity to come back, to play basketball again, and to be part of that whole magnificent Olympic experience. It's a memory I will always cherish.

—AFTER THE DREAM TEAM WON THE GOLD MEDAL IN BARCELONA, IBID.

If people around you aren't going anywhere, if their dreams are no bigger than hanging out on the corner, or if they're dragging you down, get rid of them. Negative people can sap your energy so fast, and they can take your dreams from you, too.

—IBID.

All kids need is a little help, a little hope, and somebody who believes in them.

—IBID.

Magic is who I am on the basketball court. Earvin is who I am.

—*Ibid.*

Fenton Johnson

(1 8 8 8 – 1 9 5 8)

Born in Chicago and educated at the University of Chicago, Johnson taught school briefly and had several plays performed before his first volume of poetry was published when he was twenty-four. Like Claude McKay's poems, Johnson's free verse is often marked by protest. He also published collections of essays and short stories.

We are children of the sun,
Rising sun!

—"*Children of the Sun*"

For we have been with thee in No Man's Land,
Through lake of fire and down to Hell itself;
And now we ask of thee our liberty,
Our freedom in the land of Stars and Stripes.

—"*The New Day*"

I had nothing, so I had to go to work.
All the stock I had was a white girl's education and a face that enchanted the men of both races.

—"*The Scarlet Woman*"

I am tired of work; I am tired of building up somebody else's civilization.

—"*Tired*"

I have found sweeter peace than fame.

—"*The Marathon Runner*"

You can only die each morning,
And live again in the dreams of night.
> —*"The Daily Grind"*

Have those who bore her dust to the last resting place buried with
her the gentle word *Son* that she gave to each of the seed of Ethiopia?
> —*"Aunt Jane Allen"*

It seemed to me like trying to walk on the Atlantic Ocean to obtain
recognition in the literary world.
> —*circa 1920*

Georgia Douglas Johnson

(1 8 6 6 – 1 9 6 7)

*Johnson was born in Atlanta and educated at Oberlin College, be-
coming one of the most prominent women poets of the Harlem Renaissance. Her work appeared in* The Crisis, Opportunity, *and elsewhere, and she published three volumes of poems,* The Heart of a
Woman *(1918),* Bronze *(1922), and* An Autumn Love Cycle *(1928).*

The heart of a woman falls back with the night,
And enters some alien cage in its plight,
And tries to forget it has dreamed of the stars,
While it breaks, breaks, breaks on the sheltering bars.
> —*"The Heart of a Woman"*

I'm doing this living of being black.
> —*"The Ordeal"*

The planets wear
The Maker's imprint, and with mine
I swing into their rhythmic line.
      —*IBID.*

Rise with the hour for which you were made.
      —*"HOPE"*

Shadow, shadows,
Hug me round
So that I shall not be found
By sorrow
      —*"ESCAPE"*

The strong demand, contend, prevail; the beggar is a fool!
      —*"THE SUPPLIANT"*

I want to die while you love me,
And bear to that silent bed,
Your kisses turbulent, unspent,
To warm me when I'm dead.
      —*"I WANT TO DIE WHILE YOU LOVE ME"*

The dreams of the dreamer
Are life-drops that pass
The break in the heart
To the soul's hour-glass.
      —*"THE DREAMS OF THE DREAMER"*

Not wholly this or that,
Of alien bloods am I."
      —*"COSMOPOLITE"*

Helene Johnson

(1 9 0 7 –)

Johnson was born in Boston. Her work appeared, during the Harlem Renaissance, in Opportunity, Vanity Fair, *and other magazines.*

> I love the way you hold your head,
> High sort of and a bit to one side,
> Like a prince, a jazz prince.
> —"Poem"

Would you sell the colors of your sunset and the fragrance
Of your flowers, and the passionate wonder of your forest
For a creed that will not let you dance?
—"Magalu"

Jack Johnson

(1 8 7 8 – 1 9 4 6)

Called by Arthur Ashe "the most significant black athlete in history," John Arthur Johnson was born in Galveston, Texas, and left school after the fifth grade. He became a professional boxer at nineteen and in 1908 he defeated Tommy Burns to become the world's first black heavyweight champion. When he defeated the retired champion Jim Jeffries two years later, riots broke out across the country. A powerful symbol of the independent black man, not only for his physical prowess but also for his reputation of living large, Johnson was charged with violation of the Mann Act and spent seven years in exile before returning to the United States in 1920 and serving eight months in prison.

For every point I'm given, I'll have earned two, because I'm a Negro.
—ON SELECTING A REFEREE FOR THE BURNS FIGHT, DECEMBER 26, 1908

Who told you I was yellow? You're white Tommy—white as the flag of surrender!
—TAUNT TO BURNS IN THE RING, NEW YORK TIMES, DECEMBER 27, 1908

I neve doubted the issue from the beginning. I knew I was too good for Burns. I have forgotten more about fighting than Burns ever knew.
—IBID.

Hardly a blow had been struck when I knew that I was Jeff's master. From the start the fight was mine . . . The "white hope" had failed, and as far as the championship was concerned it was just where it was before . . . except that I had established my rightful claim to it beyond all possible dispute.
—ON THE 1910 JEFFRIES FIGHT, JACK JOHNSON: IN THE RING AND OUT (1927)

Jim's face reminded me of a man who had tasted his first green olive.
—ON JIM CORBETT, SUPPORTING JIM JEFFRIES IN THEIR MATCH, JULY 4, 1910

I won from Mr. Jeffries because I outclassed him in every department . . . I was certain I would be the victor.
—NEW YORK TIMES, JULY 5, 1910

I know the horror of being hunted and haunted. I have dashed across continents and oceans as a fugitive, and have matched my wits with the police and secret agents seeking to deprive me of one of the greatest blessings a man can have—liberty.
—JACK JOHNSON: IN THE RING AND OUT

The fight between life and death is to the finish, and death ultimately is the victor . . . I do not deplore the passing of these crude old days.
—IBID.

James Weldon Johnson

(1 8 7 1 – 1 9 3 8)

Poet, novelist, essayist, and critic, Johnson was born in Florida and studied at Columbia University. He served as U.S. consul in Venezuela and Nicaragua, and while maintaining a long career with the NAACP, he wrote many works of fiction, poetry, and history and taught at Fisk and New York universities. His poem "Lift Ev'ry Voice and Sing" has often been called the Negro National Anthem.

Sing a song full of the faith that the dark past has taught us
Sing a song full of the hope that the present has brought us.
Facing the rising sun of our new day begun,
Let us march on till victory is won.
    —*"Lift Ev'ry Voice and Sing" (1900)*

Nothing that I have done has paid me back so fully in satisfaction as being the part creator of this song. I am always thrilled deeply when I hear it sung by Negro children. I am lifted up by their voices . . .
    —Along This Way *(1933)*

O black and unknown bards of long ago,
How came your lips to touch the sacred fire? . . .
Who first from out the still watch, lone and long,
Feeling the ancient faith of prophets rise
Within his dark-kept soul, burst into song? . . .
You sang far better than you knew; the songs
That for your listeners' hungry hearts sufficed
Still live—but more than this to you belongs:
You sang a race from wood and stone to Christ.
    —*"O Black and Unknown Bards" (1917)*

It would have been a notable achievement if the white people who settled this country, having a common language and heritage, seeking liberty in a new land, faced with the task of conquering untamed nature, and stirred with the hope of building an empire, had created a body of folk music comparable to the Negro Spirituals. But from whom did these songs spring—these songs unsurpassed among the folk songs of the world and, in the poignancy of their beauty, unequalled?

—Preface, The Book of Negro Spirituals *(1925)*

Whatever new thing the *people* like is pooh-poohed; whatever is *popular* is spoken of as not worth the while. The fact is, nothing great or enduring, especially in music, has ever sprung full-fledged and unprecedented from the brain of any master; the best he gives to the world he gathers from the hearts of the people, and runs it through the alembic of his genius.

—Autobiography of an Ex-Coloured Man *(1912)*

Seems lak to me de stars don't shine so bright,
Seems lak to me de sun done loss his light,
Seems lak to me der's nothin' goin' right,
  Sence you went away.

—*"Sence You Went Away"* (1900)

I am a thing not new, I am as old
As human nature.

—*"Brothers"*

This land is ours by right of birth,
This land is ours by right of toil;
We helped to turn its virgin earth,
Our sweat is in its fruitful soil

· · ·

No! stand erect and without fear,
And for our foes let this suffice—
We've bought a rightful sonship here,
And we have more than paid the price.

—*"Fifty Years"* (1917)

This is the dwarfing, warping, distorting influence which operates upon each and every coloured man in the United States. He is forced to take his outlook on all things, not from the view-point of a citizen, or a man, or even a human being, but from the view-point of a *coloured* man.

—Autobiography of an Ex-Coloured Man

New York is the most fatally fascinating thing in America.
—*Ibid.*

Evil is a force, and, like the physical and chemical forces, one cannot annihilate it; we may only change its form.
—*Ibid.*

I lived to learn that in the world of sport all men win alike, but lose differently; and so gamblers are rated, not by the way in which they win, but by the way in which they lose.
—*Ibid.*

I had made up my mind that since I was not going to be a Negro, I would avail myself of every possible opportunity to make a white man's success; and that, if it can be summed up in any one word, means "money."
—*Ibid.*

A people may become great through many means, but there is only one measure by which its greatness is recognized and acknowledged. The final measure of the greatness of all peoples is the amount and standard of the literature and art they have produced.
—The Book of American Negro Poetry *(1922)*

> This Great God,
> Like a mammy bending over her baby,
> Kneeled in the dust
> Toiling over a lump of clay
> Till He shaped it in His own image;
> Then into it He blew the breath of life,
> And man became a living soul.
> —*"The Creation" (1918)*

In a word, the stereotype is that the Negro is nothing more than a beggar at the gate of the nation, waiting to be thrown crumbs of civilization. Through his artistic efforts the Negro is smashing this immemorial stereotype faster than he has ever done through any other method he has been able to use. He is making it realized that he is the possessor of a wealth of natural endowments and that he has long been a generous giver to America. He is impressing upon the national mind the conviction that he is an active and important force

in American life; that he is a creator as well as a creature; that he has
given as well as received; that he is the potential giver of larger and
richer contributions.

—Harper's magazine, 1925

And now, O Lord, this man of God,
Who breaks the bread of life this morning—
Shadow him in the hollow of Thy hand,
And keep him out of the gunshot of the devil.

—"A Prayer," God's Trombones (1927)

Young man, Young man,
Your arm's too short to box with God

—God's Trombones

You'll have a hand-to-hand struggle with bony Death
And Death is bound to win.

—"The Prodigal Son," Ibid.

Within the past ten years Harlem has acquired a world-wide reputation . . . It is known in Europe and the Orient, and it is talked about
by nations in the interior of Africa. It is farthest known as being
exotic, colourful, and sensuous; a place of laughing, singing, and
dancing; a place where life wakes up at night.

—Black Manhattan, 1930

Some critics of the Negro—especially Negro critics—say that religion
costs him too much; that he has too many churches, and that many of
them are magnificent beyond his means; that church mortgages and
salaries and upkeep consume the greater part of the financial margin
of the race and keep its economic nose to the grindstone. All of which
is, in the main, true. And it may be that there will rise up out of that
element of the coloured clergy which realizes the potentialities of a
modern Negro Church a man with sufficient wisdom and power to
bring about a new Reformation.

—Ibid.

I have been amazed and amused watching white people dancing to a
Negro band in a Harlem cabaret; attempting to throw off the crusts
and layers of inhibitions laid on by sophisticated civilization; striving
to yield to the feel and experience of abandon; seeking to recapture a

taste of primitive joy in life and living; trying to work their way back into that jungle which was the original Garden of Eden; in a word, doing their best to pass for coloured.

—Along This Way

If the Negro is always to be given a heavy handicap back of the common scratch, or if the antagonistic forces are destined to dominate and bar all forward movement, there will be only one way of salvation for the race that I can see, and that will be through the making of its isolation into a religion and the cultivaton of a hard, keen, relentless hatred for everything white.

—*Ibid.*

Conservatism and radicalism are relative terms. It is as radical for a black American in Mississippi to claim his full rights under the Constitution and the law as it is for a white American in any state to advocate the overthrow of the existing national government. The black American in many instances puts life in jeopardy, and anything more radical than that cannot reasonably be required.

—Negro Americans, What Now? *(1934)*

I will not allow one prejudiced person or one million or one hundred million to blight my life. I will not let prejudice or any of its attendant humiliations and injustices bear me down to spiritual defeat. My inner life is mine, and I shall defend and maintain its integrity against all the powers of hell.

—*Ibid.*

ℒonnie 𝒥ohnson

(1894 – 1970)

Born in New Orleans, Johnson traveled widely in Texas and lived in Saint Louis, Chicago, New York, and elsewhere during his career. He recorded with Armstrong and Ellington during the 1920s and was noted for developing the blues guitar solo.

My nights is so lonely
days is so doggone long
My bed room is so lonely
every doggone thing is wrong
—*"Jersey Belle Blues"*

Careless love, you drove me through the rain and snow
Careless love, you drove me through the rain and snow
You have robbed me out of my silver
And out of all my gold
I'll be damned if you rob me outa my soul
—*"Careless Love"*

Mordecai Wyatt Johnson

(1 8 9 0 – 1 9 7 6)

Born in Tennessee, Johnson attended Morehouse College and Rochester Theological Seminary before graduating from the Theology School in Harvard University in 1922. A popular speaker, Johnson was for more than three decades president of Howard University and was awarded the Spingarn Medal of the NAACP in 1928.

The Negro people of America have been with us here for three hundred years. They have cut our forests, tilled our fields, built our railroads, fought our battles, and in all of their trials until now they have manifested a simple faith, a grateful heart, a cheerful spirit, and an undivided loyalty to the nation that has been a thing of beauty to behold. Now they have come to the place where their faith can no longer feed on the bread of repression and violence. They ask for the bread of liberty, of public equality, and public responsibility. It must not be denied them.

—"*The Faith of the American Negro,*" *Harvard commencement address, June 1922*

When the Negro cries with pain from his deep hurt and lays his petition for elemental justice before the nation, he is calling upon the American people to kindle about that crucible of race relationships the fires of American faith.

—*Ibid.*

Western civilization, Christianity, decency are struggling for their very lives. In this worldwide civil war, race prejudice is our most dangerous enemy, for it is a disease at the very root of our democratic life.

—*during World War II*

There will be a meeting of the great powers who will disagree, and the next noise we hear will be the screeching of elevators going up and down from heaven to hell . . . We are living under the illusion that we have the power to determine what to do with it.

—*on the atom bomb, at Duke University, January 1946*

$\mathcal{R}$obert $\mathcal{J}$ohnson

(1 9 1 1 – 1 9 3 8)

Now undergoing an enormous commercial and critical revival of his early guitar recordings, the Texas bluesman Robert Johnson led a short, troubled life before being killed by a jealous husband in 1938.

You better come on in my kitchen
baby it's going to be raining outdoors
—"*Come On In My Kitchen*"

I woke up this morning feeling around for my shoes
Know by that I got these old walking blues
    —*"WALKING BLUES"*

I feel so lonesome, you can hear me when I moan
And I feel so lonesome, you can hear me when I moan
Who's been driving my Terraplane for you since I've been gone
    —*"TERRAPLANE BLUES"*

I'm getting up this morning
I believe I'll dust my broom
Girl friend the black man you been loving,
girl friend, can get my room
    —*"I BELIEVE I'LL DUST MY BROOM"*

I've got to keep moving
blues falling down like hail
And the days keeps on 'minding me
there's a hellhound on my trail
    —*"HELLHOUND ON MY TRAIL"*

The blues
is a low-down aching heart disease
And like consumption
Killing me by degrees
    —*"PREACHING BLUES"*

You may bury my body down by the highway side
So my old evil spirit can get a Greyhound bus and ride
    —*"ME AND THE DEVIL BLUES"*

Man is like a prisoner and he's never satisfied
    —*"FROM FOUR UNTIL LATE"*

Gayl Jones

(1 9 4 9 -)

Born in Lexington, Kentucky, Jones received her M.A. and D.A. in creative writing from Brown University. She has a particular interest in black oral culture, and her short stories and novels, notably Corregidora *and* Eva's Man, *precisely capture the black idiom.*

I learned to write by listening to people talk. I still feel that the best of my writing comes from having heard rather than having read.
—IN MICHAEL HARPER AND ROBERT B. STEPTO, CHANT OF SAINTS *(1979)*

My great-grandmama told my grandmama the part she lived through that my grandmama didn't live through and my grandmama told my mama what they both lived through and my mama told me what they all lived through and we suppose to pass it down like that from generation to generation so we'd never forget.
—CORREGIDORA *(1975)*

I never told you how it was. Always their memories, but never my own.
—IBID.

You got to be true to your ancestors and you got to be true to those that come after you. How can you be true to those that come after you if there ain't none coming after you?
—EVA'S MAN *(1976)*

He's made himself both the doctor and the patient, the curer and the ill. He has made himself the priest figure, working his own magic.
—"THE RETURN: A FANTASY"

James Earl Jones

(1 9 3 1 –)

Known for his resonant voice, Jones stuttered as a child and virtually stopped speaking from the time he was six until he was fourteen. Born in Mississippi, he grew up on a farm with his grandparents in Michigan and studied acting at the University of Michigan. He earned a Tony award in 1969 for his starring role in The Great White Hope, *based on the life of Jack Johnson, and later re-created the role on screen. He has starred in works by Ibsen, Shakespeare, Steinbeck, and Athol Fugard, among others, and won a second Tony for his role in August Wilson's* Fences *in 1987. In 1985 he was elected to the Theater Hall of Fame, and in 1992 he received the National Medal for the Arts.*

One of the hardest things in life is having words in your heart that you can't utter.

—Voices and Silences *(1993)*

Out in the country, with few books or strangers, and no such thing as television, we depended on the stories we knew, and the stories we could invent and tell ourselves. I grew up with the spoken word.

—*Ibid.*

Starting with the aunts I loved as a boy, I have always idealized women. I have always held a faith and trust in the women I have worked with. Seldom have they disappointed me.

—*Ibid.*

Culture is as necessary for humanity as food . . . Once a state eliminates its access to the arts, it sets up the machinery for the decay of civilization. I would rather sacrifice well-paved roads than good theatre.

—*Ibid.*

I love to play renegades, rogues, and ramblers . . . Race does not matter.

—*IBID.*

When I read great literature, great drama, speeches, or sermons, I feel that the human mind has not achieved anything greater than the ability to share feelings and thoughts through language.

—*IBID.*

The love of reading and book learning is our bone memory.

—*IBID.*

Your own need to be shines out of any dream or creation you imagine.

—*IBID.*

Scott Joplin

(1 8 6 8 – 1 9 1 7)

Growing up in a musical family in Texarkana, Joplin studied classical piano but found work primarily in bars and brothels. In 1894 he settled in Sedalia, Missouri, where he taught college music classes. In 1899, "Maple Leaf Rag," his most famous work, ushered in the era of ragtime. In addition to dozens of ragtime tunes he is the composer of the opera Treemonisha, *which was fully staged for the first time in the 1970s, and in 1976 he was posthumously awarded a special Bicentennial Pulitzer Prize for his contribution to American music.*

Oh go 'way man
I can hypnotize dis nation
I can shake de earth's foundation
wid de Maple Leaf Rag.

—*"MAPLE LEAF RAG"*

Let me see you do the "rag time dance"
Turn left and do the "Cake walk prance"
Turn the other way and do the "Slow drag"
Now take your lady to the world's fair . . .
And do the "rag time dance."

—*"The Ragtime Dance" (1902)*

Because it has such a ragged movement. It suggests something like that.

—*why he called it "ragtime," American Musician and Art Journal December 13, 1907*

Don't play this piece fast. It is never right to play ragtime fast.

—*A musical notation*

Syncopations are no indication of light or trashy music, and to shy bricks at "hateful ragtime" no longer passes for musical culture.

—*defending his art, School of Ragtime (1908)*

When I'm dead twenty-five years, people are going to begin to recognize me.

—*in Edward A. Berlin, King of Ragtime (1994)*

Barbara Jordan

(1 9 3 6 –)

Born in Houston, Jordan attended Texas Southern University and received her J.D. from Boston University in 1959. She practiced law in Texas and was a member of the Texas legislature before being elected to the U.S. House of Representatives in 1972, where she was highly visible during the Watergate hearings. After leaving Congress in 1978 she taught for many years at the University of Texas, and in 1976 and again in 1992 was the keynote speaker at the Democratic National Convention.

The challenge facing us is not the defense of any system, be it segregated or integrated; the challenge facing us is to equip ourselves that we will be able to take our place wherever we are in the affairs of men.

—*c. 1951*

What the people want is very simple. They want an America as good as its promise.

—*speech at Harvard University, June 16, 1977*

"We the people"; it is a very eloquent beginning. But when the Constitution of the United States was completed on the seventeenth of September, 1787, I was not included in that "We, the people."

—Barbara Jordan *(1977)*

We live in a distraught present. Although we have had the courage to deplore it, we have failed to heal the gap between the middle-class Black lawyer and the Black slum dweller, who hates us almost as much as he hates whitey.

—*Ibid.*

Education remains the key to both economic and political empowerment.

—*c. 1991*

When do any of us ever do enough?

—*in Eric V. Copage, Black Pearls (1993)*

June Jordan

(1 9 3 6 –   )

Born in Harlem and raised in Bedford-Stuyvesant, Jordan attended the University of Chicago and Barnard College. A leading activist, poet, and essayist, she is the author of more than sixteen books of

poetry and prose, including the collections Civil Wars: Selected Essays, 1963–1980 *and in 1992,* Technical Difficulties. *Her work appears frequently in* The Progressive *and other journals, and she is currently a professor of Afro-American studies at the University of California, Berkeley.*

As a Black woman/feminist, I must look about me, with trembling, and with shocked anger, at the endless waste, the endless suffocation of my sisters . . . I must look about me and, as a Black Feminist, I must ask myself *Where is the love?* How is my own lifework serving to end these tyrannies, these corrosions of sacred possibility?
— *"Where Is the Love?,"* Civil Wars *(1981)*

It is a sad thing to consider that this country has given its least to those who have loved it the most.
— *"For My American Family,"* New York Newsday, *July 4, 1986*

A democratic nation of persons, of individuals, is an impossibility, and a fratricidal goal. Each American one of us must consciously choose to become a willing and outspoken part of *the people* who, together, will determine our individual chances for happiness, and justice.
— *"Waking up in the Middle of Some American Dreams," keynote address, Agenda for the 90s, Portland, Oregon, May 18, 1986*

To believe is to become what you believe.
— *Alternative Commencement Address at Dartmouth College, June 14, 1987*

We have been flexible, ingenious, and innovative or we have perished. And we have not perished.
— *"Don't You Talk about My Momma!," keynote address, Conference on the Black Family, Williams College, February 1987*

My own momma done better than she could and my momma's momma, *she* done better than I could. And *everybody's momma* done better than anybody had any right to expect she would. And that's the truth!
— *Ibid.*

If we are afraid to insist we are right, then what?
— *"Where Is the Rage?,"* The Progressive, *October 1989*

There is difference, and there is power. And who holds the power shall decide the meaning of difference.

—*"Toward a Manifest New Destiny," speech at Mount Holyoke College, December 8, 1991*

Behold my heart of darkness as it quickens now, with rage!

—*on the 1992 Los Angeles rebellion,* Technical Difficulties *(1992)*

Michael Jordan

(1 9 6 3 –)

Arguably the most talented athlete ever to play basketball, Michael Jordan helped North Carolina win the NCAA championship in 1982, and in 1985 was named Rookie of the Year for the Chicago Bulls. He helped the Bulls win a record three straight national championships and was voted most valuable player three times and was top scorer for seven straight years. On October 6, 1993, he announced his retirement, at the age of thirty.

Once I get the ball you're at my mercy. There is nothing you can say or do about it. I own the ball . . . When I'm on my game I don't think there's anybody that can stop me.

—*"Michael Jordan in His Own Orbit,"* GQ, *March 1989*

When I say, "Don't think of me as Black or White," all I'm saying is, view me as a person. I know my race.

—*Ibid.*

I have nothing more to prove in basketball. I have no more challenges that I felt I could get motivated for. It doesn't have anything to do with my father's passing, or media pressure, or anything other than that I had achieved everything in basketball that I could. And when that happened, I felt it was time to call it a career.

—PRESS CONFERENCE ANNOUNCING HIS RETIREMENT, OCTOBER 6, 1993

I always wanted to quit at the top. I never wanted to feel that foot in the back, from others trying to push me out, saying I had got too old, or that I couldn't do what I once could.

—IBID.

It made me realize how short life is, how quickly things can end, how innocently. And I thought that there are times in one's life when you have to put games aside.

—ON HIS FATHER'S DEATH, IBID.

The word "retire" means you can do anything you want. I'm not going to close the door on it . . . I will never say never. I don't close the door to any possibilities.

—IBID.

I've always believed that if you put in the work, the results will come.

—I CAN'T ACCEPT NOT TRYING (1994)

If you run into a wall, don't turn around and give up. Figure out how to climb it, go through it, or work around it.

—IBID.

I know fear is an obstacle for some people, but it is an illusion to me . . . Failure always made me try harder next time.

—IBID.

Talent wins games, but teamwork and intelligence win championships.

—IBID.

I can accept failure. Everyone fails at something. But I can't accept not trying.

—IBID.

Sharon Pratt Kelly

(1944–)

Born in Washington, D.C., Sharon Pratt received her undergraduate and law degrees from Howard University. After a career in law and the private sector, her 1990 election in Washington made her the first African American woman to become mayor of a major American city, and she has also held significant positions within the national Democratic Party.

Now it's time for us to claim ownership, to own a piece of the American rock.

—COMMENCEMENT ADDRESS, HOWARD UNIVERSITY, MAY 11, 1991

Divisiveness has no place in our politics . . . spitefulness and hatred only erode that which is truly magnificent about our country.

—IBID.

John O. Killens

(1916–)

Born in Macon, Georgia, Killens was educated at Howard University and Columbia Law School. He served in World War II and taught at Fisk, Columbia, and Howard universities. He is the author of Young-blood *and other novels, and a collection of essays,* Black Man's Burden *(1965).*

Just as surely as East is East and West is West, there is a "black" psyche in America and there is a "white" one, and the sooner we face up to this psychological, social, and cultural reality, the sooner the twain shall meet. . . . Your joy is very often our anger, and your despair our hope. Most of us came here in chains, and many of you came here to escape your chains. Your freedom was our slavery, and therein lies the bitter difference in the way we look at life.

—*"The Black Psyche" (circa 1966)*

The Negro loves America enough to criticize her fundamentally. Most white Americans simply can't be bothered.

—*Ibid.*

Integration begins the day after the minds of the people are desegregated.

—Beyond the Angry Black *(1966)*

How many are the winter soldiers of white America? . . . will the liberals of white America desert our ranks when we say that we will not love our enemies?

—*"The Black Revolution and the White Backlash," forum of the Association of Artists for Freedom, Town Hall, New York, June 15, 1964*

Who in the hell ever heard of a second-class citizen until they were invented in the United States? A person is either a citizen or he is not a citizen. You are either free or you are a slave.

—*Ibid.*

What a tiresome place America would be if freedom meant we all had to think alike or be the same color or wear that same gray flannel suit! That road leads to the conformity of the graveyard . . . We are not fighting for the right to be like you. We respect ourselves too much for that.

—*"The Black Psyche"*

A child must have a sense of selfhood, a knowledge that he is not here by sufferance, that his forebears contributed to the country and to the world.

—Beyond the Angry Black

The white man's juju is powerful stuff, but it cannot wish the Negro into invisibility.

—*"The Black Psyche"*

I believe that when the history of our times is written, it will not be so important who reached the moon first or who made the largest bomb. I believe the great significance will be that this was the century when most of mankind achieved freedom and human dignity, the age when racial prejudices became obsolete. For me, this is the Freedom Century.

—*"The Black Psyche"*

When the battle is won, let history be able to say to each one of us: He was a dedicated patriot. Dignity was his country. Manhood was his government and Freedom was his land.

—And Then We Heard the Thunder *(1963)*

History is a people's memory, and a people have a habit of remembering the very best about themselves. It is an all too human trait. But, in the final analysis, people must face their history squarely in order to transcend it.

—*c. 1969*

Time is swiftly running out, and a new dialogue is indispensable. It is so long overdue, it is already half past midnight.

—*"The Black Psyche"*

Jamaica Kincaid

(1 9 4 9 –)

Eleanor Potter Richardson left her native Caribbean at the age of sixteen to live in the United States, where she worked as a journalist and writer. She became a staff writer with The New Yorker *in 1976*

and under the name Jamaica Kincaid has published the collection of short stories At the Bottom of the River, *novels, and a memoir.*

This is how to love a man, and if this doesn't work there are other ways, and if they don't work don't feel too bad about giving up.
—*"Girl"*

Children are so quick: quick to laugh, quick to brand, quick to scorn, quick to lay claim to the open space.
—*"At Last"*

Many secrets are alive here.
—*Ibid.*

I swim in a shaft of light, upside down, and I can see myself clearly, through and through, from every angle. Perhaps I stand on the brink of a great discovery.
—*"Wingless"*

My disappointments stand up and grow ever taller. They will not be lost to me.
—*Ibid.*

I have many superstitions. I believe them all.
—*"Holidays"*

In isolation I ruthlessly plow the deep silences, seeking my opportunities like a miner seeking veins of treasures. In what shallow glimmering space shall I find what glimmering glory?
—*"Blackness"*

And again and again, the heart—buried deeply as ever in the human breast, its four chambers exposed to love and joy and pain and the small shafts that fall with desperation in between.
—*Ibid.*

This is my child sitting in the shade, her head thrown back in rapture, prolonging some moment of joy I have created for her.
—*Ibid.*

I had grown big, but my mother was bigger, and that would always be so.

—*"My Mother"*

Is life, then, a violent burst of light, like flint struck sharply in the dark? If so, I must continually strive to exist between the day and the day.

—*"At the Bottom of the River"*

Time and time again, I am filled up with all that I thought life might be—glorious moment upon glorious moment of contentment and joy and love running into each other and forming an extraordinary chain: a hymn sung in rounds.

—*Ibid.*

I stood as if I were a prism, many-sided and transparent, refracting and reflecting light as it reached me, light that never could be destroyed. And how beautiful I became.

—*Ibid.*

We were afraid of the dead because we never could tell when they might show up again.

—Annie John *(1986)*

Already her mouth was turned down permanently at the corners, as if to show that she had been born realizing that nobody else behaved properly, and as if also she had been born knowing that everything in life was a disappointment and her face was all set to meet it.

—*Ibid.*

Martin Luther King, Jr.

(1929–1968)

The grandson of a slave, and the son and grandson of Baptist minis-ters, the great civil rights leader was born Michael Luther King and attended Morehouse College, Crozer Theological Seminary, and Bos-ton University. As pastor of the Dexter Avenue Baptist Church, he rose to prominence during the Montgomery bus boycott in 1955 and the desegregation campaign in Birmingham in 1963. The author of numerous volumes, he delivered his "I Have a Dream" speech during the March on Washington in 1963 and was awarded the Nobel Peace Prize the following year, at the age of thirty-five. He continued his nonviolent protests, against discrimination, poverty, and the war in Vietnam, until his assassination, on April 4, 1968. In 1983, the anni-versary of his birth, January 15, was designated a federal holiday.

There are moral laws of the universe that man can no more violate with impunity than he can violate its physical laws.

—MOREHOUSE STUDENT ORATION, *1948*

If we are wrong—the Supreme Court of this nation is wrong.
If we are wrong—God Almighty is wrong!
If we are wrong—Jesus of Nazareth was merely a utopian dreamer
    and never came down to earth!
If we are wrong—justice is a lie!

—SPEECH DURING THE MONTGOMERY BUS BOYCOTT, DECEMBER 5, *1955*

If one day you find me sprawled and dead, I do not want you to retaliate with a single act of violence. Remember, if I am stopped, this movement will not be stopped, because God is with this movement. I urge you to continue protesting with the same dignity and discipline you have shown so far. The old law of an eye for an eye leaves every-body blind.

—STATEMENT DURING THE MONTGOMERY BUS BOYCOTT, *1955*

We must somehow learn that unearned suffering is redemptive.

—SPEECH ON HIS FRONT PORCH AFTER HIS HOME IN MONTGOMERY WAS BOMBED, JANUARY 30, 1956

Government action is not the whole answer to the present crisis, but it is an important partial answer. Morals cannot be legislated, but behavior can be regulated. The law cannot make an employer love me, but it can keep him from refusing to hire me because of the color of my skin.

—STRIDE TOWARD FREEDOM (1958)

Human progress is neither automatic nor inevitable. Even a superficial look at history reveals that no social advance rolls in on the wheels of inevitability. Every step toward the goal of justice requires sacrifice, suffering, and struggle, the tireless exertions and passionate concern of dedicated individuals.

—IBID.

We have allowed our civilization to outrun our culture, and so we are in danger now of ending up with guided missiles in the hands of misguided men.

—"THE AMERICAN DREAM" SPEECH, LINCOLN UNIVERSITY, OXFORD, PENNSYLVANIA, JUNE 6, 1961

Now is the time to make real the promises of democracy.

—c. 1961

Injustice anywhere is a threat to justice everywhere. We are caught in an inescapable network of mutuality, tied in a single garment of destiny. Whatever affects one directly affects all indirectly.

—LETTER FROM BIRMINGHAM JAIL, APRIL 16, 1963

I submit that an individual who breaks a law that conscience tells him is injust, and willingly accepts the penalty by staying in jail to arouse the conscience of the community over its injustice, is in reality expressing the very highest respect for the law.

—IBID.

Freedom is never voluntarily given by the oppressor; it must be demanded by the oppressed.

—IBID.

Nonviolence is a powerful and just weapon. It is a weapon unique in history, which cuts without wounding, and ennobles the man who wields it. It is a sword that heals.

—WHY WE CAN'T WAIT *(1963)*

I submit to you that if a man hasn't discovered something that he will die for, he isn't fit to live!

—SPEECH, COBO HALL, DETROIT, JUNE 23, 1963

The inseparable twin of racial injustice is economic injustice.

—THE STRENGTH TO LOVE *(1963)*

When in future generations men look back upon these turbulent, tension-filled days through which we are passing, they will see God working through history for the salvation of man.

—*IBID.*

One day we must come to see that peace is not merely a distant goal we seek, but that it is a means by which we arrive at that goal. We must pursue peaceful ends through peaceful means.

—SERMON, CHRISTMAS EVE, 1967

Courage faces fear and thereby masters it. Cowardice represses fear and is thereby mastered by it.

—THE STRENGTH TO LOVE *(1963)*

The belief that God will do everything for man is as untenable as the belief that man can do everything for himself. It, too, is based on a lack of faith. We must learn that to expect God to do everything while we do nothing is not faith but superstition.

—*IBID.*

Man is neither villain nor hero; he is rather both villain and hero.

—THE STRENGTH TO LOVE

I have a dream that one day, on the red hills of Georgia, sons of former slaves and the sons of former slaveowners will be able to sit down together at the table of brotherhood. I have a dream that my four little children will one day live in a nation where they will not be judged by the color of their skin but by the content of their character.

—ADDRESS AT THE MARCH ON WASHINGTON, AUGUST 28, 1963

And when that happens, and when we allow freedom to ring, when we let it ring from every village and every hamlet, from every state and every city, we will be able to speed up that day when all of God's children, black men and white men, Jews and Gentiles, Protestants and Catholics, will be able to join hands and sing in the words of that old Negro spiritual, "Free at last! Free at last! Thank God almighty, we are free at last!"

—Ibid.

We can never be satisfied as long as a Negro in Mississippi cannot vote and a Negro in New York believes he has nothing for which to vote.

—1964

The deep rumbling of discontent that we hear today is the thunder of disinherited masses, rising from dungeons of oppression to the bright hills of freedom.

—Nobel acceptance speech, December 11, 1964

Oppressed people cannot remain oppressed forever.

—Ibid.

I know some of you are asking today, "How long will it take?" I come to say to you this afternoon however difficult the moment, however frustrating the hour, it will not be long, because truth pressed to earth will rise again.

How long? Not long, because no lie can live forever.

How long? Not long, because you will reap what you sow.

How long? Not long, because the arm of the moral universe is long, but it bends toward justice.

—speech on the steps of the Alabama state capitol after the march from Selma to Montgomery, Alabama, March 26, 1965

Christianity has always insisted that the cross we bear precedes the crown we wear.

—sermon, "Beyond Discovery, Love," Dallas, Texas, September 25, 1966

We are inevitably our brother's keeper because we are our brother's brother.

—Where Do We Go From Here: Chaos or Community? (1967)

Ultimately a great nation is a compassionate nation.

—*IBID.*

I do not think of political power as an end. Neither do I think of economic power as an end. They are ingredients in the objective that we seek in life. And I think that end or that objective is a truly brotherly society; the creation of the beloved community.

—CHRISTIAN CENTURY, *JULY 13, 1966*

Somehow we must be able to stand up before our most bitter opponents and say: "We shall match your capacity to inflict suffering by our capacity to endure suffering. We will meet your physical force with soul force."

—*SERMON, CHRISTMAS EVE, 1967*

We will never have peace in the world until men everywhere recognize that ends are not cut off from means, because the means represent the idea in the making, and the end in process, and ultimately you can't reach good ends through evil means, because the means represent the seed and the end represents the tree.

—THE TRUMPET OF CONSCIENCE *(1967)*

We need a radical reordering of our national priorities.

—*CHICAGO FREEDOM MOVEMENT STATEMENT, MARCH 28, 1967*

We will place the problems of the poor at the seat of the government of the wealthiest nation in the history of mankind. If that power refuses to acknowledge its debt to the poor, it will have failed to live up to its promise to ensure "life, liberty, and the pursuit of happiness" to its citizens.

—*ANNOUNCING THE POOR PEOPLE'S CAMPAIGN, 1968*

Somehow this madness must cease.

—*IN OPPOSITION TO THE VIETNAM WAR, RIVERSIDE CHURCH, NEW YORK, APRIL 4, 1967*

Now the Judgment of God is upon us, and we must either learn to live together as brothers or we are going to perish together as fools.

—THE TRUMPET OF CONSCIENCE

A riot is at bottom the language of the unheard. It is the desperate, suicidal cry of one who is so fed up with the powerlessness of his cave existence that he asserts that he would rather be dead than ignored.

—Where Do We Go From Here?

I'd like somebody to mention that day that Martin Luther King, Jr., tried to give his life serving others . . . Yes, if you want to say that I was a drum major, say that I was a drum major for justice; say that I was a drum major for peace; I was a drum major for righteousness. And all the other things will not matter.

—on the subject of his own funeral, sermon, February 4, 1968

We've got some difficult days ahead. But it really doesn't matter with me now, because I've been to the mountaintop. And I don't mind. Like anybody, I would like to live a long life. Longevity has its place. But I'm not concerned about that now. I just want to do God's will. And He's allowed me to go up to the mountain, and I've looked over and I've seen the promised land. I may not get there with you. But I want you to know tonight that we, as a people, will get to the promised land. And I'm happy tonight. I'm not worried about anything. I'm not fearing any man. Mine eyes have seen the glory of the coming of the Lord.

—his last public address, Memphis, April 3, 1968, the night before his death

I believe that unarmed truth and unconditional love will have the final word and reality. This is why right temporarily defeated is stronger than evil triumphant.

—Nobel acceptance speech

We must accept finite disappointment, but we must never lose infinite hope.

—The Strength to Love

When I took up the cross, I recognized its meaning . . . The cross is something that you bear, and ultimately that you die on.

—speech, Penn Community College, Frogmore, South Carolina, May 22, 1967

Etheridge Knight

(1 9 3 1 –)

One of the dominant new voices of the 1960s, Knight was self-educated and published his first poems while he was an inmate in prison. After his release, he went on to become an award-winning poet, receiving grants from the Guggenheim Foundation and the National Endowment for the Arts, and has taught at several colleges.

The sounds made at night by 400 caged men are lonely and empty. A clacking typewriter, a flushing toilet, a futile curse, and drifting, distorted music from a radio. An inmate spends from fourteen to sixteen hours a day in his cell. Soon it becomes, in truth, a home.

—*"Inside These Walls,"* Black Voices from Prison *(1970)*

Each Fall the graves of my grandfathers call me, the brown hills and red gullies of Mississippi send out their electric messages, galvanizing my genes.

—*"The Idea of Ancestry"*

> To write a blues song
> is to regiment riots
> and pluck gems from graves.
> —*"Haiku"*

> Another weaver of black dreams has gone.
> —*"For Langston Hughes"*

> I boil my tears in a twisted spoon
> And dance like an angel on the point of a needle.
> —*"The Violent Space"*

He sees through stone
he has the secret
eyes this old black one
—*"He Sees Through Stone"*

The numbers operation with its blood-sucking corollaries could not exist without the aid and assistance of a corrupt political system whose bosses also grow fat off the dimes and dreams of black people. . . . The benefits to the black community from a numbers operation is a mouse's tit compared to the elephant's udder suckled by the syndicate and politicians.

—*"The Poor Pay More, Even for Their Dreams,"* Black Voices from Prison

Charles H. Langston

(fl. mid-1800s)

The brother of John Mercer Langston, Dr. Charles Langston was active in the convention movement and a strong proponent of political agitation for abolition. He was convicted of helping free a man from slavery in Ohio in 1858, but was given a reduced sentence after his impassioned defense.

I would call on every slave, from Maryland to Texas, to arise and assert their *liberties*, and cut their masters' throats if they attempt again to reduce them to slavery. Whether or not this principle is correct, an impartial posterity and the Judge of the Universe shall decide.

—*address to the Ohio State Convention, Columbus, January 15–18, 1851*

I know that the courts of this country, that the laws of this country, that the governmental machinery of this country, are so constituted as to oppress and outrage colored men . . . I was tried by a jury who were prejudiced; before a Court that was prejudiced; prosecuted by an officer who was prejudiced, and defended . . . by counsel that were prejudiced . . . I should not be subjected to the pain and penalties of this oppressive law, when I have not been tried, either by a jury of my peers, or by a jury that were impartial.

—AT HIS TRIAL IN OBERLIN, SEPTEMBER 1858

John Mercer Langston

(1829 – 1897)

Born in slavery in Virginia, Langston was emancipated during his youth and moved to Ohio, where he graduated from Oberlin in 1849. A leading abolitionist and convention man, he was president of the Equal Rights League and taught law at Howard University, where he became dean. He was later appointed American minister to Haiti and served as a congressman from Virginia in the 1890s.

While the devotion, the gallantry, and the heroism displayed by our sons, brothers, and fathers at Port Hudson, Fort Wagner, Petersburg, New Market Heights are fresh in the minds of the American people, let us spare no pains, let us not fail to make every effort in our power to secure for ourselves and our children all those rights, natural and political, which belong to us as men and as native-born citizens of America . . . Shall they return, after weary months and years of laborious service, as soldiers and sailors, bearing the scars of hard-earned victories, to tread again the old way of degradation and wrong? It must not be.

—APPEAL FROM THE EQUAL RIGHTS LEAGUE DURING THE CIVIL WAR, PHILADELPHIA, NOVEMBER 24, 1864

Nella Larsen

(1 8 9 1 – 1 9 6 4)

Larsen achieved fame during the Harlem Renaissance with the publication of the novels Quicksand *and* Passing, *which portray female characters of great psychological complexity, and she became the first African American woman to receive a Guggenheim Fellowship, in 1930. Her later work remained unpublished and she returned to a career in nursing before her death in 1964.*

These people yapped loudly of race, of race consciousness, of race pride, and yet suppressed its most delightful manifestations, love of color, joy of rhythmic motion, naïve, spontaneous laughter, harmony, radiance, and simplicity, all the essentials of spiritual beauty in the race they had marked for destruction.

—Quicksand *(1928)*

Lies, injustice, and hypocrisy are a part of every ordinary community. Most people achieve a sort of protective immunity, a kind of callousness, toward them. If they didn't, they couldn't endure.

—*Ibid.*

Why couldn't she have two lives, or why couldn't she be satisfied in one place?

—*Ibid.*

She wished to find out about this hazardous business of "passing," this breaking away from all that was familiar and friendly to take one's chances in another environment, not entirely strange, perhaps, but certainly not entirely friendly. What, for example, one did about background, how one accounted for oneself.

—Passing *(1929)*

If a man calls me a nigger it's his fault the first time, but mine if he has the opportunity to do it again.

—*Ibid.*

I feel like the oldest person in the world with the longest stretch of life before me.

—*Ibid.*

It was . . . enough to suffer as a woman, an individual, on one's own account, without having to suffer for the race as well. It was brutality, and undeserved.

—*Ibid.*

George Lawrence

(f l .   1 8 0 0 s)

A free black in New York, Lawrence delivered this address on the fifth anniversary of the abolition of the legal slave trade in the United States.

Cling to the paths of virtue and morality, cherish the plants of peace and temperance; by doing this you shall not only shine as the first stars in the firmament, and do honour to your worthy patrons, but immortalize your names. Be zealous and vigilant, be always on the alert to promote the welfare of your injured brethren; then shall providence shower down her blessings upon your heads, and crown your labors with success.

—An Oration on the Abolition of the Slave Trade, *delivered in the African Methodist Episcopal Church, New York, January 1, 1813*

There could be many reasons given, to prove that the mind of an African is not inferior to that of a European; yet to do so would be superfluous. It would be like adding hardness to the diamond, or lustre to the sun . . . No! The noble mind of a Newton could find room, and to spare, within the tenement of many an injured African.

—*IBID.*

Our day star is arisen, and shall perform its diurnal revolutions, until nature herself shall change . . . The spring is come, and the autumn nigh at hand, when the rich fruits of liberty shall be strewed in the path of every African, or descendant, and the olive hedge of peace encompass them in from their enemies.

—*IBID.*

Leadbelly (Huddie Ledbetter)

(1 8 8 5 ? – 1 9 4 9)

Born in Shreveport, Louisiana, Huddie Ledbetter left home in his teens and played with the blues singer Blind Lemon Jefferson in Texas. While imprisoned for murder in Angola Penitentiary, in 1933, he met Alan Lomax, who promoted his career when he was pardoned by the governor (who liked his singing) two years later. Richard Wright sums up the legendary figure: "Down south the white landlords called him a 'bad nigger' and they were afraid of his fists, his bitter biting songs, his twelve-stringed guitar, and his inability to take injustice and like it." He spent the last fourteen years of his life in New York and died of Lou Gehrig's disease, never having achieved true commercial success.

One dollar bill, baby, won't buy you no shoes.
—*"ONE DOLLAR BILL, BABY" (1936)*

The People's World, your name is called.
The People's World, your name is called.
I said it, your name is called to outshine the sun.
—*"OUTSHINE THE SUN" (c. 1944)*

I can pray and preach, too. I can *sure* pray.

—Library of Congress interview with Alan Lomax

If a white woman says something, it must be so, and she can say something about a colored person, if it's a thousand colored men, they kill all of 'em just for that one woman. If she ain't telling the truth, it don't make any difference. Why? 'Cause it's Jim Crow, and I know it's so 'cause the Scottsboro boys can tell you about it.

—On the incident that prompted his famous song "The Scottsboro Boys Shall Not Die" (1937)

I always sings too long and too loud.

—In Charles Wolfe and Kip Lornell, The Life and Legend of Leadbelly (1992)

One thing, folks, you all should realize,
Six foot of dirt makes us all one size,
For God made us all, and in Him we trust,
Nobody in this world is better than us.

—"Equality for Negroes" (c. 1948)

The blues is like this. You lay down some night and you turn from one side of the bed to the other: all night long. It's not too cold in that bed, and it ain't too hot. But what's the matter? The blues has got you.

—Introduction to his "Good Morning Blues," (1959)

I'll fight Jim Crow any place, any time . . . One of the songs I'm gonna sing is "We all in the same boat brother. You rock it too far to the right you fall in the waddah, rock it too far to the left you fall in the same waddah, and it's just as wet on both sides."

—Interview, Folk Music (June 1964)

I'm gonna tell you, tell you, tell you,
I'm gonna tell you, to save my soul.

—"Ha, Ha Thisaway" (1936)

Spike Lee

(1 9 5 7 –   )

Born Shelton Spike Lee in Atlanta, Lee attended Morehouse College and film school at New York University, where his early work was first produced. He came to media attention with She's Got to Have It *in 1986 and since then has produced a major, and usually controversial, film almost every year, and he has spoken out frequently on civil rights issues.*

Critics like to build you up, tear you down, and then, if you're lucky, build you up again.

—FIVE FOR FIVE *(1991)*

I collect names for characters. Names are valuable; they can be your first source of insight into a character.

—MO' BETTER BLUES *(1991)*

We wuz robbed.

—*ON BEING DENIED AN AWARD AT CANNES FOR* DO THE RIGHT THING, *1989*

I'm gonna say this, and I'll continue to say it until things change. The good ole U.S. of A. has two motherfucking standards and sets of rules: one white and one black.

—FIVE FOR FIVE

Yusuf Hawkins is Emmet Till. Both were murdered for alleged reckless eyeballing.

—*ON THE DEATH OF YUSUF HAWKINS IN BENSONHURST, QUEENS, AUGUST 1989, IBID.*

Black people have never had the power to enforce racism, and so this is something that white America is going to have to work out themselves. If they decide they want to stop it, curtail it, or do the right thing . . . then it will be done, but not until then.

—*IN ROGER EBERT,* HOME MOVIE COMPANION *(1990)*

Malcolm is a saint and he means different things to different people.
—*c. 1991*

To me, the Celtics represent white supremacy.
—*AS A CELEBRATED BASKETBALL FAN IN KEVIN NELSON,* TALKIN' TRASH *(1993)*

Our greatness, our talent has never been the question. It's been a matter of grappling for control over what we do.
—*INTERVIEW, OCTOBER 1989*

Fred Leonard

(c . 1 9 4 3 –)

As a high school student, Leonard participated in sit-ins and freedom rides in Tennessee.

I think we were all thinking maybe we should go off at the back of this bus because we thought that if we had gone off at the back maybe they wouldn't be so bad on us. But we decided no, no, we'll go off the front and take what's coming to us.
—*IN HENRY HAMPTON,* VOICES OF FREEDOM *(1990)*

Sugar Ray Leonard

(1 9 5 6 –)

Born in Wilmington, North Carolina, and raised in Wasington, D.C., Ray Charles Leonard was the son of a boxer and won his first Golden Gloves title in 1972 and an Olympic Gold Medal in 1976. An enormously popular fighter, with notable bouts against Roberto Duran and Tommy Hearns, he retired in 1984 after suffering a detached retina, and lost in a brief comeback against Marvin Hagler in 1987.

We're all endowed with God-given talents. Mine happens to be hitting people in the head.
—IN THE BLACK LIGHTS *(1986)*

We assume the risks. That's what makes a great champion. We care, but you can't let that be a burden to you.
—IN HARRY MULLAN, THE BOOK OF BOXING QUOTATIONS *(1988)*

A fighter never knows when it's the last bell. He doesn't want to face that.
—NEW YORK POST, *1987*

The only way for a fighter to get back in shape is to fight his way back.
—C. *1988*

John Lewis

(1 9 4 0 –)

A student at the American Baptist Theological Seminary when the civil rights movement escalated in the South in the early 1960s, Lewis participated in Freedom rides in Nashville and Birmingham, and became chairman of the Student Nonviolent Coordinating Committee. He delivered a memorable address during the March on Washington, August 28, 1963, and is now a congressman from Georgia.

The next time we march, we won't march on Washington, but we will march through the South, through the Heart of Dixie, the way Sherman did. We will make the action of the past few months look petty. And I say to you, WAKE UP AMERICA!

—SPEECH AT *LINCOLN MEMORIAL, AUGUST 28, 1963*

The revolution is at hand, and we must free ourselves of the chains of political and economic slavery . . . We cannot be patient, we do not want to be free gradually, we want our freedom, and we want it now.

—*IBID.*

It was like a holy crusade. It was like Gandhi's march to the sea. You didn't get tired, you really didn't get weary, you had to go. It was more than an ordinary march, to me there was never a march like this one before, and there hasn't been one since. It was the sense of community moving there . . .

—ON THE MARCH FROM *SELMA TO MONTGOMERY, 1965, IN HENRY HAMPTON,*

VOICES OF FREEDOM *(1990)*

Reginald Lewis

(1 9 4 2 – 1 9 9 3)

One of the wealthiest black businessmen in America, Lewis was a graduate of Harvard Law School and became the CEO of TLC Beatrice International Holdings in 1989. He gave millions of dollars to charitable and political causes, including $2 million to the NAACP.

It is all too little when we consider the day-to-day drama being inflicted upon many of our children who are of African or Hispanic descent and who are not yet fully included in the American dream. By working in this field in the future, I believe I am working for all Americans, because I truly believe that our society is highly vulnerable unless we join together in seeing this not as a particular problem of any one ethnic group but as something that the nation must address as part of its own spirit of renewal.

—*STATEMENT SEVERAL DAYS BEFORE HIS DEATH, IN JANUARY 1993*

Sonny Liston

(1 9 3 2 – 1 9 7 0)

Born in Pine Bluff, Arkansas, Charles Liston began his troubled life as one of his father's twenty-five children and by the age of eighteen was in prison for robbery. There, he trained as a boxer, and after his release, on September 25, 1962, he won the heavyweight title from Floyd Patterson. He held the title until his bout with Muhammad Ali in February 1964, and died of a drug overdose six years later.

I never had a dime to my name before I became a fighter. I never had friends before, or respect. Now when people see me on the street, they turn around and say, "Ain't that Sonny Liston, the fighter?"

—BOXING ILLUSTRATED, *AUGUST 1959*

In the films the good guy always wins, but this is one bad guy who ain't gonna lose.

—*BEFORE HIS TITLE FIGHT WITH PATTERSON, SEPTEMBER 25, 1962, IN WHICH HE BECAME HEAVYWEIGHT CHAMPION*

It don't matter as long as he can count up to ten.

—*ON HIS CHOICE OF REFEREE FOR THE FIGHT*

I'm ashamed to say I'm in America.

—*ON RETURNING TO THE UNITED STATES FROM A EUROPEAN TOUR AFTER THE BOMBING OF THE SIXTEENTH STREET BAPTIST CHURCH IN BIRMINGHAM, SEPTEMBER 15, 1963*

Alain Locke

(1 8 8 6 – 1 9 5 4)

Born in Philadelphia, Locke earned both his B.A. and Ph.D. from Harvard, where he was elected to Phi Beta Kappa and became the first black Rhodes Scholar. He taught for more than forty years at Howard University and is best known as the editor of the seminal work of the Harlem Renaissance, The New Negro.

Harlem is the precious fruit in the Garden, of Eden, the big apple.

—*c. 1919*

In its own setting African Art was a vital part of life—masks and costumes for the ritual dances, the festivals, the initiations, the pageants of a primitive but wholesome civilization. Africa produced things imperishably beautiful.

—THEATRE ARTS MONTHLY, *FEBRUARY 3, 1920*

The younger generation is vibrant with a new psychology; the new spirit is awake in the masses . . . Each generation . . . will have its creed.

—THE NEW NEGRO *(1925)*

The choice is not between one way for the Negro and another way for the rest, but between American institutions frustrated on the one hand and American ideals progressively fulfilled and realized on the other.

—*IBID.*

The pulse of the Negro world has begun to beat in Harlem.

—*IBID.*

The Younger Generation comes, bringing its gifts. They are the first fruits of the Negro Renaissance. Youth speaks, and the voice of the New Negro is heard.

—*"NEGRO YOUTH SPEAKS" (1925)*

Through their untarnishable beauty, they seem assured of the immortality of those great folk expressions that survive not so much through being typical of a group or representative of a period as by virtue of being fundamentally and everlastingly human.

—*"THE NEGRO SPIRITUALS" (1925)*

Art must discover and reveal the beauty which prejudice and caricature have overlaid.

—*"THE LEGACY OF THE ANCESTRAL ARTS" (1925)*

Once African art is known and appreciated, it can scarcely have less influence upon the blood descendants, bound to it by a sense of cultural kinship, than those who inherit it by tradition.

—*c. 1928*

Audre Lorde

(1 9 3 4 – 1 9 9 2)

*P*oet, essayist, feminist, educator, lesbian activist, cancer patient, mother, Lorde was born in Harlem and attended Hunter College and Columbia University. She taught at several colleges and is the author of more than a dozen volumes of poetry and essays.

> see me now
> your severed daughter
> laughing our name into echo
> all the world shall remember
>
> —"125TH ST. AND ABOMEY," THE BLACK UNICORN *(1978)*

There are no new ideas still waiting in the wings to save us as women, as human. There are only old and forgotten ones, new combinations, extrapolations and recognitions from within ourselves—along with the renewed courage to try them out.

—"POETRY IS NOT A LUXURY," CHRYSALIS, *1977*

We are African women and we know, in our blood's telling, the tenderness with which our foremothers held each other.

—"EYE TO EYE"

My work is about difference, my work is about how we learn to lie down with the different parts of ourselves, so that we can in fact learn to respect and honor the different parts of each other, so that we in fact can learn to use them moving toward something that needs being done, that has never been done before.

—RADIO INTERVIEW, *1988*

The master's tools will never dismantle the master's house.

—WIDELY QUOTED

My body
writes into your flesh
the poem
you make of me
—*"RECREATION,"* THE BLACK UNICORN

When I speak of the erotic, then, I speak of it as an assertion of the life-force of women; of that creative energy empowered, the knowledge and use of which we are now reclaiming in our language, our history, our dancing, our loving, our work, our lives.
—*"USES OF THE EROTIC: THE EROTIC AS POWER,"* CONFERENCE ON THE HISTORY OF WOMEN, MOUNT HOLYOKE COLLEGE, AUGUST 25, 1978

Every Black woman in America lives her life somewhere along a wide curve of ancient and unexpressed anger.
—SISTER OUTSIDER *(1974)*

Some problems we share as women, some we do not. You fear your children will grow up to join the patriarchy and testify against you; we fear our children will be dragged from a car and shot down in the street, and you will turn your backs upon the reasons they are dying.
—*"THE TRANSFORMATION OF SILENCE INTO LANGUAGE AND ACTION,"* MODERN LANGUAGE ASSOCIATION, DECEMBER 28, 1977

What is there possibly left for us to be afraid of, after we have dealt face to face with death and not embraced it? Once I accept the existence of dying as a life process, who can ever have power over me again?
—THE CANCER JOURNALS, *1980*

The learning process is something you can incite, literally incite, like a riot.
—*IN* VALERIE SMITH, *ET AL.,* AFRICAN-AMERICAN WRITERS *(1991)*

Sometimes the only thing I had to hold on to was knowing I could read, and that that could get me through.
—ZAMI: A NEW SPELLING OF MY NAME *(1982)*

Wherever the bird with no feet flew she found trees with no limbs.
—*"HOW I BECAME A POET,"* IBID.

—the rhythm of a litany, the rituals of Black women combing their daughters' hair.

—*Ibid.*

Battling racism and battling heterosexism and battling apartheid share the same urgency inside me as battling cancer . . . Each victory must be applauded, because it is so easy not to battle at all, to just accept and call that acceptance inevitable.

—A Burst of Light *(1988)*

We cannot afford to do our enemies' work by destroying each other.

—*"Learning from the 60s," speech during Malcolm X Weekend in Harlem, 1982*

For in order to survive, those of us for whom oppression is as American as apple pie have always had to be watchers.

—*"Age, Race, Class, and Sex: Women Redefining Difference," Amherst College,
April 1980*

I am not only a casualty, I am also a warrior . . . Of what had I *ever* been afraid?

—*"The Transformation of Silence into Language and Action,"
Modern Language Association, December 28, 1977*

I am a Black Lesbian, and I *am* your sister.

—*A frequent salutation*

Joe Louis

(1 9 1 4 – 1 9 8 1)

Born in Alabama and raised in Detroit, Joseph Louis Barrow began boxing at sixteen and turned pro in 1934, when he changed his name. He defeated both Primo Carnera and Max Baer in 1935, and became the first black man since Jack Johnson to gain the heavyweight title

when he fought James J. Braddock on June 22, 1937. He held the title
for almost twelve years, before retiring in March 1949.

Nobody ever called me nigger until I got to Detroit.
<blockquote>—ON GROWING UP IN THE SOUTH, IN A HARD ROAD TO GLORY *(1988)*</blockquote>

Yeah, I'm scared. I'm scared I might kill Schmeling.
<blockquote>—ON HIS REMATCH WITH MAX SCHMELING, JUNE 22, 1938, IBID.

(THE FIGHT WAS OVER IN TWO MINUTES, FOUR SECONDS.)</blockquote>

Once that bell rings you're on your own. It's just you and the other guy.
<blockquote>—IN HARRY MULLAN, THE BOOK OF BOXING QUOTATIONS *(1988)*</blockquote>

Reverend Joseph Lowery

(1 9 2 4 –)

During the 1960s, Lowery was active in the civil rights movement as
president of the Southern Christian Leadership Conference, based in
Birmingham, and he continues to speak out on political issues.

There is a new Ku Klux Klan out there called Killer Crack and Cocaine, and the new lynch mob is sweeping all through the Black neighborhood.
<blockquote>—"HOME AT LAST," THE CRISIS, *NOVEMBER 1986*</blockquote>

America has abandoned the strong woman of spirituality and is shacking up with the harlot of materialism.
<blockquote>—CIRCA *1989*</blockquote>

The safest sex is on the shore of abstinence. The next is with one faithful partner. If you insist on wading out into the turbulent waters of multiple sex partners—wear a life jacket.
—JET, *MARCH 1989*

The issues in the 1950s were very simple—whether you sit in a restaurant or whether you can vote . . . Now we have to find a way to simplify very complicated issues, and we haven't been able to do it yet.
—NEW YORK TIMES, *APRIL 3, 1993*

John R. Lynch

(1 8 4 7 – 1 9 3 9)

Born a slave, John Roy Lynch was one of the most prominent of Reconstruction politicians. A major in the U.S. Army during the Civil War, he became speaker of the Mississippi House of Representatives in 1872 and served in Congress from 1873 to 1877 and again in 1882–1883. In the 1882 contest, he was briefly denied his seat by Southern politicians, but was admitted by member vote.

It is an act of simple justice . . .
—*IN SUPPORT OF THE NATION'S FIRST CIVIL RIGHTS BILL*, CONGRESSIONAL RECORD, *43RD CONGRESS, 1ST SESS., JUNE 1874*

When every man, woman, and child can feel and know that his and their rights are fully protected by the strong arm of a generous and grateful Republic, then can all truthfully say that this beautiful land of ours, over which the Star Spangled Banner so triumphantly waves, is, in truth and fact, the "land of the free and the home of the brave."
—CONGRESSIONAL RECORD, *43RD CONGRESS, 2ND SESS., FEBRUARY 1875*

You may deprive me for the time being of my opportunity of making an honest living; you may take the bread out of the mouths of my hungry and dependent family; you may close the school-house door in the face of my children; yea, more, you may take that which no man can give, my life, but my manhood, my principles you cannot have!

—*DEFENDING HIS SEAT IN THE HOUSE,* CONGRESSIONAL RECORD, *APRIL 27, 1882*

The laboring people in this country can secure all the rights to which they are justly entitled without violating the law, and there is no better way to bring this about than through organization.

—THE A.M.E. CHURCH REVIEW, *OCTOBER 1886*

Claude McKay

(1889–1948)

Born in Jamaica, McKay spent much of his life in the United States, Europe, and Africa. His first work, Songs of Jamaica, *was published when he was twenty. He came to the United States in 1912 and left in 1919 for London, where* Spring in New Hampshire *was published. His volume* Harlem Shadows *was one of the inaugural works of the Harlem Renaissance; among his other works are the novels* Home to Harlem *and* Banana Bottom *and other volumes of poetry and fiction.*

> If we must die—let it not be like hogs
> Hunted and penned in an inglorious spot . . .
> If we must die, O let us nobly die,
> So that our precious blood may not be shed
> In vain: then even the monsters we defy
> Shall be constrained to honor us though dead!
>
> —*"IF WE MUST DIE" (1917)*

> Be not deceived, for every deed you do
> I could match—out-match: am I not Africa's son,
> Black of that black land where black deeds are done?
>
> —*"TO THE WHITE FIENDS"*

The white man is a tiger at my throat,
Drinking my blood as my life ebbs away . . .
—"TIGER"

Although she feeds me bread of bitterness,
And sinks into my throat her tiger's tooth,
Stealing my breath of life, I will confess
I love this cultured hell that tests my youth!
—"AMERICA"

For the new birth rends the old earth and the
      very dead are waking,
Ghosts are turned flesh, throwing off the grave's disguise,
And the foolish, even children, are made wise . . .
—"EXHORTATION: SUMMER, 1919"

Africa! long ages sleeping, O my motherland, awake!
—IBID.

Bow down my soul in worship very low
And in the holy silences be lost.
—"RUSSIAN CATHEDRAL"

I know the dark delight of being strange,
The penalty of difference in the crowd,
The loneliness of wisdom among fools . . .
—"MY HOUSE"

All wonderful things, all beautiful things, gave of their wealth to your
birth.
—"TO O.E.A."

Deep in the secret chambers of my heart
I muse my life-long hate, and without flinch
I bear it nobly as I live my part.
—"THE WHITE CITY"

For I was born, far from my native clime,
Under the white man's menace, out of time.
—"OUTCAST"

Where else could I have all this life but Harlem? Good old Harlem! Chocolate Harlem! Sweet Harlem! Harlem, I've got yo' number down.
—Home to Harlem *(1928)*

Sometimes he felt like a tree with roots in the soil and sap flowing out and whispering leaves drinking in the air.
—*Ibid.*

Jungle jazzing. Orient wrigging, civilized stepping. Shake that thing. Sweet dancing thing of primitive joy, perverse pleasure, prostitute ways, many adored variations of the rhythm, savage, barbaric, refined-eternal rhythm of the mysterious magical, magnificent—the dance divine of life. Oh, shake that thing.
—Banjo, *1929*

Color consciousness was the fundamental of my restlessness. And it was something with which my fellow-expatriates could sympathize but which they could not altogether understand . . . some even thought that I might have preferred to be white like them . . . For all their knowledge and sophistication, they couldn't understand the instinctive and animal and purely physical pride of a black person resolute in being himself.
—A Long Way from Home *(1937)*

I stripped down harshly to the naked core
of hatred based on the essential wrong!
—*unpublished, "Cycle Manuscript"*

Floyd McKissick

(1922–1991)

In 1951, McKissick became the first African American to receive a law degree from the University of North Carolina. He worked as an attorney for CORE and in 1966 became the civil rights group's chairman.

We have made the slogan Black Power into a program destined to rescue Black people from destruction by the forces of a racist society which is bent upon denying them freedom, equality, and dignity.

—*"Black Power: A Blueprint for Survival," speech at the 24th national convention of CORE, Oakland, June 30–July 4, 1967*

I liked the slogan Black Power, and it was not the first time it had been used . . . Du Bois and Richard Wright certainly had used the expression of black people getting their power. I think it scared people because they did not understand. They could not subtract violence from power . . . I don't believe in a standard for white and a standard for black. I think violence and nonviolence is equally distributed among all races.

—*In Henry Hampton, Voices of Freedom (1990)*

$\mathcal{T}$erry $\mathcal{M}c\mathcal{M}$illan

(1 9 5 1 –   )

Born in Port Huron, Michigan, McMillan is the author of the best-selling novels Mama, Disappearing Acts, *and* Waiting to Exhale. *She has taught at the University of Arizona, was a fellow at Yaddo and the MacDowell Colony, and has received grants from the PEN American Center, the National Endowment for the Arts, and other groups. She is also the editor of* Breaking Ice: An Anthology of Contemporary African-American Fiction.

It's sad to think that we've gotten to this—that we actually have to *think* about how to go about finding a man. But what's even sadder is that some men make you feel guilty for looking.

—*"Looking for Mr. Right," Essence, February 1990*

I don't trust white critics' judgment about most things that deal with black life, particularly when a black person is the creator.

—IN SPIKE LEE, FIVE FOR FIVE *(1991)*

I mean, I have my days and I have my nights, but I haven't gotten to the point where I'll take whatever I can get.

—WAITING TO EXHALE *(1992)*

It takes me forever to say my prayers these days, but I don't care, because this time around, I want to make sure God doesn't have to do any guesswork.

—*IBID.*

I'm talking about having somebody around to talk to, having somebody put their arms around you and tell you everything is going to be fine and not to worry. Even if the shit is a lie, it still feels good.

—*IBID.*

Even fools get tired of being fools at some point.

—*IBID.*

$\mathcal{H}$aki $\mathcal{M}$adhubuti

(1 9 4 2 –   )

Formerly known as Don L. Lee, Madhubuti was an important force in the Black Arts Movement (together with Amiri Baraka and Larry Neal) of the 1960s. He is the author of eleven books of poetry, essays, and criticism and is the director of the Third World Press.

Back again,
BLACK AGAIN,
Home.

—*"BACK AGAIN, HOME"*

They who humble themselves before knowledge of any kind generally end up the wiser and as voices with something meaningful to say.
—*IN* BLACK POETRY WRITING *(1975)*

> change.
> for the better into a realreal together thing.
> —*"A POEM TO COMPLEMENT OTHER POEMS"*

If black people do not *have* and *practice* their own values, customs and traditions, other people out of their own survival necessity will impose their values on us . . . *Revolutionary theory comes from revolutionary practice* and not the other way around.
—*"THE REDEVELOPMENT OF THE BLACK MIND: THE BUILDING OF BLACK EXTENDED FAMILY INSTITUTIONS,"* ENEMIES: THE CLASH OF RACES *(1978)*

the seeing eye should always see.
the night doesn't stop the stars & our enemies scope the ways of blackness in three bad shifts a day.
—*"ONE-SIDED SHOOT-OUT"*

The *family* as the first-line institution is the foundation upon which the new black consciousness and community can be built and sustained.
—*"THE REDEVELOPMENT OF THE BLACK MIND"*

To maintain the ability to admit and grow from our mistakes rather than let them defeat us represents best the inner strength of a people.
—*IBID.*

> u feel that way sometimes
> wondering:
> wondering, how did we survive?
> —*"MIXED SKETCHES"*

We believe in the concepts of *work* every day for our people; *study* every day for the development of our people; *creativity* for the beauty of our people; and *building* for the future of our people.
—*"THE REDEVELOPMENT OF THE BLACK MIND"*

Black poetry is like a razor; it's sharp and will cut deep.
—*IN* BLACK POETRY WRITING

What the black critic must bring to us is an extensive knowledge of world literature, along with a specialized awareness of his own litera- ture. He must understand that a "mature literature has a history behind it," and that that which is being written today is largely in- debted to the mature black literature that came before.
—*"The Black Critic," in Gwendolyn Brooks, Jump Bad: A New Chicago Anthology (1971)*

Black critics who do not have a tradition of social rhetoric must now become masters of an alien language, that is, if black people are to survive. And survival is what we are about.
—*Ibid.*

> we *ran* the dangercourse,
> now, it's a silent walk/a careful eye
> —*"We Walk the Way of the New World"*

Language . . . expands the brain, increases one's knowledge bank, enlarges the world, and challenges the vision of those who may not have a vision. *One of the most effective ways to keep a people en- slaved . . . is to create in that people a disrespect and fear of the written and spoken word.*
—*in Mari Evans, Black Women Writers (1984)*

> We're an African people
> hard softness burning black
> the earth's magic color our veins . . .
> —*"African Poem"*

Bravery lies in his word, his telling the truth; some say he's a poet.
—*"Only a Few Left," Negro Digest, September 1967*

Clarence Major

(1 9 3 6 –)

Born in Atlanta, Major attended the Art Institute of Chicago and has published poetry, fiction, and criticism. He is the author of the novel Emergency Exit *and has edited the* Juba to Jive: A Dictionary of Afro-American Slang *and the fiction anthology* Calling the Wind.

The black poet confronted with western culture and civilization must isolate and define himself in as bold a relief as he can. He must chop away at the white criterion and destroy its hold on his black mind because seeing the world through white eyes from a black soul causes death.

> —"A BLACK CRITERION," THE JOURNAL OF BLACK POETRY, SPRING 1967

The nightmare of this western sadism must be fought with superior energy, and black poetic spirit is a powerful weapon.

> —IBID.

Paule Marshall

(1 9 2 9 –)

The daughter of Jamaican immigrants in Bedford-Stuyvesant, New York, Marshall was graduated Phi Beta Kappa from Brooklyn College and worked at a small magazine before her first novel, Brown Girl, Brownstones, *was published. She is the author of three other novels as well as many well-known short stories, and has received a Guggenheim Fellowship and a Ford Foundation Award, as well as honors*

from the National Institute of Arts and Letters, the National Endowment for the Arts, and others.

For me, listening unnoticed in a corner of the kitchen . . . it wasn't only what the women talked about, the content, but the way they put things, the style . . . They were, in other words, practicing art of a high order, and in the process revealing at a level beyond words their understanding of and commitment to an aesthetic which recognizes that art is inseparable from life, and form and content are one.
—*INTERVIEW*, NEW LETTERS *(AUTUMN 1973)*

She was one with them: the mother and the Bajan women, who had lived each day what she had come to know. How had the mother endured, she who had not chosen death by water?
—BROWN GIRL, BROWNSTONES *(1959)*

Small island, go back where you really come from.
—*IBID.*

Perhaps she was both . . . child and woman, darkness and light, past and present, life and death—all the opposites contained and reconciled in her.
—*"TO DA-DUH IN MEMORIAM," (1966)*

There's nothing to be done with you, soul.
—*IBID.*

"You ain't people."
—*"BARBADOS,"* SOUL CLAP HAND AND SING *(1961)*

I come here and pick up with a piece of man and from then on I has read hell by heart and called every generation blessed.
—BROWN GIRL, BROWNSTONES

Once a great wrong has been done, it never dies. People speak the words of peace, but their hearts do not forgive. Generations perform ceremonies of reconciliation but there is no end.
—*EPIGRAPH*, THE CHOSEN PLACE, THE TIMELESS PEOPLE *(1969)*

309

"If we had been selfish, we couldn't have lived at all." They half-spoke, half-sang the words. They had trusted one another, had set aside their differences and stood as one against their enemies. *They had been a people!*

—<small>IBID.</small>

The combined voices of the drowned raised in a loud unceasing lament—all those, the nine million and more it is said, who in their enforced exile, their Diaspora, had gone down between this point and the homeland lying out of sight of the east. This sea mourned them.

—<small>PRAISESONG FOR THE WIDOW</small> *(1983)*

The theme of separation and loss the note embodied, the acknowledged longing it conveyed summed up feelings that were beyond words, feelings and a host of subliminal memories that over the years had proven more durable and trustworthy than the history with its trauma and pain out of which they had come. After centuries of forgetfulness and even denial, they refused to go away. The note was a lamentation that could hardly have come from the rum keg of a drum. Its source had to be the heart, the bruised still-bleeding innermost chamber of the collective heart.

—<small>IBID.</small>

The words were living things to her. She sensed them bestriding the air and charging the room with strong colors.

—<small>BROWN GIRL, BROWNSTONES</small>

Thurgood Marshall

(1 9 0 8 – 1 9 9 3)

The first African American to sit on the Supreme Court, Marshall was born in Baltimore, the grandson of slaves. He attended Howard University Law School and, as an NAACP lawyer, winning twenty-nine of the thirty-two cases he argued before the Supreme Court, he

earned his greatest victory in Brown v. Board of Education of Topeka
*(1954), which desegregated public schools. He served on the U.S.
Court of Appeals and as solicitor general before his appointment to
the Court in 1967, where for twenty-four years he supported affirmative action policies and equality of opportunity and opposed the death
penalty and government intrusion into private life.*

To oppose Plessy v. Ferguson *was merely asking for what was ours
by right—it was simple justice.*
—AFTER THE DECISION IN BROWN V. BOARD OF EDUCATION *(1954)*

Oh, yipe! What did you say?
—WHEN TOLD BY PRESIDENT LYNDON JOHNSON OF HIS APPOINTMENT TO THE COURT,
JUNE 13, 1967; COLUMBIA ORAL HISTORY INTERVIEW

Instead of making us copy out stuff on the blackboard after school
when we misbehaved, our teacher sent us down into the basement to
learn parts of the Constitution. I made my way through every para-
graph.
—INTERVIEW, 1989

I was on the verge of a nervous breakdown for a long time, but I never
quite made the grade.
—IBID.

We lived on a respectable street, but behind us there were back alleys
where the roughnecks and the tough kids hung out. When it was time
for dinner, my mother used to go to the front door and call my older
brother. Then she'd go to the *back* door and call me.
—IBID.

If the First Amendment means anything, it means that a State has no
business telling a man, sitting alone in his own house, what books he
may read or what films he may watch. Our whole constitutional heritage rebels at the thought of giving government the power to control
men's minds.
—STANLEY V. GEORGIA, APRIL 7, 1969

The measure of a country's greatness is its ability to retain compas-
ion in time of crisis. No nation in the recorded history of man has a

greater tradition of revering justice and fair treatment for all its citizens in times of turmoil, confusion, and tension than ours . . . In striking down capital punishment, this Court does not malign our system of government. On the contrary, it pays homage to it. Only in a free society could right triumph in difficult times, and could civilization record its magnificent advancement. In recognizing the humanity of our fellow beings, we pay ourselves the highest tribute . . . The Eighth Amendment is our insulation from our baser selves.

—*CONCURRING IN THE DECISION TO ABOLISH CAPITAL PUNISHMENT,*
FURMAN *v.* GEORGIA, *JUNE 29, 1972*

It is the poor and the members of minority groups who are least able to voice their complaints against capital punishment. Their impotence leaves them victims of a sanction that the wealthier, better-represented, just-as-guilty person can escape. So long as the capital sanction is used only against the forlorn, easily forgotten members of society, legislators are content to maintain the status quo.

—*IBID.*

In the short run, it may seem to be the easier course to allow our great metropolitan areas to be divided up each into two cities—one white, the other black—but it is a course, I predict, our people will ultimately regret.

—*DISSENTING IN* MILLIKEN *v.* BRADLEY, *1974*

The responsibility for enforcement of the civil provisions of the civil rights statutes rests solely with the individual.

—*c. 1975*

The enactments challenged here brutally coerce poor women to bear children whom society will scorn for every day of their lives.

—*DISSENT IN* BEAL *v.* DOE, *1977, BARRING FUNDING OF ABORTIONS FOR THE POOR*

In light of the sorry history of discrimination and its devastating impact on the lives of Negroes, bringing the Negro into the mainstream of American life should be a state interest of the highest order. To fail to do so is to insure that America will forever remain a divided society.

—*DISSENT IN* REGENTS OF UNIVERSITY OF CALIFORNIA *v.* BAKKE, *1978*

Throughout the world today there are men, women, and children interned indefinitely, awaiting trials which may never come or which may be a mockery of the word, because their governments believe them to be "dangerous." Our Constitution, whose construction began two centuries ago, can shelter us forever from the evils of such unchecked power . . . But it cannot protect us if we lack the courage, and the self-restraint, to protect ourselves.

—*DISSENTING OPINION IN* UNITED STATES *V.* SALERNO, *1987*

A majority of this Court signals that it regards racial discrimination as largely a phenomenon of the past, and that government bodies need no longer preoccupy themselves with rectifying racial injustice . . . I, however, do not believe this nation is anywhere close to eradicating racial discrimination or its vestiges.

—CITY OF RICHMOND *V.* CROSON, *1989*

History teaches that grave threats to liberty often come in times of urgency, when constitutional rights seem too extravagant to endure.

—*DISSENTING IN* FLORIDA *V.* BOSTICK, *1991*

Power, not reason, is the new currency of this Court's decision-making . . . The majority today sends a clear signal that scores of established constitutional liberties are now ripe for reconsideration, thereby inviting the very type of open defiance of our precedents that the majority rewards in this case . . . Neither the law nor the facts supporting [the law] underwent any change in the last four years. Only the personnel of this Court did.

—*DISSENTING IN* PAYNE *V.* TENNESSEE, *JUNE 27, 1991*

It would have been cheaper to shoot him right after he was arrested, wouldn't it?

—*TO JUSTICE REHNQUIST, WHO COMMENTED ON THE COST OF A DEATH ROW INMATE'S APPEAL, 1981*

Sometimes history takes things into its own hands.

—*c. 1983*

I wouldn't do the job of dog-catcher for Ronald Reagan.

—*INTERVIEW, 1989*

What's wrong with me? I'm old. I'm getting old and coming apart.

—*ON ANNOUNCING HIS RETIREMENT IN 1992*

That he did what he could with what he had.

Benjamin Mays

(1 8 9 5 – 1 9 8 4)

Orator, preacher, journalist, and reformer, Mays was born in South Carolina and was awarded Phi Beta Kappa at Bates College. He was ordained a Baptist minister before earning his M.A. and Ph.D. from the University of Chicago and his D.D. from Howard University. In 1934, he became the dean of Howard University School of Religion and in 1940 was elected president of Morehouse College. Throughout his career he was involved in legal battles for civil rights, and he documented the importance of the black church in his works The Negro's Church *and* The Negro's God.

God is absolute—not man, not race, not economics, not politics—but God. And whenever men in their arrogance and pride set themselves up as absolute, they will be beaten to the ground.

—"THE INESCAPABLE CHRIST," HOWARD UNIVERSITY, JUNE 8, 1945

If we believe in the democratic way of life as a means of perfecting change, we should be willing to trust the federal courts. This is the machinery which our founding fathers set up as one of the ways to resolve differences and adjust grievances.

—PITTSBURGH COURIER, OCTOBER 14, 1950

Man is what his dream are.

—BORN TO REBEL (1971)

We strive to desegregate and integrate America to the end that this great nation of ours, born in revolution and blood, "conceived in liberty, and dedicated to the proposition that all men are created equal," will truly become the lighthouse of freedom where none will be denied because his skin is black and none favored because his eyes are blue.

—IN COLUMBUS SALLEY, THE BLACK 100 (1993)

Willie Mays

(1 9 3 1 –)

Born in Fairfield, Alabama, Mays began playing professional baseball at seventeen with the Birmingham Black Barons. In 1951, he joined the major league with the New York (later San Francisco) Giants. In twenty-two seasons, he maintained a .302 average and hit 654 home runs, the third highest total on record. He was named Most Valuable Player in 1954 and 1965 and was elected to the Baseball Hall of Fame in 1979.

Maybe I was born to play ball. Maybe I truly was.

—EBONY, AUGUST 1955

Every time I look at my pocketbook, I see Jackie Robinson.

—WIDELY ATTRIBUTED

I don't compare 'em, I just catch 'em.

—ON HIS BEST PLAYS

I like to play happy. Baseball is a fun game, and I love it.

—SPORTING NEWS, JULY 25, 1970

They throw the ball, I hit it; they hit the ball, I catch it.

—ON HIS TECHNIQUE

I remember the last season I played. I went home after a ballgame one day, lay down on my bed, and tears came to my eyes. How can you explain that? You cry because you love her. I cried, I guess, because I loved baseball and I knew I had to leave it.

—*SABR* collection

I think I was the best baseball player I ever saw.

—Newsweek, *February 5, 1970*

I guess I talked too much.

—Willie Mays: My Life In and Out of Baseball *(1966)*

Memphis Minnie

(1 8 9 6 – 1 9 7 3)

Born in the Mississippi Delta, the early influential blues singer and guitarist Lizzie Douglas, known as Memphis Minnie, played guitar in the streets of Memphis at a very young age. In the 1930s, she traveled to Chicago, where she was part of the blues scene for more than two decades.

You know it ain't nothing in rambling
Either running around
Well I believe I'll get me a good man
Oooooo ooo, lord, and settle down

—*"Nothing in Rambling"*

Won't you be my chauffeur
I want someone to drive me/Down town
Baby drive me crazy/I can't turn him down

—*"Me and My Chauffeur Blues"*

I woke up this morning about half past five
Woke up this morning about half past five
My baby turned over, cried just like a child
—*"Frisco Town"*

Kelly Miller

(1863 – 1939)

Born in South Carolina and educated at Howard University and Johns Hopkins, Miller returned to Howard as a professor and later dean of the College of Arts and Sciences. He was the author of Race Adjustment *(1909),* An Appeal to Conscience *(1918), and* The Everlasting Stain *(1924), as well as numerous articles on education and race.*

Circumstances not only alter causes; they alter character.
—An Appeal to Conscience *(1918)*

As God uses the humbler things of life to confound the mighty, it may be that the helpless victims of cruelty and outrage shall bring an apostate world back to God . . . Righteousness exalteth a nation, but sin is a reproach to any people.
—*Ibid.*

Civilization is not a spontaneous generation with any race or nation known to history, but the torch to be handed down from race to race from age to age.
—The American Negro *(1908)*

Crime has no color, the criminal no race. He is the common enemy of society.
—*Ibid.*

Freedom of speech is the bulwark of the weak; suppression is the weapon of the strong. If Garvey's doctrines are false, combat them with the truth; if his dealings are devious, correct them with the law; if he misleads the simple, show them the more excellent way. But by no means should the oppressed become the oppressor, nor the persecuted turn persecutor.

—"A SYMPOSIUM ON GARVEY," THE MESSENGER, DECEMBER 1922

An enslaved people has not been permitted to taste of the tree of knowledge, which is the tree of good and evil. This coveted tree has been zealously and jealously guarded by the flaming sword of prejudice, kept keen and bright by avarice and cupidity.

—"HOWARD: THE NATIONAL NEGRO UNIVERSITY," THE NEW NEGRO, 1925

Advantage and opportunity confer obligation.

—IBID.

The Negro college must furnish stimulus to hesitant Negro scholarship, garner, treasure, and nourish group tradition, enlighten both races with a sense of the cultural worth and achievement of the constituency it represents, and supply the cultural guidance of the race.

—IBID.

Mamie Till Bradley Mobley

(fl. mid-1950s)

Mamie Till Bradley Mobley, the mother of Emmett Till, who was brutally lynched while visiting relatives in Mississippi in August 1955 for ostensibly speaking "disrespectfully" to a white woman, spoke out publicly when she saw her son's body.

I wanted the whole world to see what I had seen. There was no way I could describe what was in that box. No way. And I just wanted the world to see.

—AFTER VIEWING THE BODY OF HER SON, IN HENRY HAMPTON, VOICES OF FREEDOM *(1990)*

His untimely death was the call for freedom that was heard around the world.

—JET, *AUGUST 19, 1991*

William H. A. Moore

(fl. 1920s)

Born in New York City, Moore attended City College and became a journalist. His volume of poems, Dusk Songs, *was published in 1920.*

I shall will that my soul must be cleansed of hate,
I shall pray for strength to hold children close to my heart,
I shall desire to build houses where the poor will know shelter,
   comfort, beauty.
And then may I look into a woman's eyes
And find holiness, love, and the peace which passeth understanding.

—"IT WAS NOT FATE"

Invisible I wander far from the feast,
As night grows old.

—"DUSK SONG"

Toni Morrison

(1 9 3 1 –)

*B*orn Chloe Anthony Webb in Lorain, Ohio, which forms the backdrop of many of her fictional stories, Morrison attended Howard and
Cornell universities. She taught at Texas Southern and Howard before becoming an editor at Random House, when her first novel, The
Bluest Eye, was published in 1970. Her subsequent novels have won
much critical acclaim, including Song of Solomon, which received
the American Book Award, and Beloved, which was awarded the Pulitzer Prize. She has also taught at Yale, SUNY, and, since 1988, at
Princeton. In 1993 she became the first African American woman to
be awarded the Nobel Prize for Literature.

American means white, and Africanist people struggle to make the
term applicable to themselves with ethnicity and hyphen after hyphen
after hyphen.

—PLAYING IN THE DARK: WHITENESS AND THE LITERARY IMAGINATION *(1992)*

In becoming an American, from Europe, what one has in common
with that other immigrant is contempt for *me* . . . Wherever they
were from, they would stand together. They could all say, "I am not
that" . . . When they got off the boat, the second word they learned
was "nigger."

—*"THE PAIN OF BEING BLACK," TIME, MAY 22, 1989*

I really think the range of emotions and perceptions I have had access
to as a black person and a female person are greater than those of
people who are neither. My world did not shrink because I was a black
female writer. It just got bigger.

—*INTERVIEW WITH* NEW YORK TIMES

Oppressive language does more than represent violence; it is violence; does more than represent the limits of knowledge; it limits
knowledge.

—*NOBEL PRIZE ADDRESS, DECEMBER 7, 1993*

Not a house in the country ain't packed to the rafters with some dead Negro's grief.

—BELOVED (1987)

I don't think a female running a house is a problem, a broken family. It's perceived as one because of the notion that a head is a man . . . The question is not morality, the question is money. That's what we're upset about. We don't care whether they have babies or not.

—TIME, MAY 22, 1989

She is a friend to my mind. She gathers me. The pieces I am, she gathers them and gives them back to me in all the right order. It's good when you got a woman who is a friend of your mind.

—BELOVED

A little black girl yearns for the blue eyes of a little white girl, and the horror at the heart of her yearning is exceeded only by the evil of fulfillment.

—THE BLUEST EYE (1970)

Sadness was at her center, the desolated center where the self that was no self made its home.

—BELOVED

It was a fine cry—loud and long—but it had no bottom and it had no top, just circles and circles of sorrow.

—SULA (1973)

It seems to me interesting to evaluate Black literature on what the writer does with the presence of an ancestor . . . And these ancestors are not just parents, they are sort of timeless people whose relationships to the characters are benevolent, instructive, and protective, and they provide a certain kind of wisdom . . . When you kill the ancestor, you kill yourself.

— "ROOTEDNESS: THE ANCESTOR AS FOUNDATION," IN MARI EVANS, BLACK WOMEN WRITERS (1984)

The fathers may soar,
And the children may know their names.

—EPIGRAPH, SONG OF SOLOMON (1977)

Names they got from yearnings, gestures, flaws, wins, mistakes, weaknesses. Names that bore witness.

—Song of Solomon

They sang the women they knew; the children they had been; the animals they had tamed themselves or seen others tame. They sang of bosses and masters and misses; of mules and dogs and the shamelessness of life. They sang lovingly of graveyards and sisters long gone. Of port in the woods; meal in the pan; fish on the line; cane, rain and rocking chairs.

—Beloved

It did not matter which one of them would give up his ghost in the killing arms of his brother. For now he knew what Shalimar knew: If you surrender to the air, you could *ride* it.

—Song of Solomon

We are very practical people, very down-to-earth, even shrewd people. But with that practicality we also accepted what I suppose could be called superstition and magic, which is another way of knowing things.

—"Rootedness: The Ancestor as Foundation"

I don't know whether the bird you are holding is dead or alive, but what I do know is that it is in your hands. It is in your hands.

—Nobel Prize address

You can't just fly on off and leave a body.

—Sula

Devil's confusion. He lets me look good long as I feel bad.

—Beloved

He could not help being astonished by the beauty of this land that was not his. He hid in its breast, fingered its earth for food, clung to its banks to lap water and tried not to love it.

—Ibid.

The purpose of evil was to survive it.

—Sula

There is a loneliness that can be rocked. Arms crossed, knees drawn up; holding, holding on, this motion, unlike a ship's, smooths and contains the rocker. It's an inside kind—wrapped tight like skin. Then there is a loneliness that roams. No rocking can hold it down. It is alive, on its own. A dry and spreading thing that makes the sound of one's own feet going seem to come from a far-off place.

—BELOVED

Cry . . . For the living and the dead. Just cry.

—*IBID.*

The ability of writers to imagine what is not the self, to familiarize the strange and mystify the familiar, is the test of their power.

—PLAYING IN THE DARK: WHITENESS AND THE LITERARY IMAGINATION

Africanism is inextricable from the definition of Americanness—from its origins on through its integrated or disintegrating twentieth-century self . . . It is a dark and abiding presence, there for the literary imagination as both a visible and an invisible mediating force.

—*IBID.*

I simply wanted to write literature that was irrevocably, indisputably Black, not because its characters were, or because I was, but because it took as its creative task and sought as its credentials those recognized and verifiable principles of Black art.

—*"MEMORY, CREATION, AND WRITING"*

If anything I do . . . isn't about the village or the community or about you, then it is not about anything . . . It seems to me that the best art is political and you ought to be able to make it unquestionably political and irrevocably beautiful at the same time.

—*"ROOTEDNESS: THE ANCESTOR AS FOUNDATION"*

We die. That may be the meaning of life. But we do language. That may be the measure of our lives.

—*NOBEL PRIZE ADDRESS*

Jelly Roll Morton

(c . 1 8 8 5 – 1 9 4 1)

Born Ferdinand Le Menthe, probably in New Orleans, Morton was raised by his grandmother and began playing in sporting houses in Storyville when he was still in his teens. A memorable figure with a diamond set in his gold front tooth, he later played in Memphis, Saint Louis, Chicago, New York, Houston, and Los Angeles with his Red Hot Peppers and other bands.

Originator of Jazz.

—*ENGRAVED ON HIS CALLING CARD*

I'm just the whining boy
Don't deny my name.

—*WININ' BOY BLUES*

The sporting houses needed professors, and we had so many different styles that whenever you came to New Orleans, it wouldn't make any difference that you just came from Paris or any part of England, Europe, or anyplace—whatever your tunes were over there, we played them in New Orleans.

—*IN* NAT SHAPIRO AND NAT HENTOFF, HEAR ME TALKIN' TO YA

Get up from that piano. You hurtin' its feelings.

—*JIBE TO ANOTHER PIANIST TO LET HIM PLAY*

Not until 1926 did they get a fair idea of real jazz, when I decided to live in New York.

—*IN* HEAR ME TALKIN' TO YA

In 1908 Handy didn't know anything about the blues and he doesn't know anything about jazz and stomps to this day . . . I myself figured out the peculiar form of mathematics and harmonies that was strange to all the world but me.

—*DISPUTING THAT* W. C. HANDY *WAS THE* "FATHER OF THE BLUES";
IN "I DISCOVERED JAZZ IN 1902," DOWN BEAT

My contributions were many: First clown director, with witty sayings and flashily dressed, now called master of ceremonies.

—*IBID.*

I have been robbed of three million dollars all told. Everyone today is playing my stuff and I don't even get credit. Kansas City style, Chicago style, New Orleans style—hell, they're all Jelly Roll style.

—*IN* HEAR ME TALKIN' TO YA

Carol Moseley-Braun

(1 9 4 7 –)

After Braun received her law degree from the University of Chicago, she was elected to the Illinois legislature in 1978 and became assistant majority leader four years later. When the Anita Hill–Clarence Thomas hearings highlighted the underrepresentation of women in Congress, Braun, then the Cook County recorder of deeds, declared her candidacy, and in 1992 she became the first black woman to be seated in the U.S. Senate.

I don't know of one woman who hasn't been sexually harassed. Men just don't get it. It's an economic issue for women . . . It has to do with equality in the workplace.

—*ANNOUNCING HER CANDIDACY ON* "CHICAGO TONIGHT," *NOVEMBER 1991*

If I lose, I'm going to retire from politics, practice law, and wear bright leather pants.

—*HER PLANS IF SHE LOST THE SENATE RACE, IN* NEW REPUBLIC, *NOVEMBER 15, 1993*

I've always maintained that black people and women suffer from a presumption of incompetence. The burdens of proof are different. It just gets so tiresome.

—Chicago Tribune, *during potential crises in her campaign*

I feel like I've been raped by you guys already, and I just figure this rape has gone on long enough. Quite frankly, for me to continue to lie back and let you guys do this is just asinine.

—*press conference during campaign*

It's hard to be the first. It's almost as if I'm subject to a different level of inspection.

—*in* The New Republic, *November 15, 1993*

There are some sensitivities I'd like my colleagues to be aware of. If you call people to right, if you call them to the moral high ground, they can and will respond.

—*on the* Confederate *flag issue, Ibid.*

Defining myself, as opposed to being defined by others, is one of the most difficult challenges I face.

—*Ibid.*

Bob $Moses$

(1 9 3 5 –)

Born in Harlem, Moses earned an M.A. in philosophy from Harvard University. As Mississippi State Project Director for SNCC and co-director of the Mississippi Summer Project in 1964, he led voter-registration drives and was assaulted and jailed on several occasions.

You dig into yourself and the community to wage psychological warfare; you combat your own fears about beatings, shootings, and possible mob violence . . . you create a small striking force capable of moving out when the time comes, which it must, whether we help it or not.

—*Letter to Northern supporters, from Greenville, Mississippi, February 27, 1963*

This is a tremor in the middle of the iceberg—from a stone that the builders rejected.

—*Letter from prison during the Mississippi Voting Rights Campaign, November 1, 1961*

I justify myself because I'm taking risks myself, and I'm not asking people to do things I'm not willing to do . . . If you are going to do anything about it, other people are going to be killed. No privileged group in history has ever given up anything without some kind of blood sacrifice, something.

—*In Sally Belfrage, Freedom Summer (1965)*

There is a weariness . . . from constant attention to the things you are doing, the struggle of good against evil.

—*Ibid.*

Robert Russa Moton

(1 8 6 7 – 1 9 4 0)

Educated at Hampton Institute, Moton succeeded Washington as principal of Tuskegee in 1916. He is the author of Racial Good Will *(1916) and* Finding a Way Out *as well as many essays and speeches.*

It is often said that the destiny of the Negro is in the hands of Southern whites. I can tell you that the reverse is also true.

—*Finding a Way Out (1920)*

Booker Washington made a religion out of life for his people and few indeed were those who heard one of his talks who came away without getting this kind of religion.

—*"Hampton-Tuskegee: Missioners of the Masses,"* The New Negro *(1925)*

₤lijah 〈Muhammad

(1 8 9 7 – 1 9 7 5)

Born in rural Georgia, Elijah Poole left school at a young age and in 1923 moved to Detroit, where he worked in an automobile plant and met Wallace D. Fard, the founder of the Nation of Islam. After Fard disappeared in 1934, his disciple became leader of the Nation of Islam, changing his name and moving to Chicago. For the next four decades, he helped establish more than 150 temples across the United States, as well as a network of restaurants, banks, markets, and other industries. On his death, he was succeeded by his son, Wallace D. Muhammad.

A prime requisite for freedom and independence is having one's own land. There can be no freedom without a people having its own land.

—*in E. U. Essien-Udom,* Black Nationalism *(1962)*

Let us refrain from doing evil to each other, and let us love each other as brothers, as we are the same flesh and blood . . . It is a fool who does not love himself and his people.

—Message to the Black Man *(1965)*

The day has arrived that you will have to help yourselves or suffer the worst.

—Pittsburgh Courier, *September 3, 1958*

Not one of us will have to raise a sword. Not one gun would we need to fire. The great cannon that will be fired is our unity.

—MESSAGE TO THE BLACK MAN

Accept your place in the sun as it was originally before the creation of this world . . . The black man is the first and last, maker and owner of the universe.

—*IBID.*

We cannot be equal with the master until we own what the master owns. We cannot be equal with the master until we have the freedom the master enjoys. We cannot be equal with the master until we have the education the master has. Then, we can say, "Master, recognize us as your equal."

—*IBID.*

Integration means self-destruction, death, and nothing else.

—BLACK NATIONALISM

Discard your former slave-master's names and be willing and ready to accept one of Allah's Pure and Righteous Names that He Alone will give our people from His Own Mouth! A good name is, indeed, better than gold.

—A MESSAGE TO THE BLACK MAN

Islam comes after everything else fails.

—*IBID.*

*W*allace *D*. *M*uhammad

(1 9 3 4 –)

The son of Elijah Muhammad, the younger Muhammad succeeded his father as head of the Nation of Islam after the latter's death in 1975. He renamed the group the World Community of Islam.

We are not Black Muslims and never have been. We're a world community—a community that encompasses everybody.

—Cleveland Plain Dealer, *October 10, 1976*

We can't think [of separation] . . . and live in America and claim a share in the benefits of this country you know. If we are going to live in this country and claim a share in the fruits of this country, then we have to identify in the national aspirations of the people.

—*in Columbus Salley,* The Black 100 *(1993)*

$\mathcal{G}loria\ \mathcal{N}aylor$

(1 9 5 0 –)

Born in New York City, Gloria Naylor was for seven years a Jehovah's Witness missionary before she attended Brooklyn College and received her master's degree from Yale University. The Women of Brewster Place, *which received the American Book Award in 1983, was the first of her highly acclaimed novels; Naylor has taught at many universities.*

It's as if I've arrived in a place where it's all spirit and no body—an overwhelming sense of calm . . . I actually began to feel blessed.

—*on writing, in Valerie Smith, et al.,* African-American Writers *(1991)*

Now me, when I want ready-made trouble, I dig up a handsome man

—*"Mattie Michael,"* The Women of Brewster Place *(1982)*

Sometimes being a friend means mastering the art of timing. There is a time for silence. A time to let go and allow people to hurl them selves into their own destiny. And a time to prepare to pick up the pieces when it's all over.

—"ETTA MAE JOHNSON," IBID.

I am alive because of the blood of proud people who never scraped or begged or apologized for what they were. They lived asking only one thing of this world—to be allowed to be. And I learned through the blood of these people that black isn't beautiful and it isn't ugly—black is!

—"KISWANA BROWNE," IBID.

I got nothing, but you welcome to all of that.

—"THE TWO," IBID.

Linden Hills wasn't black; it was successful. The shining surface of their careers, brass railings, and cars . . . only reflected the bright nothing that was inside of them.

—LINDEN HILLS (1985)

His entire life was becoming a race against the natural—and he was winning.

—IBID.

It ain't really what you'd call change. It's all happened before and it'll happen again with a different set of facts.

—MAMA DAY (1988)

Can't nothing be wrong in bringing on life, knowing how to get under, around, and beside nature to give it a slight push. Most folks just don't know what can be done with a little will and their own hands.

—IBID.

It's only an ancient mother of pure black that one day spits out this kinda gold.

—IBID.

Think about it: ain't nobody really talking to you . . . Uh, huh, listen. Really listen this time: the only voice is your own.

—IBID.

It seems like God reached way down into his box of paints, found the purest reds, the deepest purples, and a dab of midnight blue, then just kinda trailed his fingers along the curve of the horizon and let 'em all bleed down. And when them streaks of color hit the hush-a-by green of the marsh grass with the blue of The Sound behind 'em, you ain't never had to set foot in a church to know you looking at a living prayer.

—MAMA DAY

Not only is your story worth telling, but it can be told in words so painstakingly eloquent that it becomes a song.

—IN VALERIE SMITH, ET AL., AFRICAN-AMERICAN WRITERS (1991)

Larry Neal

(1 9 3 7 – 1 9 8 1)

Born in Atlanta, Neal was raised in Philadelphia and attended Lincoln University and the University of Pennsylvania. With Amiri Baraka, he edited the important anthology Black Fire *in 1968 during the Black Arts Movement, and published several volumes of his own poetry.*

I have drunk deep of the waters of my ancestors.

—"MALCOLM X—AN AUTOBIOGRAPHY"

America is the world's greatest jailer,
and we all in jails. Black spirits contained like magnificent
birds of wonder.

—IBID.

Black women, timeless,
are sun breaths

are crying mothers
are snatched rhythms.
—*"For Our Women"*

The artist and the political activist are one. They are both shapers of
the future reality. Both understand and manipulate the collective
myths of the race. Both are warriors, priests, lovers, and destroyers.
—*in Addison Gayle, Jr.,* The Black Aesthetic, *1971*

For the blues singer, the world is his text . . . Like any artist, the
blues singer has the task of bringing order out of chaos.
—*"The Ethos of the Blues,"* The Black Scholar, *Summer 1972*

The end of formal slavery would . . . alter the slave's horizon of
experience. He would have to confront his own name.
—*Ibid.*

You see it's like this: boxing is just another kind of rhythm activity.
Like all sports is based on rhythm. Dig: if you ain't got no rhythm,
you can't play no sports.
—*"Uncle Rufus Raps on the Squared Circle,"* Partisan Review, *Spring 1972*

Now Ali understands these principles of rhythm and music. Theoreti-
cally, that's what so sweet about him. You see, he believes in riffing.
He certainly has got the body, the legs, and the mouth for it. But
Frazier is somewhere else in the musical universe. Frazier is stomp-
down blues, bacon, grits, and Sunday church.
—*Ibid.*

William C. Nell

(1 8 1 6 – 1 8 7 4)

*Abolitionist, convention delegate, and historian, Nell was the author
of one of the earliest works of African American history.*

I yield to no one in appreciating the propriety and pertinency of every *effort*, on the part of Colored Americans, in *all* pursuits, which, as members of the human family, it becomes them to share in.

—Services of Colored Americans in the Wars of 1776 and 1812 *(1851)*

Any man among us, voting for their respective candidates, virtually recognizes the righteousness of their principles, and shall be held up to public reprobation as a traitor, a hissing and a byword, a pest and a nuisance, and the offscouring of the earth.

—on the current political parties, letter to William Lloyd Garrison, The Liberator, *December 10, 1852*

Our brethren at the South should not be called *slaves,* but *prisoners of war.*

—Ibid.

To organize the militia of the country is one thing; to dishonor and outrage a portion of the citizens, on any ground, is a very different thing. To do the former, Congress is clothed with ample constitutional authority; to accomplish the latter, it has no power to legislate, and resort must be had, and has been had, to usurpation and tyranny.

—arguing for the right of African Americans to perform military service; petition sent to Massachusetts Constitutional Convention, August 1, 1853

While I would not in the smallest degree detract from the credit justly due the *men* for their conspicuous exertions in this reform, truth enjoins upon me the pleasing duty of acknowledging that to the *women,* and the *children* also, is the cause especially indebted . . . It was these mothers who accompanied me to the various school-houses, to residences of teachers and committee-men, to see the laws of the Old Bay State applied in good faith.

—fighting Jim Crow schools in Boston, September 1855

I have borne allegiance to principles, rather than men.

—The Liberator, *December 15, 1953*

Huey P. Newton

(c. 1944 –)

The son of a Baptist minister, Newton was involved in community social programs in Oakland, California, when he and Bobby Seale founded the Black Panther Party in October 1966. On October 28, 1967, he received four bullet wounds in his stomach and was arrested for the killing of a policeman. The incident led the Panthers to conduct a "Free Huey" campaign, and his conviction was overturned by the California State of Appeals in 1971.

The Black Panthers were and are always required to keep their activities within legal bounds . . . So, we studied the law about weapons and kept within our rights.

—Revolutionary Suicide *(1973)*

The police have never been our protectors . . . With weapons in our hand, we were no longer their subjects but their equals.

—*Ibid.*

We were trying to increase the conflict that was already happening and that was between the white racism, the police forces in the various communities, and the black communities in the country. And we felt that we would take the conflict to so high a level that some change had to come.

—*In* Henry Hampton, Voices of Freedom *(1990)*

I know sociologically that words, the power of the word, words stigmatize people. We felt that the police needed a label, a label other than that fear image that they carried in the community. So we used the pig as the rather low-lifed animal in order to identify the police. And it worked.

—*Ibid.*

The Niagara Movement

The Niagara Movement was founded in reaction to the accommodationist principles and political monopoly exercised by Booker T. Washington. Led by William Monroe Trotter and W. E. B. Du Bois, in July 1905, a group of twenty-nine business and educational leaders met in Ontario, where they issued a declaration of principles outlining a policy of self-determination.

We believe that no man is so good, intelligent, or wealthy as to be entrusted wholly with the welfare of his neighbor.

—*PROGRAM OF THE NIAGARA MOVEMENT, JULY 1905*

We note with alarm the evident retrogression in this land of sound public opinion on the subject of manhood rights, republican government, and human brotherhood and we pray God that this nation will not degenerate into a mob of boasters and oppressors, but rather will return to the faith of the fathers, that all men were created free and equal, with certain unalienable rights.

—*IBID.*

Any discrimination based simply on race or color is barbarous, we care not how hallowed it be by custom, expediency, or prejudice.

—*IBID.*

We regret that this nation has never seen fit adequately to reward the black soldiers who, in its five wars, have defended their country with their blood, and yet have been systematically denied the promotions which their abilities deserve.

—*IBID.*

We repudiate the monstrous doctrine that the oppressor should be the sole authority as to the rights of the oppressed. The Negro race in

America, stolen, ravished, and degraded, struggling up through difficulties and oppression, needs sympathy and receives criticism; needs help and is given hindrances, needs protection and is given mob-violence, needs justice and is given charity, needs leadership and is given cowardice and apology, needs bread and is given a stone. This nation will never stand justified before God until these things are changed.

—*IBID.*

Persistent manly agitation is the way to liberty, and toward this goal the Niagara Movement has started and asks the cooperation of all men of all races . . . [T]he voice of protest of ten million Americans must never cease to assail the ears of their fellows, so long as America is unjust.

—*IBID.*

Jessye Norman

(1 9 4 5 –)

Norman was born in Augusta, Georgia, and at the age of sixteen entered the Marian Anderson Scholarship competition in Philadelphia. Though unsuccessful, she was awarded a scholarship to Howard University and went on to the Peabody Conservatory of Music in Baltimore and received a master's degree from the University of Michigan in 1968. She pursued a successful career in Europe—she is said to be the inspiration for Jean-Jacques Beineix's film Diva—*and made her Metropolitan Opera début in 1983. She is also a popular recitalist and recording star.*

The very best thing that could happen to a voice, if it shows any promise at all, is when it is very young to leave it alone and to let it develop quite naturally, and to let the person go on as long as possible with the sheer joy of singing—rather than being concerned with what comes later; the necessary concern for vocal technique.

—INTERVIEW IN CONNOISSEUR, IN ROSALYN M. STORY, AND SO I SING: AFRICAN AMERICAN DIVAS OF OPERA AND CONCERT (1993)

I'm not interested in so-called mainstream repertory. I have not become a Verdi heroine soprano, and, of course, that's what's needed in opera houses . . . To sing roles with which I have no empathy would be wrong.

—NEW YORK TIMES INTERVIEW, 1984

If you send up a weather vane or put your thumb up in the air every time you want to do something different, to find out what people are going to think about it, you're going to limit yourself. That's a very strange way to live.

—NEW YORK TIMES INTERVIEW, 1987

I am grateful that my horizons were not narrowed at the outset.

—c. 1981

Solomon $\mathcal{N}$orthrup

(1 8 0 9 – ?)

Born free in New York, Northrup was kidnapped while on a trip to Washington, D.C., and was held in slavery in Louisiana for twelve years, until he was able to get word to his wife, who succeeded in petitioning for his freedom in 1853.

She wanted to be with her children, she said, the little time she had to live. All the frowns and threats of Freeman could not wholly silence the afflicted mother.

—ON A SLAVE AUCTION, TWELVE YEARS A SLAVE (1853)

When a new hand, one unaccustomed to the business, is sent for the first time into the field, he is whipped up smartly, and made for that day to pick as fast as he can possibly. At night it is weighed, so that his capability for cotton picking is known. He must bring in the same weight each night following. If it falls short, it is considered evidence that he has been laggard, and a greater or less number of lashes is the penalty.

—*Ibid.*

Then the fears and labors of another day begin; and until its close there is no such thing as rest. He fears he will be caught lagging through the day; he fears to approach the gin-house with his basket-load of cotton at night; he fears, when he lies down, that he will oversleep himself in the morning. Such is a true, faithful, unexaggerated picture and description of the slave's daily life, during the time of cotton-picking, on the shores of Bayou Boeuf.

—*Ibid.*

Eleanor Holmes Norton

(1 9 3 8 –)

Born in Washington, D.C., Norton received her law degree from Yale and was an attorney and activist during the 1970s. She served as chair of the Equal Employment Opportunity Commission and taught law at the Georgetown University Law Center before becoming the nonvoting D.C. delegate to the U.S. Congress in 1990.

There is a large role for the government here, and there is a role that only black people can attend to. Nobody can reconstruct the black family and bring it to its historic strength except us. We've got to demand that the programs that should be available to us in undertaking this work be made available. But also ultimately this is our job and our work . . . And there's got to be an infusion of young leadership that wants to roll up its sleeves and go to work at the *hard* problems in the black community that will take more than money.

—*IN HENRY HAMPTON,* VOICES OF FREEDOM *(1990)*

Blacks get their moral authority not only because they were pressing for their own rights, but because they did so in a way that wrote equality lessons large . . . Our freedom is precious and important, but in the end what gives our movement its majesty is the example it set throughout the world for people of color and for people who in any way were oppressed and found in that example a reason to hope and strive for a different life.

—*IBID.*

Jesse Owens

(1 9 1 3 – 1 9 8 0)

Nicknamed Jesse after his initials, James Cleveland Owens was born in rural Alabama and had earned national recognition for his athletic prowess while still in high school. He enrolled at Ohio State University and, at the national collegiate championships in May 1935, he tied or surpassed six world records. The following year he earned four Gold Medals at the Berlin Olympics in a dramatic rebuttal of Adolf Hitler's theories of white supremacy.

After I came home from the 1936 Olympics with my four medals, it became increasingly apparent that everyone was going to slap me on the back, want to shake my hand, or have me up to their suite. But no one was going to offer me a job.

—*IN COLUMBUS SALLEY,* THE BLACK 100 *(1993)*

The battles that count aren't the ones for gold medals. The struggles within yourself—the invisible, inevitable battles inside all of us—that's where it's at.

—BLACKTHINK *(1970)*

One chance is all you need.

—*IBID.*

ℒeroy (Satchel) ℙaige

(1 9 0 6 – 1 9 8 2)

From Mobile, Alabama, Paige began playing ball at the age of eighteen with the Mobile Tigers. He also played with Chattanooga, New Orleans, and the Pittsburg Crawfords. He pitched for the Cleveland Indians in the 1948 World Series and played for three seasons for the Saint Louis Browns. He was inducted into the Baseball Hall of Fame in 1971.

I used to feel so bad before I got to the clubhouse, I didn't know what to do. But when I put that ballsuit on, I don't know where I got the spark to save my life.

—*ON FACING PREJUDICE, IN DON ROGOSIN,* INVISIBLE MEN:
LIFE IN BASEBALL'S NEGRO LEAGUES *(1983)*

1. Avoid fried meats which angry up the blood.
2. If your stomach disputes you, lie down and pacify it with cool thoughts.
3. Keep the juices flowing by jangling around gently as you move.
4. Go very light on the vices, such as carrying on in society. The social ramble ain't restful.
5. Avoid running at all times.
6. Don't look back. Something might be gaining on you.

—*ON "HOW TO STAY YOUNG," WIDELY ATTRIBUTED*

Age is a question of mind over matter. It you don't mind, it doesn't matter.

— *WIDELY QUOTED*

Ain't no man can avoid being average, but there ain't no man got to be common.

— *WIDELY QUOTED*

With women, it's like this: I'm not married, but I'm in great demand.

— *WIDELY QUOTED*

It got so I could nip frosting off a cake with my fastball.

— *MAYBE I'LL PITCH FOREVER (1962)*

Just take the ball and throw it where you want to . . . Home plate don't move.

— *HIS PITCHING ADVICE*

Millionaires took over, and changed the game completely.

— *AP, FEBRUARY 3, 1981*

I never threw an illegal pitch. The trouble is, once in a while I tossed one that ain't never been seen by this generation.

— *WASHINGTON POST, JUNE 10, 1982*

Don't pray when it rains if you don't pray when the sun shines.

— *CIRCA 1945, WIDELY ATTRIBUTED*

Listen, if I had it to do all over again, I would. I had more fun and seen more places with less money than if I was Rockefeller.

— *WIDELY QUOTED AT THE TIME OF HIS DEATH*

Charlie Parker

(1 9 2 0 – 1 9 5 5)

A master improvisor, Charles Christopher Parker was born in Kansas City, Kansas, and started playing saxophone at eleven. Self-taught by listening for hours outside clubs while he was under age, he joined his first band at seventeen and worked with Hines, Monk, Gillespie, and others. In 1948 the café Birdland was named in his honor in New York, but waging a constant struggle with drugs he died at thirty-five. Still, "Bird Lives" in his enormous influence on younger artists like Miles Davis and Max Roach.

Music is your own experience, your thoughts, your wisdom. If you don't live it, it won't come out of your horn. They teach you there's a boundary line to music. But, man, there's no boundary line to art.

—*IN NAT SHAPIRO AND NAT HENTOFF,* HEAR ME TALKIN' TO YA *(1955)*

I realized by using the high notes of the chords as a melodic line, and by the right harmonic progression, I could play what I heard inside me. That's when I was born.

—*C. 1939, IN GÉRALD ARNAUD AND JACQUES CHESNEL,* MASTERS OF JAZZ *(1991)*

Any musician who says he is playing better either on tea, the needle, or when he is juiced, is a plain straight liar . . . You can miss the most important years of your life, the years of possible creation.

—*IN NAT SHAPIRO AND NAT HENTOFF,* HEAR ME TALKIN' TO YA

Junior Parker

(1 9 2 7 -   )

From West Memphis, Parker began recording the Delta sound on the Sun label with "Little Junior's Blue Flames." His best-known blues, "Mystery Train," was later recorded by Elvis Presley.

Anybody can boil up some greens, but a good cook—a good one—has a special way of seasoning 'em that ain't like nobody else's. So anybody can do it but it's only somebody who can do it their own way.

— *IN CHARLES KEIL*, URBAN BLUES *(1966)*

Gordon Parks

(1 9 1 2 -   )

Born in Fort Scott, Kansas, Parks worked at various jobs in his youth before buying a camera and becoming a successful photojournalist. He was a correspondent during World War II and in 1948 became a staff photographer for Life. *Though he never completed high school, he is the author of more than a dozen books and the recipient of more than fifty honorary degrees, and he was also the director of the films* Shaft *and* Shaft's Big Score.

Many times I wondered whether my achievement was worth the loneliness I experienced, but now I realize the price was small . . . [T]here is nothing ignoble about a black man climbing from the troubled darkness on a white man's ladder, providing he doesn't forsake the others who, subsequently, must escape that same darkness.

—"What Their Cry Means to Me," Life, May 31, 1963

In the course of a career that has thrust me into contact with virtually every kind of person and has taken me several times around the world, I have come to realize the universality of man.

—Ibid.

Most of us are wondering about the "new" Negro—and how he got this way. But he isn't new and he didn't get this way overnight. He has been stirring for a long time, while his country tucked the Emancipation Proclamation under her head for a pillow and went to sleep.

—Ibid.

America is me. It gave me the only life I know, so I must share in its survival.

—Born Black (1971)

Nothing came easy. I was just born with a need to explore every toolshop of my mind, and with long searching and hard work.

—Voices in the Mirror (1990)

Success can be wracking and reproachful, to you and those close to you. It can entangle you with legends that are consuming and all but impossible to live up to.

—Ibid.

I do find a certain fascination with the unpredictable. The transitory years we wade through are what they are—what we make of them.

—Ibid.

I'm still happy to be here, and I'm clever enough to know that my date of departure remains time's secret. I trust time. It has been my friend for a long while, and we have been through a lot together.

—Ibid.

Rosa Parks

(1 9 1 3 –   )

When this NAACP organizer refused to give up her seat to a white man on a bus in Alabama on December 1, 1955, she helped start the year-long Montgomery bus boycott, in which Martin Luther King, Jr., first came to national attention. Born in Tuskegee, Alabama, Parks has worked tirelessly for social reform.

It was not at all pre-arranged. It just happened that the driver made a demand and I just didn't feel like obeying his demand . . . I was quite tired after spending a full day working. I handle and work on clothing that white people wear. That didn't come into my mind but this is what I wanted to know: when and how would we ever determine our rights as human beings.

—WORKSHOP AT THE HIGHLANDER FOLK SCHOOL, MONTEAGLE, TENNESSEE, MARCH 1956

We didn't have any of what they called Civil Rights back then. It was just a matter of survival—existing from day to day.

—IN BLACKS IN DETROIT (1980)

I was determined to achieve the total freedom that our history lessons taught us we were entitled to, no matter what the sacrifice.

—"THE MEANING OF LIFE," LIFE, DECEMBER 1988

Memories of our lives, of our works and our deeds will continue in others.

—IBID.

ℱloyd ℛatterson

(1 9 3 5 –)

Born in North Carolina, Patterson won an Olympic Gold Medal in 1952 and earned the heavyweight title by defeating Archie Moore on November 30, 1956. On June 26, 1960, he became the first heavyweight to gain the title a second time in a rematch with Ingemar Johansson, but suffered later defeats to Sonny Liston and Muhammad Ali.

There is so much hate among people, so much contempt inside people who'd like you to think they're moral, that they have to hire prizefighters to do their hating for them. And we do. We get into a ring and act out other people's hates.

— ESQUIRE, *AUGUST 1966*

A prizefighter who gets knocked out or is badly outclassed suffers in a way he will never forget.

— *IBID.*

I felt I had let so many people down, all of America.

— *ON THE LOSS OF HIS HEAVYWEIGHT TITLE TO INGEMAR JOHANSSON, A SWEDE, JUNE 26, 1959, IN PETER HELLER, IN THIS CORNER (1973)*

It's not so bad for politicians and Pulitzer Prize poets and certain intellectuals in this country to sign petitions and speak out against the war in Vietnam, but when Cassius Clay did it he paid a heavy price for Freedom of Speech.

— *C. 1966, ON MUHAMMAD ALI'S BEING STRIPPED OF HIS TITLE*

The fighter loses more than his pride in the fight; he loses part of his future. He's a step closer to the slum he came from.

— *C. 1970*

It's easy to do anything in victory. It's in defeat that a man reveals himself.

—IN HENRY MULLAN, THE BOOK OF BOXING QUOTATIONS *(1988)*

ℛeverend 𝒩athaniel 𝒫aul

(1 7 7 5 – 1 8 3 9)

Pastor of the first African Baptist Society of Albany, Paul was a prominent abolitionist and associate of William Lloyd Garrison. He spent several months lecturing and raising support for the abolition cause in England.

The progress of emancipation, though slow, is nevertheless certain: it is certain, because that God who has made of one blood all nations of men, and who is said to be no respector of persons, has so decreed; I therefore have no hesitation in declaring from this sacred place, that not only throughout the United States of America but throughout every part of this habitable world where slavery exists, it will be abolished.

—ON THE OCCASION OF THE ABOLITION OF SLAVERY IN NEW YORK, JULY 5, 1827

I have not failed to give Uncle Sam due credit for his 2,000,000 slaves; nor to expose the cruel prejudices of the Americans to our colored race . . . And is this, they say, republican liberty? God deliver us from it.

—LETTER TO WILLIAM LLOYD GARRISON FROM ENGLAND, APRIL 10, 1833

Yes, sir, Britons shall know that there are men in America, and whole towns of them, too, who are not so destitute of true heroism but tha' they can assail a helpless woman, surround her house by night, breal her windows, and drag her to prison, for the treasonable act of teaching females of color to read!!!

—LETTER FROM ENGLAND ON THE MOBBING OF A QUAKER SCHOOL FOR BLACK CHILDREN, AUGUST 29, 1833

William Pickens

(1 8 8 1 – 1 9 5 4)

Born in South Carolina, Pickens was educated at Yale, where he was elected to Phi Beta Kappa, and at Fisk. He became dean at Morgan State University and was for more than twenty years a field secretary for the NAACP. His autobiography, Bursting Bounds, was published in 1923.

Those who quote providence are almost without exception the Negro's most active enemies.

— "THE ULTIMATE EFFECTS OF SEGREGATION AND DISCRIMINATION" (1915)

An insignificant right becomes important when it is assailed.

—IBID.

Color had been made the mark of enslavement and was taken to be also the mark of inferiority; for prejudice does not reason, or it would not be prejudice . . . If prejudice could reason, it would dispel itself.

—THE NEW NEGRO (1916)

t is not the ought-ness of this problem that we have to consider, but he is-ness!

—IN CHILDREN OF THE SLAVES (c. 1919)

'll tell you who is the greatest agitator in this country . . . the reatest agitator is injustice.

—IBID.

The moral standard of the Whites is written in the flesh and blood of three million of our race.

—*IBID.*

Lynching and mob violence are only methods of economic repression.

—*ON THE FOUNDING OF THE AMERICAN CIVIL LIBERTIES UNION, MAY 1921*

Why, I ask you, is God always shown as white? It is because He is the white man's God. It is the God of our masters. (Yes, brother, that's it.) It's the God of those who persecute and despise the coloured people. Brothers, we've got to knock that white God down and put up a black God—we've got to rewrite the Old Testament and the New from a black man's point of view.

—*IN COLUMBUS SALLEY,* THE BLACK 100 *(1993)*

The best time to do a thing is when it can be done.

—*IN ERIC V. COPAGE,* BLACK PEARLS *(1993)*

Billie Pierce

(1 9 0 7 - 1 9 7 4)

Born Willie Madison Goodson, the early jazz pianist Pierce left home at fifteen and, after traveling in the South for several years during the Depression, became a fixture in the New Orleans jazz scene.

I don't know if it was rough or not. I was rough right along with it

—*ON THE EARLY DAYS OF JAZZ, INTERVIEW OCTOBER 7, 1959*

P. B. S. Pinchback

(1 8 3 7 – 1 9 2 1)

Born in Macon, Georgia, of a white father and a black mother, Pinckney Benton Stewart Pinchback was educated as a free man in Ohio. During the Reconstruction era, he held a number of offices in Louisiana before being elected to the U.S. Senate in 1872, but was denied his seat by a vote of his colleagues. During the early 1900s, he was an ally of Booker T. Washington and was also active in the black press.

We are an element of strength and wealth too powerful to be ignored by the American People. All we need is a just appreciation of our own power and our own manhood.

—*ADDRESS TO THE CONVENTION OF COLORED NEWSPAPER MEN, CINCINNATI, OHIO, AUGUST 1875*

If the law, both constitutional and statutory, affecting the rights and privileges of the colored citizens can be defiantly ignored and disobeyed in eleven States of the Union . . . who can tell where it will end and how long it will be before elections in all of the States will be armed conflicts, to be decided by the greatest prowess and dexterity in the use of the bowie knife, pistol, shotgun and rifle?

—*IBID.*

This rolling in the dust—this truckling to power, whether wrapped up in an individual or a party, I have long since abandoned. I strike out boldly, as if born in a desert and looking for civilization. I am groping about through this American forest of prejudice and proscription, determined to find some form of civilization where all men will be accepted for what they are worth.

—*IBID.*

Ann Plato

(1 8 2 0 ? – ?)

Plato's Essays: Including Biographies and Miscellaneous Pieces in Prose and Poetry *was the first volume published by a black woman since Phillis Wheatley's* Poems on Various Subjects *almost seventy years earlier. Born in Connecticut, Plato was a teacher at the Zion Methodist Church School in Hartford and was thought to be about twenty when her book was published.*

> The greatest word that I can say,—
> I think to please, will be,
> To try and get your learning young . . .
>   —*"Advice to Young Ladies"*

> If we no more on earth do meet,
> Forget me not.
>   —*"Forget Me Not"*

> Oh! may each youthful bosom, catch the sacred fire . . .
>   *"Lines"*

We are, some of us, very fond of knowledge, and apt to value ourselves upon any proficiency in the sciences; one science, however, there is, worth more than all the rest, and that is the science of living well—which shall remain "when tongues shall cease," and "knowledge shall vanish away."
    —*"Education"*

It is owing to the preservation of books, that we are led to embrace their contents. Oral instructions can benefit but one age and one set of hearers; but these silent teachers address all ages and all nations. They may sleep for a while and be neglected; but whenever the desire

of information springs up in the human breast, there they are with
mild wisdom ready to instruct and please us.

—*Ibid.*

Adam Clayton Powell, Jr.

(1 9 0 8 – 1 9 7 2)

*Powell attended Colgate University and earned his M.A. from Co-
lumbia before receiving his Doctor of Divinity and succeeding his
father at the Abyssinian Baptist Church in New York. In 1944, he first
ran for Congress, winning the Republican, Democratic, and American Labor primaries in his district. After rising to the chairmanship of
the House Education and Labor Committee, in 1966 he was denied
his seat over a "mishandling" of funds, but his constituents re-
elected him in 1968.*

I will not be a silent congressman; I shall be vocal.

—*"Meet Adam Powell" (1944)*

We have just brought to a close the Second World War in a generation for the saving of democracy. We have a V-E Day and a V-J Day,
but we will not establish the peace until we have a V-A (Victory in
America) Day. There is no going back to yesterday. On August 6, 1945,
the old world went up in smoke over Hiroshima; we are living in a
new world, the atomic age, and there is no turning back.

—*"Let My People Go!," Houston, March 1946*

That crack of hatred, prejudice, and man's inhumanity to man. There
is not metal in the world nor skill of an artisan which can weld this
bell together so there will be no crack and its tone will be true—the
summons to pure freedom. That crack will only be closed by the unity
of blacks and whites.

—*speech at Liberty Hall, Philadelphia, July 4, 1947*

Have you ever seen a black Santa Claus?

—*URGING A CONSUMER BOYCOTT, 1963*

To demand these God-given rights is to seek black power—what I call audacious power—the power to build black institutions of splendid achievement.

—*COMMENCEMENT ADDRESS, HOWARD UNIVERSITY, MAY 29, 1966*

Once a man walked this earth and spoke with such uncommon power that He separated history into B.C. and A.D. . . . the teachings He proclaimed become newer and more challenging as the centuries roll.

—ADAM BY ADAM *(1971)*

No one can say that Christianity has failed. It has never been tried.

—MARCHING BLACKS *(1945)*

Colin Powell

(1 9 3 7 –)

Born in Harlem of Jamaican parents, Colin Luther Powell received his B.S. in geology from City College in New York, where he joined the ROTC. After serving two tours of duty in Vietnam, he held various military and political positions in Washington before he was named chairman of the Joint Chiefs of Staff by President Bush in 1989 and in 1991 orchestrated the Operation Desert Storm assault on Iraq.

While I had been fighting in Vietnam alongside brave soldiers trying to preserve their freedom, in my own land a long-simmering conflict had turned into an open fight in our streets and cities—a fight that had to be won.

—*IN COLUMBUS SALLEY,* THE BLACK 100 *(1993)*

There are no more major civil rights laws to be passed. What we are dealing with now is changing of hearts, changing of perspective and of minds.

—PARADE, *AUGUST 1989*

Americans do remember . . . we [will] never rest until everyone—every Vietnam POW and MIA—is accounted for.

—*SPEECH AT THE VIETNAM VETERANS MEMORIAL, MEMORIAL DAY, 1991*

These were not ordinary men and women and Tuskegee. If there is one thing about the history of the Tuskegee Airmen that is as unmistakable as the silhouette of a P–51, it is the fact that *these were not ordinary people*. They were *extra*ordinary men and women.

—*SPEECH AT TWENTIETH ANNUAL NATIONAL CONVENTION OF TUSKEGEE AIRMEN, DETROIT, AUGUST 1991*

The one rule I always follow: If all else fails and we have no choice, tell the truth.

—WASHINGTONIAN, *c. 1990*

Colin Powell's Rules, kept on his desk in the Pentagon:
1. It ain't as bad as you think. It will look better in the morning.
2. Get mad, then get over it.
3. Avoid having your ego so close to your position that, when your position fails, your ego goes with it.
4. It can be done!
5. Be careful what you choose. You may get it.
6. Don't let adverse facts stand in the way of a good decision.
7. You can't make someone else's choices. You shouldn't let someone else make yours.
8. Check small things.
9. Share credit.
10. Remain calm. Be kind.
11. Have a vision. Be demanding.
12. Don't take counsel of your fears or naysayers.
13. Perpetual optimism is a force multiplier.

Our strategy for going after this army is very, very simple. First we are going to cut it off, and then we are going to kill it.

—*PENTAGON PRESS CONFERENCE ON OPERATION DESERT STORM, JANUARY 23, 1991*

Though we dream of returning to our loved ones, we are ready to do our duty to our country no matter what it may be. We grieve for those we lost, and we grieve for their loved ones, and we ask that God hold them close and give them comfort.

—*MEMORIAL SERVICE FOR PERSIAN GULF SOLDIERS, CATHEDRAL OF SAINT JOHN THE DIVINE, JUNE 9, 1991*

The point I want to make to you is, role models can be black. Role models can be white. Role models can be generals. Role models can be principals, teachers, doctors, or just your parent who brought you into this world and who is trying to give you the best of everything.

—*SPEECH AT MORRIS HIGH SCHOOL IN THE SOUTH BRONX, APRIL 15, 1991*

History and destiny have made America the leader of the world that would be free. And the world that would be free is looking to us for inspiration.

—*LAST SPEECH AS CHAIRMAN OF THE JOINT CHIEFS OF STAFF, SEPTEMBER 28, 1993*

We are not committing mercenaries. We are committing sons and daughters.

—*ON DEPLOYING AMERICAN TROOPS, IBID.*

I've been a soldier all my life. I've never wanted to be anything else. I have loved every single minute of it, and I thank the nation for having given me the opportunity to serve in the proud armed forces of the United States.

—*IBID.*

Leontyne Price

(1 9 2 7 –)

Born in Mississippi, Mary Violet Leontyne Price attended the Juilliard School in New York, where she was discovered by the music critic Virgil Thomson. After performing major operatic roles in the

United States and Europe throughout the 1950s, she made her debut at the Metropolitan Opera in 1961. She participated in two presidential inaugurations and in 1982 opened a concert at Constitution Hall honoring Marian Anderson, who had been barred from singing there in 1939.

All token Blacks have the same experience. I have been pointed at as a solution to things that have not yet begun to be solved, because pointing at us token Blacks eases the consciences of millions.

—DIVAS: IMPRESSION OF SIX OPERA SUPERSTARS *(1959)*

We are positively a unique people. Breathtaking people. Anything we do, we do big!

—ESSENCE, *FEBRUARY 1975*

I prefer to leave standing up, like a well-mannered guest at a party.

—*ON HER RETIREMENT FROM THE MET, 1985*

I was in the audience and saw my door open for me. I heard it open. And I said to myself, "I don't want this night, from you, ever to be wasted."

—*ATTENDING MARIAN ANDERSON'S GROUNDBREAKING DÉBUT AT THE METROPOLITAN OPERA, JANUARY 27, 1961*

Verdi and Mozart are the best vocal pals I have. They like me and I like them.

—*IN ROSALYN M. STORY, AND SO I SING: AFRICAN AMERICAN DIVAS OF OPERA AND CONCERT (1993)*

If you are going to think black, think positive about it. Don't think down on it, or think it is something in your way. And this way, when you really do want to stretch out, and express how beautiful black is, everybody will hear you. It is overwhelming, because it is so honest, so total, and so unapologetic. So . . . *strong* . . . How can you not stand tall?—because you are saying who you are.

—*IBID.*

Be Black, shine, aim high.

—ESSENCE *AWARDS, OCTOBER 1990*

357

$\mathcal{P}$roverbs

As with other folk literature, the origin of some well-known African American proverbs is lost to time. Perhaps their source was in instructive sayings that can be traced to Africa. They had nonetheless become familiar by the time they were recorded in narrative works by such authors as Frederick Douglass, Harriet Jacobs, and Frances Ellen Harper in the nineteenth century, as well as by Zora Neale Hurston, Arna Bontemps, and Langston Hughes in the twentieth.

Tell the truth and shame the devil.

Don't trouble trouble till trouble troubles you.

Every shut-eye ain't sleep and every good-bye ain't gone.

We ain't what we ought to be, and we ain't what we want to be, and we ain't what we're going to be. But thank God we ain't what we was.

He thinks he's the only rooster know how to crow.

Nothing goes over the devil's back that don't come under his belly.

A dog who will bring a bone will carry one.

He's got spunk to the backbone.

Promises, like pie crusts, are made to be broken.

Ah ain't got to do nothin' but die and stay black.

The blacker the berry, the sweeter the juice.

He's as poor as Job's turkey.

Don't pay no tenshun to what the guinea hen say, 'cause the guinea hen cackle before she lay.

I believe in praising the bridge that carries me over.

If you've got a lot of money, you'd better salt it down.

Ways of woman and ways of snake deeper than the sea.

A whistling woman and crowing hen don't ever come to no good end.

Signification is the Nigger's occupation.

He think if it wasn't for white people there wouldn't be no daylight.

Hard work in de hot sun done called a many a man to preach.

The higher the monkey climbs, the more he shows his behind.

You can read my letters, but you sho' cain't read my mind.

Tain't much difference 'twixt a hornit an' a yaller jacket when dey bofe git under your clo'es.

I been in sorrow's kitchen and licked out all the pots.

Richard Pryor

(1 9 4 0 –)

A brilliant but volatile performer, Richard Franklin Lenox Thomas Pryor III grew up in Peoria, Illinois, in the brothel run by his grandmother. He moved to New York in 1963 and after an appearance on the "Ed Sullivan Show" earned roles in Lady Sings the Blues *(1972),* Silver Streak *(1976), and* Richard Pryor Live in Concert *(1979), as*

*well as several flops. Through an ongoing drug problem and five
dissolved marriages, he continued to perform for live audiences and
received five Grammy awards for his comedy albums. After a heart
attack in 1978 and near-fatal burn injuries in 1980, he made several
more films and albums, and now lives in near seclusion.*

It's so much easier for me to talk about my life in front of two
thousand people than it is one-to-one. I'm a real defensive person,
because if you were sensitive in my neighborhood you were something to eat.

—*IN JEFF ROVIN,* RICHARD PRYOR: BLACK AND BLUE *(1983)*

When you ain't got no money, you gotta get an attitude.

—*IBID.*

I'm gettin' paid to make an ass out of myself. What's your excuse?

—*A FREQUENT RETORT TO HECKLERS*

I'd like to make you laugh for about ten minutes—though I'm gonna
be on for an hour.

—*TO LOOSEN UP AN AUDIENCE*

Allow me to grow. Just watch and see where my growth takes me.
Maybe someday they'll say, "Look at the motherfucker! He don't say
all that shit he used to say, yet he's still saying some funny shit."
That'll be my growth.

—*ON TAKING THE WORD "NIGGER" OUT OF HIS ACT AFTER HIS FIRST TRIP TO AFRICA,*
MARCH 1979

When all of a sudden there you are, burning up . . . you don't call
on the Bank of America to help you. You don't call on nobody but
God. Dear Jesus! Lord! My Master! You know, all those people, those
names you'd forgotten.

—*AFTER THE 1980 FIRE, WIDELY THOUGHT TO BE DRUG-RELATED*

I spent a lot of time being a hustler . . . struggling, stepping, pulling, clawing. Then you get to a point where you don't have to do that
—so what do you do with your hands? I had all this stuff seething

inside of me and not being able to express that. Everything was settled that night . . . the slate was clean.

—*ON THE FIRE*, RICHARD PRYOR

A little laughter, some tears—that's good, that's *box office.*

—*ON HIS LATER WORK*, *IBID.*

I'm grateful. I really am. I could be in Peoria parking cars, hoping to get a tip. This is what I enjoy doing, so that's why I chose it—and I did it well.

—*IBID.*

℘ublic ℰnemy

Led by Chuck D and Flavor Flav, PE was one of the dominant rap groups of the 1980s, often taking a challenging stance on the status quo, which brought them both fame and controversy.

Fight the Power!

—*1989*

Don't believe the hype.

—*1988*

911 is a joke.

—*1990*

Robert Purvis

(1 8 1 0 – 1 8 9 8)

One of the most prominent activists of his time, Purvis was born to a free black mother and a wealthy Englishman and was educated at Amherst College. He unsuccessfully protested the disenfranchisement of blacks in Philadelphia in the 1830s and cofounded the American Anti-Slavery Society in 1833. Active in the Underground Railroad and president of the Philadelphia Vigilance Committee, he continued to fight to secure civil rights for African Americans after the war and throughout his long life.

It is the safeguard of the strongest that he lives under a government which is obliged to respect the voice of the weakest. When you have taken from an individual his right to vote, you have made the government, in regard to him, a mere despotism; and you have taken a step towards making it a despotism to all.

—Appeal of Forty Thousand Citizens, Threatened with Disfranchisement,
to the People of Pennsylvania, 1837

Like every other despot, this despot majority will believe in the mildness of its own sway; but who will the more willingly submit to it for that?

—Ibid.

We love our native country, much as it has wronged us; and in the peaceable exercise of our inalienable rights, we will cling to it . . . Will you starve our patriotism? Will you cast our hearts out of the treasury of the commonwealth? Do you count our enmity better than our friendship?

—Ibid.

We are not intruders here nor were our ancestors. Surely you ought to bear as unrepiningly the evil consequences of your fathers' guilt, as we those of our fathers' misfortune.

—Ibid.

In the name of humanity, in the name of justice, in the name of the God you profess to worship, who has no respect of persons, do not turn into gall and wormword the friendship we bear to yourselves by ratifying a Constitution which tears from us a privilege dearly earned and inestimably prized . . . We take our stand upon that solemn declaration, that to protect inalienable rights "governments are instituted among men, deriving their JUST POWERS from the CONSENT of the governed," and proclaim that a government which tears away from us and our posterity the very power of CONSENT, is a tyrannical usurpation which we will never cease to oppose.

—*IBID.*

No man is safe. His life—his property—and all that he holds dear, are in the hands of a mob, which may come upon him at any moment—at midnight or midday, and deprive him of his all.

—*AFTER RIOTS IN 1849*

I object to the payment of this tax, on the ground that my rights as a citizen, and my feelings as a man and a parent, have been greatly outraged in depriving me, in violation of law and justice, of the benefits of the school system which this tax was designed to sustain . . . The miserable shanty, with all its appurtenances, on the very line of the township . . . is, as you know, that most flimsy and ridiculous sham which any tool of a skin-hating aristocracy could have resorted to, to cover or protect his servility.

—*PROTESTING A SEPARATE AND UNEQUAL SCHOOL FOR HIS CHILDREN,* THE LIBERATOR, *DECEMBER 16, 1853*

No allegiance is due from any man, or any class of men, to a Government founded and administered in inequity, and that the only duty the colored men owes to a Constitution under which he is declared to be an inferior and degraded being, having no rights which white men are bound to respect, is to denounce and repudiate it, and to do what he can by all proper means to bring it into contempt.

—*RESOLUTION IN RESPONSE TO THE DRED SCOTT SUPREME COURT DECISION THAT A BLACK MAN HAD "NO RIGHTS WHICH A WHITE MAN WAS BOUND TO RESPECT," PHILADELPHIA, APRIL 3, 1857*

Should any wretch enter my dwelling, any pale-faced spectre among ye, to execute this law on me or mine, I'll seek his life, I'll shed his blood.

—*OCTOBER 17, 1859, AFTER PASSAGE OF THE FUGITIVE SLAVE ACT*

Ma Rainey

(1886–1939)

Born Gertrude Pridgett in Georgia, "the Queen of the South" went on the vaudeville stage while still in her teens. She married William (Pa) Rainey in 1904 and established a recording career in the 1920s, before retiring to manage two theaters of her own.

I can't tell you about my future, so I'm going to tell you about my past.

—"LAST MINUTE BLUES"

You'll never miss the sunshine till the rain begin to fall
Never miss the sunshine till the rain begin to fall
You'll never miss your hay till another mule be in your stall.

—"DON'T FISH IN MY SEA"

Sometimes I'm grieving from my hat down to my shoes.
I'm a goodhearted woman that's a slave to the blues.

—"SLAVE TO THE BLUES"

White folks hear the blues come out, but they don't know how it got there.

—c. 1929

A(sa) Philip Randolph

(1889-1979)

Educated at City College, Randolph founded The Messenger *with Chandler Owen in 1917 and in 1925 established the Brotherhood of Sleeping Car Porters. In 1941 he organized the March on Washington Movement to protest discrimination in the defense industry and military services. He remained active in labor causes throughout his life and helped organize the March for Jobs and Freedom in Washington on August 28, 1963.*

Violence seldom accomplishes permanent and desired results. Herein lies the futility of war.

—The Truth About Lynching *(1922)*

The regnant law of the life of political parties, like all other organisms, is self-preservation. They behave in obedience to the principle of the *greatest gain for the least effort.*

—*"The Political Situation and the Negro,"* The Crisis, August *1924*

War is the twin evil sister of Fascism . . . It is a danger, an immediate danger, a danger to the American workers, black and white, who fight and pay for all wars in blood and taxes, while the bankers and munition makers, such as the Morgans and Du Ponts, reap huge and fabulous profits.

—*Keynote address as president of the National Negro Congress, Chicago,*
February 14–16, 1936

The political committees of Wall Street . . . are constructed to serve the profit-making agencies and therefore can no more protect or advance the interests of the workers than can a sewing machine grind corn. It is poor working-class wisdom to fight big business for economic justice on the industrial field and vote for it on the political.

—*Ibid.*

The Negro peoples should not place their problems for solution down at the feet of their white sympathetic allies . . . In the final analysis, the salvation of the Negro, like the workers, must come from within.

—*IBID.*

The Future belongs to the people.

—*IBID.*

Freedom is never given; it is won.

—*KEYNOTE ADDRESS, SECOND NATIONAL NEGRO CONGRESS, 1937*

We are gathered here in the largest demonstration in the history of this nation. Let the nation and the world know the meaning of our numbers. We are not pressure groups, we are not an organization or a group of organizations, we are not a mob. We are the advance guard of a massive moral revolution for jobs and freedom.

—*SPEECH AT THE LINCOLN MEMORIAL, MARCH ON WASHINGTON, SEPTEMBER 26, 1942*

We want the full works of citizenship with no reservations. We will accept nothing less . . . This condition of freedom, equality, and democracy is not the gift of gods. It is the task of men, yes, men, brave men, honest men, determined men.

—*KEYNOTE ADDRESS TO THE POLICY CONFERENCE, MARCH ON WASHINGTON MOVEMENT, DETROIT, SEPTEMBER 26, 1942*

If Negroes secure their goals, immediate and remote, they must win them, and to win them they must fight, sacrifice, suffer, go to jail and, if need be, die for them. These rights will not be given. They must be taken.

—*IBID.*

We must develop huge demonstrations, because the world is used to big dramatic affairs. They think in terms of hundreds of thousands and millions and billions . . . Billions of dollars are appropriated at the twinkling of an eye. Nothing little counts.

—*IBID.*

This is the hour of the common man.

—*IBID.*

I have waited twenty-two years for this . . . I've waited all my life for this opportunity.

—ON THE 1963 MARCH ON WASHINGTON, IN HENRY HAMPTON, VOICES OF FREEDOM (1990)

What you needed to follow Garvey was a leap of the imagination, but socialism and trade unionism called for rigorous social struggle— hard work and programs—and few people wanted to think about that. Against the emotional power of Garveyism, what I was preaching didn't stand a chance.

—IN COLUMBUS SALLEY, THE BLACK 100 (1993)

Bernice Johnson Reagon

(1942–)

While still a student, Bernice Johnson was secretary of the local NAACP youth chapter and became a leader of the Atlanta (Georgia) Movement (1961–1962) and one of the Freedom Singers. A member of the singing group Sweet Honey in the Rock, she is now a curator at the Smithsonian Institution.

They were for freedom, I understood that, and I had been waiting.

—ON THE ORGANIZERS OF THE ALBANY MOVEMENT, IN HENRY HAMPTON, VOICES OF FREEDOM (1990)

I'd always been a singer but I had always, more or less, been singing what other people taught me to sing. That was the first time I had the awareness that these songs were mine and I could use them for what I needed . . . The voice I have now, I got the first time I sang in a movement meeting, after I got out of jail . . . and I'd never heard it before in my life.

—IN CLAYBORNE CARSON, ET AL., THE EYES ON THE PRIZE CIVIL RIGHTS READER (1991)

Singing is different than talking, because no matter what they do, they would have to kill me to stop me from singing, if they were arresting me. Sometimes they would plead and say, "Please stop singing." And you would just know your word is being heard.

—*IN* VOICES OF FREEDOM

We had been too long out of the light. It was our time.

—*IBID.*

I learned that if you bring black people together, you bring them together with a song. To this day, I don't understand how people think they can bring anybody together without a song.

—*IN CLAYBORNE CARSON, ET AL.,* THE EYES ON THE PRIZE CIVIL RIGHTS READER

J. Saunders Redding

(1906–1988)

Born in Delaware, Redding attended Morehouse and Lincoln and was awarded Phi Beta Kappa at Brown, where he also received his Ph.D. He taught for many years at the Hampton Institute and elsewhere and was a prolific critic and essayist whose works include To Make a Poet Black *and the autobiography,* No Day of Triumph.

I would not know the thing I sought until I found it. It was both something within and something without myself. Within, it was like the buried memory of a name that will not come to the tongue for utterance. Without, it was the muffled roll of drums receding through a darkling wood. And so, restricted in ways I had no comprehension of, I sought, and everywhere—because I sought among the things and folk I knew—I went unfinding.

—NO DAY OF TRIUMPH *(1944)*

Dishonesty, bigotry, hatred, degradation, injustice, arrogance, and obscenity do flourish in American life, and especially in the prescribed and proscriptive American Negro life; and it is the right and the duty of the Negro write to say so—to complain . . . History is as personal to him as the woman he loves.

—*"The Negro Writer and His Relationship to His Roots," address at the First Conference of Negro Writers, March 1959*

The pathos of man is that he hungers for personal fulfillment and for a sense of community with others.

—*Ibid.*

The final test of Afro-American studies will be the extent to which they rid the minds of whites and blacks alike of false learning, and the extent to which they promote for blacks and whites alike a completely rewarding participation in American life.

—*"The Black Youth Movement," The American Scholar (1969)*

The writer's ultimate purpose is to use his gifts to develop man's awareness of himself so that he, man, can become a better instrument for living together with other men. This sense of identity is the root by which all honest creative effort is fed.

—*"The Negro Writer and His Relationship to His Roots"*

Ishmael Reed

(1 9 3 8 –)

Reed was born in Chattanooga, Tennessee, and grew up in Buffalo, New York. He attended college briefly before working in journalism and the theater in the 1960s. His first novel, The Freelance Pall-bearers, *was published in 1967. A dominant and experimental voice in African American letters, he has published eight novels, four volumes of poetry, and several collections of essays and has taught at*

Yale, Dartmouth, Harvard, Berkeley, and several other universities in California, where he now lives.

I try to do what has never been done before.
—IN *VALERIE SMITH, ET AL.,* AFRICAN-AMERICAN WRITERS *(1991)*

listen man, i cant help it if
yr thing is over
—*"BADMAN OF THE GUEST PROFESSOR"*

the hunger of this poem is legendary
—*"BEWARE: DO NOT READ THIS POEM"*

So Jes Grew is seeking its words. Its text. For what good is a liturgy without a text?
—MUMBO JUMBO *(1973)*

I am saying Open-Up-To-Right-Here and then you will have something coming from your experience that the whole world will admire and need.

—*IBID.*

No one says a novel has to be one thing. It can be anything it wants to be, a vaudeville show, the six o'clock news, the mumblings of wild men saddled by demons.
—YELLOW BACK RADIO BROKE-DOWN *(1975)*

All art must be for the end of liberating the masses. A landscape is only good when it shows the oppressor hanging from a tree.
—*IBID.*

Strange, history. Complicated, too. It will be a mystery, history.
—FLIGHT TO CANADA *(1976)*

Regardless of the criticisms I receive from the left, the right, and the middle, I think it's important to maintain a prolific writing jab, as long as my literary legs hold up.
—WRITIN' IS FIGHTIN' *(1988)*

We learn about one another's culture the same way we learn about sex: in the streets.

—*IBID.*

Any black man, I don't care how much prominence he has, if he isn't bitter by the age of forty he has lived his life as a fool.

—RECKLESS EYEBALLING *(1986)*

Writing has made me a better man. It has put me in contact with those fleeting moments which prove the existence of soul.

—AFRICAN-AMERICAN WRITERS

shake hands now and come
out conjuring

—*"BLACK POWER POEM"*

Charles Lenox Remond

(1810–1873)

Born of West Indian parents, Remond became a leading abolitionist and a prominent member of the Anti-Slavery Society.

Slavery is trembling, prejudice is falling, and I hope will soon be buried—buried beyond resurrection; and we will write over its grave as over Babylon—"Prejudice, the mother of abominations, the liar, the coward, the tyrant, the waster of the poor, the brand of the white man, the bane of the black men, is fallen! is fallen!"

—*LETTER TO THOMAS COLE, JULY 3, 1838*

The grievances of which we complain, be assured, sir, are not imaginary, but real—not local, but universal—not occasional, but continual, everyday matter-of-fact things—and have become, to the disgrace of our common country, matters of history.

—ADDRESS TO MASSACHUSETTS LEGISLATURE PROTESTING SEGREGATED TRAVELING ACCOMMODATIONS, FEBRUARY 1842

We owe no allegiance to a country which grinds us under its iron hoof and treats us like dogs. The time has gone by for colored people to talk of patriotism: He used to be proud that that first blood shed in the American Revolution (that of Attucks, who fell in Boston) was that of a colored man. He used to be proud that his grandfather, on his mother's side, fought for liberty in the Revolutionary War. But that time had passed by.

—RESPONSE TO THE DRED SCOTT DECISION, PHILADELPHIA, APRIL 3, 1857

To-day there are, on the Southern plantations, between three and four millions, to whom the popular Fourth of July in the United States of America is a most palpable insult.

—ANTI-SLAVERY DISCOURSE TO THE MASSACHUSETTS ANTISLAVERY SOCIETY, THE LIBERATOR, JULY 10, 1857

I have only to speak for myself; to speak for freedom for myself; to determine for freedom for myself; and in doing so, I speak and determine for the freedom of every slave on every plantation, and for the fugitives on my right hand; and in so speaking, I speak for those before me as emphatically as I can for the blackest man that lives or suffers in our country.

—IBID.

If the Union shall be dissolved, if for no other purpose than for the emancipation of the slave, it will be glory enough for me to engage in it . . . I am among the number who would embrace this day, this moment, to strike the last fetter from the limbs of the last slave, if it were in my power to do so, and leave the consequences to those at whose instigation it has been fastened upon them.

—IBID.

Max Roach

(1 9 2 5 –   )

One of the greatest of all jazz drummers, Roach played with Ellington, Basie, and Parker in the 1940s, and during the next decade collaborated with Clifford Brown and Sonny Rollins. From the 1960s, his art became infused with political themes, and he refused to record in the United States from 1970 to 1976 in protest against the economic exploitation of musicians.

What "jazz" means to me is the worst kind of working conditions, the worst in cultural prejudice . . . The term "jazz" has come to mean the abuse and exploitation of black musicians.
> —"WHAT 'JAZZ' MEANS TO ME," THE BLACK SCHOLAR, SUMMER 1972

My point is that we much decolonize our minds and re-name and re-define ourselves . . . In all respects, culturally, politically, socially, we must re-define ourselves and our lives, in our own terms.
> —IBID.

Jazz is a very democratic musical form. It comes out of a communal experience. We take our respective instruments and collectively create a thing of beauty.
> —"JAZZ MEN: A LOVE SUPREME," EBONY MAN, APRIL 1987

The American drummer is a one-man percussion orchestra.
> —JAZZ MAGAZINE, JUNE 1988

Paul Robeson

(1898 – 1976)

*A*thlete, scholar, actor, singer, and tireless advocate for his people, Robeson was born in Princeton, New Jersey, of a family whose forebears were active in the early American and Civil War eras. He graduated from Columbia Law School but began a career in the theater, starring in Othello *and* The Emperor Jones *on Broadway and traveling to Europe, Africa, and Russia. He returned to the United States in 1939 and spoke out on labor issues, lynching, and African independence before his passport was denied, in 1950, depriving him of an international forum.*

In my music, my plays, my films, I want to carry always this central idea: to be African.
—*IN E. G. COUSINS,* WHAT I WANT FROM LIFE *(1934)*

The American Negro has changed his temper. Now he wants his freedom. Whether he is smiling at you or not, he wants his freedom.
—NEW YORK TIMES, *APRIL 12, 1944*

It is unthinkable that American Negroes could go to war on behalf of those who have oppressed them for generations against the Soviet Union which in one generation has raised our people to full human dignity.
—*STATEMENT AT* WORLD PEACE CONGRESS, PARIS, *APRIL 20, 1949*
(The statement led to near riots at his appearance soon after, in Peekskill, New York.)

My father was a slave and my people died to build this country, and I'm going to stay right here and have a part of it, just like you. And no fascist-minded people like you will drive me from it. Is that clear?
—*TESTIMONY BEFORE THE* HOUSE UN-AMERICAN ACTIVITIES COMMITTEE, *JUNE 12, 1956*

Freedom is a hard-bought thing and millions are in chains, but they strain toward the new day drawing near.

—HERE I STAND *(1958)*

Yes, here is my homeground—here and in all the Negro communities throughout the land. Here I stand.

—*IBID.*

I saw no reason my convictions should change with the weather.

—*IBID.*

We ask for nothing that is not right, and herein lies the great power of our demand.

—*IBID.*

How long? The answer is: *As long as we permit it.*

—*IBID.*

To be free—to walk the good American earth as equal citizens, to live without fear, to enjoy the fruits of our toil, to give our children every opportunity in life—that dream which we have held so long in our hearts is today the destiny that we hold in our hands.

—*IBID.*

The patter of their feet as they walk through Jim Crow barriers to attend school is the thunder of the marching men of Joshua, and the world rocks beneath their tread.

—*ON THE CHILDREN IN LITTLE ROCK*

Through my singing and acting and speaking, I want to make freedom ring. Maybe I can touch people's hearts better than I can their minds, with the common struggle of the common man. Most of all, I want to help my homeland realize that it will grow only as it lets all its people do their full part in making it rich and strong.

—*IN* 13 AGAINST THE ODDS *(1976)*

Frank Robinson

(1 9 3 5 –   )

Born in Beaumont, Texas, Robinson joined the minors out of high school and in his first year with the Cincinnati Reds led the league in runs scored and was chosen Rookie of the Year for 1956. After a career in Cincinnati and Baltimore, in 1974 he became the first black manager of a major league team. He is the only player to have been voted MVP in both National and American Leagues, and in 1982 he was elected to the Hall of Fame.

Close don't count in baseball. Close only counts in horseshoes and grenades.

—*WIDELY QUOTED*

If I had one wish I was sure could be granted, it would be that Jackie Robinson could be here, seated alongside me today.

—*ON BECOMING MANAGER IN 1974, IN RUSSELL SCHNEIDER,*
FRANK ROBINSON: THE MAKING OF A MANAGER (1976)

I always tried to do the best. I knew I couldn't always be the best, but I tried to be. I expect that of my players today and of my kids. My wife says I shouldn't expect that of my children, but I don't think that's asking too much.

—*ON HIS ELECTION TO THE HALL OF FAME, JANUARY 14, 1982*

Jackie Robinson

(1919 – 1972)

In 1947, Jack Roosevelt Robinson became the first black player in the major leagues. Born in Georgia, he attended UCLA, where he ran track and played football, baseball, and basketball. After serving as an army officer from 1942 to 1944, he played for the Kansas City Monarchs in the Negro League. In 1945 he was signed by the Brooklyn Dodgers and played in the World Series the following year. With a .311 career average, he was the first black player elected to the Hall of Fame.

Are you looking for a Negro who won't fight back?

—*ON BEING TAPPED BY BRANCH RICKEY FOR THE MAJOR LEAGUES*

At the beginning of the World Series of 1947, I experienced a completely new emotion when the National Anthem was played. This time, I thought, it is being played for me, as much as for anyone else. This is organized major league baseball, and I am standing here with all the others, and everything that takes place includes me.

—*THIS I BELIEVE (1972)*

I've been riding on Cloud Nine since the election, and I don't think I'll ever come down. Today, everything is complete.

—*ON BECOMING THE FIRST BLACK PLAYER ELECTED TO THE BASEBALL HALL OF FAME,*
JULY 23, 1962

The way I figured it, I was even with baseball and baseball with me. The game had done much for me, and I had done much for it.

—*I NEVER HAD IT MADE (1972)*

I don't think anyone in or out of sports could ever seriously accuse Willie Mays of offending white sensitivities. But when he was in California, whites refused to sell him a house in their community. They loved his talent, but they didn't want him for a neighbor.

—*Ibid.*

I know that I am a black man in a white world. In 1972, in 1947, at my birth in 1919, I know that I never had it made.

—*Ibid.*

I'm not concerned with your liking or disliking me . . . All I ask is that you respect me as a human being.

—*In Peter Beilenson, Grand Slams and Fumbles, (1989)*

The many of us who attain what we may and forget those who help us along the line—we've got to remember that there are so many others to pull along the way. The farther they go, the further we all go.

—*Baseball Has Done It (1964)*

Athletes die twice.

—*On His Retirement*

Sugar Ray Robinson

(1 9 2 0 – 1 9 8 9)

Born Walker Smith, Jr., in Detroit, Robinson grew up in New York and took the name Ray Robinson from a retired fighter's hastily procured registration card; he got his nickname from a reporter who told his manager, "That's a real sweet fighter you've got there. As sweet as sugar." Robinson gained the world title in several weights before his retirement, in 1965, and was described by a New York Mirror reporter as "the greatest combination of brains, brawn, and boxing skill the modern prize ring has seen."

Hurting people is my business.
—STATEMENT TO NEW YORK BOXING COMMISSION, MAY 23, 1962,
AFTER FATALLY INJURING ANOTHER BOXER

Fighting, to me, seems barbaric. It seems to me like the barbarous days when men fought in a pit and people threw money down to them. I don't really like it. I enjoy out-thinking another man and out-maneuvering him, but I still don't like to fight.
—IN W. C. HEINZ, ONCE THEY HEARD THE CHEERS (1979)

Jake La Motta and I fought six times. We almost got married.
—IN PETER HELLER, IN THIS CORNER (1973)

Getting hit.
—TO A REPORTER'S QUESTION, "WHAT DO YOU LIKE LEAST ABOUT BOXING?"

Unless you've been in the ring when the noise is for you, there's no way you'll ever know what it's like.
—IN HARRY MULLAN, THE BOOK OF BOXING QUOTATIONS (1988)

You always say "I'll quit when I start to slide," and then one morning you wake up and realize you've done slid.
—ON HIS RETIREMENT AT AGE FORTY-ONE, DECEMBER 1965

A broke fighter is a pitiful sight . . . most fighters end up broke . . . I certainly don't intend to finish my career battered and broke.
—HOW HE STARTED HIS CAREER, EBONY, NOVEMBER 1950

Only me was left . . . I went through four million dollars, but I have no regrets.
—HOW HE ENDED HIS CAREER, IN DAVE ANDERSON, SUGAR RAY ROBINSON (1970)

Sonny Rollins

(1 9 3 0 –   )

In a career of constant self-reflection and occasional withdrawal, Rollins emerged as a master of bop in the 1950s with Saxophone Colossus. *Born in the Virgin Islands, he recorded with Charlie Parker and Miles Davis, among others, and in his improvisation he quotes liberally from all musical forms, including his native Caribbean sound.*

America is deeply rooted in Negro culture: its colloquialisms; its humor; its music. How ironic that the Negro, who more than any other people can claim America's culture as his own, is being persecuted and repressed; that the Negro, who has exemplified the humanities in his very existence, is being rewarded with inhumanity.

—Freedom Suite

I think music should be judged on what it is. It should be very high and above everything else. It is a beautiful way of bringing people together, a little bit of an oasis in this messed-up world.

—June 1971 interview, in Arthur Taylor, Notes and Tones *(1977)*

I simply want to reach a level where I will never cease to make progress. I know I will not be satisfied with myself every evening. I know that it is impossible, but I am trying to improve my standard. I should be better than I am. So that, even the bad evenings, I may never be bad enough to despair.

—interview, Jazz magazine, March 1987

This way he has of doing the extraordinary is what I dig in people. They say he can't do it and he does it in the face of odds. That's what I admire in him. He's got some great strength someplace.

—on Muhammad Ali, June 1971 interview, in Arthur Taylor, Notes and Tones

Diana Ross

(1 9 4 4 –)

In her native Detroit, Ross formed a singing group while still in high school and attracted the attention of Motown's Barry Gordy, who signed up the group in 1961. The first of its many number one hits, "Where Did Our Love Go?," followed three years later. Ross sang with the Supremes until 1970, when she launched a solo career that has included numerous successful albums and Oscar-nominated acting performances in the films Lady Sings the Blues *(1971) and* Mahogany *(1975).*

I really, deeply believe that dreams do come true. Often, they might not come when you want them. They come in their own time.
—SECRETS OF A SPARROW *(1993)*

I was lucky, and if I have any bad memories, I hope they're not true.
—*IBID.*

If I have someone who believes in me, I can move mountains.
—*IBID.*

I certainly had more opportunities than my grandparents or their grandparents. But as a black woman in the entertainment business, I know all too well about discrimination and prejudice . . . That's because the one thing none of us has been able to destroy completely is hate. If God gave me one job in life, it is to help create a world in which we are all just people.
—*IBID.*

Time is moving too fast, and I have too many things I want to do. I think once you stop wanting to create, wanting to work and push forward, you become old. And then you die.
—*IBID.*

Learning to "let go and let God" has been a tremendous lesson for me.

—Ibid.

I am on the verge of something. Each day I can just feel it. Something special is about to happen. Expect a miracle today.

—Ibid.

I am a private person living a public life.

—Ibid.

Carl Rowan

(1 9 2 5 –)

Born into poverty in a coal-mining town in Tennessee, Rowan was one of the first black naval officers in World War II and during the civil rights movement became a ground-breaking journalist for the Minneapolis Tribune. *He was named ambassador to Finland in 1963 by President Kennedy and head of the U.S. Information Agency in 1964, becoming the first African American to attend meetings of the Cabinet meetings and the National Security Council. As a syndicated columnist and political commentator, he continues to play an active role in public affairs today.*

I do not believe that man was born to hate and be hated; I cannot believe that the race problem is an inevitable concomitant of democratic life.

—c. 1951

I have come to inform, to provide, to prod, to inspire—to become factor in that great process through which the people of a democrac make the decisions that spell life or death for nations, and even civilizations.

—ON BECOMING THE FIRST BLACK SYNDICATED COLUMNIST, 1965

A society is never in more peril than when the people lose the ability to identify a genuine threat to personal liberty.

—CHICAGO DAILY NEWS, JUNE 14, 1969

It is difficult to determine whether Mr. Reagan is absurdly stubborn, a slow learner who has landed a job that is above his level of competency, or just an ideologue imprisoned in a maze of right-wing clichés.

—NEWSPAPER COLUMN, MARCH 1982

Breaking barriers! Just as no man is an island in the sea of human hopes and hatreds, so no man is capable of bashing alone the roadblocks to justice and human freedom.

—BREAKING BARRIERS (1991)

Neither death, the passage of time, nor anything else will ever end the suspicion, the speculation, about who really killed Dr. King. I shall go to *my* grave believing that Hoover . . . and others in the FBI had a role in silencing the black man they professed to fear but surely hated.

—IBID.

I never could accept the idea that I was a failure at anything. No one told me then to never look back; I just never looked back. Triumphs were where I found them.

—IBID.

The question of the early 1940s is still the question of today. How do deprived, poorly educated kids escape temptations and deprivation, survive foolish and often unlawful escapades, and get anyplace close to an even chance in the race that privileged Americans like to call "the pursuit of happiness"? We have yet to find a meaningful answer.

—IBID.

Josephine St. Pierre Ruffin

(1 8 4 2 – 1 9 2 4)

Born in Boston, Josephine married Saint Pierre Ruffin, the first black judge in Massachusetts, and as the mother of five became a major force in the black women's club movement. A member of the (white) New England Women's Club, she founded the New Era Club and edited its journal, The Women's Era, *and led the First National Conference of Colored Women in 1895. She became vice president of the National Association of Colored Women in 1896 and remained active in the organization until her death.*

One of the saddest things about the sad condition of affairs in the South has been the utter indifference which Southern women, who were guarded with unheard-of fidelity during the war, have manifested to the mental and moral welfare of the children of their faithful slaves.

> —"An Open Letter to the Educational League of Georgia," June 1889

All over America there is to be found a large and growing class of earnest, intelligent, progressive colored women, women who, if not leading full useful lives, are only waiting for the opportunity to do so, many of them warped and cramped for lack of opportunity, not only to do more but to *be* more.

> —address to the First National Conference of Colored Women, Boston, July 29–31, 1895

Too long have we been silent under unjust and unholy charges; we cannot expect to have them removed until we disprove them through *ourselves.*

> —Ibid.

Our woman's movement is [a] woman's movement in that it is led and directed by women for the good of women and men, for the benefit of *all* humanity . . . We want, we ask the active interest of our men, and, too, we are not drawing the color line . . . we are not alienating or withdrawing, we are only coming to the front, willing to join any others in the same work and cordially inviting and welcoming any others to join us.

—*IBID.*

We are justified in believing that the success of this movement for equality of the sexes means more progress toward equality of the races.

—*ON THE ISSUE OF WOMAN SUFFRAGE*, THE CRISIS, *AUGUST 1915*

David Ruggles

(1 8 1 9 – 1 8 4 9)

The editor in the 1830s and '40s of the journals Mirror of Liberty *and* Genius of Freedom, *Ruggles was the secretary of the New York Vigilance Committee, which sought to rescue blacks who were kidnapped into slavery.*

The whites have robbed us [the blacks] for centuries—they made Africa bleed a river of blood!—they have torn husbands from their wives—wives from their husbands—parents from their children—children from their parents—brothers from their sisters—sisters from their brothers, and bound them in chains—forced them into holds of vessels—subjected them to the most unmerciful tortures: starved and murdered, and doomed them to endure the horrors of slavery! Still, according to . . . logic, the whites have virtuous "characters" and we are *brutes!*

—THE "EXTINGUISHERS" EXTINGUISHED,
WRITTEN IN RESPONSE TO AN ANTI-ABOLITION PAMPHLET, 1834

Why is it that it seems to you so "repugnant" to marry your sons and daughters to colored persons? Simply because public opinion is against it. *Nature* teaches no such "repugnance," but experience has taught me that education only does.

—*IBID.*

A man is sometimes lost in the dust of his own raising.

—*IBID.*

Let us to the Press Devoted Be,
Its *Light* will *Shine* and *Speak Us Free.*

—*"APPEALS" (1835)*

While we are subject to be thus inhumanly practised upon, no man is safe; we must look to our own safety and protection from kidnappers, remembering that "self-defence is the first law of nature."

—*PROTESTING KIDNAPPING,* NEW YORK SUN, *JULY 1836*

While every man's hand is against us, our every hand is against each other, I speak plainly, because truth will set us free. Are we not guilty of cherishing, to an alarming extent, the sin of sectarian, geographical, and complexional proscription? . . . If we hope for redemption from our present condition, we must repent, turn, and UNITE in the hallowed cause of reform.

—THE LIBERATOR, *SEPTEMBER 24, 1841*

In our cause, mere words are nothing—action is everything.

—THE LIBERATOR, *AUGUST 13, 1841*

RuPaul

(1 9 6 0 s –   )

RuPaul André Charles had been performing for eleven years when the LP Supermodel of the World *became a major hit in 1993 and the performer a cult figure.*

With hair, heels, and attitude, honey, I am through the roof.
— ON BEING ALMOST SEVEN FEET TALL WITHOUT SHOES, NEW YORK TIMES, *JULY 11, 1993*

I don't have to explain myself. My frequency is very common and is open to anybody who wants to tune in.
— *IBID.*

You're born naked and the rest is drag.
— *IBID.*

Everybody say "Love"!
— OFTEN QUOTED

John B. Russwurm

(1 7 9 9 – 1 8 5 1)

Born in Jamaica, Russwurm graduated from Bowdoin College in 1826 and the following year founded the first African American newspaper, Freedom's Journal, *with Samuel Cornish. He left in 1829 for Liberia, where he edited the* Liberian Herald *and became superintendent of schools.*

Empires rise, and fall, flourish, and decay. Knowledge follows revolutions and travels over the globe. Man alone remains the same being, whether placed under the torrid suns of Africa, or in the more congenial temperate zone. A principle of liberty is implanted in his breast, and all efforts to stifle it are as fruitless as would be the attempt to extinguish the fires of Etna.

—*"The Condition and Prospects of Hayti," delivered at his commencement from Bowdoin, September 6, 1826*

It is in vain to stem the current; degraded men will rise in his native majesty, and claim his rights. They may be withheld from him now, but the day will arrive, when they must be surrendered.

—*Ibid.*

Remind me not of moral duties, of meekness and generosity. Show me the man who has exercised them under these trials, and you point to one who is more than human.

—*Ibid.*

Bayard Rustin

(c. 1910–1987)

Born in Pennsylvania of Quaker heritage, Rustin attended Wilberforce University and was a labor organizer in the 1930s. He helped plan the 1941 March on Washington Movement and spent two years in jail as a conscientious objector during World War II. A proponent of nonviolence, he was active during the civil rights era and was an aide to Martin Luther King, Jr., for seven years. From 1964 until his death, he headed the A. Philip Randolph Institute in New York, dedicated to social change.

By equality I do not mean "separate but equal," a phrase created by segregationists in order to prevent the attainment of equality. I mean equality based upon an integrated social order in which black people, proud of their race and their heritage, shall have no door closed to them.

—IN COLUMBUS SALLEY, THE BLACK 100 *(1993)*

It wasn't the Harry Belafontes and the greats from Hollywood that made the march. What made the march was that black people voted that day with their feet.

—ON THE 1963 MARCH ON WASHINGTON, IN HENRY HAMPTON, VOICES OF FREEDOM *(1990)*

I'm prepared to be a Tom, if it's the only way I can save women and children from being shot down in the street, and if you're not willing to do the same, you're fools.

—SPEECH TO A CROWD IN AN ATTEMPT TO AVERT VIOLENCE IN HARLEM, NEW YORK HERALD TRIBUNE, *JULY 20, 1964*

All mankind is my community . . . Loving your enemy is manifest in putting your arms not around the man but around the social situation, to take power from those who misuse it—at which point they can become human too.

—IN SALLY BELFRAGE, FREEDOM SUMMER *(1965)*

I believe that the Negro's struggle for equality in America is essentially revolutionary. While most Negroes—in their hearts—unquestionably seek only to enjoy the fruits of American society as it now exists, their quest cannot *objectively* be satisfied within the framework of existing political and economic relations . . . How are these radical objectives to be achieved? The answer is simple, deceptively so: *through political power.*

—"FROM PROTEST TO POLITICS: THE FUTURE OF THE CIVIL RIGHTS MOVEMENT," COMMENTARY, *FEBRUARY 1965*

The Lord has his hands on you, and that is a dangerous, dangerous thing.

—DOWN THE ROAD CHICAGO, *1970*

To be afraid is to behave as if the truth were not true.
—*"Meaning of Birmingham," The Liberator, June 1973*

The real radical is that person who has a vision of equality and is willing to do those things that will bring reality closer to that vision . . . In such a social order there will no longer be walls, representing fear and insecurity, to separate people from one another. Such walls, whether constructed by whites or by blacks, are built to oppress and repress, but never to liberate.
—*in Columbus Salley, The Black 100 (1993)*

$\mathcal{S}$onia $\mathcal{S}$anchez

(1 9 3 4 –   )

Born in Birmingham, Alabama, Sanchez attended Hunter College and New York University. During the 1960s she was active in CORE, and her first volume of poetry, Homecoming, *was published in 1969. She has since published half a dozen volumes and has taught at Rutgers, Amherst, and Temple University. She was married for some time to the poet Etheridge Knight.*

The most fundamental truth to be told in any art form, as far as Blacks are concerned, is that America is killing us. But we continue to live and love and struggle and win.
—*"Ruminations / Reflections," in Mari Evans, Black Women Writers (1984)*

> We are the dead
> ones the slow
> fast suicides
> of our time.
> —*"Old Words"*

So much of growing up is an unbearable waiting. A constant longing for another time. Another season.

— "GRADUATION NOTES," FROM UNDER A SOPRANO SKY *(1987)*

                    i know i am
          black.
                    beautiful.
                              with meaning.
                    — "NIGGER"

When he spoke we listened and we heard and knew and felt and lived and loved and we were.

— ON MALCOLM X, IN HENRY HAMPTON, VOICES OF FREEDOM *(1990)*

                    blk/
                    lovers   cannot   live
               in wite power that removes
               them from they blk/selves
          "— ANSWER TO YO / QUESTION OF AM *I* NOT YO / WOMAN
                    EVEN IF U WENT ON SHIT AGAIN—"

I write to tell the truth about the Black condition as I see it. Therefore I write to offer a Black woman's view of the world . . . So the values in my work reflect the values I live by and work for. I keep writing because I realize that until Black people's social reality is free of oppression and exploitation, I will not be free to write as one who's not oppressed or exploited. That is the goal. That is the struggle and the dream.

— "RUMINATIONS / REFLECTIONS"

          no mo tellen the man he is
                              a dead/die/en/motha
          fucka.
                    just a sound of drums.
                    — "LISTENEN TO BIG BLACK AT S.F. STATE"

                                becuz yo/body
                    stops its earth
                                    movements
                                            does not
                    mean it dies.
                            —*"HOSPITAL / POEM"*

                            black
                        magic is your
                        touch
                                making
                        me breathe.
                            —*"BLACK MAGIC"*

Black people will have no beginning or end if each generation does
the job it must do to change the world.
                            —*"RUMINATIONS/REFLECTIONS"*

                    we have come to
                    believe that we are
                    not. to be we
                    must be loved or
                    touched and proved
                    to be.
                            —*"OLD WORDS"*

The joy of poetry is that it will wait for you. Novels don't wait for you.
Characters change. But poetry will wait. I think it's the greatest art.
                —*IN HENRY HAMPTON, VOICES OF FREEDOM (1990)*

                    come. let us ascend from the
                    middle of our breath
                    sacred rhythms
                    inhaling peace.
                            —*"HOMECOMING"*

Arthur Schomburg

(*1 8 7 4 – 1 9 3 8*)

From San Juan, Puerto Rico, Schomburg came to the United States in 1891 and worked in law and business. In 1911, he cofounded the Negro Society for Historical Research and in 1922 became the president of the American Negro Academy. The author of a critical study of Phillis Wheatley, he was an extraordinary collector of works by people of color, a legacy that formed the foundation of the Schomburg Center for Research in Black Culture in New York.

We need the historian and philosopher to give us with trenchant pen, the story of our forefathers, and let our soul and body, with phosphorescent light, brighten the chasm that separates us. We should cling to them just as blood is thicker than water.

—RACIAL INTEGRITY *(1913)*

It is the season to devote our time to kindling the torch that will inspire us to racial integrity.

—*IBID.*

The American Negro must remake his past in order to make his future . . . History must restore what slavery took away.

—*"THE NEGRO DIGS UP HIS PAST,"* THE NEW NEGRO *(1925)*

The bigotry of civilization which is the taproot of intellectual prejudice begins far back and must be corrected at its source.

—*IBID.*

The blatant Caucasian racialist with his theories and assumptions of race superiority and dominance has in turn bred his Ethiopian counterpart—the rash and rabid amateur who has glibly tried to prove half the world's geniuses to have been Negroes and to trace the pedigree of nineteenth-century Americans from the Queen of Sheba. But fortu-

nately to-day there is on both sides of a really common cause less of
the sand of controversy and more of the dust of digging.

—Ibid.

Already the Negro sees himself against a reclaimed background, in a
perspective that will give pride and self-respect ample scope, and
make history yield for him the same values that the treasured past of
any people affords.

—Ibid.

Dred Scott

(1795–1858)

*Born into slavery in Southampton, Virginia, Scott became the center
of an important legal case when he sued for freedom on the basis of
his having lived for a time in free territory. The Supreme Court denied his request, stating that a black man had "no rights a white man
was bound to respect."*

Your petitioner therefore prays your Honorable Court to grant him
leave to sue as a poor person, in order to establish his right to freedom.

—petition, July 1, 1847

$\mathcal{H}$azel $\mathcal{S}$cott

(1 9 2 0 – 1 9 8 1)

A musical prodigy, Scott auditioned on piano for the Juilliard School at the age of eight and spent much of her career in Europe. Married briefly to Adam Clayton Powell, Jr., she was close to Billie Holiday and many other jazz greats and, like Dizzy Gillespie, was a member of the Baha'i faith.

I have always respected everyone's religion. As I say, there is only one God and a lot of confused people.

—INTERVIEW IN NEW YORK, DECEMBER 1972, IN ARTHUR TAYLOR, NOTES AND TONES *(1977)*

I've always known I was gifted, which is not the easiest thing in the world for a person to know, because you're not responsible for your gift, only for what you do with it.

—IBID.

I think we musicians are emissaries. Every time we go before the public, we're there to make converts. We can either be ugly and contemptuous in our behavior, which will turn people off, or else we can carry ourselves with dignity and pride.

—IBID.

It's not just in the United States but all through the Western Hemisphere that you get the black man's art form, which is the beat of Africa.

—IBID.

I think integration is greatly overrated. I don't think there is any such thing as integration, because you can't integrate a person's mind.

—IBID.

When the whites of this country ask us, "What do you want?" We must answer, "We want some of what you've got; that's what we want, and we deserve a chance to have it." It's that simple.

—*IBID.*

Scottsboro Boys

Andy and Leroy Wright, Olen Montgomery, Ozie Powell, Charlie Weems, Clarence Norris, Haywood Patterson, Eugene Williams, Willie Roberson

In the spring of 1931, nine young men were arrested and convicted by an all-white jury of the rape of two white women. The case caused widespread protests, and after a series of trials in 1935 the Supreme Court ruled that the exclusion of African Americans from the jury lists violated the defendants' Fourteenth Amendment rights. The men were retried, and five of them were convicted; in 1955, a state judge claimed that confidential information not released in the trial proved their innocence.

The courtroom was one big smiling white face.

—*AFTER THE CONVICTION, HAYWOOD PATTERSON, IN JAMES GOODMAN,*
STORIES OF SCOTTSBORO *(1994)*

We have been sentenced to die for something we ain't never done. Us poor boys been sentenced to burn up on the electric chair for the reason that we is workers—and the color of our skin is black.

—THE NEGRO WORKER, *MAY 1932*

Bobby Seale

(1 9 3 7 –)

Born in Texas, Seale served in the U.S. Air Force and was working at the North Oakland Neighborhood Anti-Poverty Center when he and Huey Newton founded the Black Panther Party in October 1966. In 1968 he ran for the California state legislature and was one of the Chicago Eight, charged with disrupting the 1968 Democratic National Convention.

First we had to accept the fact that we might get killed or go to jail. But we were also sensitive to the fact that peaceful demonstrators were being brutalized all across this country. Their rights were being violated.

—IN HENRY HAMPTON, VOICES OF FREEDOM *(1990)*

The enslavement of black people from the very beginning of this country, the genocide practiced on the American Indians and the confining of the survivors on reservations, the savage lynching of thousands of black men and women, the dropping of atomic bombs on Hiroshima and Nagasaki, and now the cowardly massacre in Vietnam, all testify to the fact that toward people of color the racist power structure of America has but one policy: repression, genocide, terror, and the big stick.

—EXECUTIVE MANDATE NUMBER ONE OF THE BPP, STATE CAPITOL, SACRAMENTO, CALIFORNIA,
MAY 2, 1967

A people who have suffered so much for so long at hands of a racist society must draw the line somewhere. We believe that the black communities of America must rise up as one man to halt the progression of a trend that leads inevitably to their total destruction.

—IBID.

Seize the Time.

—SLOGAN, AND TITLE OF HIS 1968 AUTOBIOGRAPHY

Betty Shabazz

(1 9 2 0 –   )

Betty Shabazz was a member of the Nation of Islam when she met Malcolm X in 1956. They were married in January 1958 and had four children. She is now a professor at Medgar Evers College in Brooklyn.

What should be remembered about Malcolm is his love of humanity, his willingness to work. He stressed the fact that our young people—all young people, not just blacks—need to accept the responsibility to do what is best to salvage civilization . . . Surely people of goodwill can come together to salvage the world.

—*IN HENRY HAMPTON,* VOICES OF FREEDOM *(1990)*

Ntozake Shange

(1 9 4 8 –   )

Born Paulette Williams, the poet-playwright attended Barnard College, where a sense of alienation led to several suicide attempts. In 1971, she assumed the name Ntozake ("she who brings her own things") Shange ("one who walks with lions"). Her Broadway "choreopoem," for colored girls who have considered suicide when the rainbow is enuf, *received an Obie, and she is the author of the novels* Sassafras, Cypress and Indigo, *and* Betsey Brown, *as well as numerous plays and volumes of poetry and criticism.*

somebody/anybody
sing a black girl's song . . .

she's been dead so long
closed in silence so long
she doesn't know the sound
of her own voice
her infinite beauty . . .

sing the song of her possibilities
sing a righteous gospel
let her be born
let her born
& handled warmly.

—*"DARK PHRASES,"* FOR COLORED GIRLS WHO HAVE CONSIDERED SUICIDE WHEN THE RAINBOW IS ENUF
(1976)

this is my space/i am not movin
—*"NAPPY EDGES" (1978)*

hold yr head like it was ruby sapphire.
—*"I'M A POET WHO,"* FOR COLORED GIRLS

i cdn't stand bein sorry & colored at the same time
it's so redundant in the modern world.
—*"NO MORE LOVE POEMS #1,"* FOR COLORED GIRLS

thinkin wont do me a bit of good tonite
i need to be loved
—*"NO MORE LOVE POEMS #4," IBID.*

Where there is a woman there is music.
—SASSAFRAS, CYPRESS AND INDIGO *(1982)*

cda clothed the naked & fed the hungry/with dance i saw tonite . . .
mean i saw the black people move the ground & set stars beneath
hey feet . . . what we do all the time/it's how we remember what
annot be said.
—*IBID.*

Give gifts to those who should know love.
—*IBID.*

The nice thing about segregation was the colored could be all together, where the air and the blossoms were their own, as clear as it was impossible for white folks to put a veil over the sun.
— BETSEY BROWN *(1985)*

The song moved as if it weren't used ta having shoes on its feet.
— *IBID.*

That's what love did. It came down on you like rain or sunshine.
— *IBID.*

Po' white trash with guns gonna escort us to our classes and make us eat the flag, while they tell us how slavery wasn't quite so bad.
— *IBID.*

Nobody's ordinary. Each one of us is special and it's the coming together of alla that that makes the world so fine.
— *IBID.*

Women who can see over the other side are never far from each other.
— *IBID.*

Mamas only do things cause they love you so much. They can't help it. It's flesh to flesh, blood to blood. No matter how old you get, how grown and on your own, your mama always loves you like a newborn.
— *IBID.*

a poem should happen to you like/cold water or a kiss.
— *c. 1984*

We shall see no evil. We shall strangle it.
— SEE NO EVIL *(1984)*

i found god in myself
& i loved her/i loved her fiercely
— *"A LAYING ON OF HANDS,"* FOR COLORED GIRLS

Grow in your own patch. Stay put and blossom.
— BETSEY BROWN

Reverend Al Sharpton

(1955–)

Born in Crown Heights, Sharpton was a child prodigy, delivering his first sermon at the age of four. As a young man he was influenced by Adam Clayton Powell, Jr., and worked for some time for the singer James Brown. He has protested the treatment of the cases of Tawana Brawley, Yusef K. Hawkins, and others in the court system and in 1992 made a strong showing in the New York Democratic senatorial primary.

No justice. No peace.

—*HIS OFT-QUOTED PROTEST*

I yelled when I was hungry, I yelled when I was wet. I yelled when all those little black bourgeois babies stayed dignified and quiet. I learned before I got out of the maternity ward that you've got to holler like hell sometimes to get what you want.

—New York Times Magazine, *JANUARY 24, 1993*

It was time to bring down the volume and bring up the program.

—*ON HIS RUN FOR THE SENATE, IBID.*

There is nothing hip or slick about being ignorant. And there is nothing hip or slick about going around killing each other for no good reason.

—*SPEECH AT JOHN MARSHALL HIGH SCHOOL, ROCHESTER, NEW YORK, OCTOBER 1992*

I am a watchman. I've been designated to stand on the wall and tell what I see.

—New York Times, *JANUARY 25, 1994*

Reverend Fred Shuttlesworth

(1 9 2 2 –)

As minister of the Bethel Baptist Church in Birmingham and a leader in the city's civil rights movement, Shuttlesworth was attacked on several occasions and his home was bombed twice. Born in Alabama, he was the founder of the Alabama Christian Movement for Human Rights and a cofounder of the Southern Christian Leadership Conference. In 1963 he was one of the organizers of the Birmingham Movement.

Birmingham is where it's at, gentlemen, I assure you, if you come to Birmingham, we will not only gain prestige but really shake the country. If you win in Birmingham, as Birmingham goes, so goes the nation.

—INVITING DR. MARTIN LUTHER KING, JR., AND THE SCLC TO BIRMINGHAM, 1963;
IN HENRY HAMPTON, VOICES OF FREEDOM (1990)

The Movement Must Move.

—SLOGAN OF THE BIRMINGHAM MOVEMENT

When I see it on TV, that you have called it off, I will get up out of this, my sick bed, with what little ounce of strength I have, and lead them back into the street.

—ON LEARNING, WHILE HOSPITALIZED FOR INJURIES SUSTAINED IN BIRMINGHAM, THAT THE PROTEST
MIGHT BE CALLED OFF; IN HENRY HAMPTON, VOICES OF FREEDOM

It was tragic, but in every war innocent people get killed . . . But maybe that's why we win, because Dr. King said unearned suffering has to be redemptive.

—ON THE 16TH STREET CHURCH BOMBING IN BIRMINGHAM, SEPTEMBER 15, 1963;
IN HENRY HAMPTON, VOICES OF FREEDOM

We have taken the Bull out of old *Bull* Connor and made a steer out of him.

—*c. 1963*

They could outlaw an organization, but they couldn't outlaw the movement of a people determined to be free.

—BIRMINGHAM: PEOPLE IN MOTION *(1966)*

Roscoe Conkling Simmons

(d . 1 9 5 1)

A nephew of Booker T. Washington by marriage, "the golden-voiced orator" was active in politics—seconding the nomination for Herbert Hoover at the Republican National Convention in 1932—and for more than twenty years wrote "The Untold Story," a column in the Chicago Defender.

The Senate means debate! . . . That's me!
The Senate means disputation! . . . That's me!
The Senate needs *eloquence!* . . . AND GOD KNOWS THAT'S ME!

—*DURING AN UNSUCCESSFUL CAMPAIGN BID FOR THE ILLINOIS SENATE, 1932*

Nina Simone

(1 9 3 3 –   )

Born *Eunice Waymon in North Carolina and educated at the Juilliard School, Simone is an accomplished pianist as well as an elastic singer; her repertoire extends from gospel to jazz, soul to pop.*

Music is a gift and a burden I've had since I can remember who I was.
— *INTERVIEW IN PARIS, DECEMBER 1970, IN ARTHUR TAYLOR,* NOTES AND TONES *(1977)*

Everything that happened to me as a child involved music. It was part of everyday life, as automatic as breathing.
— *I PUT A SPELL ON YOU (1992)*

Jazz is not just music, it's a way of life, it's a way of being, a way of thinking. I think that the Negro in America is jazz. Everything he does—the slang he uses, the way he walks, the way he talks, his jargon, the new inventive phrases we make up to describe things—all that to me is jazz just as much as the music we play.
— *IN ARTHUR TAYLOR,* NOTES AND TONES

Charlie Parker and Billie Holiday are our father and mother.
— *IBID.*

How do you explain what it feels like to get on the stage and make poetry that you know sinks into the hearts and souls of people who are unable to express it?
— *IBID.*

Slave Narratives (wpa)

During the 1930s, the Federal Writers Project of the Works Project Administration enlisted researchers to interview and collect the oral histories of surviving slaves so that their memories would not be lost. Their accounts were published in several volumes, including Before Freedom *(1989).*

Honey, us wasn't ready for the big change that come. The birds had nests in the air, the foxes had holes in the ground, and the fishes had beds under the great falls, but us colored folks was left without any place to lay our heads.

—VIOLET GUNTHARPE, WINNSBORO, SOUTH CAROLINA

When the Yankees come and take all that away, all us had to thank them for was a hungry belly and Freedom.

—IBID.

The folks who know me always call me Sarah Poindexter. I got it honestly, like other honest slaves who never know what their real name was, and so I keeps it to the end of the road.

—SARAH POINDEXTER, COLUMBIA, SOUTH CAROLINA

The rule on the place was: Wake up the slaves at daylight, begin work when they can see, and quit work when they can't see.

—PETER CLIFTON, WINNSBORO, SOUTH CAROLINA

For God's sake, don't be catch with pencil and paper. That was a major crime. You might as well had killed your marster or missus.

—ELIJAH GREEN, CHARLESTON, SOUTH CAROLINA

General Sherman? I *seen* him. He had a big name, but he warn't such a big man. He was a little spare-made man.

—Willis Williams, Conway, South Carolina

I see the lines of sorrow had plowed on that old [master's] face, and I remembered he'd been a captain on horseback in that war. It come into my remembrance the song of Moses: "The Lord had triumphed glorily and the horse and his rider have been throwed into the sea."

—Savilla Burrell, Winnsboro, South Carolina

I don't know how we live, yet we is.

—Ann Perry, Charleston, South Carolina

Robert Smalls

(1 8 3 9 – 1 9 1 5)

Born a slave in Beaufort, South Carolina, Smalls became a hero during the Civil War when he led the Confederate gunboat The Planter *out of Charleston Harbor. He served in Congress from 1875 to 1887, longer than any of the other black Reconstruction legislators.*

The United States Government is not powerless, and surely she will not be silent in an emergency like this . . . In this centennial year will she stand idly by and see her soil stained with the blood of defenseless citizens, and witness the bitter tears of women and children falling upon the murdered bodies of their loved ones? God forbid that such an attitude will be assumed toward the colored people of the South by the "best Government the world ever saw."

—Seeking to secure black troops to protect black citizens from violence, Congressional Record, *July 1876*

Bessie Smith

(1894 – 1937)

"The Empress of the Blues" was born in Chattanooga and began performing at the age of nine. In 1912 she joined Ma Rainey's show and started a career on the road. Her first record was issued in 1923, and over the next five years she became the highest paid black entertainer in the world. Though she adapted her style, she never quite recovered from the Depression and the waning popularity of the blues. Known for her prodigious appetite for alcohol and the company of both sexes—"I never saw so much life left in someone who had lived so much," one singer remarked—she died from injuries sustained in a car accident in rural Mississippi.

No time to marry, no time to settle down;
I'm a young woman, and I ain't done runnin' aroun'.
—*"Young Woman Blues" (1927)*

Have you ever seen peaches grow on sweet potato vine;
Yes, step in my backyard and take a peep at mine.
—*"Sorrowful Blues" (1924)*

If it wasn't for the poor man, mister rich man, what would you do?
—*"Poor Man's Blues" (1930)*

There's a devil in my soul, and I'm full of bad booze;
I'm out here for trouble. I've got the Black Mountain Blues.
—*"Black Mountain Blues" (1930)*

I have given and helped more people in and out of the profession than I ever hope to be repaid for on earth, but I will get my reward later from the man higher up.
—*Letter to the Pittsburgh Courier in response to an unfavorable article on her treatment of her cast, May 14, 1927*

The funk is flyin'.
—IN CHRIS ALBERTSON, BESSIE (1972)

I ain't never *heard* of such shit!
—A FREQUENT RETORT, WIDELY ATTRIBUTED

I'm the *star* of the show, I'm Bessie Smith, and these fuckin' bastards won't let me have any money.
—WIDELY REPORTED INCIDENT IN WHICH SMITH POUNDED ON THE FLOOR OF THE APOLLO THEATER UNTIL SHE WAS GIVEN AN ADVANCE; FALL 1936

It's a long old road, but I know I'm gonna find the end.
—"LONG OLD ROAD" (1931)

Anne Spencer

(1 8 8 2 – 1 9 7 5)

Born in West Virginia, Spencer was a social worker and poet whose writings were published during the Harlem Renaissance. She was educated at the Virginia Seminary in Lynchburg, where she later taught, and had a great love of the garden.

Let me learn now where Beauty is;
I was born to know her mysteries . . .
—"QUESTING"

I saw your heart,
And altared there in its darksome place
Were the tongues of flame the ancients knew . . .
—"LADY, LADY"

Is any prophet come to teach a new thing
Now in a more apt time?
—*"Before the Feast of Shushan"*

It is dangerous for a woman to defy the gods;
To taunt them with the tongue's thin tip,
Or strut in the weakness of mere humanity,
Or draw a line daring them to cross.
—*"Letter to My Sister"*

I proudly love being a Negro woman—it's so involved and interesting.
We are the PROBLEM—the great national game of TABOO.
—Caroling Dusk *(1927)*

Leon Spinks

(1 9 5 3 –)

Born in Saint Louis, Spinks won the light heavyweight Olympic Gold Medal in 1976. Only two years into his professional career, he captured the world heavyweight title from Muhammad Ali, in a fifteen-round split decision on February 15, 1978. He held the title for only seven months, losing it to Ali on September 15.

To experience the agony of defeat makes you stronger. It's like taking one step back and two steps forward. To experience the agony of defeat makes you appreciate the experience of winning. That's what makes a champion.
—*In Harry Mullan,* The Book of Boxing Quotations *(1988)*

I'm not the greatest, I'm the latest.
—*Ibid.*

Spirituals

Though the precise origins of the spirituals are now uncertain, there is no question that they remain one of the most significant legacies of the African American people. They were written down for the first time after the Civil War and continue to be performed by major artists to audiences around the world.

Go down Moses,
Way down in Egyptland,
Tell old Pharaoh,
"Let my people go!"
— *"Go Down Moses"*

Joshua commanded de chillen to shout
An' de walls come tumblin' down.
— *"Joshua Fit de Battle ob Jerico"*

God gave Noah de Rainbow sign,
Don't you see?
God gave Noah de Rainbow sign,
No more water but fire next time.
— *"I Got a Home in Dat Rock"*

Roll Jordan, roll,
Roll Jordan, roll,
I wanter go to heav'n when I die
To hear ol' Jordan roll.
— *"Roll Jordan, Roll"*

Old Satan is mad an' I'm so glad,
Sen' dem angels down,

He missed de soul he thought he had,
Oh, sen'a dem angels down.
—*"MY WAY'S CLOUDY"*

My Lord, He calls me,
He calls me by the thunder,
The trumpet sounds within-a my soul.
—*"STEAL AWAY TO JESUS"*

I know moon-rise, I know star-rise,
Lay dis body down.
I walk in de moonlight, I walk in de starlight,
To lay this body down.
—*"I KNOW MOON-RISE"*

Oh, don't you want to go to that gospel feast,
That promised land where all is peace?
—*"DEEP RIVER"*

My Lord, what a morning,
When the stars begin to fall . . .
You'll hear the trumpet sound,
To wake the nations underground,
Look in my God's right hand.
When the stars begin to fall.
—*"MY LORD, WHAT A MORNING"*

We'll run and never tire,
Jesus set poor sinners free.
—*"DOWN IN THE VALLEY"*

I look'd over Jordan, an' what did I see,
'Comin' for to carry me home,
A band of angels comin' after me,
Comin' for to carry me home.
—*"SWING LOW, SWEET CHARIOT"*

Ride in, kind Savior!
No man can hinder me.
Oh, Jesus is a mighty man!
No man can hinder me . . .

Oh, old Secesh done come and gone!
No man can hinder me.
— *"Ride In, Kind Savior"*

No more driver's lash for me,
No more, no more,
No more driver's lash for me,
Many thousand gone.
— *"Many Thousand Gone"*

Rise and shine and give God the glory
For the year of Jubilee.
— *"Rise and Shine"*

Some of these mornings bright and fair,
I thank God I'm free at last,
Going to meet my Jesus in the middle of the air,
I thank God I'm free at last.
— *"I Thank God I'm Free at Last"*

We'll soon be free,
When de Lord will call us home . . .
We'll fight for liberty,
When de Lord will call us home.
— *"We'll Soon Be Free"*

Gonna shout trouble over,
When I get home.
Gonna shout trouble over,
When I get home . . .
No mo prayin, no mo dyin,
When I get home.
No mo prayin and no mo dyin,
When I get home.
— *"Gonna Shout"*

One more river
And that's the river of Jordan
One more river
There's one more river to cross.
— *"One More River to Cross"*

Michael row the boat ashore
Hallelujah!
—"MICHAEL ROW THE BOAT ASHORE"

Brudder, keep your lamp trimmin' and a-burnin',
Keep your lamp trimmin' and a-burnin',
Keep your lamp trimmin' and a-burnin',
For dis world mos' done.
—"DIS WORLD MOS' DONE"

For death is a simple ting,
And he go from door to door,
And he knock down some, and he cripple up some,
And he leave some here to pray.
O do, Lawd, remember me!
O do, Lawd, remember me!
—"DO, LAWD"

O Lord, I want to be in that number
When the saints go marching in.
—"WHEN THE SAINTS GO MARCHING IN"

Oh! take your nets and follow me
For I died for you upon the tree!
Shout along, chillen!
Shout along, chillen!
Hear the dying Lamb!
—"SHOUT ALONG, CHILDREN"

If you cain't bear no crosses, you cain't wear no crown,
Way beyond the moon . . .
I'ze gotta mother in de Beaulah land, she's callin me,
Way beyond de sun.
—"WHEN-A MAH BLOOD RUNS CHILLY AND COL'"

Sometimes I feel like a motherless child,
A long ways from home,
A long ways from home . . .
Sometimes I feel like a feather in the air,

And I spread my wings and I fly,
I spread my wings and I fly.
— *"Motherless Child"*

All God's Chillun got-a wings . . .
Ev'ry body talkin' bout heav'n ain't goin' dere,
— *"All God's Chillun Got Wings"*

Gimme dat ol' time religion,
It's good enough for me . . .
It will do when de world's on fiah,
An it's good enough for me.
— *"Gimme Dat Ol' Time Religion"*

In dat mornin' when I rise,
Dat mornin' when I rise,
In dat mornin' when I rise,
Give me Jesus.
— *"Give Me Jesus"*

Wade in de water, children,
Wade in de water, children,
Wade in de water, children,
God's a-gwineter trouble de water.
— *"God's A-Gwineter Trouble de Water"*

De People keep-a comin' an' de train done gone.
— *"Mary Had a Baby"*

I want to die easy when I die,
I want to die easy when I die,
Shout salvation as I die,
I want to die easy when I die.
— *"I Want to Die Easy When I Die"*

Nobody knows de trouble I see, Lord,
Nobody knows like Jesus.
— *"Nobody Knows de Trouble I See"*

Just like the tree that's planted by the water,
We shall not be moved.

—*"WE SHALL NOT BE MOVED"*

There's a star in the Eas' on Christmas morn,
Rise up Shepherd an' follow.
It will lead to de place where de Savior's born,
Rise up Shepherd an' follow.

—*"RISE UP SHEPHERD AN' FOLLOW"*

We are clim'in' Jacob's ladder,
We are clim'in' Jacob's ladder,
We are clim'in' Jacob's ladder,
Soldiers of the cross.

—*"WE ARE CLIM'IN' JACOB'S LADDER"*

De gospel train's a-comin',
I hear it's jus' at han',
I hear de car wheels movin',
An' rumblin trough de lan'.
Git on board, little chillen,
Dere's room for many a mo'.

—*"GIT ON BOARD, LITTLE CHILLEN"*

Shelby Steele

(1 9 4 6 –)

Work by this leading essayist and black conservative political thinker has appeared in Harper's, *the* New York Times Magazine, *the* Washington Post, American Scholar, *and elsewhere. He won a National Magazine Award in 1989 and is now a professor of English at San Jose State University in California. His collections of essays,* The Content of Our Character *(1990), received the National Book Critics Circle Award.*

From this point on, the race's advancement will come from the efforts of its individuals.

—*"I'M BLACK, YOU'RE WHITE, WHO'S INNOCENT,"* HARPER'S, *JUNE 1988*

What both black and white Americans fear are the sacrifices and risks that true racial harmony demands. This fear is the measure of our racial chasm.

—*IBID.*

Personal responsibility is the brick and mortar of power.

—*"RACE-HOLDING,"* THE CONTENT OF OUR CHARACTER

One of the heaviest weights that oppression leaves on the shoulders of its former victims is simply the memory of itself . . . Not only does the enemy-memory pull us backward, it also indirectly encourages us to remain victims so as to confirm the power of the enemy we remember and believe in.

—*"THE MEMORY OF ENEMIES," IBID.*

Being "black" in no way spared me the necessity of being myself.

—*"EPILOGUE," IBID.*

The promised land guarantees nothing. It is only an opportunity, not a deliverance.

—*IBID.*

Carl Stokes

(1 9 2 7 –)

Born in a housing project in Cleveland, Stokes dropped out of school and earned a living by working at factory jobs and boxing. After serving in the army, he received his high school, college, and law degrees and in 1962 became the first black Democrat in the Ohio House of Representatives. After an unsuccessful bid in 1965, he be-

came the mayor of Cleveland in 1967, the first black mayor of a major city in America.

So many of the people were expressing in different kinds of ways about the confidence that they had, both that I would win and that when I won that I'd be able to correct all the wrongs and problems that beset them. And when you realize that people have that sort of feeling about you, that you're going to be some sort of savior from their dilemma, it's very sobering, because it imposes a great responsibility upon you.

—ON HIS *1965* CAMPAIGN, IN HENRY HAMPTON, VOICES OF FREEDOM *(1990)*

Carl, it must have been rather difficult for you to say that the candidate wasn't like God.
Yes, it was. But I didn't mean it.

—EXCHANGE WITH AN AIDE AFTER A FUMBLE IN HIS *1965* CAMPAIGN

My election on November 7, 1967, had a great deal of meaning to America because this was a city in which the black population was a distinct minority. It illustrated the ability of white people to vote for a black candidate for mayor. To black people, it introduced a whole new echelon of political power.

—IN HENRY HAMPTON, VOICES OF FREEDOM

I knew my own situation, my own town, and I knew I had it in my hand. Once I got it, I knew I could do things that no civil rights march ever did.

—IN CLAYBORNE CARSON, ET AL., THE EYES ON THE PRIZE CIVIL RIGHTS READER *(1991)*

Mary Church Terrell

(1 8 6 3 – 1 9 5 4)

Born in Memphis, Terrell received her M.A. from Oberlin and taught at Wilberforce University and at the high school in Washington, D.C., soon to be named for Paul Laurence Dunbar. She became the first black woman appointed to the Board of Education and was a founding member of the Niagara Movement and the NAACP, and the first president of the National Association of Colored Women. Throughout her long life she fought for woman suffrage and against discrimination in public accommodations in the nation's capital.

Lifting as We Climb.

—*MOTTO OF THE NATIONAL ASSOCIATION OF COLORED WOMEN*

No people need ever despair whose women are fully aroused to the duties which rest upon them and are willing to shoulder responsibilities which they alone can successfully assume.

—*"WHAT ROLE IS THE EDUCATED NEGRO WOMAN TO PLAY IN THE UPLIFTING OF HER RACE,"*
TWENTIETH-CENTURY NEGRO LITERATURE, 1902

Through the children of today we believe we can build the foundation of the next generation upon such a rock of morality, intelligence, and strength, that the floods of proscription, prejudice, and persecution may descend upon it in torrents and yet it will not be moved.

—*IBID.*

Through our clubs colored women hope to improve the social atmosphere by showing the enormity of the double standard of morals, which teaches that we should turn the cold shoulder upon a fallen sister, but greet her destroyer with open arms and a gracious smile.

—*IBID.*

Seeking no favors because of our color or patronage because of our needs, we knock at the bar of justice and ask for an equal chance.

—*Ibid.*

Lynching is the aftermath of slavery.

—*"Lynching from a Negro's Point of View,"* The North American Review, *June 1904*

The whole country seems tired of hearing about the black man's woes. The wrongs of the Irish, of the Armenians, of the Roumanians and Russian Jews, of the exiles of Russia, and of every other oppressed people upon the face of the globe, can arouse the sympathy and fire the indignation of the American public, while they seem to be all but indifferent to the murderous assaults upon the negroes in the South.

—*Ibid.*

Surely nowhere in the world do oppression and persecution based solely on the color of the skin appear more hateful and hideous than in the capital of the United States, because the chasm between the principles upon which this Government was founded, in which it still professes to believe, and those which are daily practiced under the protection of the flag, yawn so wide and deep.

—*"What It Means to Be Colored in the Capital of the United States,"* The Independent, *January 24, 1907*

Nothing could be more inconsistent than that colored people should use their influence against granting the ballot to women, if they believe the colored men should enjoy this right which citizenship confers.

—*on the issue of woman suffrage,* The Crisis, *August 1915*

While most girls run away from home to marry, I ran away to teach.

—A Colored Woman in a White World *(1940)*

Men do not gather grapes of thorn nor figs of thistle.

—*Ibid.*

After people have been freed, it is a cruel injustice to call them by the same name as they bore as slaves.

—*"Please Stop Using the Word 'Negro,'"* letter to the editor, Washington Post, *May 14, 1949*

Clarence Thomas

(1948 –)

*B*orn in Pin Point, Georgia, Thomas was raised by his grandfather and briefly studied for the priesthood before attending Holy Cross College in Massachusetts. He graduated from Yale Law School and had held a number of political posts when he was nominated to the U.S. Circuit Court of Appeals in Washington in 1990. A year later, President Bush nominated him to the Supreme Court to fill the position left by Thurgood Marshall. After volatile hearings, in which he was accused of sexual harassment by Anita Hill, Thomas was confirmed by the Senate to become the one hundred and sixth Supreme Court justice.

I am the product of hatred and love—the hatred of the social and political structure which dominated the segregated, hate-filled city of my youth, and the love of some people—my mother, my grandparents, my neighbors and relatives—who said by their actions, "You can make it, but first you must endure."

—*COMMENCEMENT SPEECH AT SAVANNAH STATE COLLEGE, JUNE 9, 1985*

Do not be lured by sirens and purveyors of misery who profit from constantly regurgitating all that is wrong with black Americans and blaming these problems on others . . . Do not become obsessed with all that is wrong with our race. Rather, become obsessed with looking for solutions to our problems. Be tolerant of all positive ideas; their number is much smaller than the countless number of problems to be solved. We need *all* the help we can get.

—*IBID.*

I was raised to survive under the totalitarianism of segregation, not only without the active assistance of government but with its active opposition . . . Self-sufficiency and spiritual and emotional security were our tools to carve out and secure freedom.

—*c. JULY 1990*

Mr. Chairman, in my forty-three years on this earth, I have been able with the help of others and with help of God to defy poverty, avoid prison, overcome segregation, bigotry, racism, and obtain one of the finest educations available in this country. But I have not been able to overcome this process. This is worse than any obstacle or anything that I have ever faced . . . I never asked to be nominated. It was an honor. Little did I know the price, but it is too high.

—*First statement to the Senate Judiciary Committee, October 11, 1991*

The Supreme Court is not worth it. No job is worth it. I am not here for that. I am here for my name, my family, my life, and my integrity.

—*Second statement to the Senate Judiciary Committee, October 11, 1991*

This is a circus. It's a national disgrace. And from my standpoint, as a black American, it is a high-tech lynching for uppity blacks who in any way deign to think for themselves, to do for themselves, to have different ideas, and it is a message that unless you kowtow to an old order, this is what will happen to you. You will be lynched, destroyed, caricatured by a committee of the U.S. Senate rather than hung from a tree.

—*Ibid.*

Howard Thurman

(1899–1981)

Known as a powerful orator, Thurman was born in Florida and was educated at Morehouse College, Rochester Theological Seminary, and Haverford College. He served as dean of the chapel at Howard University from 1932 to 1944 and later at Boston University, and he is the author of nineteen volumes.

Commitment means that it is possible for a man to yield the nerve center of his consent to a purpose or cause, a movement or an ideal, which may be more important to him than whether he lives or dies.

—Disciplines of the Spirit *(1963)*

At the core of life is a hard purposefulness, a *determination* to live.

—*Ibid.*

It is my belief that in the presence of God, there is neither male nor female, white or black, Gentile or Jew, Protestant or Catholic, Hindu, Buddhist, or Moslem, but a human spirit stripped to the literal substance of itself before God.

—*in Marcus Hanna Boulware, ed.,* The Oratory of Negro Leaders *(1969)*

Perhaps the authentic moral stature of a man is determined by his choice of weapons which he uses in his fight against the adversary. Of all weapons, love is the most deadly and devastating, and few there be who dare trust their fate in its hands.

—*Ibid.*

No external force, however great and overwhelming, can at long last destroy a people if it does not first win the victory of the spirit against them.

—*Ibid.*

A dream is the bearer of a new possibility, the enlarged horizon, the great hope.

—Disciplines of the Spirit

Community cannot for long feed on itself; it can only flourish with the coming of others from beyond, their unknown and undiscovered brothers.

—Search for a Common Ground *(1971)*

He who fears is literally delivered to destruction.

—*in Janet Cheatham Bell,* Famous Black Quotations *(1986)*

To love is to make of one's heart a swinging door.

—Recapture the Spirit *(1963)*

Wallace Thurman

(1 9 0 2 – 1 9 3 4)

Born in Salt Lake City and educated in California, Thurman was active as a journalist, dramatist, and literary editor during the Harlem Renaissance. He was the author of short stories and the novels The Blacker the Berry, Interne; *his satiric portrait of the period,* Infants of the Spring, *was perhaps more effective as an acerbic comment than as a novel.*

This is indeed an accidental cosmos . . .
—*"Grist in the Mill" (c. 1926)*

The American Negro feels that he has been misinterpreted and caricatured so long by insincere artists that once a Negro gains the ear of the public he should expend his spiritual energy feeding the public honeyed manna on a silver spoon . . . Negroes in America feel certain that they must always appear in public butter side up, in order to keep from being trampled in the contemporary onward march.
—*"Negro Artists and the Negro,"* The New Republic, *August 31, 1927*

If but a few live coals are found in a mountain of ashes, no one should be disappointed. Genius is a rare quality in this world, and there is no reason why it should be more ubiquitous among Blacks than Whites.
—*Ibid.*

She should have been a boy, then the color of her skin wouldn't have mattered so much, for wasn't her mother always saying that a black boy could get along, but that a black girl would never know anything but sorrow and disappointment?
—The Blacker the Berry *(1929)*

Time and distance—strange things, immutable, yet conquerable.
—*Ibid.*

The God we, or rather most Negroes, worship is a patriarchal white man, seated on a white throne, in a spotless white Heaven, radiant with white streets and white-apparelled angels eating white honey and drinking white milk.

—*Ibid.*

Color prejudice and religion are akin in one respect. Some folks have it and some don't, and the kernel that is responsible for it is present in us all.

—*Ibid.*

Piano treble moaning, bass rumbling like thunder. A swarm of people, motivating their bodies to express in suggestive movements the ultimate consummation of desire.

—*Ibid.*

The Negro and all things negroid had become a fad, and Harlem had become a shrine to which feverish pilgrimages were in order . . . Seventh Avenue was the gorge into which Harlem cliff dwellers crowded to promenade. It was heavy laden, full of life and color, vibrant and leisurely.

—*Ibid.*

Being a Negro writer these days is a racket and I'm going to make the most of it while it lasts. Sure I play the fool . . . They fall for it. About twice a year I sell a story. It is acclaimed. I am a genius in the making. Thank God for this Negro literary renaissance. Long may it flourish!

—Sweetie May, a character based on Zora Neale Hurston, Infants of the Spring

We are mere journeymen, planting seeds for someone else to harvest.

—on the Harlem Renaissance, c. 1929

Melvin Tolson

(1900–1966)

Tolson attended Fisk and Lincoln universities and received his M.A. from Columbia. He taught at Tuskegee and Langston University and was poet laureate of Liberia, for which he wrote the Libretto for the Republic of Liberia. *He is best known for his volume* Harlem Gallery *and also wrote the column "Caviar and Cabbage" for the* Washington Tribune *from 1937 to 1944.*

The New Negro
Breaks the icons of his detractors,
Wipes out the conspiracy of silence,
Speaks to *his* America . . .
—"DARK SYMPHONY," RENDEZVOUS WITH AMERICA *(1944)*

Europe is an empty python hiding in the grass.
—LIBRETTO FOR THE REPUBLIC OF LIBERIA *(1953)*

Through a glass darkly I saw the face
of a fantast, heard the undated voice of a poet crying,
among scattered bones in a stony place,
"No man cares for my soul!"
—"ZETA," HARLEM GALLERY *(1965)*

. . . I am conscious of the noiseless tread
of the Yazoo tiger's ball-like pads behind me
in the dark
as I trudge ahead,
up and up . . . that Lonesome Road . . . up and up.
—"PSI," HARLEM GALLERY

How could a civilization be "gone with the wind" unless there was something to MAKE it go?
—"GONE WITH THE WIND *IS MORE DANGEROUS THAN* BIRTH OF A NATION,"
WASHINGTON TRIBUNE, *MARCH 23, 1940*

A civilization is always judged in its decline.

—<small>IN MARI EVANS, BLACK WOMEN WRITERS</small> (1984)

Jean Toomer

(1 8 9 4 – 1 9 6 7)

Nathan Eugene Toomer was born into a prestigious family in Washington, D.C., and worked at various jobs before taking a position as a superintendent of schools in Georgia, the setting for his masterpiece, Cane, *one of the landmarks of the Harlem Renaissance. Though Toomer continued to write prose and poetry, only one additional volume was published, which did not enjoy the success of his earlier work.*

In my body were many bloods, some dark blood, all blended in the fire of six or more generations. I was, then, either a new type of man or the very oldest. In any case, I was inescapably myself.

—<small>UNPUBLISHED AUTOBIOGRAPHY</small>

A visit to Georgia last fall was the starting point of almost everything of worth that I have done. I heard folk-songs from the lips of Negro peasants. I saw the rich dusk beauty that I had heard many false accounts about, and of which til then I was somewhat skeptical. And a deep part of my nature, a part that I had repressed, sprang suddenly to life and responded to them.

—<small>THE LIBERATOR</small>, 1922

> An everlasting song, a singing tree,
> Caroling softly souls of slavery . . .
>
> —"<small>SONG OF THE SON,</small>" <small>CANE</small> (1923)

When one is on the soil of one's ancestors, most anything can come to one.

—Cane

> Cotton bales are the fleecy way
> Weary sinn'ers bare feet trod,
> Softly, softly to the throne of God.
> —"Cotton Song"

No eyes that have seen beauty ever lose their sight.

—Cane

The folk-spirit was walking in to die on the modern desert. That spirit was so beautiful. Its death was so tragic. Just this seemed to sum up life for me. And this was the feeling I put into "Cane." "Cane" was a swan-song. It was a song of the end.

— "On Being an American," The Wayward and the Seeking

> Their voices rise . . . the chorus of the cane
> Is caroling a vesper to the stars.
> —"Georgia Dusk"

The souls of old folks have a way of seein' things.

—Cane

I am not less poet; I am more conscious of all that I am, am not, and might become.

— "Remember and Return," Ibid.

Talk about it only enough to do it. Dream about it only enough to feel it. Think about it only enough to understand it. Contemplate it only enough to be it.

—Essentials: Definitions and Aphorisms (1931)

Once a man has tasted creative action, then thereafter, no matter how safely he schools himself in patience, he is restive, acutely dissatisfied with anything else. He becomes as a lover to whom abstinence is intolerable.

—Cynthia Kerman and Richard Eldridge, The Lives of Jean Toomer (1987)

I began feeling that I had in my hands the tools for my own creation.
—*UNPUBLISHED AUTOBIOGRAPHY*

We never know we are beings till we love. And then it is we know the powers and the potentialities of human existence, the powers and potentialities of organic, conscious, solar, cosmic matter and force. We, together, vibrate as one in harmony with man and with the cosmos.
—THE LIVES OF JEAN TOOMER

Perhaps . . . our lot on the earth is to seek and to search. Now and again we find just enough to enable us to carry on. I now doubt that any of us will completely find and be found in this life.
—*c. 1951*

Brother, life is water that is being drawn off.
—CANE

I feel that in time, in its social phase, my art will aid in giving the Negro to himself.
—*LETTER TO SHERWOOD ANDERSON, 1923*

William Monroe Trotter

(1 8 7 2 – 1 9 3 4)

A Phi Beta Kappa graduate of Harvard and editor of the Boston Guardian, *Trotter was an outspoken opponent of Booker T. Washington and once spent thirty days in jail for disrupting a meeting at which Washington was speaking. He was one of the founding members of the Niagara Movement and, in November 1914, had a controversial meeting with President Woodrow Wilson to protest discrimination in government offices in Washington.*

What man is a worse enemy to a race than a leader who looks with equanimity on the disfranchisement of his race in a country where other races have universal suffrage by constitutions that make one rule for his race and another for the dominant race . . . Let our spiritual advisers condemn this idea of reducing a people to serfdom to make them good.

—on Booker T. Washington, "Why Be Silent" (1902)

Silence is tantamount to being virtually an accomplice in this the treasonable act of this Benedict Arnold of the Negro race. O, for a black Patrick Henry to save his people from this stigma of cowardice; to rouse them from their lethargy to a sense of danger; to score the tyrant and to inspire his people with the spirit of those immortal words: "Give Me Liberty or Give Me Death."

—Ibid.

Only two years ago you were heralded as perhaps the second Lincoln and now the Afro-American leaders who supported you are hounded as false leaders and traitors to their race. What a change segregation has wrought!

—statement to the president, November 12, 1914

Have you a "new freedom" for white Americans and a new slavery for your Afro-American fellow citizens?

—a reference to Wilson's Four Freedoms, Ibid.

Sojourner Truth

(c . 1 7 9 7 – 1 8 8 3)

Born Isabella Baumfree into slavery in New York, Sojourner Truth worked on behalf of the Union cause during the Civil War and later for freemen's relief. She lectured at camp meetings and conventions in more than twenty states as a strong proponent of equal rights for both African American citizens and women.

Those are the same stars, and that is the same moon, that look down upon your brothers and sisters, and which they see as they look up to them, though they are ever so far away from us, and each other.

—NARRATIVE OF SOJOURNER TRUTH *(1878)*

Now the war begun.

—*ON BEING SOLD TO A HARSH MASTER, IBID.*

I was sure God would help me to get him. Why, I felt so *tall within*—I felt as if the *power of a nation* was with me!

—*DETERMINING TO FIND HER STOLEN CHILD, IBID.*

When I left the house of bondage I left everything behind. I wa'n't goin' to keep nothin' of Egypt on me, an' so I went to the Lord an' asked him to give me a new name. And the Lord gave me Sojourner because I was to travel up an' down the land showin' the people their sins an' being a sign unto them. Afterward I told the Lord I wanted another name 'cause everybody else had two names; and the Lord gave me Truth, because I was to declare the truth to the people.

—*IBID.*

I have ploughed, and planted, and gathered into barns, and no man could head me! And ain't I a woman? I could work as much and eat as much as a man—when I could get it—and bear the lash as well! And ain't I a woman? I have borne thirteen children, and seen 'em mos' all sold off to slavery, and when I cried out with my mother's grief, none but Jesus heard me! And ain't I a woman?

—*ADDRESS TO THE OHIO WOMEN'S RIGHTS CONVENTION, AKRON, OHIO, MAY 29, 1851*

If my cup won't hold but a pint and yours holds a quart, wouldn't you be mean not to let me have my little half measure full?

—*IBID.*

If the first woman God ever made was strong enough to turn the world upside down all alone, these women together ought to be able to turn it back, and get it right side up again.

—*IBID.*

We'll have our rights; see if we don't; and you can't stop us from them; see if you can. You may hiss as much as you like, but it is comin'. Women don't get half as much rights at they ought to; we want more, and we will have it.

—ADDRESS TO THE FOURTH NATIONAL WOMAN'S RIGHTS CONVENTION, NEW YORK, SEPTEMBER 7, 1853

I am sittin' among you to watch; and every once and awhile I will come out and tell you what time of night it is.

—IBID.

I come from another field—the country of the slave.

—ADDRESS TO THE FIRST ANNUAL MEETING OF THE AMERICAN EQUAL RIGHTS ASSOCIATION, NEW YORK, MAY 9, 1867

I feel that if I have to answer for the deeds done in my body just as much as a man, I have a right to have just as much as a man. There is a great stir about colored men gettin' their rights, but not a word about the colored women; and if colored men get their rights, and not colored women theirs, you see the colored men will be masters over the women, and it will be just as bad as it was before.

—IBID.

I have been forty years a slave and forty years free, and would be here forty years more to have equal rights for all. I suppose I am kept here because something remains for me to do; I suppose I am yet to help to break the chain.

—IBID.

We do as much, we eat as much, we want as much.

—IBID.

When we get our rights we shall not have to come to you for money, for then we shall have money enough in our own pockets.

—IBID.

am glad to see that men are getting their rights, but I want women o get theirs, and while the water is stirring I will step into the pool.

—IBID.

I have lived on through all that has taken place these forty years in the antislavery cause, and I have pleaded with all the force I had that the day might come that the colored people might own their own soul and body. Well, the day has come, although it came through blood. It makes no difference how it came—it did come.

—*Ibid.*

Taxes, you see, be taxes.

—*Ibid.*

It doesn't seem hard work to vote, though I have seen some men that had a hard time of it.

—*Ibid.*

I am not going to die, I'm going home like a shooting star.

—*c. 1883*

Harriet Tubman

(c . 1 8 2 0 – 1 9 1 3)

Born Ariminta Ross on the Eastern Shore of Maryland, Tubman escaped slavery at the age of twenty-five. She returned to the South nineteen times to spirit almost three hundred people to Canada on the Underground Railroad, "the midnight sky and the silent stars" serving as witness to her devotion to freedom. During the Civil War, she acted as a Union scout and spy, and then settled in Auburn, New York, where she ran a home for the aged.

'Pears like I prayed all de time, about my work, eberywhere; I was always talking to de Lord.

—*in Sarah Bradford*, Harriet Tubman: The Moses of Her People *(1886)*

I had reasoned dis out in my mind; there was one of two things I had a *right* to, liberty, or death; if I could not have one, I would have the other; for no man should take me alive; I should fight for my liberty as long as my strength lasted, and when the time came for me to go, the Lord would let them take me.

—*Ibid.*

I had crossed de line of which I had so long been dreaming. I was free; but dere was no one to welcome me to de land of freedom, I was a stranger in a strange land . . .

—*Ibid.*

Dead niggers tell no tales. You go on or die!

—*Ibid.*

Twan't *me,* 'twas *de Lord!* Jes' so long as he wanted to use me, he would take keer of me, an' when he didn't want me no longer, I was ready to go; I always tole him, I'm gwine to hole stiddy on to you, an' you've got to see me trou.

—*Ibid.*

Yes, John saw de City. Well, what did he see? He saw twelve gates, didn't he? Three of dose gates was on de north; three of 'em was on de east; an' three of 'em was on de west; but dere was three more, an' dem was on de *south;* an' I reckon, if dey kill me down dere, I'll get into one of dem gates, don't you?

—*Ibid.*

Dey may say, 'Peace, Peace,' as much as dey likes, *I know it's gwine to be war!*

—*Ibid.*

On my underground railroad I never ran my train off the track. And I never lost a passenger.

—*c. 1840*

f I never see you again I'll see you in the kingdom.

—*Letter to Mary Wright, May 29, 1896*

ℋenry ℳcℕeal 𝒯urner

(1 8 3 4 – 1 9 1 5)

Born free in South Carolina, Turner was self-educated and ordained in the Methodist Episcopal Church, preaching throughout the South before the Civil War. When he was elected to the Georgia legislature during Reconstruction, Southern Democrats attempted to deny him his seat. In later life, Turner made four trips to Africa and was a strong proponent of colonization.

I am a member of this body. Therefore, sir, I shall neither fawn nor cringe before any party, nor stoop to beg . . . I am here to demand my rights, and to hurl thunderbolts at the men who would dare to cross the threshold of my manhood.

—SPEECH DELIVERED IN THE GEORGIA LEGISLATURE TO DEMAND HIS SEAT, SEPTEMBER 3, 1868

You may expel us, gentlemen, but I firmly believe that you will some-day repent it. The black man cannot protect a country, if the country doesn't protect him; and if, tomorrow, a war should arise, I would not raise a musket to defend a country where my manhood is denied.

—IBID.

In some places in America black is supposed to symbolize the devil and white symbolize God. But this is wrong, for the devil is white and never was black.

—BALTIMORE AFRO-AMERICAN, MAY 16, 1988

I believe that the two or three millions of us should return to the land of our ancestors, and establish our own nation, civilization, laws, customs . . . What the black man needs is a country.

—DECEMBER 1895

For as long as whites enforce equality in the price of railroad tickets, and in every other particular, where we are required to pay and do, and be punished, some of us will believe that equality should be carried to a finish.

—c. 1895

Every race of people since time began who have attempted to describe God by words or painting, or by carvings, have conveyed their idea that the God who made them and shaped their destinies was symbolized in themselves, and why should not the Negro believe that he resembles God as much as other people?

—"God Is a Negro," The Voice of Mission, February 1898

No verdict of guilt from a drunken lawless mob should be accepted by a civilized country; and when they do accept it they become a barbarous people.

—in David Culp, Twentieth-Century Negro Literature (1902)

Nat Turner

(1800–1831)

Born in Southampton County, Virginia, Turner experienced religious visions in his youth. On August 21, 1831, he led an armed revolt through the nearby countryside, "sparing neither age nor sex." When the group was captured, fifteen members were hanged at once. Turner remained a fugitive for two months and made his famous "Confessions" a few days before he was hanged on November 11, 1831.

I had too much sense to be raised, and, if I was, I would never be of any service to any one as a slave.

—"Confessions of Nat Turner"

I saw white spirits and black spirits engaged in battle, and the sun was darkened—the thunder rolled in the heavens, and blood flowed in streams—and I heard a voice saying, "Such is your luck, such you are called to see; and let it come rough or smooth, you must surely bear it."

—*Ibid.*

I heard a loud noise in the heavens, and the Spirit instantly appeared to me and said the Serpent was loosened, and Christ had laid down the yoke He had borne for the sins of men, and that I should take it on and fight against the Serpent, for the time was fast approaching when the first should be last and the last should be first.

—*Ibid.*

I am loaded here with chains, and willing to suffer the fate that awaits me.

—*Ibid.*

Tina Turner

(1 9 3 9 –   )

Annie Mae Bullock was born in rural Tennessee and sang in church choirs and local contests before she met the pianist Ike Turner, when she was sixteen. She married him two years later, and the Ike and Tina Turner Revue enjoyed a string of hits like "Fool in Love," "Proud Mary," and "River Deep, Mountain High." After years of abuse Tina Turner divorced her husband in 1976 and achieved new success in the films Tommy *and* Mad Max Beyond Thunderdome, *as well as with the album* Private Dancer, *which won several Grammy awards. A film of her life,* What's Love Got to Do with It?, *was released to popular acclaim in 1993.*

I didn't have anybody, really, no foundation in life, so I had to make my own way. Always, from the start. I had to go out in the world and become strong, to discover my mission in life.

—I, TINA *(1986)*

I never said "Well, I don't have this and I don't have that." I said, "I don't have this *yet*, but I'm going to get it."

—Ibid.

Sometimes you've got to let *everything* go—purge yourself. I did that. I had nothing, but I had my freedom . . . If you are unhappy with anything . . . whatever is bringing you down, get rid of it. Because you'll find that when you're free, your true creativity, your true self comes out.

—Ibid.

The real power behind whatever success I have now was something I found within myself—something that's in all of us, I think, a little piece of God just waiting to be discovered.

—Ibid.

Mike Tyson

(1 9 6 6 –   )

Iron Mike Tyson spent a troubled youth on the streets of New York before he began training at the age of thirteen. In November 1986, he became the youngest fighter to win the WBF heavyweight title, and in January 1988 he retired Larry Holmes in a fourth-round knockout. After a brief troubled marriage to the actress Robin Givens, he received a six-year sentence for a rape conviction in 1992.

I can't change myself. I'm Mike Tyson. I'm a regular kid from the ghetto striving to do something positive with myself. I happen to fight well.

—<small>IN HARRY MULLAN</small>, THE BOOK OF BOXING QUOTATIONS (1988)

I just love to fight. I like to hurt people.

—Ibid.

I just took out the garbage, like I always do.
—AFTER HIS TITLE FIGHT WITH TREVOR BERBICK, NOVEMBER 22, 1986

I think religion is going to change my life. Baptism is an unbelievable experience.
—ON HIS 1988 BAPTISM BY JESSE JACKSON, IN ARTHUR ASHE, A HARD ROAD TO GLORY (1988)

It makes you want to cry to see old friends who failed to beat the trap into which they were born. I could so easily have become one of them. I was running wild and I was either going to end up locked away in prison, or dead.
—IN HARRY MULLAN, THE BOOK OF BOXING QUOTATIONS (1988)

Experience is sometimes better than money.
—JET, NOVEMBER 14, 1988

United Negro College Fund

In 1983, this scholarship organization adopted one of the most famous slogans in advertising history.

A mind is a terrible thing to waste.

Sarah Vaughan

(1914 – 1990)

A legendary talent, Sassy Vaughan was born in Newark and sang with church choirs and at parties before she was discovered by Billy Eckstine at amateur night at the Apollo Theater in October 1942. Fond of the nightlife, and with several husbands to her credit, "the Divine One" worked with Charlie Parker and Dizzy Gillespie under the band leader Earl Hines and later with Eckstine, and recorded many jazz standards before her death from lung cancer in 1990.

It's singing with soul that counts.
—Down Beat, *May 30, 1957*

Choir singing's a wonderful thing for what ails you. There's a lot of meaning in a hymn if you think about it when you're singing it. And the music is there, just about as beautiful as it can be.
—New York Post *interview, c. 1946*

I like to pick good notes. The right note is not always the best note for me. I like to hear the good notes.
—in Leslie Gourse, Sassy *(1993)*

God is good.
—on her talent, widely attributed

I drink booze, I smoke cigarettes, I stay high, I stay up all night, I hang out.
—on how she maintained her voice; Sassy

I'd like to go broke again, and this time I'd like to spend all the money myself.
—Ibid.

I don't think black or white. I have to tell you that. I think of human beings, people . . . My mother raised me that way.

—*Ibid.*

Music is not perfect. When it's perfect, it's too . . . it's not right.

—*National Public Radio interview, c. 1987*

I've been singing all my life, and I've never really thought about anything else since that amateur hour. But I'm the same way now that I was when I was eighteen. I don't go for that star suff. All the stars are in heaven.

—*Down Beat, May 1982*

It sure is a nice feeling to know that people will remember you after you've gone—that you'll manage to be a little bit of history.

—*interview with the jazz critic Leonard Feather, in Sassy*

$\mathcal{D}$enmark Vesey

(? – 1 8 2 2)

Born in the West Indies, Vesey purchased his own freedom in 1800 and worked as a sailor and carpenter. He was the organizer of one of the most significant early uprisings in Charleston, South Carolina, and was executed in 1822.

We are free, but the white people here won't let us be so; and the only way is to rise up and fight the whites.

—*from testimony at his trial, 1822*

Alice Walker

Poet, essayist, and novelist, Alice Walker was born in Eatonton, Georgia, and attended Spelman College and Sarah Lawrence College. She is the author of the Pulitzer Prize–winning The Color Purple, *among other novels, as well as several volumes of poetry and prose. She has also been an important force as a critic and essayist.*

To acknowledge our ancestors means we are aware that we did not make ourselves, that the line stretches all the way back, perhaps to God, or to Gods. We remember them because it is an easy thing to forget; that we are not the first to suffer, rebel, fight, love, and die. The grace with which we embrace life, in spite of the pain, the sorrows, is always a measure of what has gone before.
—*"In These Dissenting Times,"* Revolutionary Petunias *(1970)*

Shit, nobody's as powerful as we make them out to be. We got our own souls, don't we?
—The Third Life of Grange Copeland *(1970)*

Most of what I'm saying is *you got to hold tight a place in you where they can't come* . . . We keep killing ourselves for people that don't even mean nothing *to* us!
—*Ibid.*

Black women were always imitating Harriet Tubman—escaping to become something unheard of.
—Meridian *(1976)*

Is there no place in a revolution for a person who *cannot* kill?
—*Ibid.*

When they stop to wash off the blood and find their throats too choked with the smell of murdered flesh to sing, I will come forward and sing from memory songs they will need once more to hear. For it is the song of the people, transformed by the experiences of each generation, that holds them together, and if any part of it is lost, the people suffer and are without soul.

—*Ibid.*

All the people who are as alone as I am will one day gather at the river. We will watch the evening sun go down. And in the darkness maybe we will know the truth.

—*Ibid.*

It is not my child who has purged my face from history and herstory and left mystory just that, a mystery; my child loves my face and would have it on every page, if she could, as I have loved my own parents' faces above all others, and refused to let them be denied, or myself to let them go.

—"One *Child of One's Own*," in Janet Sternburg, The Writer on Her Work *(1980)*

Poetry, I have discovered, is always unexpected and always as faithful and honest as dreams.

—We Have a Beautiful Mother *(1991)*

You better not never tell nobody but God. It'd kill your mammy.

—The Color Purple *(1982)*

I am preoccupied with the spiritual, the survival *whole* of my people. But, beyond that, I am committed to exploring the oppressions, the insanities, the loyalties, and the triumphs of Black women.

—in John O'Brien, Interviews with Black Writers *(1973)*

I believe in the soul. Furthermore, I believe it is prompt accountability for one's choices, a willing acceptance of responsibility for one's thoughts, behavior, and actions that makes it powerful.

—*afterword to second edition of* Grange Copeland *(1988)*

I just say, Never mine, never mine, long as I can spell G-o-d I got somebody along.

—The Color Purple

She look like she ain't long for this world but dressed well for the next.

—*IBID.*

White folks is a miracle of affliction.

—*IBID.*

I think it pisses God off if you walk by the color purple in a field somewhere and don't notice it.

—*IBID.*

Why any woman give a shit what people think is a mystery to me.

—*IBID.*

I'm pore, I'm black, I may be ugly and can't cook, a voice say to everything listening. But I'm here.

—*IBID.*

There is no book more important to me than this one.

—*ON HURSTON'S* THEIR EYES WERE WATCHING GOD

When we have children you do everything in your power to make them feel unwanted from the moment they are born . . . Abortion, for many women, is more than an experience of suffering beyond anything most men will ever know, it is an act of mercy, and an act of self-defense.

—*"THE RIGHT TO LIFE: WHAT CAN THE WHITE MAN SAY TO THE BLACK WOMAN?," SPEECH, WASHINGTON, D.C., APRIL 8, 1989*

She understood, finally, that the respect she owed her life was to continue, against whatever obstacles, to live it, and not to give up any particle of it without a fight to the death, preferably *not* her own. And that this existence extended beyond herself to those around her because, in fact, the years in America had created them One Life.

—MERIDIAN

Madame C. J. Walker

(1867–1919)

Born Sarah Breedlove, Walker was orphaned at seven, married at fourteen, and widowed at twenty. In 1905 she began marketing hair products, and soon launched a cosmetics and cosmetology school business that would make her the first self-made woman millionaire in America.

Don't sit down and wait for the oportunities to come; you have to get up and make them.

—c. 1914

America doesn't respect anything but money . . . What our people need is a few millionaires.

They are positively the only remedies on the market that do not record a single failure to do all that they are recommended to do.

—"Why This Company Succeeded," 1924 Year Book and Almanac, *published by the Madame C. J. Walker Mfg. Co.*

THE SECRET OF A HAPPY LIFE
Lord help me live from day to day
In such a self-forgotten way
That when I kneel to pray
My prayer shall be for—OTHERS

—HER MOTTO

$\mathcal{D}$avid Walker

(1 7 8 5 – 1 8 3 0)

*T*he author of one of the most powerful documents in early American history, Walker was born free in North Carolina and settled in
Boston, where he was a merchant and abolitionist. His wide-ranging
Appeal *recalled the founding principles of the Republic and posed the
threat of armed insurrection in making its case for abolition. Its
impact was enormous, and Walker was found dead near his shop on
June 28, 1830.*

I write without the fear of man, I am writing for my God, and fear
none but himself.

> —WALKER'S APPEAL, IN FOUR ARTICLES *(1829)*

They think because they hold us in their infernal chains of slavery,
that we wish to be white, or of their color—but they are dreadfully
deceived—we wish to be just as it pleased our Creator to have made
us.

> —*IBID.*

God will not suffer us always to be oppressed. Our sufferings will
come to an *end,* in spite of all the Americans this side of *eternity.*

> —*IBID.*

Fortune and misfortune, two inseparable companions, lay rolled up in
he wheel of events.

> —*IBID.*

Can the Americans escape God Almighty? If they do, can he be to us a
God of Justice?

> —*IBID.*

If you commence, make sure you work—do not trifle, for they will
not trifle with you—they want us for their slaves and think nothing of

murdering us in order to subject us to that wretched condition—
therefore, if there is an *attempt* made by us, kill or be killed.

—Ibid.

The bare name of educating the coloured people, scares our cruel
oppressors almost to death.

—Ibid.

When God Almighty commences his battle on the continent of America, for the oppression of his people, tyrants will wish they never were
born.

—Ibid.

Man is a peculiar creature—he is the image of his God, though he
may be subjected to the most wretched condition upon earth, yet the
spirit and feeling which constitute the creature, man, can never be
entirely erased from his breast, because God who made him after his
own image, planted it in his heart.

—Ibid.

Let no man of us budge one step, and let slave-holders come to beat
us from our country. America is more our country, than it is the
whites—we have enriched it with our *blood and tears*.

—Ibid.

I believe there are some true-hearted sons of Africa, in this land of
oppression, but pretended *liberty!!!!!*

—Ibid.

Some of you [whites] on the continent of America, will yet curse the
day that you ever were born. You want slaves, and want us for your
slaves!!! My colour will yet root some of you out of the very face of the
earth!!!!!!

—Ibid.

Treat us like men, and there is no danger but we will all live in peace
and happiness together. For we are not like you, hard-hearted, un
merciful, and unforgiving. What a happy country this will be, if the
whites will listen.

—Ibid.

Margaret Walker

(1 9 1 5 -)

*B*orn in Alabama, Walker was one of the most important poets to emerge in the 1930s, and her volume For My People *won the Yale Younger Poets Award in 1942. She captures the struggles of Southern blacks in much of her work and is also the author of* Jubilee, *the bestselling, extensively researched novel about several generations of a black family in the Civil War–era South.*

I want to write the songs of my people . . . I want to frame their dreams into words; their souls into notes.

—*WRITTEN AT AGE NINETEEN,* THE CRISIS, *APRIL 1934*

Let a new earth rise. Let another world be born. Let a bloody peace be written in the sky . . . Let the martial songs be written, let the dirges disappear. Let a race of men now rise and take control.

—*"FOR MY PEOPLE"*

Our children . . . do not allow us to remain cowards, complacent, nor withdrawn. They force us to face the bitterness and dare us to explain the pain. Much as it hurts, we owe them the truth.

—*"HOW I TOLD MY CHILD ABOUT RACE,"* NEGRO DIGEST, *AUGUST 1951*

My grandmothers are full of memories.

—*"LINEAGE"*

How many years since 1619 have I been singing Spirituals
How long have I been praising God and shouting hallelujahs?

—*"SINCE 1619"*

I want my careless song to strike no minor key; no fiend to stand between my body's Southern song—the fusion of the South, my body's song and me.

—*"SOUTHERN SONG"*

There were bizarre beginnings in old lands for the making of me.
—*"Dark Blood"*

We have been believers believing in our burdens and our demigods too long. Now the needy no longer weep and pray; the long-suffering arise, and our fists bleed against the bars with a strange insistency.
—*"We Have Been Believers"*

The Word of fire burns today
On the lips of our prophets in an evil age.
—*"Prophets for a New Day"*

Beautiful were your sand-papering words against our skins!
—*"For Malcolm X"*

Talk had feet and could walk, and gossip had wings and could fly.
—Jubilee *(1966)*

Love stretches your heart and makes you big inside.
—*Ibid.*

I look up at the stars,
and I look at my scars,
and I look at my children
and I wonder . . .
—*slave song, Ibid.*

Once we were slaves, and now we are not and the South remains angry.
—How I Wrote Jubilee and Other Essays on Life and Literature *(1972)*

Once the human spirit is washed clean of prejudices, once the basic needs of people are considered, and not the pocketbooks of the few or the power of a handful; once institutionalized religion is liberated into religious meaning, of necessity there must begin to bloom upon the earth something spiritually more durable than any of the mystic conceptions of religion that humankind has thus far brought forth. Then no person will look at another with fear, patronage, condescension, hatred, or disparagement, under pain of one's own spiritual death.
—*Ibid.*

All around me was prejudice. To understand the issues out of which it grew became my life's preoccupation.

—*IBID.*

I sing these fragments of living that you may know by these presents that which we feared most has come upon us.

—*"TODAY"*

The poetry of a people comes from the deep recesses of the unconscious, the irrational and the collective body of our ancestral memories.

—BLACK WORLD, *DECEMBER 1971*

Fats Waller

(1 9 0 4 – 1 9 4 3)

Thomas Waller came to prominence in Harlem during the 1920s playing "stride" piano and organ. A high-spirited vocalist and the composer of such well-known standards as "Ain't Misbehavin' " and "Black and Blue," he led his own band from 1934 until his death.

They stopped me from swinging in church, so I had to swing outside.

—*c. 1935*

What did I do?
To be so black and blue?

—*"BLACK AND BLUE"*

What key are you struggling in?

—*A SIGNATURE PUT-DOWN*

Lady, if you got to ask, you ain't got it.

—*ASKED TO EXPLAIN RHYTHM*

One never know, do one?

—HIS CLASSIC LINE FROM STORMY WEATHER

Is this real, this fascination? Are my dreams holding you fast?

—C. 1936

I'm very glad to see that jazz has finally come back to his pappy, Melody . . . It is my contention, and always has been, that the thing that makes a tune click is the melody, and give the public four bars of that to dig their teeth into, and you have a killer-diller.

—IN NAT SHAPIRO AND NAT HENTOFF, HEAR ME TALKIN' TO YA (1955)

I'd like to close with a message to my dear little wife—get that man outta there, honey, 'cause I'm coming home directly.

—RADIO BROADCAST, C. 1950

To live the life I love.

—HIS MOTTO

Eric Walrond

(1 8 9 8 – 1 9 6 6)

Born in British Guiana, Walrond came to New York in 1918, where he attended City College and worked as a journalist for Garvey's Negro World *and for* Opportunity. *He published numerous essays in leading magazines, as well as* Tropic Death *(1926), a collection of stories.*

The American negro of today believes intensely in America . . . He is pinning everything on the hope, illusion or not, that America will some day find its soul, forget the negro's black skin, and recognize him as one of the nation's most loyal sons and defenders.

—"THE NEW NEGRO FACES AMERICA," NEW YORK TIMES CULTURAL HISTORY MAGAZINE, FEBRUARY 1923

With its rise, its struggles, its beginnings; its loves, its hates, its visionings, its tossings on the crest of the storming white sea; its orgies, its gluttonies; its restraints, its passivities; its spiritual yearnings—it is beautiful . . . It is wise, is this black city.

—ON HARLEM, *"THE BLACK CITY,"* THE MESSENGER, *JANUARY 1924*

The blows rain. The men sang . . .

—*"SUBJECTION"*

Samuel Ringgold Ward

(1 8 1 7 – 1 8 6 6)

The son of escaped slaves from Maryland, Ward was self-educated and entered the Presbyterian ministry in New York. Standing six feet tall, he was a striking and popular abolitionist speaker. He vowed that "Sam Ward . . . will never be taken alive" and was a frequent contributor to the black press and a conductor on the Underground Railroad. Because of his lifelong fugitive status, he traveled to Canada, England, and Jamaica, where he lived from the mid-1850s until his death.

There are many attempts to get up compromises—and there is no term which I detest more than this, it is always the term which makes right yield to wrong; it has always been accursed since Eve made the first compromise with the devil.

—*SPEECH ON THE FUGITIVE SLAVE BILL, FANEUIL HALL, BOSTON,* THE LIBERATOR, *APRIL 5, 1850*

Such crises as these leave us the right of Revolution, and if need be, that right we will, at whatever cost, most sacredly maintain.

—*IBID.*

The business of catching slaves, or kidnapping freemen, is an open warfare upon the rights and liberties of the black men of the North.

Let them know that to enlist in that warfare is present, certain, inevitable death and damnation.

—The Impartial Citizen, *October 1850*

One of my earliest and firmest determinations, one yet unshaken by years of poverty, and progressing premature old age, was *to serve my own people, to the extent of my very limited ability—whensoever, howsoever, and wheresoever, I might have opportunity.*

—The Aliened American, *April 9, 1853*

The question now mooted and to be settled, is, how long shall this important, increasing, progressive, class of American-born citizens be trodded under foot? . . . Shall the great fundamental principles of this Republic, ever be practically applied alike to whites and to blacks?

—*Ibid.*

When the God of the Poor and Needy shall arise to overwhelm this people, by the inflicting of long deferred but too well deserved judgments, at the hands of the *spoiler* and not the *spoiled,* will an account for all this iniquity be required.

—*Ibid.*

I have often been called a nigger, and some have tried to make me believe it; and the only consolation that has been offered me for being called nigger was that when I die and go to heaven, I shall be white. But if I cannot go to heaven as black as God made me, let me go down to hell and dwell with the Devil forever.

—Autobiography of a Fugitive Slave, *1855*

My father and I talked very freely of his death. He had always maintained that a Christian ought to have his preparation for his departure made, and completed in Christ, before death, so as when death should come he should have nothing to do BUT TO DIE. "That," said my father, "is enough to do at once."

—*Ibid.*

My private opinion is, that he who would have enslaved me would have "caught a Tartar": for my peace principles never extended so far as to *either seek or accept peace at the expense of liberty.*

—*Ibid.*

Yes, reader, we who are slaveborn derive a comfort and solace from the death of those dearest to us, if they have the sad misfortune to be BLACKS and AMERICANS, that you know not.

—*IBID.*

What an ever-present demon the spirit of hate is.

—*IBID.*

$\mathcal{B}$ooker $\mathcal{C}$. Washington

(1 8 5 6 – 1 9 1 5)

Born into slavery, Washington became the most prominent African American of his day, dispensing enormous political patronage through his Tuskegee Machine and the National Negro Business League, and writing a dozen books, including his immensely popular autobiography, Up From Slavery. *His controversial Atlanta Exposition Address, which outlined his pragmatic philosophy, found many critics but nonetheless would be echoed in later calls for mutual aid and economic self-empowerment.*

Brains, property, and character for the Negro will settle the question of civil rights . . . Educate the black man, mentally and industrially, and there will be no doubt of his prosperity.

—*"THE EDUCATIONAL OUTLOOK IN THE SOUTH," SPEECH TO THE NATIONAL EDUCATION ASSOCIATION, MADISON, WISCONSIN, JULY 16, 1884*

Throw aside every non-essential and cling only to the essential—his pillar of fire by night and his pillar of cloud by day shall be property, economy, education, and Christian character.

—*FUTURE OF THE AMERICAN NEGRO (1889)*

Character, not circumstances, makes the man.

—*JANUARY 31, 1896*

It seems to me that it is best to lay hold of the things we can put right rather than those we can do nothing but find fault with.

—*Fifth Tuskegee Conference, 1896*

The highest test of the civilization of any race is in its willingness to extend a helping hand to the less fortunate. A race, like an individual, lifts itself up by lifting others up.

—*Ibid.*

I cannot remember a single instance during my childhood or early boyhood when our entire family sat down to the table together, and God's blessing was asked, and the family ate a meal in a civilized manner.

—Up from Slavery *(1901)*

From some of the things that I have said one may get the idea that some of the slaves did not want freedom. This is not true. I have never seen one who did not want to be free, or one who would return to slavery.

—*Ibid.*

After the coming of freedom there were two points upon which practically all the people on our place were agreed . . . that they must change their names, and that they must leave the old plantation for at least a few days or weeks in order that they might really feel sure that they were free.

—*Ibid.*

When a white boy undertakes a task, it is taken for granted that he will succeed. On the other hand, people are usually surprised if the Negro boy does not fail. In a word, the Negro youth starts out with the presumption against him.

—*Ibid.*

There was never a time in my youth, no matter how dark and discouraging the days might be, when one resolve did not continually remain with me, and that was a determination to secure an education at any cost.

—*Ibid.*

I have learned that success is to be measured not so much by the position that one has reached in life as by the obstacles which he has overcome while trying to succeed.

—*IBID.*

It seemed to me as I watched this struggle between members of the two races, that there was no hope for our people in this country. The "Ku Klux" period was, I think, the darkest part of the Reconstruction days.

—*IBID.*

No white American ever thinks that any other race is wholly civilized until he wears the white man's clothes, eats the white man's food, speaks the white man's language, and professes the white man's religion.

—*IBID.*

My experience is that there is something in human nature which always makes an individual recognize and reward merit, no matter under what colour of skin merit is found.

—*IBID.*

In the long run, the world is going to have the best, and any difference in race, religion, or previous history will not long keep the world from what it wants.

—*IBID.*

To those of my race who underestimate the importance of cultivating friendly relations with the Southern white man, who is their next-door neighbor, I would say, "Cast down you bucket where you are"—cast it down in making friends in every manly way of the people of all races by whom we are surrounded."

—*ATLANTA INTERNATIONAL EXPOSITION ADDRESS, SEPTEMBER 18, 1895*

No race can prosper till it learns that there is as much dignity in tilling a field as in writing a poem. It is at the bottom of life we must begin, and not at the top. Nor should we permit our grievances to overshadow our opportunities.

—*IBID.*

455

In all things that are purely social we can be as separate as the fingers, yet one as the hand in all things essential to mutual progress.

—*Ibid.*

No race that has anything to contribute to the marketplace of the world is long in any degree ostracized.

—*Ibid.*

The wisest among my race understand that the agitation of questions of social equality is the extremest folly, and that progress in the enjoyment of all the privileges that will come to us must be the result of severe and constant struggle rather than of artificial forcing.

—*Ibid.*

This country demands that every race shall measure itself by the American standard. By it a race must rise or fall, succeed or fail, and in the last analysis mere sentiment counts for little.

—*Commencement Address at Harvard University, June 24, 1896*

No race of people ever got upon its feet without severe and constant struggle, often in the face of the greatest disappointment.

—*"The Case of the Negro," speech at Tuskegee, 1902*

You can't hold a man down without staying down with him.

—*Speeches of Booker T. Washington (1932)*

When you meet an American Negro who's not Methodist or a Baptist, some white man's been tampering with his religion.

—*Ibid.*

Never let work drive you, master it and keep in complete control.

—*Ibid.*

More and more we must learn to think not in terms of race or color or language or religion or of political boundaries, but in terms of humanity. Above all races and political boundaries there is humanity.

—*Up from Slavery*

I am willing to be misjudged, if need be, if I can accomplish a little good.

—*Letter to the Louisiana Constitutional Convention, February 19, 1898*

Harold Washington

(1 9 2 2 – 1 9 8 7)

Raised and educated in Chicago, Washington dominated its political life for three decades. He began his career in 1954 as an assistant counsel for the city, was elected to the Illinois House in 1965 and the state Senate in 1976, and in 1980 to the U.S. Congress. He had just been re-elected to that seat by an enormous margin in 1982 when he announced his candidacy for mayor and in April 1983 became Chicago's first black mayor.

Finally, "the city that works" doesn't work anymore . . . I see a Chicago in which the neighborhoods are once again the center of our city, in which businesses boom and provide neighborhood jobs, in which neighbors join together to help govern their neighborhood and their city. Some may say this is visionary—I say *they* lack vision.

—*PRESS CONFERENCE ANNOUNCING HIS CANDIDACY FOR MAYOR, NOVEMBER 10, 1982*

This has truly been a pilgrimage. We never stopped believing that we were part of something good that has never happened before.

—*ON HIS ELECTION, APRIL 1983*

Most of our problems can be solved. Some of them will take brains, and some of them will take patience, but all of them will have to be wrestled with like an alligator in the swamp.

—*INAUGURAL SPEECH, APRIL 20, 1983*

I'm an optimist, not just because I have a positive view of life, but because there is so much about this city that promises achievement. We are a multiethnic, multiracial, multilanguage city and that is a source of stability and strength . . . In our ethnic and racial diversity, we are all brothers and sisters in a quest for greatness.

—*IBID.*

The idea one hundred and twenty years ago that Black votes would be the key to the presidential election would have seemed like wild-eyed conjecture.

—"SPEAKING OUT: THE BLACK VOTE," EBONY, NOVEMBER 1983

Ethel Waters

(1896-1977)

Raised in Philadelphia, Waters married unhappily at the age of thirteen but became an enormously pupular singer, dancer, and stage and screen actress. She was the first black woman to star on Broadway; she appeared in Cabin in the Sky *and* Member of the Wedding, *among other films, and wrote the autobiographies* His Eye Is on the Sparrow *and* To Me It's Wonderful *(1972).*

I can come where I please
I can go where I please
I can flit, fly, and flutter, like the birds in the trees.
—*"His Eye Is on the Sparrow" (1925)*

I was a tough child. I was too large and too poor to fit, and I fought back.

—*in "Ethel Waters," by William Gardner Smith, Phylon (1950)*

I could depend a lot on my shaking, though I never shimmied vulgarly and only to express myself.

—His Eye Is on the Sparrow *(1951)*

Bessie's shouting brought worship wherever she worked.

—*on Bessie Smith, in Nat Shapiro and Nat Hentoff, Hear Me Talkin' to Ya (1955)*

When I was a honky-tonk entertainer, I used to work from nine until unconsciousness. I was just a young girl, and when I tried to sing anything but the double-meaning songs, they'd say, "Oh, my God, Ethel, get hot!"

—*INTERVIEW WITH EARL WILSON*

I ask the Lord for so much that I guess I keep him scufflin'.

—*HIS EYE IS ON THE SPARROW*

$\mathcal{M}$axine Waters

(1 9 3 8 –)

Born in Saint Louis, Waters moved to Los Angeles after her gradua- tion from high school and later earned a degree from California State University. She was a delegate to the Democratic National Conven- tion in 1972 and in 1976 was elected to the California State Assem- bly. In 1990, she was elected to Congress, where she is a strong advocate for minorities and the poor, and she gained national promi- nence during the Los Angeles uprising in 1991.

The riots in Los Angeles and in other cities shocked the world. They shouldn't have. Many of us have watched our country—including our government—neglect the problems, indeed the people, of our inner cities for years—even as matters reached a crisis stage . . . For years, they have been crying out for help. For years, their cries have not been heard.

—*TESTIMONY BEFORE THE SENATE BANKING COMMITTEE AFTER THE LOS ANGELES RIOTS, MAY 14, 1992*

The challenge for us is to put together our own legislative agenda, not simply support or not support the agenda of the House.

—*ON THE NEW ROLE OF BLACK POLITICIANS*, WASHINGTON POST, *SEPTEMBER 19, 1993*

Ida B. Wells (Barnett)

(1 8 6 2 – 1 9 3 1)

Born into slavery, Ida B. Wells Barnett waged a fearless "crusade for justice" and, as a journalist and author, spoke out boldly against lynching, particularly in her comprehensive account, A Red Record. *Married in 1895 to the lawyer and publisher Ferdinand Lee Barnett, she was also active in the women's club movement and was a founding member of the NAACP.*

I have firmly believed all along that the law was on our side and would, when we appealed to it, give us justice. I feel shorn of that belief and utterly discouraged, and just now, if it were possible, would gather my race in my arms and fly away with them. O God, is there no redress, no peace, no justice in the land for us?

—*AFTER LOSING A COURT CASE PROTESTING* JIM CROW *TRAIN CARS, FROM HER DIARY,*
APRIL 11, 1887

In slave times the Negro was kept subservient and submissive by the frequency and severity of the scourging, but, with freedom, a new system of intimidation came in vogue; the Negro was not only whipped and scourged; he was killed.

—CRUSADE FOR JUSTICE: THE AUTOBIOGRAPHY OF IDA B. WELLS
(PUBLISHED POSTHUMOUSLY, 1970)

Nobody in this section of the country believes the old threadbare lie that Negro men rape white women. If Southern white men are not careful, they will over-reach themselves and public sentiment will have a reaction; a conclusion will then be reached which will be very damaging to the moral reputation of their women.

—*FROM THE EDITORIAL IN* MEMPHIS FREE SPEECH, *MAY 25, 1892,*
THAT CAUSED HER OFFICE TO BE RANSACKED AND HER LIFE THREATENED

True chivalry respects all womanhood, and no one who reads the record, as it is written in the faces of the million mulattoes in the South, will for a minute conceive that the southern white man had a very chivalrous regard for the honor due the women of his own race or respect for the womanhood which circumstances placed in his power.

—*FROM* A RED RECORD *(1895)*

It becomes the painful duty of the Negro to reproduce a record which shows that a large portion of the American people avow anarchy, condone murder, and defy the contempt of civilization.

—*IBID.*

Out of their own mouths shall the murderers be condemned.

—*IBID.*

I felt that one had better die fighting against injustice than to die like a dog or rat in a trap. I had already determined to sell my life as dearly as possible if attacked. I felt if I could take one lyncher with me, this would even up the score a little bit.

—CRUSADE FOR JUSTICE

The more I studied the situation, the more I was convinced that the Southerner had never gotten over his resentment that the Negro was no longer his plaything, his servant, and his source of income.

—*IBID.*

In the death of Frederick Douglass we lost the greatest man that the Negro race has ever produced on the American continent.

—*IBID.*

I had already found that motherhood was a profession by itself, just like schoolteaching and lecturing, and that once one was launched on such a career, she owed it to herself to become as expert as possible in the practice of her profession.

—*IBID.*

I had always felt that the man who bought votes was just as much to be condemned as the man who sold them.

—*IBID.*

I would consider it an honor to spend whatever years are necessary in prison as the one member of the race who protested, rather than to be with all the 11,999,999 Negroes who didn't have to go to prison because they kept their mouths shut.

—*ON THE LYNCHING OF BLACK VETERANS OF WORLD WAR I; IBID.*

Many people wonder at the crime wave sweeping over our country, at the horrible murders committed by young bandits, and the cold-blooded taking of life by the men and women of this generation with white skins. Strange they do not seem to realize that this is simply a reaping of the harvest which has been sown by those who administer justice.

—*AFTER THE EAST SAINT LOUIS RIOTS, 1917; IBID.*

But why don't you pray to live and ask to be freed? The God you serve is the God of Paul and Silas, who opened their prison gates, and if you have all the faith you say you have, you ought to believe that he will open your prison door too.

—*TO THE MEN IMPRISONED AFTER THE ARKANSAS RIOT OF 1922. THEY WERE ALL FREED; IBID*

Let the Afro-American depend on no party, but on himself for his salvation.

—*"IOLA'S SOUTHERN FIELD," THE NEW YORK AGE, NOVEMBER 18, 1892.*

Threats cannot suppress the truth.

—A RED RECORD

Cornel West

(1 9 5 3 –)

An ordained minister, Cornel West was until 1988 Professor of Religion and Director of Afro-American Studies at Princeton University. He recently joined the faculty of Harvard as Professor of African-American Studies and the Philosophy of Religion. A charismatic speaker, he is the author of Keeping Faith, Prophetic Fragments, *and the bestselling* Race Matters.

Let us hope and pray that the vast intelligence, imagination, humor, and courage of Americans will not fail us. Either we learn a new language of empathy and compassion, or the fire this time will consume us all.

—RACE MATTERS *(1993)*

We need leaders—neither saints nor sparkling television personalities—who can situate themselves within a larger historical narrative of this country and our world, who can grasp the complex dynamics of our peoplehood and imagine a future grounded in the best of our past, yet who are attuned to the frightening obstacles that now perplex us. Our ideals of freedom, democracy, and equality must be invoked to invigorate all of us, especially the landless, propertyless, and luckless.

—*IBID.*

The major enemy of black survival in America has been and is neither oppression nor exploitation but rather the nihilistic threat—that is, loss of hope and absence of meaning. For as long as hope remains and meaning is preserved, the possibility of overcoming oppression stays alive.

—*"NIHILISM IN BLACK AMERICA," IBID.*

Black people have always been America's wilderness in search of a promised land.

—*IBID.*

Where there is no vision, the people perish; where there is no framework of moral reasoning, the people close ranks in a war of all against all.

—*"THE PERILS OF RACIAL REASONING," IBID.*

Humility is the fruit of inner security and wise maturity.

—*"THE CRISIS OF BLACK LEADERSHIP," IBID.*

Malcolm X sharply crystallized the relation of black affirmation of self, black desire for freedom, black rage against American society, and the likelihood of early black death.

—*"MALCOLM X AND BLACK RAGE," IBID.*

The power of the civil rights movement under Martin Luther King was its universalism. Now, instead of the civil rights movement being viewed as a moral crusade for freedom, it's become an expression of a particular interest group. Once you lose that moral high ground, all you have is a power struggle, and that has never been a persuasive means for the weaker to deal with the stronger.

—New York Times, *April 3, 1991*

$\mathcal{P}hillis\ \mathcal{W}heatley$

(c . 1 7 5 3 - 1 7 8 4)

Kidnapped as a child in Africa, Wheatley arrived in Boston in 1761 and within sixteen months had learned to read and write English. She began composing verse at fourteen, and when no American publisher would accept her poems, she traveled to England. There, Poems on Various Subjects, Religious and Moral, the first book by an African American author, was published in 1773. She was freed upon the death of her master in the mid-1770s, but died in poverty some years later.

'Twas mercy brought me from my *Pagan* land
    —*"On being brought from Africa to America"*

But here I sit, and mourn a grov'ling mind
That fain would mount and ride upon the wind.
    —*"To Maecenas"*

Wash'd in the fountain of redeeming blood,
You shall be sons, and kings, and priests to God.
    —*"On the Death of the Rev. Mr. George Whitefield"*

Imagination! who can sing thy force?
Or who describe the swiftness of thy course?

Soaring through air to find the bright abode,
Th'empyreal palace of the thund'ring God,
We on thy pinions can surpass the wind
And leave the rolling universe behind.
                    —*"On Imagination"*

In every human Breast, God has implanted a Principle, which we call
Love of Freedom; it is impatient of Oppression, and pants for Deliverance; and by the Leave of our Modern Egyptians I will assert, that the
same Principle lives in us.
            —*letter to Samson Occom, February 11, 1774*

No more, *America,* in mournful strain
Of wrongs, and grievance unredress'd complain,
No longer shall thou dread the iron chain,
Which wanton *Tyranny* with lawless hand
Had made, and with it meant t'enslave the land
                        . . .
I, young in life, by seeming cruel fate
Was snatch'd from *Afric's* fancy'd happy seat:
What pangs excruciating must molest,
What sorrows labour in my parent's breast?
Steel'd was that soul and by no misery mov'd
That from a father seiz'd his babe belov'd:
Such, such my case. And can I then but pray
Others may never feel tyrannic sway?
        —*"To the Right Honourable William, Earl of Darmouth"*

This Eternity how dreadful, how delightful!
                —*letter to John Thornton, December 1, 1773*

But thou! Temptation hence away,
With all thy fatal train
Nor once seduce my soul away,
By thine enchanting strain.
            —*"A Farewell to America"*

Proceed, great chief, with virtue on thy side,
Thy ev'ry action let the goddess guide.

A crown, a mansion, and a throne that shine,
With gold unfading, WASHINGTON! be thine.
— *"TO HIS EXCELLENCY GENERAL WASHINGTON"*

To every Realm shall *Peace* her Charms display,
And Heavenly *Freedom* spread her golden Ray.
— *"LIBERTY AND PEACE"*

Wisdom is higher than a fool can reach.
— *"ON VIRTUE"*

Each human heart inspire:
To act in bounties unconfin'd
Enlarge the close contracted and,
And fill it with thy fire.
— *"AN HYMN TO HUMANITY"*

Let us not sell our birthright for a thousand worlds, which indeed would be as dust upon the balance.
— *LETTER TO OBOUR TANNER, OCTOBER 30, 1773*

The world is a severe schoolmaster, for its frowns are less dang'rous than its smiles and flatteries, and it is a difficult task to keep in the path of Wisdom.
— *LETTER TO JOHN THORNTON, OCTOBER 30, 1774*

William Whipper

(1 8 0 1 – 1 8 8 5)

Born to a servant in the household of a Pennsylvania lumberman, Whipper was self-educated and became enormously successful in business and real estate. Active in the convention and abolition movements and the Underground Railroad, he was editor of The National Reformer *and was an early advocate of nonviolence and universal peace.*

All moral principles are universal in their nature, and application: they embrace "all men" without distinction.

—*c. 1835*

The practice of non-resistance to physical aggression, is not only consistent with reason, but the surest method of obtaining a speedy triumph of the principles of universal peace.

—*"AN ADDRESS ON NON-RESISTANCE TO OFFENSIVE AGGRESSION," THE COLORED AMERICAN, SEPTEMBER 16, 1937*

It is self-evident, that when the greatest difficulties surround us, we should summon our noblest powers.

—*IBID.*

The rich bequest of Heaven to man, was a natural body, a reasonable soul, and an immortal mind. With these he is rendered capable through the wisdom of Providence, of ascending to the throne of angels, or descending to the abyss of devils.

—*IBID.*

There is scarcely a single fact more worthy of indelible record, than the utter inefficiency of human punishments, to cure human evils. The history of wars exhibits a hopeless, as well as a fatal lesson, to all such enterprises . . . Human bodies have been lacerated with whips and scourges—prisons and penitentiaries have been erected for the immolation of human victims—the gibbet and halter have performed their office—while the increase of crime has kept pace with the genius of punishment.

—*Ibid.*

Our reasoning powers ought to be the helm that should guide us through the shoals and quicksands of life . . . If amidst these difficulties we can but possess our souls in patience, we shall finally triumph over our enemies.

—*Ibid.*

The spirit of passion has become so implanted in human bosoms, that the laws of our country give countenance to the same, by exhibiting lenity for those who are under its influence. This is doubtless a great error in legislation, because it not only pre-supposes the irrationality of man, but gives him a plea of innocence, in behalf of his idiotism.

—*Ibid.*

The love of power is one of the greatest human infirmities, and with it comes the usurping influence of despotism, the mother of slavery.

—*Ibid.*

With God, all is order—with man, all confusion.

—*Ibid.*

In our onslaught upon what we term separate institutions, we too frequently lose sight of the fact that to our church, association, and school we are at this hour chiefly indebted for whatever of preparation we have made for the great battle to today.

—*c. 1855*

Walter (Francis) White

(1893-1955)

Active in the local branch of the NAACP after his graduation from Atlanta University, White moved to New York in 1918 as an assistant secretary of the NAACP and spent a lifetime investigating riots and lynchings in Georgia, Arkansas, Chicago, Detroit, and elsewhere. His books include a study of lynching, Rope and Faggot, *the novels* The Fire in the Flint *(1924) and* Flight *(1955), and his autobiography,* A Man Called White *(1948).*

In the final analysis, lynching and mob violence, disfranchisement, unequal distribution of school funds, the Ku Klux Klan, and all other forms of racial prejudice are for one great purpose—that of keeping the Negro in the position where he is economically exploitable.

—The Crisis, *April 1923*

In any American village, North or South, East or West, there is no problem which cannot be solved in half an hour by the morons who lounge about the village store.

—"I Investigate Lynchings," The American Mercury

Intolerance can grow only in the soil of ignorance: from its branches grow all manner of obstacles to human progress.

—Rope and Faggot *(1929)*

The Negro must, without yielding, continue the grim struggle *for* integration and *against* segregation for his own physical, moral, and spiritual well-being and for that of white America and of the world at large.

—in Columbus Salley, The Black 100 *(1993)*

James Whitfield

(1 8 2 3 – 1 8 7 8)

Abolitionist writer and pro-colonization poet, writer, and orator, Whitfield was the author, most notably, of America and Other Poems *(1853).*

America, it is to thee
Thou boasted land of liberty—
It is to thee I raise my song
Thou land of blood and crime and wrong.
—*"America"*

John Edgar Wideman

(1 9 4 1 –)

Wideman grew up in the Homewood section of Pittsburgh and attended the University of Pennsylvania before winning a Rhodes Scholarship, in 1963. He has taught at Pennsylvania and the University of Wyoming, and his highly acclaimed works include the novel Sent for You Yesterday, *which won the PEN/ Faulkner Award, and the autobiographical* Brothers and Keepers.

What seems to ramble begins to cohere when the listener understands the process, understands that the voice seeks to recover everything, that the voice proclaims *nothing is lost,* that the listener is not passive but lives like everything else within the story.
—*"The Beginning of Homewood"*

I'm on my own feet. Learning to stand, to walk, learning to dance.
—Sent for You Yesterday *(1983)*

Fever grows in the secret places of our hearts, planted there when one of us decided to sell one of us to another.
—*"Fever" (1989)*

He already knows he will suffer for whatever he knows.
—Damballah *(1981)*

He publishes one book—the text of suffering—over and over again. He disguises it between new boards, in different shapes and sizes, prints on varying papers, in many fonts, adds prefaces and postscripts to deceive the buyer, but it's always the same book.
—*"Fever"*

The strong survive. The ones who are strong and *lucky*.
—Brothers and Keepers *(1984)*

Prison time must be hardtime, a metaphorical death, a sustained, twilight condition of death-in-life. The prisoner's life is violently interrupted, enclosed within a parenthesis. The point is to create the fiction that he doesn't exist. Prison is an experience of death by inches, minutes, hours, days.
—*Ibid.*

The streets had been my stomping ground, my briar patch. The place I'd fled from with all my might, the place always snatching me back.
—*Ibid.*

Every step and the way you take it here on enemy ground is a lesson.
—*Ibid.*

ℛoger Wilkins

(1 9 3 2 –   )

The nephew of the civil rights leader Roy Wilkins, Roger Wilkins was born in Kansas City, Missouri, and was an official in the Justice Department during the 1960s. He won a Pulitzer Prize for his Watergate editorials for the Washington Post *and is now a professor of political science at George Mason University in Virginia.*

I was an American boy, though I did not fully comprehend that . . . I was fully shaped and formed by America, and America is both powerful and racist.

—A Man's Life *(1982)*

I have been an explorer and I sailed as far out into the white world as a black man of my generation could sail . . . I could not stand white people shutting doors in my face, so I pushed through plenty of them.

—*Ibid.*

America loves to have black heroes because it tells America that we're fair and that the doors are open.

—*"Frontline," April 1991*

We have had preference programs in this country, and we still have them, and the preferred are white men. But somehow in the debate all the victims are white men worried that black men are going to take their jobs. The only place in America where blacks have taken jobs in a major way from whites is the National Basketball Association.

—New York Times, *April 3, 1991*

The struggle of life is not won with one glorious moment like Reggie Jackson's five straight home runs in a recent World Series—wonderful and thrilling though that was—but a continual struggle in which you keep your dignity intact and your powers at work, over the long course of a lifetime.

—A MAN'S LIFE

Roy Wilkins

(1 9 0 1 – 1 9 8 1)

Wilkins was active in the NAACP for more than thirty years, and as its executive, from 1955 to 1977, led it into alliances with other rights groups in a rapidly changing political environment. Born in Saint Paul, he was briefly a journalist before joining the NAACP in 1931, and also served as the editor of The Crisis, *after Du Bois's resignation, from 1934 until 1949.*

Negroes are still being registered one by one and only after long litigation. We must transform this retail litigation method of registration into a wholesale administration procedure registering all who seek to exercise their democratic birthright. The time is long overdue to sweep the last vestiges of voting restrictions into the sea.

—*TESTIMONY ON THE VOTING RIGHTS ACT BEFORE THE HOUSE JUDICIARY COMMITTEE, MARCH 24, 1965*

NAACP strategy . . . will continue, regardless of setbacks, to be one of pressing, on all fronts, in every field of endeavor, and by every productive method for the freedom of the individual to win equality under the Constitution and the Declaration of Independence.

—*ON THE EVE OF THE GARY, INDIANA, CONVENTION, MARCH 1972*

Of all violence, official violence is the most destructive. It not only takes life, but it does so in the name of the people and as the agent of the society. It says, therefore, this is our way, this is what we believe, we stand for nothing better.

—Search and Destroy: A Report by the Commission of Inquiry into the Black Panthers and the Police (1973)

In a free society the police must be accountable to the people.

—*Ibid.*

$\mathcal{B}$ert Williams

(1876–1922)

With George Walker, Williams was one of the most successful entertainers of his time. He toured Europe and appeared on Broadway with the Ziegfeld Follies.

The sight of people in trouble is nearly always funny. This is human nature . . . The man with the real sense of humor is the man who can put himself in the spectator's place and laugh at his own misfortune.

—"The Comic Side of Trouble," American Magazine, January 1918

Humor is the one thing in the world it is impossible to argue about, because it is all a matter of taste.

—*Ibid.*

I ain't never done nothing to nobody
I ain't never got nothing from nobody, no time
and until I get something from somebody, sometime
I don't intend to do nothing for nobody, no time.

—"Nobody" (c. 1922)

In truth, I have never been able to discover that there was anything disgraceful in being a colored man. But I have often found it inconvenient—in America.

—*"The Comic Side of Trouble"*

Fannie Barrier Williams

(1 8 5 5 – 1 9 4 4)

Born in Brockport, New York, Williams studied at the New England Conservatory of Music in Boston and the School of Fine Arts in Washington. She worked as a teacher before her marriage and then became active in the women's club movement, becoming the first black women admitted to the Women's Club of Chicago.

Afro-American women of the United States have never had the benefit of a discriminating judgment concerning their worth as women made up of the good and bad of human nature. What they have been made to be and not what they are, seldom enters into the best or worst opinion concerning them.

—*"The Club Movement Among Colored Women of America,"*
A New Negro for a New Century *(1900)*

The club movement . . . is something deeper than a mere imitation of white women. It is nothing less than the organized anxiety of women who have become intelligent enough to recognize their own low social conditions and strong enough to initiate the forces of reform.

—*Ibid.*

Women who have always lived and breathed the air of ample freedom and whose range of vision has been world-wide, will scarcely know what it means for women whose lives have been confined and dependent to feel the first consciousness of a relationship to the great social forces that include whole nationalities in the sweep of their influences. To feel that you are something better than a slave, or a descendant of an ex-slave, to feel that you are a unit in the womenhood of a great nation and a great civilization, is the beginning of self-respect and the respect of your race.

—*Ibid.*

It is the same old fight of light against darkness and progress against caste. Prejudice resists all that tends to soften the heart and enlighten the mind. It defies logic. It has no part with charity.

—"Club Movement Among Negro Women," in Progress of a Race *(1903)*

The colored women of the country have borne the burden of more misery than has ever been imposed upon womankind by a Christian nation. She knows herself and asks for the assistance and encouragement of those who are more or less responsible for this burden, yet there are thousands of free strong women in this country who would refuse her appeal.

—*Ibid.*

It is scarcely possible to enumerate the many ways in which an ambitious colored young woman is prevented from being all that she might be in the higher directions of life in this country.

—"A Northern Negro's Autobiography," The Independent *July 14, 1904*

Whether I live in the North or the South, I cannot be counted for my full value, be that much or little. I dare not cease to hope and aspire and believe in human love and justice, but progress is painful and my faith is often strained to the breaking point.

—*Ibid.*

George Washington Williams

(1 8 4 9 – 1 8 9 1)

Born in Pennsylvania, Williams joined the Union Army when he was in his teens and after the war entered Newton Theological Seminary in Massachusetts. He led congregations in Boston, Washington, and Cincinnati, and his growing interest in history led him to write two major works, which became the foundation of the study of African American history.

The Creator gave all nations arts and sciences. Where nations have turned aside to idolatry, they have lost their civilization.

—*c. 1876*

Not as a blind panegyrist of my race, nor as a partisan apologist, but for a love for *"the truth of history"* I have striven to record the truth, the whole truth, and nothing but the truth.

—History of the Negro Race in America *(1883)*

The war between the British colonies in North America and the mother country gave the Negro an opportunity to level, by desperate valor, a mountain of prejudice . . . History says he did it.

—*Ibid.*

The part enacted by the Negro soldier in the war of the Rebellion is the romance of North American history. It was midnight and noonday without a space between; from the Egyptian darkness of bondage to the lurid glare of civil war; from clanking chains to clashing arms; from passive submission to the cruel curse of slavery to the brilliant aggressiveness of a free solder; from a chattel to a person; from the shame of degradation to the glory of military exaltation; and from deep obscurity to fame and martial immortality.

—A History of the Negro Troops in the War of Rebellion: 1861–1865 *(1888)*

My language is not plainer than the truth, my philippic is not more cruel than the crimes exposed, my rhetoric is not more fiery than the trials through which these black troops passed, nor my conclusions without warrant of truth or justification of evidence.

—*Ibid.*

The Negro soldier had seen his red-letter day, and his title to patriotic courage was written in his own blood.

—*Ibid.*

Marion Williams

(1 9 2 8 – 1 9 9 4)

The pioneering gospel singer joined her church choir at the age of three and sang with the famed Clara Ward Singers while she was a teenager. She was a strong influence on Aretha Franklin and Little Richard, among others, and in 1993 received both the Kennedy Center Honors and a "genius grant" from the MacArthur Foundation.

I don't have nothing against other people and what they do, but I don't want no part of singing secular music. I was offered $100,000 to make one blues record, and I turned it down. I sing for the Lord, and that's enough for me.

—*c. 1993*

$\mathcal{R}$obert Williams

(1 9 2 5 –   )

After serving in the army, Williams returned to North Carolina, where he worked as a machinist and engaged in a campaign of letters to the editor of Charlotte newspapers, protesting discrimination. After he became president of the Union County NAACP chapter, he advocated armed self-defense, which caused the NAACP to suspend him. Williams fled to Cuba in 1961 after an outbreak of violence in Monroe, North Carolina.

We cannot rely on the law. We can get no justice under the present system. If we feel that injustice is done, we must right then and there, on the spot, be prepared to inflict punishment on the people. Since the federal government will not bring a halt to lynching in the South, and since the so-called courts lynch our people legally, if it's necessary to stop lynching with lynching, then we must be willing to resort to that method.

—ON THE STEPS OF THE COURTHOUSE, AFTER WHITE SUSPECTS WERE RELEASED FOR THE SAME CRIME
FOR WHICH A BLACK MAN WAS CONVICTED, MONROE, NORTH CAROLINA, MAY 5, 1959

Laws served to deter crime and protect the weak from the strong in a civilized society. Where there is a breakdown of law, where is the force of deterrent? Only highly civilized and moral individuals respect the rights of others . . . Nonviolence is a very potent weapon when the oppressor is civilized, but nonviolence is no repellent for a sadist.

—LIBERATION, SEPTEMBER 1959

It is instilled at an early age that men who violently and swiftly rise to oppose tyranny are virtuous examples to emulate. I have been taught by my government to fight. Nowhere in the annals of history does the record show a people delivered from bondage by patience alone.

—IBID.

What some people don't understand is that in the South we're fighting for our lives. I'm in this struggle to win, and I'll win it any way I can.

—*INTERVIEW WITH JULIAN MAYFIELD, IN "CHALLENGE TO NEGRO LEADERSHIP," COMMENTARY, APRIL 1961*

We have proved that a hooded man who thinks a white life is superior to a black life is not so ready to risk his white life when a black man stands up to him.

—*IBID.*

The majority of white people in the United States have literally no idea of the violence with which Negroes in the South are treated daily —nay, hourly. This violence is deliberate, conscious, condoned by the authorities. It has gone on for centuries and is going on today, every day, unceasing and unremitting. It is our way of life.

—NEGROES WITH GUNS *(1962)*

All those who dare to attack are going to learn the hard way that the Afro-American is not a pacifist; that he cannot forever be counted on not to defend himself. Those who attack him brutally and ruthlessly can no longer expect to attack him with impunity.

—*IBID.*

It is possible for a people to rise above their aspirations. If we think we cannot, we most certainly cannot . . . Sweetest fruits of liberty are plucked by those who readily display boldness and daring.

—*"USA: THE POTENTIAL OF A MINORITY REVOLUTION,"* THE CRUSADER MONTHLY NEWSLETTER, *MAY–JUNE 1964*

August Wilson

(1945–)

*B*eginning *with* Ma Rainey's Black Bottom, *which won the Drama Critics Circle Award for best play in 1986, the poet and playwright Wilson has composed a cycle of dramas re-creating the African American experience in the twentieth century. One of the country's most distinguished dramatists, he has received two Pulitzer Prizes, five Drama Critics Circle Awards, and a Tony.*

Me and this horn . . . we tight. If my daddy knowed I was gonna turn out like this, he would've named me Gabriel.
> —*LEVEE*, MA RAINEY'S BLACK BOTTOM *(1984)*

Style ain't nothing but keeping the same idea from beginning to end. Everybody got it.
> —*TOLEDO, IBID.*

Good times done got more niggers killed than God got ways to count.
> —*IBID.*

I might be a different kind of fool, but I ain't gonna be the same fool twice.
> —*IBID.*

Life ain't shit. You can't put it in a paper bag and carry it around with you. It ain't got no balls. Now, death, death got some style! Death will kick your ass and make you wish you never been born! That's how bad death is!
> *LEVEE, IBID.*

You got to move on down the road from where you sitting . . . and all the time you got to keep an eye out for that devil who's looking to buy up souls. And hope you get lucky and find him!
> —*IBID.*

Death ain't nothing but a fastball on the outside corner.
—*TROY,* FENCES *(1986)*

Searching out the New Land. That's what the old folks used to call it. See a fellow moving around from place to place . . . woman to woman . . . called it searching out the New Land.
—*BONO, IBID.*

Women be where the men is so they can find each other.
—*SETH,* JOE TURNER'S COME AND GONE *(1988)*

Make his feet say my name on the road.
—*MATTIE, IBID.*

This fellow here look like he owe the devil a day's work and he's trying to figure out how he gonna pay him.
—*SETH, IBID.*

Desperate women ain't nothing but trouble for a man.
—*JEREMY, IBID.*

It's a blessing when you learn to look at a woman and see in maybe just a few strands of her hair, the way her cheek curves . . . to see in that everything there is out of life to be gotten. It's a blessing to see that.
—*BYNUM, IBID.*

I done seen bones rise up out the water. Rise up and walk across the water.
—*IBID.*

When you look at a fellow, if you taught yourself to look for it, you can see his song written on him. Tell you what kind of man he is in the world.
—*IBID.*

That's all you need in the world is love and laughter. That's all anybody needs. To have love in one hand and laughter in the other.
—*BERTHA, IBID.*

I done strung along and strung along. Going this way and that. Whatever way would lead me to a moment of peace. That's all I want. To be
as easy with everything. But I wasn't born to that. I was born to a time
of fire.
                    —*Boy Willie*, The Piano Lesson *(1990)*

You got the preacher on the one hand and the gambler on the other.
Sometimes there ain't too much difference in them.
                    —*Wining Boy, Ibid.*

See, a nigger that ain't afraid to die is the worse kind of nigger for the
white man. He can't hold that power over you.
                    —*Boy Willie, Ibid.*

He say if you afraid of the truth to get back in the shadows 'cause you
never will see the light.
                    —*Risa*, Two Trains Running *(1992)*

Niggers is the most hard-working people in the world. Worked three
hundred years for free.
                    —*Holloway, Ibid.*

When you get to be a saint there ain't nothing else you can do but
die. The people wouldn't have it any other way.
                    —*Ibid.*

Freedom is heavy. You got to put your shoulder to freedom. Put your
shoulder to it and hope your back hold up.
                    —*Memphis, Ibid.*

Every nigger you see done been to jail one time or another. The white
man don't feel right unless he got a record on these niggers.
                    —*Wolf, Ibid.*

I found out life's hard but it ain't impossible.
                    —*West, Ibid.*

That's all you got. You got love and you got death. Death will find you
. . . it's up to you to find love . . . That's 'cause love cost. Love got
a price to it. Everybody don't want to pay.
                    —*Holloway, Ibid.*

ℱlip Wilson

*O*ne of twenty-four children, Clerow Wilson grew up in Jersey City, New Jersey, where he spent time in reform school before testing his comedic talents while in the air force. He appeared regularly at the Apollo Theater in the 1960s, and after frequent stints on "The Tonight Show" hosted the popular "The Flip Wilson Show" in the early 1970s. He has also recorded several comedy albums.

The devil made me do it.
> —*A FREQUENT RETORT OF THE CHARACTER GERALDINE*

Here come de judge.
> —*SIGNATURE EXCLAMATION*

ℋarriet Wilson

(1 8 0 8 – c . 1 8 7 0)

*H*arriet Wilson's novel Our Nig, *printed in 1859, is thought to be the first novel by an African American author published in the United States (though several others had already appeared in England). Wilson was probably born in Fredericksburg, Virginia. She was married, deserted by her husband, lost a child, and lived in frail health much of her life, incidents mirrored in her autobiographical novel.*

In offering to the public the following pages, the writer confesses her inability to minister to the refined and cultivated, the pleasure suppied by abler pens . . . I sincerely appeal to my colored brethren universally for patronage, hoping they will not condemn this attempt of their sister to be erudite, but rally around me a faithful band of supporters and defenders.

—*from the preface to* Our Nig

No one had a kinder heart, one capable of loving more devotedly. But to think how prejudiced the world are [sic] toward her people; that she must be reared in such ignorance as to drown all the finer feelings. When I think of what she might be, of what she will be, I feel like grasping time till opinions change, and thousands like her rise to a noble freedom.

—Our Nig

*O*prah *W*infrey

(1 9 5 4 –   )

Though she had a troubled childhood, Winfrey excelled in school, won a college scholarship, and began working in radio and television, rising quickly at stations in Nashville, Baltimore, and Chicago. The syndicated "Oprah Winfrey Show" has made her one of the world's wealthiest and most popular entertainment figures. She also heads her own production company and has starred in the films The Color Purple *and* The Women of Brewster Place.

Luck is a matter of preparation.

—*c. 1984, in Nellie Bly,* Oprah! *(1993)*

I believe that it is necessary to not be restricted in your work based on your color, and as long as you tell the truth in your work and your art, people have no right to tell you how to do it.

—*Ibid.*

I learned that I could not look to my exterior self to do anything for me. If I was going to accomplish anything in life, I had to start from within.

—*speech to the American Women's Economic Development Corporation, New York, February 25, 1989*

I've discovered if you treat people the way you wish to be treated at all times, you will get exactly what the universe has intended.

—*Ibid.*

Surround yourself with only people who are going to lift you higher.

—*Ibid.*

If you want to accomplish the goals of your life, you have to begin with the spirit.

—*Ibid.*

Always continue the climb. It is possible for you to do whatever you choose, if you first get to know who you are and are willing to work with a power that is greater than ourselves to do it.

—*Ibid.*

I, like a lot of people here, spent a lot of time trying to be somebody I was not . . . The world awaits what you have to give.

—*commencement speech at Morehouse College, May 21, 1989*

I come here celebrating every African, ever colored, black, Negro American everywhere that ever cooked a meal, ever raised a child, ever worked in the fields, ever went to school, ever sang in a choir, ever loved a man or loved a woman, every corn-rowed, every Afroed, every wig-wearing, pigtailed, weave-wearing one of us. I come celebrating the journey, I come celebrating the little passage, the movement of our women people.

—*as mistress of ceremonies, Convention of the National Council of Negro Women, Washington, D.C., December 3, 1989*

You don't have to have laws that say, "You can't come here or go sit there in this place" in order to be a slave. The only thing that can free you is the belief that you can be free.

—*STATEMENT AT THE "EBONY/JET SHOWCASE," AUGUST 24–26, 1990*

Children cannot stand alone; none of us can. There's not a one of us in this room, no matter how smart we are . . . No matter how diligent or persistent you have been, there is not one of us who made this journey toward success by ourselves.

—*GOING PUBLIC ON HER ABUSE AS A CHILD; SPEECH BEFORE THE CALIFORNIA BAR ASSOCIATION, NOVEMBER 1991*

I'm a truth seeker. That's what I do every every day on the show—put out the truth. Some people don't like it, they call it sensational, but I say life is sensational.

—*c. 1991, IN OPRAH!*

If you come to fame not understanding who you are, it will define who you are.

—*IBID.*

Think like a queen. A queen is not afraid to fail. Failure is another steppingstone to greatness.

—*COMMENCEMENT ADDRESS AT SPELMAN COLLEGE, MAY 1993*

I still have my feet on the ground, I just wear better shoes.

—*IN OPRAH!*

You *can* have it all. You just can't have it all at one time.

—LADIES' HOME JOURNAL, *MAY 1990*

George C. Wolfe

(1 9 5 6 –   )

Wolfe received his B.A. in directing from Pomona College and his M.F.A. from New York University. The recipient of numerous awards, he is best known for Spunk *(based on the writings of Zora Neale Hurston) and* The Colored Museum, *and as the acclaimed director of* Jelly's Last Jam, *Tony Kushner's* Angels in America, *and Anna Deavere Smith's* Twilight: Los Angeles, 1992.

Each and every one of 'em had pain in his future and blood on his path.

—*"A Soldier with a Secret,"* The Colored Museum

God created black people and black people created style.

—*"The Gospel According to Miss Roj,"* Ibid.

We traded in our drums for respectability. So now it's just words.

—*Ibid.*

I can't live inside yesterday's pain, I can't live without it.

—*"The Party,"* Ibid.

I must be able to smile on cue. And watch the news with an impersonal eye. I have no stake in the madness.

—*"Symbiosis,"* Ibid.

If only he had been born into a better world than this. A world where there are no well-worn couches and no well-worn mamas and nobody overemotes. If only he had been born into an all-black musical.

—*"The Last Mama-on-the-Couch Play,"* Ibid.

Carter Woodson

Born in Virginia to former slaves, Woodson, was the oldest of nine children. Though he was unable to attend school until he was twenty, he received his B.A. and M.A. from the University of Chicago and his Ph.D. from Harvard in 1912. Called "the father of Negro history," he founded the Association for the Study of Negro Life and History in 1915 and, the following year, its Journal of Negro History. *He was the author or editor of more than ten volumes on African American subjects, and in 1926 organized Negro History Week, which is now celebrated as Black History Month in February.*

We have a wonderful history behind us . . . It reads like the history of a people in a heroic age . . . We are going back to that beautiful history and it is going to inspire us to greater achievements.

—IN COLUMBUS SALLEY, THE BLACK 100 *(1993)*

In the first place, we need to attain economic independence. You may talk about rights and all that sort of thing. The people who own this country will rule this country. They always have done so and they always will.

—*c. 1922*

We should emphasize not Negro History, but the Negro in history. What we need is not a history of selected races or nations, but the history of the world void of national bias, race hate, and religious prejudice.

—ON FOUNDING NEGRO HISTORY WEEK, *1926*

Negroes have and always have had their own ideas about purpose, chance, time, and space, about appearance and reality, and about freedom and necessity. The effort of the Negro to interpret man's relation to the universe shows just as much intelligence as we find in the philosophy of the Greeks. There were many Africans who were as wise as Socrates.

—*"The Miseducation of the Negro,"* The Crisis, *August 1931*

For me, education means to inspire people to live more abundantly, to learn to begin with life as they find it and make it better.

—*Ibid.*

$\mathcal{R}$ichard Wright

(1 9 0 8 – 1 9 6 0)

Growing up amid extreme poverty in Mississippi and forced to leave school for periods of time to work, Wright became one of the most influential writers of the twentieth century. In 1927 he moved to Chicago, where he began to publish poetry and prose and joined the Communist Party, from which he would later break. His first book, Uncle Tom's Children, *was published in 1938, followed two years later by his best-known work,* Native Son. *He published many other volumes of fiction, essays, and autobiography, and in 1974, disillusioned with the pervasiveness of racism in America, moved to Paris, where he spent the rest of his life.*

Negroes who have lived South know the dread of being caught alone upon the streets in white neighborhoods after the sun has set. In such a simple situation as this the plight of the Negro in America is graphically symbolized.

—*"The Ethics of Living Jim Crow,"* 1937

My Jim Crow education assumed quite a different form. It was no longer brutally cruel, but subtly cruel. Here I learned to lie, to steal, to dissemble. I learned to play that dual role which every Negro must play if he wants to eat and live.

—*Ibid.*

It was not really a fight; it was an act of revenge, of dominance, of complete mastery. The black puppet glided from his corner and simply wiped his feet on the white puppet's face. The black puppet was contemptuous, swift; his victory was complete, unquestionable, decisive; his blows must have jarred the marrow not only in the white puppet's but in Hitler's own bones.

—ON THE JOE LOUIS–MAX SCHMELING FIGHT, NEW MASSES JULY 5, 1938

With a supreme act of will springing from the essence of his being, he turned away from his life and the long train of disastrous consequences that had flowed from it and looked wistfully upon the dark face of ancient waters upon which some spirit had breathed and created him, the dark face of the waters from which he had been first made in the image of a man with a man's obscure need and urge; feeling that he wanted to sink back into those waters and rest eternally.

—NATIVE SON (1940)

To live, he had created a new world for himself, and for that he was to die.

—IBID.

Had not this voice of hate been sounding long before he was born; and would it not still sound long after he was dead?

—IBID.

Injustice which lasts for three long centuries and which exists among millions of people over thousands of square miles of territory, is injustice no longer; it is an accomplished fact of life.

—IBID.

You can't make me do nothing but die!

—IBID.

This Court should not sit to fix punishment for this boy; it should sit to ponder why there are not more like him!

—IBID.

Another civil war in these states is not impossible and if the misunderstanding of what this boy's life means is an indication of how men

of wealth and property are misreading the consciousness of the sub-
merged millions today, one may truly come.

—*IBID.*

In self-defense he shut out the night and day from his mind, for if he
had thought of the sun's rising and setting, of the moon or the stars,
or clouds of rain, he would have died a thousand deaths before they
took him to the chair. To accustom his mind to death as much as
possible, he made all the world beyond his cell a vast grey land where
neither night nor day was, peopled by strange men and women whom
he could not understand, but with those lives he longed to mingle
once before he went.

—*IBID.*

Life for us is a daily warfare and . . . we are hard like soldiers . . .
We are always in battle, but the tidings of victory are few.

—Twelve Million Black Voices *(1941)*

Each day when you see us black folk upon the dusty land of your
farms or upon the hard pavement of your city streets, you usually take
it for granted and think you know us, but our history is far stranger
than you suspect, and we are not what we seem.

—*IBID.*

Blues, spirituals, and folk tales recounted from mouth to mouth . . .
all these formed the channels through which the racial wisdom
flowed.

—*"Blueprint for Negro Literature,"* Amistad 2 *(1971)*

He would not mind dying now if he could only find out what this
meant, what he was in relation to all the others that lived, and the
earth upon which he stood.

—Native Son

$\mathcal{T}$heodore $\mathcal{S}$. Wright

(1 7 9 7 – 1 8 4 7)

A freeman from Providence, Rhode Island, Wright was educated at the Free African School in New York and at Princeton Theological Seminary. Ordained in 1825, he spoke fervently from the pulpit for abolition and civil rights. With Samuel Cornish and David Ruggles, he organized the New York Vigilance Committee and was active in the convention movement and the black press.

It is of small moment to me, what I am called to encounter . . . Let every epithet which vile and unprincipled men can devise be heaped upon me—let me be assailed by the hand of ruthless and even beardless violence—and I will smile, and be happy, so long as I may stand forth to the view of Infinite Excellence, and of pure minded men, clad in the robes of moral worth.

—*LETTER TO THE REVEREND ARCHIBALD ALEXANDER AT PRINCETON, OCTOBER 11, 1836, AFTER A WHITE MAN TRIED TO EVICT HIM FROM AN ADDRESS AT THE SEMINARY*

It is an easy thing to ask about the vileness of slavery at the South, but to call the dark man a brother, heartily to embrace the doctrine advanced in the second article of the Constitution, to treat all men according to their moral worth, to treat the man of color in all circumstances as a man and brother—that is the test.

—*ADDRESS TO THE NEW YORK STATE ANTI-SLAVERY SOCIETY, UTICA, SEPTEMBER 20, 1837*

Let every man take his stand, burn out this prejudice, live it down, talk it down, everywhere consider the colored man as a man, in the church, the stage, the steamboat, the public house, in all places, and the death-blow to slavery will be struck.

—*IBID.*

Malcolm X

*B*orn Malcolm Little, Malcolm X went to prison at the age of twenty-one. There he converted to Islam and, after his release, became one of the Nation of Islam's most effective ministers. After his breach with Elijah Muhammad and his pilgrimage to Mecca in 1963 (as El-Hajj Malik El-Shabazz) he founded the Organization of Afro-American Unity to provide a less exclusionary forum. He was assassinated on February 21, 1965, and his famous autobiography appeared after his death.

Revolution is like a forest fire. It burns everything in its path.
—*INTERVIEW WITH A. B. SPELLMAN, MONTHLY REVIEW, MAY 1964*

We have never been involved in any kind of violence whatsoever. We have never initiated any violence against anyone, but we do believe that when violence is practiced against us we should be able to defend ourselves. We don't believe in turning the other cheek.
—*IBID.*

We are all brothers of oppression, and today brothers of oppression are identified with each other all over the world.
—*IBID.*

You wouldn't be in this country if some enemy hadn't kidnapped you and brought you here. On the other hand, some of you think you came here on the *Mayflower.*
—*SPEECH, DETROIT, APRIL 12, 1964*

If I'm teaching someone to hate, I'm teaching them to hate the Ku Klux Klan. But here and in America, they have taught us to hate ourselves.
—*SPEECH, LONDON SCHOOL OF ECONOMICS*

Without education, you are not going anywhere in this world.
—*speech, Militant Labor Forum, New York, May 29, 1964*

I'm a field Negro. If I can't live in the house as a human being, I'm praying for a wind to come along.
—*Selma, Alabama, February 4, 1965*

Early in life I had learned that if you want something, you had better make some noise.
—*The Autobiography of Malcolm X (1965)*

All Negroes are angry and I am the angriest of them all.
—*Ibid.*

In the ghettoes the white man has built for us, he has forced us not to aspire to greater things, but to view life as *survival.*
—*Ibid.*

The black man, original man, built great empires and civilizations and cultures while the white man was still living on all fours in caves.
—*Ibid.*

We didn't land on Plymouth Rock, my brothers and sisters— Plymouth Rock landed on *us!*
—*Ibid.*

I firmly believe that Negroes have the right to fight against these racists, by any means that are necessary.
—*Ibid.*

This Muslim's X symbolized the true African family name that he never could know. For me, my X replaced the white slavemaster name of "Little" which some blue-eyed devil named Little had imposed upon my paternal forebears. The receipt of my X meant that forever after, in the nation of Islam, I would be known as Malcolm X. Mr. Muhammad taught that we would keep this X until God Himself returned and gave us a Holy Name from His own mouth.
—*Ibid.*

How deeply the religion of Islam had reached down into the mud to lift me up, to save me from being what I inevitably would have been.

—*Ibid.*

Everything that happens—Islam teaches—is written.

—*Ibid.*

It has been my belief that I, too, will die by violence. I have done all that I can to be prepared.

—*Ibid.*

Andrew Young

(1 9 3 2 –)

Born in New Orleans, Andrew Jackson Young, Jr., graduated from Hartford Theological Seminary in 1955 and was an associate of Dr. Martin Luther King, Jr., until King's death. He headed the Birmingham Campaign and helped draft the Civil Rights Act and Voting Acts of 1964 and 1965. In 1972, he was elected a Georgia representative to Congress, where he served until 1977, when Jimmy Carter appointed him U.S. ambassador to the UN. He served as mayor of Atlanta from 1981 to 1989 and is now a business consultant.

We are not here to do you any harm. We merely want to have a word of prayer at this place where our ancestors were brought and sold as slaves, to ask God to help us end slavery in all its forms.

—*At a March in Saint Augustine, Florida, summer 1964*

No nation as rich as ours should have so many people isolated on islands of poverty in such a sea of material wealth.

—A Way Out of No Way *(1994)*

Death is inevitable. We are fortunate if we are able to contribute to the values and ideals of our lives even in the act of dying. Martyrdom has always been one of the powerful mysteries of life.

—Ibid.

In a world where change is inevitable and continuous, the need to achieve that change without violence is essential for survival.

—Ibid.

There can be no democracy without truth. There can be no truth without controversy, and there can be no change without freedom.

—Ibid.

No matter when the killing stops, there will still be some people left on each side who will have to learn to live together. There are really no winners and losers in any conflict.

—Ibid.

There is an acceptable risk for war that is considered one's patriotic duty. Few men and women are able to see the risk for peace as a more powerful patriotic responsibility.

—Ibid.

My hope for my children must be that they respond to the still, small voice of God in their own hearts.

—Ibid.

Democracy, to be effective, requires that leaders perform heroically.

—Ibid.

I can only explain my own life and the events of the times in which I've lived in the context of faith—a biblical faith that continues to see the hand of God working in the affairs of the children of creation.

—Ibid.

Index of Speakers

Index
of
Subjects

240, 244, 247, 277, 286, 402,
471
Survival, 15, 24, 26, 36, 63, 74,
130, 322, 346, 495, 497

Talk, 13, 48, 368, 372, 448
Taxes, 158, 219, 235, 363, 365, 432
Tears, 11, 48, 49, 190, 227, 282,
448
Temptation, 100, 383, 465
Time, 24, 50, 140, 183, 233, 273,
331, 345, 381, 397, 423
Tired, 99, 132, 145, 188, 197, 250,
292, 305, 327, 346
Tradition, 169, 171, 204
Trouble, 155, 208, 245, 330, 358,
412, 414, 482
Truth, 60, 62, 93, 131, 140, 157,
177, 197, 205, 281, 355, 358,
390, 487, 497

Unity, 84, 131, 172, 175

Vanity, 46, 47, 87, 117
Viet Nam, 7, 9, 46, 139, 172, 276,
347–48, 354, 355, 397
Violence, 58, 82, 83, 94, 104, 105,
106, 139, 152, 162, 163, 175,
191, 207, 228, 229, 260, 276,
281, 304, 320, 350, 365, 435,
441, 469, 473, 479, 480, 496
Virtue, 11, 96, 102, 150, 152, 286
Voting, 45, 71, 130, 139, 158, 187,
279, 300, 326, 334, 362, 417,
419, 429, 432, 458, 461, 496

Walking, 16, 35, 41, 51, 80, 86,
121, 160, 219, 262, 448, 471,
482
War, 9, 99, 119, 149, 156, 172,
181, 183, 184, 191, 199, 219–20,
231, 242, 261, 284, 333, 336,
353, 354, 355, 356, 362, 365,
372, 374, 384, 402, 430, 434,
477, 478, 497
Washington, Booker T., 328, 336,
403, 453–56
Waters, 28, 102, 105, 118, 164,
222, 226, 243, 309, 332, 428,
482
White people, 6, 9, 25, 26, 30, 32,
39, 43, 63, 64, 71, 77, 83, 84,
89, 95, 104, 106, 112, 116, 123,
124, 141, 142, 150, 158, 173,
175, 178, 180, 181, 183, 188,
199, 201, 208, 221, 222, 226,
227, 235, 255, 259, 267, 272,
273, 288, 290, 302, 303, 327,
350, 364, 385, 393, 396, 416,
417, 429, 434, 440, 443, 455,
472, 480, 493
Wilderness, 28, 84, 157, 160
Wind, 19, 55, 64, 80, 102, 119,
130, 226, 308, 464, 465, 495
Winter, 128, 272
Wisdom, 11
Women, 12, 13, 14, 24, 42, 45, 48,
67, 80, 81, 85, 86, 88, 94, 95,
100, 104, 106, 135, 137, 142,
170, 186, 198, 203, 211, 215,
224, 226, 227, 239, 251, 263,
264, 268, 288, 296, 297, 298,
299, 309, 312, 319, 321, 332,
384, 385, 398, 399, 400, 418,
423, 430, 431, 441, 443, 460,
461, 475, 476
Words, 120–21, 129, 135, 136, 138,
162, 164, 181, 226, 247, 263,
264, 310, 332, 386
Work, 88, 99, 104, 106, 114, 130,
152, 181, 188, 193, 197, 226,
250, 296, 300, 301, 306, 339,
445, 486

Index

of

Famous Lines

Abortions will not let you forget. —Gwendolyn Brooks
Age is a question of mind over matter. —Satchel Paige
Ain't I a woman? —Sojourner Truth
All God's chillun got wings. —Spiritual
Cast down your bucket where you are . . . —Booker T. Washington
Common ground! —Jesse Jackson
Don't believe the hype. —Public Enemy
Don't look back. Something might be gaining on you. —Satchel Paige
Don't pray when it rains if you don't pray when the sun shines.
—Satchel Paige
Fight the power. —Public Enemy
The fire next time . . . —Spiritual
Float like a butterfly, sting like a bee. —Muhammad Ali
Free at last, free at last . . . —Martin Luther King, Jr.
Go down, Moses. —Spiritual
God bless the child that's got his own. —Billie Holiday
[This is] a high-tech lynching. —Clarence Thomas
I, too, sing America. —Langston Hughes
I ain't got no quarrel with the Viet Cong. —Muhammad Ali
I hate to see de ev'nin' sun go down. —W. C. Handy
I have a dream. —Martin Luther King, Jr.
I know why the caged bird sings. —Paul Laurence Dunbar
If Beale Street could talk . . . —W. C. Handy
If there is no struggle, there is no progress. —Frederick Douglass
If we must die— —Claude McKay
I'm the greatest. —Muhammad Ali
Imagination! who can sing thy force? —Phillis Wheatley
In all things purely social we can be as separate as the fingers.
—Booker T. Washington
Is this America? —Fannie Lou Hamer
It don't mean a thing if it ain't got that swing. —Duke Ellington
It is not light that is needed, but fire. —Frederick Douglass
I've been to the mountain top. —Martin Luther King, Jr.
I've known rivers. —Langston Hughes
Keep hope alive. —Jesse Jackson
Keep your eyes on the prize. —Freedom song
Let your motto be resistance! —Henry Highland Garnet
Madison Avenue is afraid of the dark. —Nat (King) Cole
A mind is a terrible thing to waste. —United Negro College Fund
Nobody knows the trouble I've seen. —Spiritual
O black and unknown bards. —James Weldon Johnson
One never know, do one? —Fats Waller
Only the BLACK WOMAN can say "When and where I enter . . ."
—Anna Julia Cooper
The problem of the Twentieth Century is the problem of the color line.
—W. E. B. Du Bois
Roll, Jordan, roll. —Spiritual
Seize the time. —Bobby Seale
Sometimes I feel like a motherless child. —Spiritual

The strong men . . . coming on / The strong men gittin' stronger.

—Sterling Brown

That fantastic period when Harlem was in vogue. —Langston Hughes
To be young, gifted, and black. —Lorraine Hansberry
Up you mighty race . . . —Marcus Garvey
Wake up, America. —John Lewis
We are clim'in' Jacob's ladder. —Spiritual
We need the storm, the whirlwind, and the earthquake. —Frederick Douglass
We shall not be moved. —Freedom song
We shall overcome. —Martin Luther King, Jr.
We want poems that kill. —Amiri Baraka
We wear the mask that grins and lies . . . —Paul Laurence Dunbar
We wish to plead our own cause. —Samuel E. Cornish
We'll soon be free. —Spiritual
What happens to a dream deferred? —Langston Hughes
What is Africa to me: —Countee Cullen
What to the American slave is your Fourth of July? —Frederick Douglass
Yet do I marvel at this curious thing: —Countee Cullen
You have seen how a man was made a slave . . . —Frederick Douglass
Your arm's too short to box with God. —James Weldon Johnson

Selected Bibliography

Abdul-Jabbar, Kareem. *Kareem*. New York: Warner, 1990.

Ali, Muhammad, with Richard Dunham. *The Greatest*. New York: Random House, 1976.

Anderson, Marian. *My Lord, What a Morning*. Madison: The University of Wisconsin Press, [1956], 1992.

Angelou, Maya. *I Know Why the Caged Bird Sings*. New York: Random House, 1970.

——. *Poems*. New York: Bantam, 1986.

Aptheker, Herbert. *A Documentary History of the Negro People*. 4 volumes. New York: Citadel Press, 1951–1974.

Arnaud, Gérald, and Jacques Chesnel. *Masters of Jazz*. Edinburgh: Chambers, 1991.

Asante, Molefi Kente. *Afrocentricity*. rev. ed. Trenton, NJ: Africa World Press, 1988.

Ashe, Arthur. *A Hard Road To Glory*. rev. ed. New York, Amistad Press, 1993.

Baldwin, James. *The Fire Next Time*. New York: Dial, 1963.

——. *Notes of a Native Son*. Boston: Beacon, 1955.

Bambara, Toni Cade. *The Salt Eaters*. New York: Vintage, 1981.

Baraka, Amiri. *Amiri Baraka Reader*. William J. Harris, ed. New York: Thunder's Mouth, 1992.

Basie, Count and Murry, Albert. *Good Morning Blues*. New York: Donald I. Fine, Inc. 1985.

Bego, Mark. *Aretha Franklin: The Queen of Soul*. New York: St. Martin's, 1989.

Bell, Derrick. *And We Are Not Saved: The Elusive Quest for Racial Justice.* New York: Basic Books, 1987.

———. *Faces at the Bottom of the Well: The Permanence of Racism.* New York: Basic Books, 1992.

Bennett, Lerone, Jr. *Before the Mayflower.* 5th rev. ed. Chicago: Johnson, 1982.

Berlin, Edward A. *King of Ragtime: Scott Joplin and His Era.* New York: Oxford, 1994.

Black Women in Nineteenth-Century American Life: Their Words, Their Thoughts, Their Feelings. Bert James Loewenberg and Ruth Bogin, eds. University Park: Pennsylvania State University Press, 1976.

Bly, Nellie. *Oprah! Up Close and Down Home.* New York: Zebra, 1993.

Bontemps, Arna, and Langston Hughes, eds. *The Book of Negro Folklore.* New York: Dodd Mead, 1965.

Bradford, Sarah. *Harriet Tubman: The Moses of Her People.* New York: Citadel Press, [1886], 1991.

Brown, Claude. *Manchild in the Promised Land.* New York: Macmillan, 1965.

Brown, James, with Bruce Tucker. *The Godfather of Soul.* New York: Macmillan, 1986.

Brown, Sterling. *The Collected Poems of Sterling Brown.* New York: Harper & Row, 1980.

Brown, Sterling, et al., eds. *The Negro Caravan.* New York: Dryden Press, 1941.

Brown, William Wells. *Narrative of William Wells Brown.* New York: New American Library, [1856], 1993.

Carmichael, Stokely, and Charles V. Hamilton. *Black Power: The Politics of Liberation in America.* New York: Vintage Books, 1967.

Chapman, Abraham, ed. *Black Voices: An Anthology of Afro-American Literature.* New York: New American Library, 1968.

Charles, Ray, and David Ritz. *Brother Ray.* New York: Da Capo, [1978], 1992.

Chesnutt, Charles W. *The Collected Stories of Charles W. Chestnutt.* William L. Andrews, ed. New York: New American Library, [1899], 1992.

———. *The Marrow of Tradition.* Eric J. Sundquist, ed. New York: Penguin, [1901], 1993.

Cleaver, Eldridge. *Soul on Ice.* New York: McGraw-Hill, 1968.

Cloe, Bill. *John Coltrane.* New York: Da Capo, [1976], 1993.

Cone, James. *Black Theology and Black Power*. New York: Seabury Press, 1969.

Cooper, Anna Julia. *A Voice from the South*. New York: Oxford University Press, [1892], 1988.

Copage, Eric V. *Black Pearls: Daily Meditations Affirmations, and Inspirations for African-Americans*. New York: Morrow, 1993.

Cosby, Bill. *Childhood*. New York: Doubleday, 1991.

————. *Fatherhood*. New York: Doubleday, 1986.

————. *Love and Marriage*. New York: Doubleday, 1989.

————. *Time Flies*. New York: Doubleday, 1987.

Crow, Bill. *Jazz Anecdotes*. New York: Oxford University Press, 1990.

Cullen, Countee, ed. *Caroling Dusk: An Anthology of Verse by Black Poets*. New York: Citadel Press, [1927], 1993.

————. *My Soul's High Song: The Collected Writings of Countee Cullen*. Gerald Early, ed. New York: Anchor, 1991.

Dahl, Linda. *Stormy Weather: The Music and Lives of a Century of Jazzwomen*. New York: Pantheon, 1984.

Davis, Miles. *Miles*. New York: Simon & Schuster, 1990.

Davis, Sharon. *I Heard It Through the Grapevine: Marvin Gaye, The Biography*. Edinburgh, Scotland: Mainstream Publishing, 1991.

Delany, Sarah, and A. Elizabeth, with Amy Hill Hearth. *Having Our Say: The Delany Sisters' First 100 Years*. New York: Kodansha, 1993.

Dineen, Catherine. *Michael Jackson*. London: Omnibus Press, 1993.

Douglass, Frederick. *Narrative of the Life of Frederick Douglass*. New York: Signet, [1845], 1968.

Du Bois, W. E. B. *Writings*. Nathan Huggins, ed. New York: Literary Classics of the United States, 1986.

Dunbar, Paul Laurence. *The Complete Poems of Paul Laurence Dunbar*. New York: Dodd, Mead, 1905.

Dunham, Katherine. *A Touch of Innocence*. Chicago: University of Chicago Press, [1959], 1994.

Duster, Alfreda M., ed. *Crusade for Justice: The Autobiography of Ida B. Wells*. Chicago: The University of Chicago Press, 1970.

Early, Gerald, ed. *Lure and Loathing: Essays on Race, Identity and the Ambivalence of Assimilation*. New York: Allen Lane, 1993.

————, ed. *Speech and Power*. 2 vols. Hopewell, NJ: Ecco Press, 1992, 1993.

Edelman, Marian Wright. *The Measure of Our Success: A Letter to My Children and Yours*. Boston: Beacon Press, 1992.

Ellington, Edward K. *Music IS My Mistress*. New York: Doubleday, 1973.

Ellison, Ralph. *Invisible Man*. New York: Random House, 1952.

————. *Shadow and Act*. New York: Random House, 1964.

Estell, Kenneth, ed. *African America: Portrait of a People*. Detroit: Visible Ink Press, 1994.

Eure, Joseph D., and Richard M. Jerome. *Back Where We Belong: Selected Speeches by Minister Louis Farrakhan*. Philadelphia: PC International Press, 1989.

Evans, Mari, ed. *Black Women Writers: 1950–1980*. New York: Doubleday, 1984.

The Eyes on the Prize Civil Rights Reader. Clayborne Carson, David J. Garrow, Gerald Gill, Vincent Harding, and Darlene Clark Hine, eds. New York: Viking Penguin, 1991.

Fauset, Jessie Redmon. *Plum Bum*. Boston: Beacon Press, [1928], 1990.

Franklin, John Hope. *Race and History: Selected Essays*. Baton Rouge: Louisiana State University Press, 1989.

Garvey, Marcus. *Philosophy and Opinions of Marcus Garvey*. New York: Atheneum, 1991.

Gates, Jr., Henry Louis, ed. *Bearing Witness: Selections from African-American Autobiography in the Twentieth Century*. New York: Pantheon, 1991.

————. ed. *The Classic Slave Narratives*. New York: Penguin, 1987.

————. *Colored People: A Memoir*. New York: Knopf, 1994.

————. *Figures in Black*. New York: Oxford University Press, 1989.

————. *The Signifying Monkey*. New York: Oxford University Press, 1988.

————. ed. *Three Classic African-American Novels*. New York: Vintage, 1990.

Giddings, Paula. *Where and When I Enter: The Impact of Black Women on Race and Sex in America*. New York: William Morrow, 1984.

Goldman, Roger, and David Gallen. *Thurgood Marshall: Justice for All*. New York: Carroll & Graf, 1992.

Goss, Linda, and Marian E. Barnes, eds. *Talk That Talk*. New York: Simon & Schuster, 1989.

Grant, Joanne. *Black Protest.* New York: Ballantine, 1968.

Gregory, Dick. *Nigger.* New York: Dutton, 1964.

Hampton, Henry, and Steve Fayer. *Voices of Freedom.* New York: Bantam, 1990.

Haley, Alex. *Roots.* New York: Doubleday, 1977.

Handy, W. C., ed. *Blues: An Anthology.* New York: Da Capo, [1926], 1990.

Hansberry, Lorraine. *To Be Young, Gifted and Black.* New York: Signet, 1970.

Harding, Vincent. *There Is a River.* New York: Harcourt Brace Jovanovich, 1981.

Harper, Michael S. and Robert B. Stepto. *Chant of Saints:* Urbana: University of Illinois Press, 1979.

Holiday, Billie, with William Duffy. *Lady Sings the Blues.* New York: Penguin, [1956], 1984.

hooks, bell, and Cornel West. *Breaking Bread: Insurgent Black Intellectual Life.* Boston: South End Press, 1991.

Horne, Lena, and Richard Schickel. *Lena.* New York: Limelight, [1965], 1986.

Huggins, Nathan. *Harlem Renaissance.* New York: Oxford University Press, 1971.

Hughes, Langston. *The Langston Hughes Reader.* New York: George Braziller, 1958.

Hurston, Zora Neale. *Dust Tracks on the Road.* Bloomington: Indiana University Press, 1942.

————. *I Love Myself When I Am Laughing.* Alice Walker, ed. New York: The Feminist Press, 1979.

————. *Mules and Men.* New York: Harper & Row, [1935], 1990.

————. *Their Eyes Were Watching God.* New York: Harper & Row, [1937], 1990.

Jamison, Judith. *Dancing Spirit: An Autobiography.* New York: Doubleday, 1993.

Johnson, Charles. *Middle Passage.* New York: Viking, 1990.

Johnson, James Weldon. *Autobiography of an Ex-Colored Man.* New York: Vintage, [1912], 1989.

————. *Black Manhattan.* New York: Da Capo, [1930], 1991.

————. *The Book of American Negro Poetry.* rev. ed. New York: Harcourt Brace, 1931.

————. *The Books of American Negro Spirituals.* New York: Da Capo, [1925, 1926], 1991.

Jones, James Earl. *Voices and Silences.* New York: Scribners, 1993.

Jordan, June. *Technical Difficulties.* New York: Vintage, 1994.

Kaplan, Sidney, and Emma Nogrady Kaplan: *The Black Presence in the Era of the American Revolution.* 2nd ed. Amherst: The University of Massachusetts Press, 1989.

Kincaid, Jamaica. *Annie John.* New York: Farrar, Straus & Giroux, 1985.

————. *At the Bottom of the River.* New York: Farrar, Straus & Giroux, 1991.

King, Martin Luther, Jr. *Testament of Hope: The Essential Writings of Martin Luther King, Jr.* James M. Washington, ed. New York: Harper & Row, 1986.

Larsen, Nella. *An Intimation of Things Distant: The Collected Fiction of Nella Larsen.* Charles R. Larson, ed. New York: Anchor, 1992.

Lerda, Gerda, ed. *Black Women in White America: A Documentary History.* New York: Pantheon, 1972.

Locke, Alain, ed. *The New Negro.* New York: Atheneum, [1925], 1992.

Lorde, Audre. *Sister Outsider: Essays and Speeches.* Freedom, CA: The Crossing Press, 1984.

McMillan, Terry. *Waiting to Exhale.* New York: Viking, 1992.

Magill, Frank N. *Masterpieces of African-American Literature.* New York: HarperCollins, 1992.

Morrison, Toni. *Beloved.* New York: Knopf, 1987.

————. *Playing in the Dark: Whiteness and the Literary Imagination.* Cambridge: Harvard University Press, 1992.

Muhammad, Elijah. *Message to the Black Man.* Chicago: United Brothers, 1965.

Mullan, Harry. *The Book of Boxing Quotations.* London: Stanley Paul, 1988.

Nathan, David H. *Baseball Quotations.* New York: Ballantine, 1993.

Naylor, Gloria. *Linden Hills.* New York: Ticknor & Fields, 1985.

————. *The Women of Brewster Place.* New York: Viking, 1982.

Nelson, Kevin. *Talkin' Trash: Basketball's Greatest Insults.* New York: Fireside, 1993.

Parks, Gordon. *Voices in the Mirror.* New York: Doubleday, 1990.

Randall, Dudley, ed. *The Black Poets.* New York: Bantam, 1971.

Riley, Dorothy Winbush. *My Soul Looks Back, 'Less I Forget.* New York: HarperCollins, 1993.

Robeson, Paul. *Here I Stand.* Boston: Beacon, [1958], 1988.

———. *Paul Robeson Speaks.* Philip S. Foner, ed. New York: Citadel, 1978.

Rose, Phyllis. *Jazz Cleopatra: Josephine Baker in Her Times.* New York: Doubleday, 1989.

Ross, Diana. *Confessions of a Sparrow.* New York: Villard, 1993.

Rovin, Jeff. *Richard Pryor: Black and Blue.* New York: Bantam, 1983.

Rowan, Carl T. *Breaking Barriers: A Memoir.* Boston: Little, Brown, 1991.

Sackheim, Eric. *The Blues Lines: A Collection of Blues Lyrics.* Hopewell, NJ: Ecco Press, [1969], 1993.

Salley, Columbus. *The Black 100.* New York: Citadel Press, 1993.

Schwerin, Jules. *Got to Tell It: Mahalia Jackson, Queen of Gospel.* New York: Oxford, 1992.

Shange, Ntozake. *Betsey Brown.* New York: St. Martin's, 1985.

———. *for colored girls who have considered suicide/when the rainbow is enuf.* New York: Collier, [1977], 1989.

Shapiro, Nat, and Nat Hentoff. *Hear Me Talkin' to Ya.* New York: Rinehart, 1955.

Shockley, Ann Allen. *Afro-American Women Writers 1746–1933.* New York: New American Library, 1989.

Smith, Valerie, Lea Baechler, and A. Walton Litz. *African-American Writers.* New York: Scribners, 1991.

Stanton, Elizabeth Cady, et al. *History of American Woman Suffrage.* New York: Fowler & Wells, 1881–1922.

Steele, Shelby. *The Content of Our Character: A New Vision of Race in America.* New York: St. Martin's, 1990.

Story, Rosalyn M. *And So I Sing: African-American Divas of Opera and Concert.* New York: Amistad Press, 1993.

Thurman, Wallace. *The Blacker the Berry.* New York: Macmillan, [1929], 1970.

Toomer, Jane. *Cane.* New York: Liveright, [1923], 1975.

Truth, Sojourner. *The Narrative of Sojourner Truth.* [1850]. Margaret Washington, ed. New York: Vintage, [1850], 1993.

Turner, Tina. *I, Tina*. New York: William Morrow, 1989.

Van Sertima, Ivan. *They Came Before Columbus*. New York: Random House, 1976.

Vincent, Theodore. *Voices of a Black Nation*. Trenton, NJ: Africa World Press, 1990.

Walker, Alice. *The Color Purple*. New York: Harcourt Brace Jovanovich, 1982.

—. *Her Blue Body Everything We Know: Earthling Poems 1965–1990* Complete. San Diego: Harcourt Brace Jovanovich, 1991.

—. *In Search of Our Mothers' Gardens*. San Diego: Harcourt Brace Jovanovich, 1983.

—. *Living by the Word: Selected Writings 1973–1987*. Orlando, Fl: Harcourt Brace Jovanovich. 1988.

—. *Meridian*. New York: Harcourt Brace Jovanovich, 1976.

Walker, David. *An Apeal to the Colored Citizens of the World*. Boston, 1829.

Walker, Margaret. *Jubilee*. Boston: Houghton Mifflin, 1966.

Washington, Booker T. *Up from Slavery*. New York: Penguin, [1901], 1986.

Wheatley, Phillis. *The Collected Works of Phillis Wheatley*. John Shields, ed. New York: Oxford University Press, 1988.

White, Walter. *Rope and Faggot*. New York: Alfred A. Knopf, 1929.

Wilson, August. *Fences*. New York: New American Library, 1986.

—. *Joe Turner's Come and Gone*. New York: New American Library, 1988.

—. *Ma Rainey's Black Bottom*. New York: New American Library, 1985.

—. *The Piano Lesson*. New York: New American Library, 1990.

Wilson, Harriet. *Our Nig: or, Sketches from the Life of a Free Black*. Henry Louis Gates, Jr., ed. New York: Vintage, [1859], 1983.

Wideman, John Edgar. *Brothers and Keepers*. New York: Holt, Rinehart & Winston, 1984.

—. *The Homewood Trilogy*. New York: Avon Books, 1991.

Wilkins, Roger. *A Man's Life*. New York: Simon & Schuster, 1982.

Wilkins, Roy. *Standing Fast*. New York: Viking, 1982.

Wolfe, Charles, and Kip Lornell. *The Life and Legend of Leadbelly*. New York: HarperCollins, 1992.

Woodson, Carter G. *The Mis-Education of the Negro*. Washington, D.C.: Associated Publishers, 1933.

Wright, Richard. *Early Works*. Arnold Rampersad, ed. New York: Literary Classics of the United States, 1991.

Malcolm X. *The Autobiography of Malcolm X*. Alex Haley, ed. New York: Grove, 1965.

————. *By Any Means Necessary*. George Breitman, ed. New York: Pathfinder, 1970.

————. *Malcolm X Speaks*. New York: Merit, 1965.

Young, Andrew. *A Way Out of No Way*. Nashville: Thomas Nelson, 1994.

Deirdre Mullane, who has worked for more than ten years in book publishing, has edited numerous volumes on African and African American subjects, including Woza Afrika!, *a collection of plays by South African playwrights;* Apartheid: A History; *the biography* Winnie Mandela; *the collected speeches of Oliver Tambo; and novels by the Nigerian writer Buchi Emecheta. Most recently, she edited* Crossing the Danger Water: Three Hundred Years of African-American Writing, *also available from Anchor Books. She lives in New York City.*

Acknowledgments

*F*or permission to reprint extensive excerpts from the collected works of individual poets, the author gratefully acknowledges:

Angelou, Maya: Excerpts from "Thank You, Lord," "Still I Rise," and "On Aging" from *And Still I Rise* by Maya Angelou. Copyright © 1978 by Maya Angelou. Reprinted by permission of Random House, Inc. Excerpts from "Alone" and "Elegy" from *Oh Pray My Wings Are Gonna Fit Me Well* by Maya Angelou. Copyright © 1975 by Maya Angelou. Reprinted by permission of Random House, Inc. Excerpts from "A Georgia Song" and "Weekend Glory" from *Shaker, Why Don't You Sing?* by Maya Angelou. Copyright © 1983 by Maya Angelou. Reprinted by permission of Random House, Inc. Excerpt from "On the Pulse of Morning" from *On the Pulse of Morning* by Maya Angelou. Copyright © 1993 by Maya Angelou. Reprinted by permission of Random House, Inc.

Baraka, Amiri: Excerpts from "Notes for a Speech," "Preface to a Twenty-Volume Suicide Note," and "State/Meant" from *The LeRoi Jones/ Amiri Baraka Reader* by Amiri Baraka. Copyright © 1991 by Amiri Baraka. Used by permission of the publisher, Thunder's Mouth Press.

Braithwaite, William Stanley: Excerpts from "Rhapsody" and "Sic Vita" from *The Selected Poems of William Stanley Braithwaite* by William Stanley Braithwaite. Copyright 1948 by William Stanley Braithwaite. Renewed © 1975 by Katherine K. Arnold and Arnold D. Braithwaite. Reprinted by permission of The Putnam Publishing Group.

Brooks, Gwendolyn: Excerpts from "What Shall I Give My Children?" "The Second Sermon on the Warpland," "Young Heroes: Keorapetse Kgositsile (Willie)," "Riot: The Third Sermon on the Warpland," "Riot: An Aspect of Love, Alive in the Ice and Fire," "To Be in Love," and "Boys Black" from *Blacks*. Reissued 1991 by Third World Press, Chicago. Reprinted by permission of the author.

Brown, Sterling: Excerpts from "Old Lem," "Long Gone," and "Strong Men" from *The Collected Poems of Sterling A. Brown*, edited by Michael S.